THE IMPROVEMENT OF MANKIND

*The Social and Political Thought
of John Stuart Mill*

JOHN M. ROBSON

Although John Stuart Mill is generally and properly known as a philosopher and political economist, his writings actually cover a wide variety of subjects. In this book Professor Robson brings together the most important strands of Mill's thought in an attempt to show that it contains a basic unity of approach, at the heart of which is his ethical system. Mill's ethical position depends on his understanding of the relation between practice and theory, and reflects his own experience, especially his "mental crisis," his appreciation of poetry, and his friendship with Harriet Taylor (who later became his wife). The study brings out the importance of the three phases in Mill's life: his early period of adherence to the ideas of James Mill and Bentham; his period of assimilation of the influences of Coleridge, Carlyle, Comte, and de Tocqueville; and finally his period of mature fame, when he published his *System of Logic*, *Principles of Political Economy*, *On Liberty*, *Representative Government*, *Utilitarianism*, and other works still central in the British liberal tradition and still used as university texts.

Mill's eminence makes his thought important to anyone interested in recent political, social, economic, and philosophical trends; and his life, as his *Autobiography* demonstrates, has its own fascination for the general reader as well as for the student of the nineteenth century.

JOHN M. ROBSON was born and educated in Toronto, graduating from the University of Toronto (B.A. 1951, M.A. 1953, PH.D. 1956). After lecturing at the University of British Columbia and the University of Alberta, he joined the staff at Victoria College, University of Toronto, where he is now Professor of English. He is Associate Editor of the *Collected Works* of John Stuart Mill, and has also edited Edmund Burke's *Appeal from the New to the Old Whigs*, *J. S. Mill: A Selection*, and *Editing Nineteenth-Century Texts*.

The Improvement of Mankind

*The Social and Political Thought of
John Stuart Mill*

UNIVERSITY OF TORONTO
DEPARTMENT OF ENGLISH

Studies and Texts No. 15

The
Improvement
of
Mankind

❋

The Social and Political Thought of
John Stuart Mill

❋

JOHN M. ROBSON

University of Toronto Press

Routledge & Kegan Paul

© University of Toronto Press 1968

SBN 8020 1529 8

Printed in Great Britain
by Hazell Watson & Viney Ltd,
Aylesbury, Bucks

London : Routledge & Kegan Paul

SBN 7100 6219 2

To A.P.W.R and A.S.P.W.

Preface

LOOKING BACK on his career, Mill comments in his *Autobiography* (155) that after about 1840 he has "no further mental changes to tell of, but only," he hopes, "a continued mental progress" of which the results, "if real," will best be found in his writings. Some years before the beginning of this final period the "only actual revolution" which had ever taken place in his modes of thinking "was already complete" (133). In his view there were, then, three main periods in his life. The first period of his "mental progress" was that of his Benthamite education and his narrow proselytizing for the Philosophic Radical cause, lasting from the time of his earliest memories (about 1809) to his "mental crisis" in 1826–27. The "revolution" occurred during the subsequent years, up to about 1835, but its results were not fully consolidated until the completion of his *System of Logic* (first offered for publication in 1841). The final or third period was from 1840 until his death in 1873 (or more strictly until he last worked on the *Autobiography* early in 1870).

Each of these periods has its own importance and, for the student of Mill's thought, the first two have a cumulative significance. As his own generous acknowledgements indicate, Mill learned much from many, and hardly any element in his final synthesis is uniquely his. The study of influences and sources is far from complete (and the study of his influence is not far advanced), although valuable work has been done in some areas. Mill's extensive reading has been often noted but never fully analyzed, and some important parts of his life require biographic elucidation. Furthermore, Mill's place in the history of ideas has not been settled, and analysis and discussion, attack and defence, of the various areas of his thought will long continue.

I mention these outstanding tasks only to say that I do not here undertake them. My desire while working on this book has been to understand him; my attempt now is to show the central importance of the utilitarian ethic, as Mill defined it, to his theoretical and practical work. In spite of the great amount written on him, I believe that no commentator has successfully revealed the unity of his thought (or to be more Gallic, the unity of his life and doctrine). One reason is that he wrote on more subjects than most critics are interested in. How is one to treat a man who writes books on logic and political economy, reviews of Tennyson's poetry and Grote's *History of Greece*, articles on French politics and botanical finds, letters on mathematical problems and the government of Indian principalities? This diversity of interest and competence has led to charges of inconsistency from those who have not had the opportunity or inclination or ability to encounter Mill's full range of interest and so to place his views in the proper context. I am not here attempting to dismiss charges of internal and verbal inconsistency, although even these are, as my argument will indicate, overstressed by many commentators. A man must grow and a man must change: it is difficult to understand what people are demanding when they ask for consistency. Sir Thomas Browne argues that it is "reasonable for every man to vary his opinion according to the variance of his reason, and to affirm one day what he denied another." One need not go this far, nor agree with Emerson and Whitman that consistency is a small-minded weakness, but it is often more profitable to try to untangle knots than simply to point to them.

A second reason for the relatively little attention paid to the unity of Mill's thought is to be seen in the view, prevalent in his lifetime and since, that he was an intellectual refugee from the land of the Benthamee, a prophet *manqué* who distorted a coherent (if unpleasant) body of doctrine by introducing new and incompatible elements. In attempting to enlarge Bentham's philosophy, it has been held, Mill overbalanced without strengthening the utilitarian structure. Such an attitude leads again to a search for inconsistencies, a search which is soon rewarded. Here is a so-called thinker who, while supporting an objective ethic, admits qualitative distinctions; who, while following Ricardo in economic theory, welcomes communistic experiments; who, while advocating a democratic representative government, objects to the secret ballot.

For these reasons, and also because academic divisions are common and comfortable, most of the work on Mill has been done in segregated areas (often with equally great facility), wherein similarities and parallels are indicated, and the question of extramural coherence is ignored. There is, however, a unity underlying Mill's mature thought, a unity both of purpose and method, hidden often in a welter of detail, seldom explicitly formulated, but always present. And no false or foreign scheme need be imposed, for Mill himself tells us how to put the pieces together.

The first clue to his purpose is easily recognized, and almost equally easily misrepresented and undervalued. Mill constantly cites the principle of utility as the sole test of actions and the proper end of plans. His re-iteration, it should be emphasized, is not only rhetorical; his schemes, his lessons, his example all have reference to the greatest happiness of the greatest number. One implication of the principle has special importance : devotion to the utilitarian end implies a belief in the possibility of social improvement and moral progress. As Mill always sees this improvement and progress in terms of the individual, his works take on a peculiar in-sistence upon individuality and freedom, but these have the status of secondary ends for Mill – utility alone is primary.

A second clue is perhaps less obvious, certainly less commented on, but scarcely less important. His plans always have a practical bias; while valuing theory highly, he makes a clear distinction (as his father did not always do) between it and practice. In recent years there has, in fact, been some mention of this matter, and Mill has been held up by Mr. Maurice Cowling as incapable of understanding the distinction. This view results, in my opinion, from an inadequate consultation of texts, and a failure to distinguish between the periods in Mill's life.

A third clue to the unity of Mill's thought is found in his dependence upon induction to discover "truth." He welcomes the dialectic of ex-perience, holding that experiments, founded on partial knowledge and hypothesis, are the best available means to the optimum social happiness. Inductive philosophy is fact-hungry, and trial, even if it ends in error, pro-duces facts. But the social experiments must be made by choice; Mill pretends to no pontifical status. Throughout his work, then, is to be de-tected a tolerance and an eagerness to learn; although he desires a scientific sociology as means, he has no wish to see society controlled by science.

The clues lead to a conclusion : Mill's labours were informed through-out by the belief that practical measures, if they arise out of and are tested by experience, and if they are designed to benefit and to be implemented by individuals, can and will result in the greatest happiness of the greatest number. Mere belief, however, is not moral action; the would-be reformer needs a method. This is outlined in the last chapter of his *System of Logic*: "Of the Logic of Practice, or Art." The tasks and procedures of the effective social reformer should be divided into three activities: ends must be described, means designed, and means applied. Mill assigns the first and the last of these to the "Artist," the second to the "Scientist." The Artist formulates an end and describes it to the Scientist. The latter, having isolated laws, discovers means which, in accordance with these known laws, will work towards the end. The Artist accepts these means from the Scientist, tests their desirability, and then tries to implement them.

This apparently theoretical and formal scheme, applied generally to Mill's works, reveals a genuine, and not an imposed, unity. I would suggest that his plans for social improvement were seen by him in this light; that is, they were conceived in accordance with the utilitarian end, were tested for practicability in terms of social laws and developments, and finally were examined for practicability and desirability with respect to the particular situation. Then he tried to persuade others to adopt them in practice.

According to this scheme, it should be noted, sociology is subordinate to ethics. Throughout his work Mill maintains the same priority. Only thus can he preserve the individualistic bias of his thought, for the individual is basic in his ethics. But while this relation is easily perceived, another is often obscured by the bulk of his writings on political subjects. To Mill politics are subordinate to sociology. His political schemes, therefore, never stand by themselves; they are supported by his social philosophy, which in turn rests on his ethical philosophy. Similarly, John Ruskin's criticism of the abstractness and inhumanity of Mill's approach to economics is the result of his failure to see that for Mill economics is subordinate to sociology and finally to ethics. This hierarchy strengthens the unity of Mill's thought.

To argue that Mill reached consistent conclusions by means of a unified method is not, of course, to imply that he was "original" in his facts and premises. I have tried to forestall such an implication by the arrangement of my argument, but some misunderstanding is almost inevitable, because of the range of secondary material not here included. I have looked at the first two periods of his life (up to about 1828, and from 1828 to 1840) not as important in themselves, though they are, but as background to his mature thought. The chapters dealing with these periods are therefore not full studies of influence and growth, and I have been less than generous in indicating the work already done on Mill and French thought by Iris Mueller, on Mill, Carlyle, and the Saint-Simonians by Dwight Lindley and others, on Mill and de Tocqueville by H. O. Pappé, J.-P. Mayer and others, on Mill and Comte by Adelaide Weinberg, on the development of Mill's *Logic* by Oskar Kubitz, and so on. I should also mention that my approach dictates a bias concerning those who influenced Mill, and it must not be thought that my brief accounts do justice to the authors from whom he learned and borrowed. I can hope only that I have been as fair as he was. Also, although these chapters are not intended to be definitive biographical accounts, the chronological order is generally borne out by the quotations and references, which in Chapter I derive mainly from the first period of his life, in Chapters II, III, IV, and VI from the second period, and in Chapters V and VII from the third period. Frequent reference to his earlier work is necessary throughout, but such references in the middle chapters are mainly useful as indications of what he was revolting against, and what form the revolt took. In the later chapters they are useful either as contrasts or as indications of the extent to which his revolt led back to his origins. A justification of this procedure is provided by his own synthesizing powers : though he borrowed extensively and adapted freely, the unity which he found in his materials was found by him alone, and it is this unity which is explored in my account. The despairing student of influences may conclude that there is nothing new under the sun, but he is wrong – there is always the unique individual who, seeing the sun, is illuminated (or burnt) by it.

In the account of Mill's mature thought I have relied heavily on quotations from and summaries of his writings. In doing so I have again been ungenerous in not sufficiently noting the contributions to Mill scholarship by Alexander Bain, R. P. Anschutz, Karl Britton and many others. I have not simply repeated their arguments, nor have I indicated, except in my list of recommended books, my agreement with them. I have not, of course, knowingly borrowed ideas or words from them without acknowledgment.

The extent of quotation may place me, like other commentators on Mill, in the position of an anthologist. Insofar as this is a valid judgment,

I have tried at least to provide a comprehensive anthology, with clear indications of the place and importance of the quoted passages. In trying to establish unity one must wallow in heavy references before emerging with evidence : I hope too much mud has not clung to the following pages. Some will think I have fallen short of Mill's rigorous canons of proof; others will think I have not emerged. To the former I can offer pages of rejected footnotes; to the latter I can only quote a chance remark of the late Professor A. S. P. Woodhouse : "There is an irreducible minimum of irrelevant exactitude in scholarly footnoting."

J.M.R.

Victoria College, 1967

Acknowledgments

WITHOUT PREJUDICE to their careers and reputations, I should like to thank all those who have assisted me in thought and deed. My primary debt is to the late A. S. P. Woodhouse, who first encouraged me to work on Mill, and until his death enriched my understanding and appreciation of the immense value of humane studies. In various and direct ways I have profited from the counsel and friendship of F. E. L. Priestley and Francis Mineka; of the host of others who might be mentioned, I recall with special pleasure the help of Joseph Hamburger, Peter Jackson, Dwight Lindley, Pedro Schwartz, and Adelaide Weinberg. Any failure to make this a better book reflects on my stubbornness and not on their abilities. Librarians at the British Museum, the University of London Library, the British Library of Political and Economic Science, Somerville College, Yale, and Toronto have been generous of time and effort. The staff of the University of Toronto Press, and especially Francess G. Halpenny and Ron Schoeffel, need not be reminded of how much they have done for me; I wish that all authors might have as pleasant relations with a publisher as mine have been. For grants in aid of research I am indebted to the Royal Society of Canada, the Canada Council, and the Humanities Research Council of Canada, who also have generously aided in the publication of this work using funds provided by the Canada Council. The University of Toronto and Victoria College have helped in providing typing expenses. In a book on Mill that treats incidentally of Comte, one must be cautious in attributing aid to one's *ange gardien*, but the fact is that living with her, our children, and this book in one house has proved a possible, stimulating, and gratifying course of *hygiène cérébrale*. My dedication is to her, and to Professor Woodhouse.

Contents

✳

II: MILL IN MATURITY

5

Moralist / 117

6

Method : Scientist and Artist / 160

7

Mill's Views on Society and Politics / 182

Government: Amount / 202

Government: Selection and Composition / 222

Socialism / 245

I

Mill's Early Years

1

The Benthamite
Influence

FEW MEN are born and educated into a creed as was John Stuart Mill. In the beginning, it may safely be said, he was a utilitarian. James Mill and Jeremy Bentham focused their attention on him as the instrument of the reforms they would not live to make. Their intention, in James Mill's words, was to train the "poor boy" to be "a successor worthy of both of us." [1] Few pains were spared and few pleasures given to ensure the result, and while the gloom of the Mill home has doubtless been exaggerated, for the eldest children at least cakes and ale came far behind Q.E.D.'s. [2]

For twenty years John Mill was under the intellectual and moral domination of his elders, and traces of that domination remained long after he had asserted his independence. Any study of his thought, and especially of his political and ethical thought, must therefore begin with an account of their influence on him.

In 1806, when John was born, his father, having forsaken the Scottish Presbyterian ministry for which he had been trained, was making a precarious living in London by journalism. A man of keen wit and personal charm, strong and acerbic in style, he knew himself intellectually en-

[1] James Mill to Bentham, 28/7/12, in Bentham's *Works*, ed. Bowring (Edinburgh, 1843), X, 473.

[2] While John Mill's account of his father and of family life is not to be accepted without reservation, the passages in the *Early Draft* of his *Autobiography* cited by the editor, Professor Stillinger, cannot but chill one's sympathy for the father of a not-ungrateful son (see *Early Draft* [University of Illinois Press, 1961], 13).

dowed beyond his station and marriage.[3] His allegiance with Bentham, beginning in 1808, promised a chance for improvement hitherto denied him, and he sensibly and assiduously cultivated the attachment. In 1810 Bentham offered Mill and his growing family a refuge in a house in his garden, once occupied by Milton, but it proved unsatisfactory, and the Mills moved to Newington Green.[4] The slight distance did not impede the relation, and during the winter and spring months James Mill continued to visit the Hermit's retreat in Queen Square Place, Westminster. Also from Newington Green to Bentham, appropriately enough, came the earliest extant letter from John Mill, aged six, asking to borrow Hooke's *Roman History*[5] – and even more appropriately, the letter seems to have been enclosed in the one from James Mill to Bentham cited above, which was an acceptance of the latter's offer to look after John should his father die.

The intimacy between the two had ripened from the time in 1809 when Bentham took Mill and his family to Barrow Green for the summer months. This practice continued until 1814, when Bentham rented Ford Abbey in Devon where he, with the Mills, spent the months from July well into January, until the opening months of 1818. From the time that John first began to learn Greek at the age of three, then, it is clear that he was never far from the feet of the master. Little is known about his early years, in spite of the amount of educational detail that he summarizes in his *Autobiography*, but that little is almost all drawn from James Mill's epistolary account of the workdays (holidays there were not) spent in Bentham's country residences. Fairly early in the account John appears, usually not lumped with "Mrs. Mill and the brats," but as "my poor boy," and then "John." In the summer of 1813 Bentham took James and John Mill on a summer tour which the latter recalled long after in his *Autobiography*, and early in the Ford Abbey period he made their intimacy year-round by obtaining for them 1 Queen Square, which adjoined his own property.

[3] On the latter point, see the testimony of a sometimes unreliable witness, Harriet Grote, in the *Amberley Papers*, ed. Bertrand and Patricia Russell (London, 1937), I, 421.

[4] For a slightly fuller account of the relations between the Mills and Bentham, see my "John Stuart Mill and Jeremy Bentham, with Some Observations on James Mill," in *Essays in English Literature from the Renaissance to the Victorian Age* (University of Toronto Press, 1964), 245–68. That essay has been extensively used in this chapter.

[5] Francis E. Mineka, ed., *The Earlier Letters of John Stuart Mill*, in *Collected Works*, XII (University of Toronto Press, 1963; London : Routledge & Kegan Paul), 3.

The regular routine demanded by Bentham, and the supply of library and (during the summers) domestic help made the great educational experiment possible, but while it went on often in Bentham's house, little of it can have gone on under his eye. The precocious, proud, awkward boy, his conscience always speaking in his father's voice,[6] might occasionally play chess, or even battledore and shuttlecock, with the eccentric old man who had himself been a precocious, proud, awkward boy with a domineering father; but Bentham, the bachelor born in 1748, and Mill, born in 1806, can have had little understanding of each other at this time.[7] Although the children were heard as well as seen, the households were, in sensible nineteenth-century style, dominated by adult needs. Of his family, James Mill writes to David Ricardo in 1815, "the history is two words – *semper idem*. We study, walk, eat, drink and sleep, and that is all." [8] John Mill later remarked that he had never learned to play,[9] but before his father is condemned, as he almost always is, to the hell of domestic despots, it should at least be asked what the virtues of learning to play are. John was trained for work, and the training had effect.

His first period of independence came in 1820–21, when he was sent to France. There he lived with the family of Sir Samuel Bentham, Jeremy's brother, and showed that no immediate supervision was needed to keep him working.[10] And when he returned home the final turn of the lathe was applied. He began a course of reading under John Austin, Bentham's best legal disciple, and soon started his serious writing career in the *Westminster Review*, the periodical founded by Bentham to give voice to the opinions of the Philosophic Radicals. Living in his father's house, just a wall away from Bentham, his other activities had an obvious reference: he spoke at the Mutual Improvement Society, of which Bentham was Honorary President,[11] founded the Utilitarian Society, of which Bentham

[6] See Stillinger, *Early Draft*, 19.

[7] The other Mill children seem to have remembered only Bentham's kindness; see Caroline Fox, *Memories of Old Friends* (2nd ed.; London, 1882), I, 162.

[8] David Ricardo, *Works*, ed. P. Sraffa, VI (Cambridge, 1952), 309 (10/10/15).

[9] Caroline Fox, *Memories*, I, 163–4.

[10] See Anna J. Mill, *John Mill's Boyhood Visit to France* (University of Toronto Press, 1960), for a full account of this period.

[11] For references to this rather elusive Society, see Bentham, *Works*, X, 488–9, 505–6; a letter of James Mill's, referring to the correspondence found in the former of these, indicates his interest in the Society (British Museum Add. MS. 35,153, f.13r.). One of Bentham's amanuenses, John Colls, was a member; see Bentham Papers, University College, London, clxiii. 48.

was patron and secular diety, and defended the true faith in debates at the Co-operative Society and in the London Debating Society. His writing appeared in many papers, and in 1825 he began the monumental task of editing Bentham's *Rationale of Judicial Evidence*. His father, after the publication of his *History of India*, had entered the Examiner's Office of the East India Company, and John joined him there in 1823 on his seventeenth birthday, disappointing those who had hoped that he might have a brilliant university career, but fulfilling the hopes of his father, who saw the independent possibilities of the India House, and thought that John could at least continue with his legal studies.[12]

To understand all this activity one has to look back to 1821. As Mill says in his *Autobiography*, his education up to then "had been, in a certain sense, already a course of Benthamism." (In the *Early Draft*, 74, he is more accurate, saying "in a great measure" rather than "in a certain sense.") As early as his eleventh year he had begun to uphold the "Roman democratic party" in a history he was writing with the aid of "such lights" as his father had given him, and the choice of the subjects he studied from that time – Logic, Political Economy, the Philosophy of Mind, and so on – indicates the bias clearly enough. He had also read his father's Benthamite account of jurisprudence in the Supplement to the *Encyclopædia Britannica*, and studied Bentham's *Chrestomathic Tables* while in France.[13] But not until 1821, when he read Dumont's French redaction of Bentham – and, although he does not make the point clearly, until he saw the details and applicability of the utilitarian doctrine through Austin's tutoring – did he reach a "turning point" in his mental history. Bentham's work "gave unity to my conceptions of things," he says in a well-known passage. "I now had opinions; a creed, a doctrine, a philosophy, in one among the best senses of the word, a religion; the inculcation and diffusion of which could be made the principal outward purpose of a life." [14]

[12] See my "John Stuart Mill and Jeremy Bentham," 255–8.

[13] See Anna J. Mill, *John Mill's Boyhood Visit to France*, 29.

[14] *Autobiography* (Columbia University Press, 1924), 47. In the *Early Draft* (75–6), "one among the best senses" reads "one (& the best) sense". It is interesting to compare this passage with Bentham's account of the effect on him of reading Book III of Hume's *Treatise*: ". . . I well remember, no sooner had I read that part of the work which touches on [the foundation of virtue in utility], than I felt as if scales had fallen from my eyes." *Fragment on Government*, in *Works*, I, 268n.

John Roebuck, Mill's early friend and disciple,[15] says that at this time Mill, although "acquainted with the state of the political world," was, "as might have been expected, the mere exponent of other men's ideas, these men being his father and Bentham. . . ." [16] Mill's own recollection confirms the judgment: "'I conceive that the description so often given of a Benthamite, as a mere reasoning machine, though extremely inapplicable to most of those who have been designated by that title, was during two or three years of my life not altogether untrue of me." [17]

The best evidence is found in Mill's early writings, which are made of Bentham's opinions in James Mill's tones. John Mill insisted that his education had trained him, through constant insistence on active participation in thought and debate on all subjects, to think for himself, but the fruits of this training were not felt for some time. Before he was twenty years of age, the ascendancy of James Mill over him ensured that his conclusions, while fully developed and clearly understood, could not be independent. Being embodied in a system, James Mill's opinions were so organized as to reinforce one another, and they thus exerted a cumulative force. The boy could not well maintain his own ground in argument with his father, of course, and the very fact that argument and discussion played so large a part in his education made him even more an advocate of his father's and Bentham's opinions than he would have been under a system of rote.

The extent of Mill's debt to his elders' thought and style is seen in his first articles in the *Westminster Review* and in the earliest of his debating speeches. The material of his father's *Essay on Government*, for example, appears in his "Law of Libel and Liberty of the Press" (1825), and (with some modifications) in his "Speech on the Influence of the Aristocracy" (1825). His ready acceptance of the economic views of the Philosophic Radicals is seen in his articles on Political Economy from 1824 to 1827,[18] and in his debates against the Owenites.[19] His political agreement is shown

[15] From Roebuck's MS. notebook (in the possession of Professor Francis Hyde), describing his reading and writing during his early years in London, it is clear that John Mill, in imitation of his father's education of him (and of Ricardo), was training Roebuck to be a good Philosophical Radical.

[16] *Life and Letters of John Arthur Roebuck*, ed. R. E. Leader (London, 1897), 28.

[17] *Autobiography*, 76.

[18] See the first six articles in *Essays in Economics and Society, Collected Works*, IV (University of Toronto Press, 1967).

[19] For information about Mill's debating speeches, see Karl Britton and John M. Robson, "Mill's Debating Speeches," *Mill News Letter*, I (1965), 2ff.

in his review of Brodie's *History of the British Empire* (1825), and in his "Speech on the Church" (1828). His youthful enthusiasm as well as the group's rhetorical confidence is shown when he parades his beliefs: "Knowledge has triumphed," he says in 1823. "It has worked the downfall of much that is mischievous. It is vain to suppose that it will pass by and spare any institution the existence of which is pernicious to mankind." [20] The virtue of the middle class, one of James Mill's characteristic themes, is proclaimed in a letter to the *Black Dwarf*: ". . . I really cannot admit that the middling classes of this country are more indifferent than the working classes to the blessings of good government; and I am sure that in every other country of Europe the middle classes ALONE feel any desire for a better government than they possess." [21]

One of his most revealing borrowings is the word "security." For the Philosophic Radicals the term is crucial: they desired security for person and property, for free economic development, and for good government. John Mill learned the lesson well. For example, in his continuation of his father's attack on the *Edinburgh Review*, he argues that mere verbal recognition of the people's right to sovereignty will not bring them nearer to good government, which they can approach only by obtaining "real and efficient *securities* for it." Again, writing on the law of libel, he says: "What is the constitution? merely the aggregate of the securities for good government, which are provided by the existing law, whatever those securities may be, more or less complete." [22]

Here lies an important clue to the Benthamite position: securities are needed because man is basically selfish; they can be provided by his reason, the tool for devising means to social betterment. The great opponent to this betterment is not selfishness, which is in fact the best guarantee of advance, but confusion, vagueness, and stupidity about ends and means. The traditional powers in the state, the aristocracy, landowners, and churchmen, protected their "sinister interest" in the *status quo* by fostering a morality based on confusion, vagueness, and stupidity. Bentham sought to sweep away this system by propagating a rational, objective ethic which, through the legal and political institutions of the country, would forward the general interest.

[20] "On the Utility of Knowledge," *Autobiography*, ed. Laski (London, 1924), 274.
[21] "Question of Population," *Black Dwarf*, 11 (1823), 795-6.
[22] *Westminster Review*, 1 (1824), 506; *ibid.*, 3 (1825), 309-10. Cf. *ibid.*, 1 (1824), 508; 2 (1825), 378; 3 (1826), 288, 304.

Mill never lost this concern for the general interest, "the greatest happiness of the greatest number," or "utility," which he had learned from his elders. Whatever his final disagreements with his father and Bentham, he continued their attempt to change existing society into the best possible society through utilitarianism. The qualification, "possible," is important: Bentham's practical sense [23] operated on his conception of the end to be attained; Mill's means, as will later be shown, and not to any appreciable extent his end, were modified by his conception of the possible. Social utility, however, in its widest acceptation, is the belief that informs the work of them both, and is in truth the main inheritance of Mill from Bentham. For, although the phrase is interpreted differently by them, "the greatest happiness of the greatest number" is the end and test of actions for both.

To understand Mill, therefore, it is necessary to look at least briefly at Bentham's ethic. [24] His description of the end of social improvement is informed with a sad wisdom: its heart is practicability:

[23] Cf. George Catlin, *History of the Political Philosophers* (London, 1950), 167, and Henry Sidgwick, "Bentham and Benthamism in Politics and Ethics," *Fortnightly Review*, n.s. 21 (1877), 638: Bentham, Sidgwick says, is "one of the *most*" and "the *least* idealistic of practical philosophers," depending on one's viewpoint. See also the "General Preface" to Bentham's *Works*, I, ix. One of the greatest difficulties here is the common but usually misleading distinction between "practical" and "theoretical." Bentham, of course, is both. He theorized about practical affairs, and often his theories were impracticable, though his followers put them to good practical use. It should be remembered (see 35ff. below) that both he and James Mill believed that sound theory and good practice must coincide.

[24] While much valuable work has been done on Bentham, much more remains to be done, and will probably wait upon the recently begun collected edition of his works. There is, for example, no satisfactory biography beyond C. W. Everett's *The Education of Jeremy Bentham* (Columbia University Press, 1931), and no really major work on him except perhaps Elie Halévy's *Growth of Philosophic Radicalism* (London, 1952), which has other ends in view. Mary Mack's *Jeremy Bentham* (London, 1962) makes an attempt to bring his thought into focus through a study of his early years, but suffers from confusion and ill-founded generalizations. This is not the place, and I am not able, to give a full account of Bentham's development and thought; my comments are governed by the influence of Bentham on Mill. It should be remarked, however, that Bentham's debts in ethics have been traced, and are easily summarized: utility is part of the dominant English tradition stemming from Locke and developed by Hume; the principle of utility, in one formulation or another, is to be found in Locke, Hutcheson, Gay, Hume, Helvetius, Beccaria, and in Priestley (where Bentham says he found it); he also says, according to Bowring, that the connection between utility and happiness was so strong that quite early in his career he "could scarcely fancy the ideas separated in the mind of any man" (*Deontology* [London, 1834], I, 303). The definition of happiness in terms of pleasure

Perfect happiness belongs to the imaginary regions of philosophy, and must be classed with the universal elixir and the philosopher's stone. In the age of greatest perfection, fire will burn, tempests will rage, man will be subject to infirmity, to accidents, and to death. It may be possible to diminish the influence of, but not to destroy, the sad and mischievous passions. The unequal gifts of nature and of fortune will always create jealousies: there will always be opposition of interests; and, consequently, rivalries and hatred. Pleasures will be purchased by pains; enjoyments by privations. Painful labour, daily subjection, a condition nearly allied to indigence, will always be the lot of numbers. Among the higher as well as the lower classes, there will always be desires which cannot be satisfied; inclinations which must be subdued: reciprocal security can only be established by the forcible renunciation by each one, of every thing which might wound the legitimate rights of others. If we suppose, therefore, the most reasonable laws, constraint will be their basis: but the most salutary constraint in its distant effect is always an evil, is always painful in its immediate operation. . . .

Let us seek only for what is attainable: it presents a career sufficiently vast for genius; sufficiently difficult for the exercise of the greatest virtues. We shall never make this world the abode of perfect happiness: when we shall have accomplished all that can be done, this paradise will yet be, according to the Asiatic idea, only a garden; but this garden will be a most delightful abode, compared with the savage forest in which men have so long wandered.[25]

Bentham's means are appropriate to this limited objective. He saw the "maximization" of social happiness as resulting from manipulation of the available and manageable elements. Hence his interest in legal reform.[26] Happiness, being composed of pleasures, is increased by adding pleasures and removing pains. The social interactions of human beings

---

and pain is in Helvetius and Beccaria, and the mechanism of combination, association, is in Hartley. Bentham, like Mill, is quite generous in acknowledging his debts (see, e.g. Works, I, 242, 268n). For extensive treatments, see the works cited, and Leslie Stephen, The English Utilitarians (London, 1900), I; Emery Neff, Carlyle and Mill (Columbia University Press, 1926); Graham Wallas, "Jeremy Bentham," Political Science Quarterly, 38 (1923), 45–56, and "Bentham as Political Inventor," Contemporary Review, 129 (1926), 308–19; and Karl Britton, John Stuart Mill (London, 1953).

[25] The Influence of Time and Place in Matters of Legislation, Works, I, 194. Cf. Mill's remarks concerning his father's attitude towards life, Autobiography, 34.

[26] Roughly one-half of Bentham's manuscripts are on legal matters; of the other half, a large batch is concerned with the Panopticon struggle, much with abstract speculation on logic and language, and only a small proportion with ethical questions as distinct from legal ones. Cf. A. Taylor Milne, Catalogue of the Manuscripts of Jeremy Bentham in the Library of University College, London (2nd. ed.; London, 1962), passim; and Thomas Whittaker, Report on the Bentham MSS. at University College, London, with Catalogue (London, 1892), 1.

produce pain through conflicts; these may be lessened by defining carefully all anti-social acts, penalizing them in proportion to their harmful-
ness, and giving power to some public body to judge and punish. Seeking
efficiency, rapidity, and thoroughness, Bentham devoted himself to a
rationalization of the law in terms of social utility. The grand plan is
clear: "The general object which all laws have, or ought to have, in common, is to augment the total happiness of the community; and therefore,
in the first place, to exclude, as far as may be, every thing that tends to
subtract from that happiness: in other words, to exclude mischief." [27]

Here, as so often, the word "ought" is puzzling. It may mean simply
that, having accepted a certain goal, legislators "ought" rationally to
choose means which will achieve it. But it more likely has its full moral
significance: that is, legislators have a moral duty to seek the total happiness of the community, and all their laws "ought" to forward that
happiness. In that case, the legislator and the moralist are one. Bentham
is, however, as careless as most people in using the word. He tells Dumont
that he has put "ought" in the place of Hume's "is," [28] but merely changing the word indicates little if, as sometimes appears, he did not distinguish between the normative and the descriptive. In the *Deontology*,
published by Bowring as Bentham's moral treatise,[29] the onslaught on the
word has the true Benthamite ring: "The talisman of arrogance, indol-
ence, and ignorance, is to be found in a single word ['ought'], an authoritative imposture, which in these pages it will be frequently necessary
to unveil. . . . If the use of the word be admissible at all, it 'ought' to be
banished from the vocabulary of ethics." [30] In *The Influence of Time and
Place in Matters of Legislation*, however, he admits a distinction "between
matters of fact and the matter of right, or rather of expediency; between
what has taken place, and what ought to have taken place." [31]

[27] *Principles of Morals and Legislation, Works,* I, 83.

[28] "The difference between Hume and me is this: the use he made of it [the
principle of utility] was – to account for that which *is*, I to show what *ought to be.*"
(Bentham Papers, University College, London, MS 10.)

[29] While I think that here the *Deontology* reflects Bentham's views, the work
cannot be accepted as Bentham's. Mill rejected it as a Bowringite hash of Bentham's views, and his opinion is supported by Stephen (I, 325), Whittaker (4) and the
present editors of Bentham's manuscripts. The best comment is in a letter from Place
to Wheatley: "It is no work of my very dear and good old master, but of that wild
poetical surface man Bowring." Graham Wallas, *Francis Place* (London, 1918), 84n.

[30] *Deontology* I, 31–2.   [31] *Works,* I, 189.

The difficulty remains, but an explanation is to hand, if one broadens the discussion a little. "Ought" and "is" come closest to identity for Bentham just in the place where he substitutes one for the other. "Nature," he says with Helvetius, "has placed mankind under the governance of two sovereign masters, *pain* and *pleasure*. It is for them alone to point out what we ought to do, as well as to determine what we shall do." [32] Man's relatively simple nature cannot be fundamentally altered. Once the way in which his actions are determined has been recognized, there is no point in saying that he "ought" to act in another way. Only an explanation of motivation is needed before the "ought" can be substituted for the "is." This explanation, in the form of the pleasure-pain calculus and associationism, Bentham found developed in his predecessors. In this way, by begging the moral question, Bentham makes the normative and the descriptive identical for the individual.

But what of society, and the individual in his social relations? Although man's nature cannot be changed, society's can. In the larger area there is room for the legislator, who defines "ought," and does not define it as "is." Here, really, the perennial dichotomy in naturalistic utilitarianism appears. The "ought" with which the legislator is concerned is seen in terms of the greatest happiness of society while the "ought" which approaches (for Bentham) "is" refers to the happiness of the individual.

On one matter bearing intimately on this discussion Bentham is completely clear: there can be no question about his acceptance of the priority of self-regarding over social motives in man. Moreover, as has been suggested, he rejoices in the primacy of selfishness.

In this general predominance of self-regarding over social interest, when attentively considered, there will not be found any just subject of regret, any more than of contestation; for it will be found, that but for this predominance, no such species as that which we belong to could have existence: and that, supposing it, if possible, done away, insomuch that all persons, or most persons, should find respectively, some one or more persons, whose interest was respectively, through the whole of life, dearer to them, and as such more anxiously and constantly watched over than their own, the whole species would necessarily, within a very short space of time, become extinct.[33]

A clue to the interior of the labyrinth [of politics] has been found: it is the principle of self-preference. Man, from the very constitution of his nature,

[32] *Principles of Morals and Legislation, Works,* I, 1.
[33] *Book of Fallacies, Works,* II, 482.

prefers his own happiness to that of all other sensitive beings put together: but for this self-preference, the species could not have had existence.[34]

> If it be through the happiness of another, or others, in whatsoever numbers, that man pursues his own happiness, still the direct, and immediate, and nearest object of pursuit is not the less his own happiness: the happiness of others is but a means to that relatively universal end.[35]

One consequence of this belief is the rejection of progress in individual morality, as commonly understood, for while reason can improve the individual's chances of success in the world, such improvement is not moral, and is certainly not without a final and not far-distant term. Social morality, if understood as the beneficial operation of a machine, can be improved simply by being made more efficient; the moralist and legislator need only oil the parts. Legislation defines the method of social advance, and as it is perfected in design and operation, so friction diminishes and the output of happiness increases. In all cases, of course, the judgment of an action's morality depends on its consequences; also, for Bentham, the agent's intentions and habitual behaviour are studied only so that they may be controlled.

The young John Mill found no difficulty, and would seem to have found some pleasure, in adopting the selfish psychology of the school. One example, drawn from his debates with the Owenites, will illustrate. Rather than attacking, he says, he would defend Owen's system to his last breath if he thought it the only hope for "those cheering anticipations of the indefinite improvement of mankind" which he has always cherished. But there is a better hope which makes "such drastic remedies" unnecessary:

> there is a principle in man, far more constant & far more universal than his love for his fellows – I mean his love for himself: & without excluding the one principle, I rest my hopes chiefly on the latter. Let self interest be or be not a principle which it is possible to eradicate from the bosom not of one man only but of all: no one at least will deny that it is a powerful principle – in the present state of things almost an all-powerful one; & if so it is surely not very wise to court opposition from it when you might have it on your side. Let things be so arranged that the interest of every individual shall exactly accord with the interest of the whole – thus much it is in the power of laws and institutions to effect; &, this done, let every individual be so educated as to know his own interest. Thus by the simultaneous action of a vast number of

[34] *Memoirs, Works*, X, 80. Bowring's quotation marks omitted in this and the next quotation.   [35] *Ibid.*, 532.

agents, everyone drawing in the direction of his own happiness, the happiness of the whole will be attained.[36]

At this point Pringle-Pattison's description of Bentham's problem is applicable to Mill as well: "Unadulterated selfishness as the motive, universal benevolence as the end – these are the two fixed poles of Bentham's thought."[37] Bentham's answer is to try to create a harmony of interests through the application of "moral arithmetic." While each seeks his own happiness, there must be some means of attaching pain to antisocial acts. Punishment is always painful, by definition, but it must not produce more pain than it prevents through deterence. A calculus designed to measure pains and pleasures according to common criteria would be invaluable. So Bentham decides on his seven measuring sticks, and to help the Deontologist puts them into mnemonic form:

> Intense, long, certain, speedy, fruitful, pure–
> Such marks in *pleasures* and in *pains* endure.
> Such pleasures seek, if *private* be thy end:
> If it be *public*, wide let them *extend*.
> Such *pains* avoid, whichever be thy view:
> If pains *must* come, let them *extend* to few.

(*Works*, I, 16n.)

This arithmetic is applicable both to the private person and to the legislator; the difference lies in the number of persons to whom the pleasures and the pains apply. The legislator is concerned with the greatest happiness of the greatest number; the private person with his happiness alone. There is no true development of a harmony of interest between one individual and others.[38]

Later John Mill tried to establish such a harmony as one of the main tenets of his ethics; he was haunted in the attempt by the pleasure-pain calculus and by its justification, the objectivity of judgments based on consequences.[39] For rational objectivity had been the key to reform, the great weapon in the Philosophic Radicals' onslaught against the wicked giants of the established system, and John Mill, however the details of his beliefs altered, remained a reformer and an opponent of entrenched privilege. And his greatest moment of conviction as a Benthamite was

[36] "Further Reply to the Debate on Population," *Archiv für Sozialwissenschaft und Sozialpolitik*, 62 (1929), 238–9; corrected from the MS.

[37] *The Philosophical Radicals* (Edinburgh, 1907), 16. Cf. Stephen, *The English Utilitarians*, I, 315.

[38] Cf. Neff, who argues that for Bentham "an artificial identity of interests is by definition inapplicable" in private ethics.   [39] See 33ff. below.

prompted by Bentham's appeal away from subjectivism and privilege. His acceptance of utilitarianism as "a creed," "a religion" resulted, he says in the *Autobiography* (45–6), from his reading of

the chapter in which Bentham passed judgment on the common modes of reasoning in morals and legislation, deduced from phrases like 'law of nature,' 'right reason,' 'the moral sense,' 'natural rectitude,' and the like, and characterized them as dogmatism in disguise, imposing its sentiments upon others under cover of sounding expressions which convey no reason for the sentiment, but set up the sentiment as its own reason. It had not struck me before, that Bentham's principle put an end to all this. The feeling rushed upon me, that all previous moralists were superseded, and that here indeed was the commencement of a new era in thought.

As will be made evident later, the passage in the chapter Mill mentions came to epitomize for him Bentham's position. An abbreviated version will indicate its mode of attack:

1. One man says, he has a thing made on purpose to tell him what is right and what is wrong; and that it is called a *moral sense*: and then he goes to work at his ease, and says, such a thing is right, and such a thing is wrong – why? 'because my moral sense tells me it is.'

2. Another man comes and alters the phrase: leaving out *moral*, and putting in *common*, in the room of it. . . .

3. Another man comes, and says, that as to a moral sense indeed, he cannot find that he has any such thing: that however he has an *understanding*, which will do quite as well. . . .

4. Another man says, that there is an eternal and immutable Rule of Right. . . .

5. Another man, or perhaps the same man . . . says, that there are certain practices conformable, and others repugnant, to the Fitness of Things. . . .

6. A great multitude of people are continually talking of the Law of Nature. . . .

7. Instead of the phrase, Law of Nature, you have sometimes, Law of Reason, Right Reason, Natural Justice, Natural Equity, Good Order. Any of them will do equally well. . . .

8. We have one philosopher, who says, there is no harm in any thing in the world but in telling a lie: and that if, for example, you were to murder your own father, this would only be a particular way of saying, he was not your father. . . .

9. The fairest and openest of them all is that sort of man who speaks out, and says, I am of the number of the Elect. . . .[40]

[40] *Introduction to the Principles of Morals and Legislation* (London, 1823), I, 29n–31n. Mill appears to have used this edition (the one now in his library, Somerville College, Oxford) rather than that in Bentham's *Works*, I, 8n–9n, into which Bentham has inserted the names of the various moralists attacked.

This is undoubtedly the "portion of Bentham's 'Introduction' " which Mill was reading when studying under Austin,[41] and its effect appears first in his own work in 1827 in a note to his edition of Bentham's *Rationale* (I, 126n–127n), where he says that such phrases as those attacked by Bentham are *"covers for dogmatism"* and "cloaks for ipse-dixitism" (Bentham's own terms). He assigns those who employ them to the *"dogmatical school* of ethics," distinguishing them from "those who think that morality is not the province of dogmatism, but of reason, and that propositions in ethics need proof, as much as propositions in mathematics."

In the 1820s, for Mill as for the other Philosophic Radicals, the ethical basis of their programme was obscured by its usefulness as a political weapon. Not the conversion of everyone to the utilitarian standard, but the placing of utilitarians in positions of power was at issue. They assumed – in the event not very wisely – that those elected under their system of representative government would be utilitarians, or at least readily amenable to utilitarian pressure through "securities." The classic statement of their programme is in James Mill's *Essay on Government*, which he said with perhaps pardonable pride was a textbook "of the young men of the Union at Cambridge"; the statement may be exaggerated, but the work was the textbook of the young men of the left in the London Debating Society.

Its argument is well known: since the end of government is the greatest happiness of the greatest number, the primary question is the adaptation of means to this end. Men, banding together to protect one another, delegate to a small number of themselves the power to protect them all, and thus institute government. Given such a situation, how can the end best be secured? The main danger is abuse of power, and Mill successively demolishes the arguments in favour of the three simple forms of government, monarchical, aristocratic, and democratic, as not providing practical securities. Theories of balance and mixture of powers are similarly dismissed, and Mill goes on, in a chapter quite boldly entitled "In the Representative System alone the Securities for good Government are to be found," to present the programme of the Philosophic Radicals. The best securities, he argues, are first a limitation of the time anyone has in power, so that the gain from improper actions is smaller than the loss sustained by the agent, as a member of the community, through the abuse,

[41] *Earlier Letters*, XII, 13.

and smaller than the loss he will sustain through punishment. Second and more important, is the broadening of the electorate to ensure that the interest of the electors is equivalent to that of the community as a whole. (He excludes men under forty and women from the electorate.) To the objection that the people are incapable of acting in their own interest he replies that, even if the objection is valid, it is better to give power to those who make mistakes than to those who act according to their own sinister interest. Knowledge, furthermore, will correct the mistakes and their consequent evils by indicating where the true interest of individuals lies, and such knowledge is possessed already by the enlightened middle class.[42]

Bentham was apparently converted by James Mill to democratic and representative beliefs, and it is not surprising that his argument is the same in almost all details. Insisting as always on the close connection between ethics and politics, in means as well as ends, he asserts in his *Constitutional Code* that

> The right and proper end of government in every political community, is the greatest happiness of all the individuals of which it is composed, say, in other words, the greatest happiness of the greatest number. . . .
> The *actual* end of government is, in every political community, the greatest happiness of those, whether one or many, by whom the powers of government are exercised.

To prove the last assertion he, like James Mill, appeals to experience without citing any, and also to "the general, indeed the all-comprehensive, principle of human nature," self-interest. He continues: "for causing it [the rulers' interest] to take that direction, in which it will be subservient

---

[42] It is possible that the *Essay on Government* may in fact be, or be in large part based on, the "unpublished dialogue on Government, written by [James Mill] on the Platonic model," mentioned by J. S. Mill in his *Autobiography*, 45. (He too worked on a Platonic dialogue on the subject while on his early French trip; again the matter may be related.) The essay as it stands has a rather unusual form, being dependent in great measure on questions, objections, and their answers. If this connection could be established, part of the difficulty in understanding the Philosophic Radicals' pleasure in the essay might be removed. Its strength as an argumentative work lies in its concise, but ill-connected, presentation of tenets which were passionately held by Mill's closest associates. It had little power to persuade those not already persuaded; it could, however, have cleared difficulties from the novice's path, and it certainly provided material for debate and argument with opponents. A full study of it also waits on an appreciation of the significance of its appearance as an encyclopaedia article, and an untangling of its bibliographic history.

to the universal interest, the nature of the case affords no other method, than that which consists in the bringing of the particular interest of rulers into accordance with the universal interest." Of these three passages, says Bentham, the "first declares, what *ought to be*, the next, what *is*, the last, the *means* of bringing what is into accordance with what ought to be." [43] The basis of the argument, and Bentham adds, of the *Constitutional Code* as a whole, is the primacy of the principles embodied in the first two statements, that is, the greatest happiness principle and the self-preference principle. Political theory is concerned solely with the means of bringing the two into consonance. As James Mill says in the *Westminster Review*: "In legislation the only enquiry is, how to make the interest of men and their duty coincide." [44]

With Mill, Bentham holds that the first essential is the destruction of the influence of sinister interests. These, while opposed to the general interest, are of course the result, for Bentham, of the perfectly laudable desire of the individual for his own happiness. But in the social and political area an artificial identity of interests must be produced. This identity is achieved by making the legislative body correspond in composition to the body politic: the interest of the law-makers, as James Mill argues, will then coincide with that of the law-obeyers. Only in a democracy is this condition satisfied, and only a representative democracy is possible. Being a practical man, Bentham after coming to these conclusions devoted himself to the institution of a democratic representative government. Also, being a practical man and a law-abiding citizen with a healthy respect for property, he favoured reform through constitutional means, and not through revolution.[45] By definition (and definition too often has pride of place over fact for the Philosophic Radicals) the government of England was in the hands of those with sinister interests. The problem was to define those interests, expose them, and finally remove them from power. The clear light of reason, plus some public pressure induced by legitimate exaggeration through the press, should dissolve and crush the malevolent

[43] *Constitutional Code, Works*, IX, 5–6. Cf. Halévy's discussion, 404–5.

[44] "Periodical Literature," *Westminster Review*, 1 (1824), 213.

[45] For a fresh and persuasive look at the Philosophic Radicals' theory and tactics of political change, see Joseph Hamburger, *James Mill and the Art of Revolution* (Yale University Press, 1963). Bentham was made a citizen of France after the Revolution, but he sympathized far more with the aims of the revolutionaries than their means, and contributed armaments only in the form of perfect codes of laws. Cf. Neff, 84.

bodies supported only by fictions. At least in print, Bentham seems to have shared with James Mill an almost absolute trust in the power of logical ratiocination to persuade, and to persuade to action.

The sinister forces were, for Bentham and Mill, the aristocratic bodies in state and church, who controlled not only the Church and the House of Lords, but also the House of Commons, the landed property, and the law courts.[46] The House of Commons being most important and most readily available for reform, the Radicals devoted much time to revealing the unsatisfactory composition of the lower House. The Whigs and Tories, in their view, were basically identical, being interested only in the spoils of office, and not in the general welfare. James Mill, writing (in the third person, as he often did) to his friend Thomson, says he "would despise himself if he cared one farthing which was uppermost of two individual factions who are only contending with one another for the privilege of preying upon the rest of their countrymen. . . ."[47] Under the present constitution, of course, the parties were merely manifesting uncontrolled the political consequences of the laws of human nature. As Bentham notes:

All parties are, in fact, at all times, resolvable into two: that which is in possession, and that which is in expectancy, of the sweets of government. Between the two, there is always the semblance of a difference; for the party which, being out of office, acts against office with its abuses, cannot act against it without acting to an extent more or less considerable for the People. There is, therefore, always the semblance of a difference; but with regard to the People's interests, there is never anything more than a semblance.[48]

These opinions are gathered into a head in James Mill's great onslaught on the *Edinburgh Review* in the first number of the *Westminster* (continued in the second by his son, who had collected the materials for both articles). There he examines the Constitution from the Radical point of

[46] See for example, "Philip Beauchamp" (i.e., George Grote, on the basis of Bentham's manuscripts), *Analysis of the Influence of Natural Religion* (London, 1822), 140: "One of the most noxious properties . . . in the profession of men to which natural religion gives birth, is its coincidence and league with the sinister interests of earth. . . . Prostration and plunder of the community is indeed the common end of both." Cf. Halévy, 294, and G. L. Nesbitt, *Benthamite Reviewing* (New York, 1934), 69.

[47] Quoted in Alexander Bain, *James Mill* (London, 1882), 167 (22/2/18).

[48] *Memoirs, Works*, X, 81. According to Bowring (*ibid.*, 79) this was written in 1822, that is, before James Mill developed the same thought in the first issue of the *Westminster*.

view, pointing out that the aristocracy, supported by the Church and the legal profession, controls both Houses of Parliament, and he goes on to discuss the party struggle in almost exactly the same way as Bentham, with special reference to the false appeal to the people by both parties. Finally he turns to the Whig Party and the *Edinburgh Review*, its mouthpiece, as manifesting this sort of hypocrisy: lacking popular sympathies and a broad view, they shilly-shally, trim, and waver, now appealing to the public at large, now temporizing, and now revealing the aristocratic beliefs really typical of them.

Here again, as always, securities are needed.[49] The modifications required in the representation of the people, simple in nature if difficult to attain in practice, are best seen as "securities for good government." The programme may finally be reduced to Bentham's concise statement: "In truth," he says, "representation requires only four things to be perfect – Secrecy, Annuality, Equality, Universality."[50] These are the means to the goal; once achieved, they will reduce and finally destroy the sinister interests, and the reign of justice, peace and happiness – that is, the reign of utility – will begin.

These then, are the beliefs, and this the programme, in and for which John Mill was educated. He embraced and propagated them with all the fervour and strength of his youth. But just as he was entering manhood, his enthusiasm escaped almost overnight.

[49] James Mill, "Periodical Literature," 222 and *passim*. See also Bentham, *Works*, I, 76, 302; II, 269–70; IX, 11–13. Cf. C. M. Atkinson, *Jeremy Bentham* (London, 1905), 105–6.   [50] *Memoirs, Works*, X, 587.

2

Mental Crisis
and
Resolution

EXCEPTING the sentence in which Mill says he began to learn Greek at three years of age, probably no part of his *Autobiography* is as well known as his account of the depression which seized him in the winter of 1826–7. Its significance matches its fame, for his career as an independent thinker began with a resolution of the problems the depression made him face. In the autumn of 1826, he says,

I was in a dull state of nerves, such as everybody is occasionally liable to; unsusceptible to enjoyment or pleasurable excitement; one of those moods when what is pleasure at other times, becomes insipid or indifferent; the state, I should think, in which converts to Methodism usually are, when smitten by their first 'conviction of sin.' In this frame of mind it occurred to me to put the question directly to myself: 'Suppose that all your objects in life were realized; that all the changes in institutions and opinions which you are looking forward to, could be completely effected at this very instant: would this be a great joy and happiness to you?' And an irrepressible self-consciousness distinctly answered, 'No!' At this my heart sank within me: the whole foundation on which my life was constructed fell down. All my happiness was to have been found in the continual pursuit of this end. The end had ceased to charm, and how could there ever again be any interest in the means? I seemed to have nothing left to live for. (94)

Much has been written on what Mill called "a crisis in [his] mental history," which is usually simply referred to as his "mental crisis." It has not been sufficiently noted that the latter phrase connotes more to the twentieth-century reader than Mill probably intended, and it is useful to recall that from all the evidence, his normal routine was unaffected for some time; when he withdrew from some of his activities two or three years later there were other, obviously valid reasons. And it is not merely facetious to note that the "dull state of nerves" came on during the influenza season when, as Michael Packe says, following Voltaire, the east wind blows and "Englishmen hang themselves in dozens." [1]

Actually the reasons for the onset of the depression are not difficult to find. He had certainly been overworking, having just completed the monumental labour of editing the five volumes of Bentham's *Rationale* from nearly illegible manuscripts, and reading law to fill lacunæ in the manuscripts. He had been writing regularly for the *Westminster* and for the *Parliamentary Review* as well as for newspapers; he continued to learn his job at the East India House (never, it must be admitted, very onerous – but still a job); he debated and argued with friends and opponents morning and evening; and he continued to take a large part in the education of his sisters and brothers. A close look at his labours in these years is enough of itself to bring on a state of depression in the viewer.

Looked at more as Mill himself saw it, the depression is again easily explained. He had been launched in life with a perfect formal scheme for curing society's ills. He threw himself into the curative work without hesitation, and did not discover for some years that the implementation of the scheme for providing universal happiness was not providing his own happiness. He was at the age when men are impatient, unwilling to accept delays or to compromise with supposed stupidity, unable to look far beyond the moment, and the utilitarian programme seemed to move too slowly. Had he been six years younger, the triumph of the Philosophic Radicals with the passing of the Reform Act of 1832 would at least have modified his distress. (The failure of that Act to change the moral complexion of England might still have led to depression in the following years.) He needed some kind of triumph, and it was not forthcoming. Almost certainly he was envious of his father, though the envy was repressed, hidden under clear admiration, which included admiration of James Mill's methods. So he began a self-defeating analysis of his position, self-defeating because the analysis had already been made with great care by the father on behalf of the son. From the analytic point of view, there was nothing wrong: he had been given all the correct associations that could be given in the imperfect state of society into which he had been

[1] Michael Packe, *John Stuart Mill* (London, 1954), 80, citing Voltaire's *Lettres choisiés* (Paris, n.d.), I, 115.

born; he had a moral task before him; he had the tools to get on with the job – nothing was wrong.

But a state of sin is a state of sin, and Mill felt himself to be in one. From unadulterated selfishness to universal benevolence: he could not find the way. He did not want to do evil (at least consciously), and yet he did not want to do good. He had, as he says, "nothing left to live for." Quite baldly, he felt cut off from his fellow-man, alienated, lonely, and deeply unhappy. His few friends could not, or were not asked for, help, and his father was, wisely it would appear, not applied to, his remedies already having failed.[2] Rest was no immediate aid, nor were books – until one book gave him release, and led him to poetry. Marmontel's *Mémoires* revealed to him that he could react emotionally,[3] and he found some pleasure in "the ordinary incidents of life" and "enjoyment, not intense, but sufficient for cheerfulness, in sunshine and sky, in books, in conversation, in public affairs. . . ." [4] There were recurrences of the distress, but gradually time and business buried the pain, and poetry and sympathy brought the pleasure to birth.

Explanations of how Mill got out of his "mental crisis" are more complex than explanations of how he got into it. By all odds the most interesting to the modern mind is Professor Levi's psychoanalytic account, which begins with the parallel between the account in Marmontel and Mill's own situation vis-à-vis his father. Once the explanation has been offered, the very words of Mill's account become obvious evidence: in Marmontel the passage which brought him to tears concerns the death of a father, the subsequent distress of the family, "and the sudden inspiration" by which Marmontel, "then a mere boy, felt and made them feel that he would be everything to them – would supply the place of all that they had lost." [5]

[2] From this time, while no estrangement can safely be posited, there was certainly a lack of sympathy between father and son. They quarrelled over John's friendship with Roebuck and Graham, and it is even possible that he did not join in his father's quarrel with Bentham a few years later, although they withdrew from the *Westminster Review* together. See my "John Stuart Mill and Jeremy Bentham," 253–4, but also 258.

[3] I should like to think that Bentham, who had early translated one of Marmontel's novels, lent Mill the *Mémoires*.

[4] *Autobiography*, 99.

[5] *Ibid.* See A. W. Levi, "The 'Mental Crisis' of John Stuart Mill," *Psychoanalytic Review*, 32 (1945), 86–101; cf. Samuel Feuer, *Psychoanalysis and Ethics* (Springfield, 1955), 55–60. Gertrude Himmelfarb, in her collection of Mill's essays, *Essays on Politics and Culture* (New York, 1962), xix–xx, sensitively and sensibly, if a bit

Mill's emotional release freed him for new experience, but it was not itself that experience; not having our terms and cunning, he could not identify a repressed death-wish towards his father, and so understanding – if that is the proper word – could not clear the clouds of guilt – if that is the proper word. Furthermore, the release was not from external circumstances: James Mill still lived, and John's familial duties remained what they had been.

It is most likely that rest and relaxation also aided his recovery. He finished editing Bentham's *Rationale*, wrote less (he debated more, but found new friends and stimulus of a different kind in the London Debating Society), and began to take walking tours with such friends as Cole and Grant. The journals of these tours, uninspiring in themselves, show Mill with his own friends rather than with his father, and bear ample testimony to his finding "enjoyment, not intense, but sufficient for cheerfulness, in sunshine and sky. . . ." His increasingly large circle of acquaintance took him away from himself by taking him away from the self who had been totally absorbed in the "movement," and also introduced him to new ideas. Even, it seems probable, his awareness of the validity of criticisms of his father's ideas gave him further reason to live, by giving him a task of reconciliation involving personal satisfaction.[6] He began what it took him more than a decade to accomplish, the revaluation from new perspectives of his intellectual inheritance. This process gave him increasing confidence, and the confident man is seldom morose.

But these explanations need to be joined by another and more complex explanation if one is to understand the "revolution" in his opinions which resulted from his depression, and which led directly to his mature ethical position. This explanation also begins with Mill's account in the *Autobiography* (99–101), where he explains the two marked effects his experience had on his opinions and character. First, he was led to adopt a theory of life like that of Carlyle, dependent on "anti-self-consciousness."

---

tendentiously, extends the discussion to include Mill's reaction to his father's actual death in 1836.

[6] In the London Debating Society he certainly met attacks on the Philosophic Radicals, and perhaps even such direct assaults on James Mill's *Essay on Government* as is contained in Leveson Smith's *Remarks upon an Essay on Government by James Mill* (London, 1827), which foreshadows many of the points raised by Macaulay in 1829 in his famous articles against James Mill. Leveson Smith was a member of the London Debating Society, and his little essay was published posthumously from a manuscript that may possibly have originally been a debating speech.

Never, of course, did he waver in his "conviction that happiness is the test of all rules of conduct, and the end of life." He continues:

But I now thought that this end was only to be attained by not making it the direct end. Those only are happy (I thought) who have their minds fixed on some object other than their own happiness; on the happiness of others, on the improvement of mankind, even on some art or pursuit, followed not as a means, but as itself an ideal end. Aiming thus at something else, they find happiness by the way. The enjoyments of life (such was now my theory) are sufficient to make it a pleasant thing, when they are taken *en passant*, without being made a principal object. Once make them so, and they are immediately felt to be insufficient. They will not bear a scrutinizing examination. Ask yourself whether you are happy, and you cease to be so. The only chance is to treat, not happiness, but some end external to it, as the purpose of life. Let your self-consciousness, your scrutiny, your self-interrogation, exhaust themselves on that; and if otherwise fortunately circumstanced you will inhale happiness with the air you breathe, without dwelling on it or thinking about it, without either forestalling it in imagination, or putting it to flight by fatal questioning. This theory now became the basis of my philosophy of life. And I still hold to it as the best theory for all those who have but a moderate degree of sensibility and of capacity for enjoyment, that is, for the great majority of mankind.

The second change was equally significant for his personal development, and more important ultimately for his thought. He began to give for the first time "the internal culture of the individual" a place "among the prime necessities of human well-being," and so "ceased to attach almost exclusive importance to the ordering of outward circumstances, and the training of the human being for speculation and for action." He continues:

I had now learnt by experience that the passive susceptibilities needed to be cultivated as well as the active capacities, and required to be nourished and enriched as well as guided. I did not, for an instant, lose sight of, or undervalue, that part of the truth which I had seen before; I never turned recreant to intellectual culture, or ceased to consider the power and practice of analysis as an essential condition both of individual and of social development. But I thought that it had consequences which required to be corrected, by joining other kinds of cultivation with it. The maintenance of a due balance among the faculties, now seemed to me of primary importance. The cultivation of the feelings became one of the cardinal points in my ethical and philosophical creed. And my thoughts and inclinations turned in an increasing degree towards whatever seemed capable of being instrumental to that object.

I now began to find meaning in the things which I had read or heard about the importance of poetry and art as instruments of human culture.

The two effects actually worked together: Mill, by connecting altruism with personal cultivation, established the important and indispensable relation between personal emotions and ethical theory. What made the relation living and constant for Mill was poetry, the missing link in his earlier attempts to connect abstract theory with a way of life.

Having failed to find inspiration in Byron's poetry, he says he was surprised to find in Wordsworth, to whom he turned during a recurrence of depression in 1828, the specific for his condition.[7] The reasons, he says in re-examining his reaction, were that Wordsworth's poetry appealed to "one of the strongest" of his "pleasurable susceptibilities, the love of rural objects and natural scenery" (especially of mountains, his "ideal of natural beauty"), and it was also, and more importantly, "a medicine" for his state of mind, expressing "not mere outward beauty, but states of feeling, and of thought coloured by feeling, under the excitement of beauty." This comment in the *Autobiography* (103–4) recalls his earlier remark (50) that he had always been at least passively susceptible to poetry or oratory "which appealed to the feelings on any basis of reason." Here is the key to his response: an appeal to feeling on the basis of reason remained for him the essential task of poetry, essential in two ways, as defining the "essence" of the poet (or of poetry), and as answering to individual and social necessities. Mill had found, through personal experience, that the poet is peculiarly useful in promoting individual adherence to and action for the greatest happiness of the greatest number.

Initially, as has been seen, poetry was medicinal for Mill in arousing, as had Marmontel's *Mémoires*, feelings which he thought he lacked or had lost. Wordsworth's poetry, coming after his depression, showed him that his education had ignored the affective for the intellectual. In it he found the "very culture of the feelings" for which he was searching, as well as "a source of inward joy, or sympathetic and imaginative pleasure . . ." (*Autobiography*, 104). Without feeling there was no desire, without desire no motivation, without motivation no action, without action no morality. For Bentham and James Mill morality depended on selfish feelings, because only these, in their view, were strong and constant enough to make a science of morality possible. But the younger Mill had found that the

[7] Here again the importance of the Debating Society for Mill is demonstrated; he had presumably read Byron for his speech against Roebuck, 19 Jan., 1827, on the topic "Whether the writings of Lord Byron had an immoral tendency" (Mill's speech, defending Byron, is now lost), and he studied Wordsworth for his speech (lasting two hours) in defence of Wordsworth, on 30 Jan., 1829.

science thus derived had no power to motivate; he turned his attention to the unselfish feelings; and henceforth the "art" or practice of morality was as important to him as the "science" or theory.[8] Eventually he came to believe that while the selfish feelings, as contributing to prudence and probity, were important to the legislator, only altruistic feelings are truly moral.

Because Mill had worried about the diminution of motivation in a progressive world, his discovery of a perpetual source of ethical joy in poetry was especially valuable. He had wondered, he says in the *Autobiography* (102), whether, "if the reformers of society and government could succeed in their objects, and every person in the community were free and in a state of physical comfort, the pleasures of life, being no longer kept up by struggle and privation, would cease to be pleasures." This peculiarly nineteenth-century attitude (open to religious, philosophical, and psychological interpretations) held no more terrors for him once the perennial and universally available source of affective culture was revealed to him. His analysis of the poetic character in his early essays shows his attitude towards the ways in which moral feeling is sustained. Briefly, the position is this: the poet has a fine and quick susceptibility to pleasure and pain, especially to pleasure. His unique mode of mental association, through emotions, gives him an appeal, unlike other benefactors of mankind, not primarily to the intellect; to be truly great, however, he must also cultivate his powers of thought.[9]

Whatever the literary merits of this analysis, which is recognizably

[8] The major importance of the distinction between "art" and "science" for Mill is discussed at length, 64ff. below. Bentham, it would appear, did not usually care to discriminate between them in ethics (see, e.g., *Principles of Morals and Legislation, Works*, I, 148). James Mill, in his *Fragment on Mackintosh* (London, 1835), 177–8, defends himself and Bentham from the charge of incompleteness as moral thinkers by saying that they were concerned with "the theory of morals, not the practice. They [again he writes in the third person] had to expound those phenomena of our nature which involve the judgment we form of actions as right and wrong. Their duty was exposition solely. Inculcation is the province of the practical moralist. . . ." As educators of John Mill, however, they were inculcators, and the charge of incompleteness is still valid.

[9] See "On Genius," *Monthly Repository*, 6 (1832); "What is Poetry?" *ibid.*, 7 (1833); "Writings of Junius Redivivus," *ibid.*; "Writings of Junius Redivivus," *Tait's Edinburgh Magazine*, 3 (1833); "The Two Kinds of Poetry," *Monthly Repository*, 7 (1833); and "Tennyson's Poems," *London and Westminster Review*, 1 & 30 (1835). There is also relevant material in his contemporary writings in the *Examiner*. The important material in his letters to Carlyle is discussed in the text following.

Romantic,[10] its value for Mill's ethical position cannot be denied. Believing himself deficient in sensibility, he strove to cultivate in himself a poetic receptivity, and while he succeeded in opening himself to poetic culture, he did not make the mistake of confusing his own powers with those of the poet. This point emerges clearly in his early correspondence with Carlyle, which is a seed-bed of ideas, especially in 1832 and 1833, the years when most of Mill's published comments on poetry appeared. He begins the topic by mentioning (17 July, 1832) that he, unlike Carlyle, is called to logic rather than art (the higher "vocation"), and adds that only in the artist's hands does "Truth" become "impressive, and a living principle of action." [11] But different ages call for different talents, and in the present time, he feels, when only the understanding is cultivated and trusted, people are influenced most easily by lessons in logical garb. So, he says in a letter written 18 May, 1833:

my word again is partly intelligible to many more persons than yours is, because mine is presented in the logical and mechanical form which partakes most of this age and country, yours in the artistical and poetical (at least in one sense of those words though not the sense I have been recently giving them) [12] which finds *least* entrance into any minds now, except when it comes before them as mere dilettantism and pretends not to make any serious call upon them to change their lives.[13]

The "serious call" – the phrase probably reflects the Nonconformist influence on him at the time – is found, then, in the "artistic and poetical" word as well as in the "logical and mechanical" one. He mentions the same day to W. J. Fox his "growing want of interest in all the subjects" which he understands, coupled with "a growing sense of incapacity *ever* to have real knowledge of, or insight into the subjects in which alone [he will] ever again feel a strong interest," [14] and on 5 July he writes again to Carlyle to explain what he meant by calling him Poet and Artist:

I conceive that most of the highest truths, are, to persons endowed by nature in certain ways which I think I could state, intuitive; that is, they need neither explanation nor proof, but if not known before, are assented to as soon as

[10] For further discussions of Mill's theory of poetry, see M. H. Abrams, *The Mirror and the Lamp* (New York, 1953), esp. 23–5, 333–5, and my "John Stuart Mill's Theory of Poetry," *University of Toronto Quarterly*, 29 (1960), 420–38, which is partly reproduced here.

[11] *Earlier Letters*, XII, 113.

[12] Presumably Mill refers to his "What is Poetry?" which had appeared in the preceding January.   [13] *Earlier Letters*, XII, 155–6.   [14] *Ibid.*, 157.

stated. Now it appears to me that the poet or artist is conversant chiefly with *such* truths and that his office in respect to truth is to declare *them*, and to make them *impressive*. This, however, supposes that the reader, hearer, or spectator is a person of the kind to whom those truths *are* intuitive. Such will of course receive them at once, and will lay them to heart in proportion to the impressiveness with which the artist delivers and embodies them. But the other and more numerous kind of people will consider them as nothing but dreaming or madness: and the more so, certainly, the more powerful the artist, *as* an artist: because the means which are good for rendering the truth impressive to those who know it, are not the same and are often absolutely incompatible with those which render it intelligible to those who know it not. Now this last I think is the proper office of the logician or I might say the metaphysician, in truth he must be both. The same person may be poet and logician, but he cannot be both in the same composition: and as heroes have been frustrated of glory 'carent quia vate sacro,' so I think the *vates* himself has often been misunderstood and successfully cried down for want of a Logician in Ordinary, to supply a logical commentary on his intuitive truths. The artist's is the highest part, for by him alone is real *knowledge* of such truths conveyed: but it is possible to convince him who never could *know* the intuitive truths, that they are not inconsistent with anything he *does* know; that they are even very *probable*, and that he may have faith in them when higher natures than his own affirm that they are truths.

His own task, he says again, is the humbler one of the man of speculation:

I am not in the least a poet, in any sense; but I can do homage to poetry. I can to a very considerable extent feel it and understand it, and can make others who are my inferiors understand it in proportion to the measure of their capacity. I believe that such a person is more wanted than even the poet himself; that there are more persons living who approximate to the latter character than to the former. . . . Now one thing not useless to do would be to exemplify this difference by enlarging in my logical fashion upon the difference itself: to make those who are not poets, understand that poetry is higher than Logic, and that the union of the two is Philosophy. . . .[15]

Carlyle still not being satisfied with the explanation (or perhaps the praise), Mill writes again (2 August, 1833): "By logic . . . I meant the antithesis of Poetry or Art: in which distinction I am learning to perceive a twofold contrast: the *literal* as opposed to the *symbolical*, and *reasoning* as opposed to *intuition*. Not the *theory* of reasoning but the *practice*. In reasoning I include all processes of thought which are *processes* at all, that is, which proceed by a series of steps or links." [16]

The distinction is clear – the speaker of the Word as against the weaver of arguments – and clearly leaves the Artist in the position of preaching

[15] *Ibid.*, 163. Cf. *ibid.*, 219 (2/3/34).   [16] *Ibid.*, 173.

to the converted. It would appear that the weight of conversion rests on the thin shoulders of the Logician. Insight is translated into syllogism, for comprehension must precede true belief. With belief (in Newman's pregnant terms) certainty can give way to certitude, and then action can follow. The full importance of these remarks waits upon an examination of the influence of Harriet Taylor, which had begun before they were written, and also upon an elucidation of the final chapter of his *Logic*, the first major work of his career, on which he had begun work in the early 1830s. One conclusion can usefully be anticipated, however: while clarification and analysis, the work of the Logician or Scientist (as Mill came to call him), are requisite, it is finally the Artist who tries to induce a current of morality into the community.

One further element in Mill's theory of poetry needs special consideration in connection with his ethics: his view of imagination. Sometimes he accepts the meaning given by his father, that is, "train of ideas." Sometimes, too, he uses it in the common way, as signifying a "train of ideas" which is not believed accurately to reflect "reality." But when he applies the term to the poet, it is used to describe an active power. He refers, for example, to "that kind of self-observation which is called *imagination*" and which, like "simple *observation*," and "a more complicated process of analysis and induction," is a method of extracting "the knowledge of general truth from our own consciousness."[17] A similar meaning is indicated in "What is Poetry?" (62): "What [great poets] know has come by observation of themselves; they have found *there* one highly delicate, and sensitive, and refined specimen of human nature, on which the laws of human emotion are written in large characters, such as can be read off without much study. . . ." But beneath this power of observation must lie another if the poet is to avoid narrowness; this more basic power, that of imagination, needs the information gathered by a cultivated intellect but, being active, is not limited by such information. This meaning is evident in his discussion of acting, which has obvious relevance to poetry as well: "A great actor must possess imagination, in the higher and more extensive meaning of the word: that is, he must be able to conceive correctly, and paint vividly within himself, states of external circumstances, and of the human mind, into which it has not happened to himself to be thrown."[18] He agrees with Pemberton, an actor,

17 "On Genius," 652.   18 "French Theatre," *Examiner*, 22 May, 1831, 325.

that in acting, as in every thing else, genius does not consist in being a copyist; even from nature: That the actor of genius is not he who observes and imitates what men of particular characters, and in particular situations, *do*, but he who can, by an act of imagination, actually *be* what they *are*: who can so completely understand, and so vividly conceive, the state of their minds, that the conception shall call up in his own the very emotions, and thereby draw from him the very sounds and gestures, which would have been exhibited by the imaginary being whom he is personifying. Such a man's representation of nature will have a consistency and keeping in it, and will reach depths in the human heart, which no man's opportunities and powers of mere outward observation could ever have enabled him to attain to.[19]

Here again Mill sets off imagination from "outward observation," but clearly some such observation is necessary for the portrayal of other men. He is suggesting, actually, that passive copying or reporting is not art; art lies in the active sharing in the feelings of the imitated or described person; and this sharing is achieved through imagination. Pemberton has the "faculty" or "power," says Mill, "to call up by a voluntary effort of imagination, what he not unhappily terms *secondary* feelings, that is, feelings suggested by a vivid conception of similar feelings in others: and by thus *realizing* for the time being, an imaginary character, to give a profoundly true dramatic representation of it."[20] Elsewhere Mill even introduces the crucial term "creative imagination," but adds little to his previous suggestions: "The faculty of thus bringing home to us a coherent conception of beings unknown to our experience, not by logically *characterizing* them, but by a living *representation* of them, such as they would, in fact, *be*, if the hypothesis of their possibility could be realized – is what is meant, when anything is meant, by the words creative imagination."[21]

In the discussion of Tennyson, from which this last passage is taken, Mill points out that the reader must co-operate with the poet by suspending his "critical understanding" and giving his "spontaneous feelings fair play," surrendering his "imagination to the guidance of the poet. . . ."[22] He will then feel with, sympathize with, the characters in the portrayed situation to the extent that the poet is able to recreate the feelings in his readers by first creating them imaginatively in himself.

It must be noted that while Mill sees the necessity of unity of

[19] "Pemberton," *ibid.*, 3 June, 1832, 358.
[20] *Ibid.* Cf. "Bentham," *Dissertations and Discussions*, I, 353.
[21] "Tennyson's Poems," 421n.   [22] *Ibid.*, 409.

conception and execution for the highest art, he does not see imagination as the controlling, unifying power. Neither can the acute sensitivity of the poet by nature be relied on for unity of effect or even of tone. For Mill the greatest poet must use what is finally his highest gift, the intellect; it cannot create poetry, but masterworks cannot be created without it. It governs the essential, but essentially random, emotions and associations; it selects, discards, and adds. Without the horse, feeling, the rider, intellect, gets nowhere, but without the rider's spurs, the horse goes anywhere. So, as Mill warns Tennyson, and as he hints to Carlyle, "poetical" conclusions must be supported by evidence, especially when philosophical questions are raised. But equally, philosophers are warned not to deny the validity of poetry, for philosophic systems must be both "comprehensive" and "commanding":

Let our philosophical system be what it may, human feelings exist : human nature, with all its enjoyments and sufferings, its strugglings, its victories and defeats, still remain [sic] to us; and these are the materials of all poetry. Whoever, in the greatest concerns of human life, pursues truth with unbiassed feelings, and an intellect adequate to discern it, will not find that the resources of poetry are lost to him because he has learnt to use, and not abuse them. They are as open to him as they are to the sentimental weakling, who has no test of the true but the ornamental. And when he once has them under his command, he can wield them for purposes, and with a power, of which neither the dilettante nor the visionary have the slightest conception.[23]

The control comes from the philosophy (intellect); the power from the poetry (feeling).

This account of Mill's poetic theory, brief as it is, will indicate that his state of mind in the years 1832–35 was far removed from that of 1826–27, when he had "nothing left to live for." It is not too much to say that poetry gave him something to live for, by lending initial force to his awakening altruism. The full implications can, however, only emerge after the new influences on him in the early 1830s are assessed (see Chapters iii and iv). The decade 1830 to 1840 was that in which he put together the strands of the past with the filaments of the present, and it ended with the assertion of his independent position.

Contemporary with the new influences was the reassessment of the old. That reassessment is properly seen in connection with Mill's new knowledge and his final position, but first one must look again at his rela-

[23] *Ibid.*, 423. Cf. *Earlier Letters*, XII, 312 (to Bulwer, 23/11/36).

tions with his father and Bentham, for his attitude to them is intimately connected with both his resolution of his mental depression and his combination of old and new.

It will be recalled that, in a passage quoted above (15), Mill attributes his full and willing conversion to Benthamism to his reading of a passage in which Bentham assails all other moral philosophies as based on the sands of vagueness, mystification, and privilege. Curiously, whenever he returned to an evaluation of Bentham, it was this passage he cited, and his reaction to it can be used as a convenient touchstone to reveal his attitude as a whole.[24] Although James Mill was evidently personally estranged from Bentham after the ascendancy of John Bowring in the Master's affections, there is no evidence, apart from his withdrawal from the *Westminster* and his unequivocal distaste for Bowring, that John Mill was similarly estranged. There is even some evidence to the contrary.[25] In any case, he was asked to write Bentham's obituary for the *Examiner*, and he complied with a resounding eulogy (10 June, 1832, 371–2). Bentham's death occurred just when the triumph of the Reform Bill was assured, and the obituary, appearing as it did in the *Examiner*, then an organ of the Philosophic Radicals, is understandably enthusiastic about Bentham's place in the reform movement. But Mill characteristically looks to the moral basis of the movement, and in assessing Bentham's merits, he gives prominent place to his own particular interest. "Mr. Bentham's real merit," he comments, "in respect to the foundation of morals, consists in his having cleared it more thoroughly than any of his predecessors, from the rubbish of pretended natural law, natural justice, and the like, by which men were wont to consecrate as a rule of morality, whatever they felt inclined to approve of without knowing why."

Within a year, however, as new thoughts poured in and out of him, he reached the height of his apostasy in an anonymous discussion of Bentham in Bulwer's *England and the English*. In the "rubbish" referred to in the obituary he had found some hidden treasures:

The principle of utility . . . stands no otherwise demonstrated in his writings, than by an enumeration of the phrases of a different description which have been commonly employed to denote the rule of life, and the rejection of them all, as having no intelligible meaning, further than as they may involve a tacit reference to considerations of utility. Such are the phrases 'law of nature,'

---

[24] For a brief examination of Mill's reliability as a judge of Bentham, see my "John Stuart Mill and Jeremy Bentham," 246–7.   [25] See *ibid.*, 253–4.

'right reason,' 'natural rights,' 'moral sense.' All these Mr. Bentham regarded as mere covers for dogmatism; excuses for setting up one's own *ipse dixit* as a rule to bind other people. 'They consist, all of them,' says he, 'in so many contrivances for avoiding the obligation of appealing to any external standard, and for prevailing upon the reader to accept the author's sentiment or opinion as a reason for itself.'

This, however, is not fair treatment of the believers in other moral principles than that of utility.[26]

In 1838, closing in on his own independent position, he is less sure of the value of Bentham's opponents; moreover his treatment indicates that having taken Bentham off his pedestal, Mill was able to avoid the extremes common to statements about canonical works, and to conduct the examination in terms appropriate to any influential writer. In his "Bentham" (1838) he cites part of the same sentence about "avoiding the obligation of appealing to any external standard," and says, "we could scarcely quote anything more strongly exemplifying both the strength and weakness of his system of philosophy" than the passage as a whole, which he reproduces at length. He then comments:

Few, we believe, are now of opinion that these phrases and similar ones have nothing more in them than Bentham saw. But it will be as little pretended, now-a-days, by any person of authority as a thinker, that the phrases can pass as reasons, till after their meaning has been completely analysed, and translated into more precise language: until the standard they appeal to is ascertained, and the *sense* in which, and the *limits* within which, they are admissible as arguments, accurately marked out.[27]

By 1852, when he wrote his attack on Whewell's moral views, his fame was established, and his position secure. He again quotes the crucial passage, this time at even greater length, and without any introductory qualification,[28] simply as part of his defence of Bentham. And seven years later, in his reprint of "Bentham," he alters the comment of 1838 quoted above, retaining only the first and last words: "Few will contend that this is a perfectly fair representation of the *animus* of those who employ the various phrases so amusingly animadverted on; but that the phrases

[26] Edward Lytton Bulwer, *England and the English* (London, 1833), II, 322. Cf. Mill's note to Bentham's *Rationale* quoted at 16 above.

[27] *London and Westminster Review*, 7 & 29 (1838), 477. Notice the consonance of these remarks with Mill's assessment of his own abilities in the letters to Carlyle quoted at 28–9 above.

[28] *Westminster Review*, n.s. 2 (1852); the passage is reprinted without change in *Dissertations and Discussions*, II, 467–70.

contain no argument, save what is grounded on the very feelings they are adduced to justify, is a truth which Bentham had the eminent merit of first pointing out." [29]

Whatever injustice is done to Bentham by this limited treatment, it at least makes clear that in his middle age, his personal doubts over, Mill returned again to his earlier enthusiasm for Bentham. He saw himself – and here the passage from the *Principles of Morals and Legislation* is most important – as Bentham's ally in a continued battle against just the kind of variable and unverified moral judgments attacked in the passage. He found that Bentham's ethics needed correction by the addition of a private morality founded on personal development, but once this addition was made, he was able fully to appreciate the virtue of Benthamite thought in the public area where mischief was still caused by fools and knaves who hid their sinister interests under loosely formulated moral appeals, or mistook words for facts.

One other element in Mill's reassessment of his teachers is equally significant: the question of method. Here, though Bentham is important, the main light falls on James Mill, and casts shadows back to John Mill's boyhood. In giving instances of his father's great educational expectations, Mill mentions

his indignation at my using the common expression that something was true in theory but required correction in practice; and how, after making me vainly strive to define the word theory, he explained its meaning, and showed the fallacy of the vulgar form of speech which I had used; leaving me fully persuaded that in being unable to give a correct definition of Theory, and in speaking of it as something which might be at variance with practice, I had shown unparalleled ignorance. In this he seems, and perhaps was, very unreasonable; but I think, only in being angry at my failure. A pupil from whom nothing is ever demanded which he cannot do, never does all he can.[30]

What this pupil did, in fact, was concentrate on the particular problem in an almost obsessive way.

The fallacy, if fallacy it be, is also found described in Bentham's *Book of Fallacies*, which John Mill knew. There, as Sidney Smith's adaptation of it in his "Noodle's Oration" shows, the argument is a polemical one. But the problem for John Mill was a logical one, and what he found in his father's writings on the matter did not long satisfy him. Theory, James Mill says in his "Education," is the "*whole* of the knowledge, which we

[29] *Dissertations and Discussions*, I, 344–5.   [30] *Autobiography*, 22.

possess upon any subject, put into that order and form in which it is most easy to draw from it good practical rules. Let any one examine this definition, article by article, and show us that it fails in a single particular. To recommend the separation of practice from theory is, therefore, simply, to recommend bad practice." [31] The "great task of the philosopher" is "that of theorizing the whole. . . ." He works "to observe exactly the facts; to make a perfect collection of them, nothing omitted that is of any importance, nothing included of none; and to record them in that order and form, in which all that is best to be done in practice can be most immediately and certainly perceived." If this statement was at least in part a tactical one,[32] John Mill did not take the admonition as tactical, and so when he found his father's theories assailed by Macaulay and others he took a long hard look at the relations between theory and practice. His principal conclusions were two: first, that more care in preparing theory is necessary than his father thought, and that even when prepared with the greatest care, theories in the moral sciences are subject to modification; second, that the relation between theory and practice must be studied from the practical as well as the theoretical side. Both of these conclusions deserve attention.

In his *Autobiography* (110), Mill admits that the attacks on his father's and Bentham's theory of government had shown him that the theory was not all-inclusive, but until he read Macaulay's attack in the *Edinburgh Review* in 1829 he thought that the theory was not defective in itself, and could be corrected in application. Macaulay's three able and slashing articles (he would have been content with one, if the *Westminster* had not replied) relentlessly exposed the methodological and logical faults of the *Essay on Government*. In his usual fashion, Macaulay informs his articles with wit and verve, and the whole performance is entertaining, although it did not amuse the Philosophic Radicals. Without any conciliatory gestures, he states his position with clarity and force: "Our objection to the Essay of Mr Mill is fundamental. We believe that it is utterly impossible to deduce the science of government from the principles of human nature." [33] How is man to reach valid conclusions in such

[31] *Essays* (London, n.d.), 5. (In this edition, "Not for Sale," the essays are paginated separately.) Cf. *Deontology*, I, 57.

[32] Cf. John Mill's comment (*Autobiography*, 111) that his father should have replied to Macaulay: " 'I was not writing a scientific treatise on politics, I was writing an argument for parliamentary reform.' "

[33] "Mr Mill's Essay on Government," *Edinburgh Review*, 49 (1829), 185.

inquiries? By substituting, Macaulay says, induction for deduction. We must proceed

by that method, which, in every experimental science to which it has been applied, has signally increased the power and knowledge of our species, – by that method for which our new philosophers would substitute quibbles scarcely worthy of the barbarous respondents and opponents of the middle ages, – by the method of Induction; – by observing the present state of the world, – by assiduously studying the history of past ages, – by sifting the evidence of facts, – by carefully combining and contrasting those which are authentic, – by generalizing with judgment and diffidence, – by perpetually bringing the theory which we have constructed to the test of new facts, – by correcting, or alto-gether abandoning it, according as those new facts prove it to be partially or fundamentally unsound. Proceeding thus, – patiently, – diligently, – candidly, – we may hope to form a system as far inferior in pretension to that which we have been examining, and as far superior to it in real utility, as the prescrip-tions of a great physician, varying with every stage of every malady, and with the constitution of every patient, to the pill of the advertising quack, which is to cure all human beings, in all climates, of all diseases.[34]

He sums up his attitude to the Utilitarians in short compass: "almost all their peculiar faults arise from the utter want both of comprehensive-ness and of precision in their mode of reasoning." [35]

James Mill's response, if his son's account is to be trusted, was typical of the man. "He treated Macaulay's argument as simply irrational; an attack upon the reasoning faculty; an example of the saying of Hobbes, that when reason is against a man, a man will be against reason." [36] But when Sir James Mackintosh, in his *Dissertation on the Progress of Ethical Philosophy*, repeated Macaulay's arguments in a less penetrating way, James Mill was stung into preparing the great polemic of his *Fragment on Mackintosh*. This is for the most part an attack on Mackintosh's in-solence in treating the ethical system of the Utilitarians, but Mill turns briefly to a defence of the *Essay on Government*. Here he shows either a reluctance to come to terms with the major objections, or a misunder-standing of them. He remarks, for example, that the *Essay* is a "case of the strictest adherence to the precepts of Bacon," for its argument de-scends from generals to particulars, and this method, with its reverse, is the only proper procedure in politics. This weak and undeveloped position is followed by a similarly weak, though legitimate statement that in the

[34] *Ibid.*, 188–9.

[35] "Utilitarian Theory of Government, and the 'Greatest Happiness Principle,' " *Edinburgh Review*, 50 (1829), 100.   [36] *Autobiography*, 111.

Essay, necessarily a short work, he could only establish the main point without going into minute details.

Still there was no answer to the questions which Macaulay had raised in a passage which, because of its importance to the younger Mill, and despite its length, deserves quotation :

How does he [James Mill] arrive at those principles of human nature from which he proposes to deduce the science of government? We think that we may venture to put an answer into his mouth; for in truth there is but one possible answer. He will say – By experience. But what is the extent of this experience? Is it an experience which includes experience of the conduct of men intrusted with the powers of government; or is it exclusive of that experience? If it includes experience of the manner in which men act when intrusted with the powers of government, then those principles of human nature from which the science of government is to be deduced, can only be known after going through that inductive process by which we propose to arrive at the science of government. Our knowledge of human nature, instead of being prior in order to our knowledge of the science of government, will be posterior to it. And it would be correct to say, that by means of the science of government, and of other kindred sciences – the science of education, for example, which falls under exactly the same principle – we arrive at the science of human nature.

If, on the other hand, we are to deduce the theory of government from principles of human nature, in arriving at which principles we have not taken into account the manner in which men act when invested with the powers of government, then those principles must be defective. They have not been formed by a sufficiently copious induction. . . . [T]he most satisfactory course is to obtain information about the particular case; and whenever this can be obtained, it ought to be obtained. . . . Mr Mill springs at once to a general principle of the widest extent, and from that general principle deduces syllogistically every thing which is included in it. . . . But the true philosopher, the inductive reasoner, travels up to it slowly, through those hundred sciences, of which the science of government is one.[37]

So the principle charges are clear, and the defence, thus far, is negligible. James Mill, and with him his associates and disciples, who not only accepted his doctrine initially but, when its errors were indicated, failed to defend it adequately or to modify it sufficiently, assumed too much, simplified too greatly, and argued too glibly. The deductions which they used exclusively were based on a minimal experience and were faulty, and their conclusions, categorically stated, were frequently illegitimate.

[37] "Bentham's Defence of Mill," *Edinburgh Review*, 49 (1829), 289–91. (Macaulay mistakenly thought Bentham the author of the first defence in the *Westminster*.)

Under the cover of formal logic, they cloaked an argument which, even when reduced to its most acceptable syllogistic form, had no internal consistency, while both assumptions and conclusions had not been verified by history or experience.

Initially it seems to have been his elders' failure to answer these attacks satisfactorily that led John Mills to examine their method, but when he came finally to expound his own position in his *Logic* the same criticisms appear, shorn of course of their asperity. He could not substitute Macaulay's method for his father's, it need hardly be said, for Macaulay was a Whig and a trimmer; in spite of the indebtedness he admits to Macaulay's articles, Mill tends to undervalue them. But admitting that there are some weak spots in Macaulay's argument, and that he had no clear ideas about the problems involved in sociological method, one must still recognize many of his ideas in the last book of Mill's *Logic*.

In this book Mill, in dealing with the misconceptions lying behind fallacious theories of politics and sociology, gives his explanation and defence of his father's position. He devotes a chapter to each of two invalid theories, the "Chemical" and "Geometrical." The first of these is the more widespread, and really the more pernicious. It is the attitude of the man in the street and the politician, of those generally who accept Baconian experimentation as the correct method of procedure, that is, of persons

not much accustomed to scientific investigation : practitioners in politics, who rather employ the commonplaces of philosophy to justify their practice, than seek to guide their practice by philosophic principles : or imperfectly educated persons, who, in ignorance of the careful selection and elaborate comparison of instances required for the formation of a sound theory, attempt to found one upon a few coincidences which they have casually noticed.[38]

The requirements of a sound induction need more careful study than such persons think necessary. As experiment is impossible in the moral sciences, and its conditions could not be adequately fulfilled even if it were possible, there remains only the expedient of watching what nature produces, and what has been produced by man for reasons other than experimental. "We cannot adapt our logical means to our wants, by varying the circumstances as the exigencies of elimination may require. If the spontaneous instances, formed by contemporary events and by the successions of phenomena recorded in history, afford a sufficient variation

[38] *Logic*, II, 479 (VI, viii, 1).

of circumstances, an induction from specific experience is attainable; otherwise not." [39] The question is then simply, do the records of history, and the evidence of the present day, afford enough material? Mill demonstrates that they cannot, and argues that prior deduction, establishing a causal chain, is necessary in sociological investigations. Experience serves to explain only that part of the effect not already known to proceed from previously ascertained causes. But, says Mill, if some political truths can be explained by the laws of human nature, why not all? In short, the experimental method can here be of use solely as a verification of the conclusions drawn from general laws.

Having thus disposed of the "Chemical" method, Mill turns his attention to the consideration which first led him to write a logic of the moral sciences, that is, the method used by James Mill and Bentham in their political theories. To him his teachers were not, of course, men "imperfectly educated," or likely to fall into the trap of philosophical commonplaces. Their error, that of adopting a "Geometrical or Abstract" method, was a subtle one :

It never could have suggested itself but to persons of some familiarity with the nature of scientific research; who, – being aware of the impossibility of establishing, by casual observation or direct experimentation, a true theory of sequences so complex as are those of the social phenomena, – have recourse to the simpler laws which are immediately operative in those phenomena, and which are no other than the laws of the nature of the human beings therein concerned.[40]

They properly, in John Mill's view, treated the science of society as deductive, but – and here is the younger Mill's special point – they failed to give enough attention to the subject matter of their deductions, and did not see, because their scientific education had not proceeded far enough, the complications involved in various types of deductive investigation. They therefore selected for politics the geometrical method, rather than that which the younger Mill believes proper, the astronomical, or more generally, the method of natural philosophy. The "geometricians" err in assuming that the phenomena of politics are uncomplicated. In geometry itself there is no need to provide for conflicting forces, but there is most certainly a need in sociology. In geometry, whatever "is once proved true is true in all cases, whatever supposition may be made in regard to any other matter." [41] The acceptance of its method in politics

[39] Ibid., 471-2 (VI, vii, 2).   [40] Ibid., 479 (VI, viii, 1).   [41] Ibid., 480 (VI, viii, 1)

therefore leads to narrow premises; its practitioners assume that social phenomena are always the result of one force alone, one single property of human nature.

Actually two classes of political theorists are guilty of adopting the geometrical method. One group, sometime allies of the Philosophic Radicals, but always castigated in the writings of the latter as unscientific, are briefly dismissed by Mill here. While their support in practical measures was not refused,[42] he too had little use for the Natural-Rights men, those who

deduce political conclusions not from laws of nature, not from sequences of phenomena, real or imaginary, but from unbending practical maxims. Such, for example, are all who found their theory of politics on what is called abstract right, that is to say, on universal precepts. . . . Such, in like manner, are those who make the assumption of a social contract, or any other kind of original obligation, and apply it to particular cases by mere interpretation.[43]

Their fundamental error lies in their treatment of an Art as though it were a Science, which leads them to the anomaly of a deductive Art. This group, therefore, are doubly in error, for they use geometrical methods, and base original premises of their argument upon false principles.

This account is merely preliminary to the most important part of Mill's argument, which is devoted to the other class of geometrical reasoners, adherents of "the interest-philosophy of the Bentham school." They base their theory of government on one premise, "that men's actions are always determined by their interests." But what does "interest" mean? (James Mill had retorted to Mackintosh that he intended only the "rough and common acceptation.") If, John Mill says, "interest" means "anything which a person likes," there is nothing more profound in the concept than that men's wishes determine their actions.[44] This simple meaning seems to be that held by some of Bentham's followers, but in politics "interest" must mean "private, or worldly, interest." In this case, the assertation that men's actions are always determined by their interests is far from universally true. (Mill admits that in politics the tenet of the school is not without value, for many men, man in the mass, and series of rulers will "be governed in the bulk of their conduct by their personal interests.")[45]

[42] An example of Mill's tenet that people disagreeing on fundamental principles may agree on practical measures and intermediate ends; see 124, 142 below.

[43] *Logic*, II, 481 (VI, viii, 2).　　　　　　[44] Macaulay also points this out.

[45] Cf. *Logic*, II, 139–41 (III, xxiii, 7); much of Book VI is, as Kubitz points out, prepared for in Book III.

The interest-philosophers also infer that the only rulers "who will govern according to the interest of the governed, are those whose selfish interests are in accordance with it." And they add a third proposition,

that no rulers have their selfish interest identical with that of the governed, unless it be rendered so by accountability, that is, by dependence on the will of the governed. In other words . . . that the desire of retaining or the fear of losing their power, and whatever is thereon consequent, is the sole motive which can be relied on for producing on the part of rulers a course of conduct in accordance with the general interest.

The school's theory, therefore, is composed of three syllogisms and depends on two general premises. In each of these premises "a certain effect is considered as determined only by one cause, not by a concurrence of causes. In the one, it is assumed that the actions of average rulers are determined solely by self-interest; in the other, that the sense of identity of interest with the governed, is produced and producible by no other cause than responsibility."

The account is a fair one, but the summary comment would have been unthinkable for Mill fifteen years earlier: "Neither of these propositions," he says, "is by any means true; the last is extremely wide of the truth." As to the first, ignoring the effect of philanthropy and duty upon rulers' actions (for, he characteristically remarks, such motives are not to be relied on),

the character and course of their actions is largely influenced (independently of personal calculation) by the habitual sentiments and feelings, the general modes of thinking and acting, which prevail throughout the community of which they are members; as well as by the feelings, habits, and modes of thought which characterize the particular class in that community to which they themselves belong.

The maxims and traditions passed down from other rulers are also an important element in determining their modes of action.

The second proposition, that identity of interest is only to be produced by responsibility, is even less admissible as a universal truth. Speaking only of "identity in essentials," and not of visionary and impracticable perfect identity, Mill instances cases in which the personal interest of a ruler – the consolidation of his power – has led him to act in ways which accord with the general interest. The establishment of strong central powers in Europe in the Middle Ages, resulting in the suppression of resistance to law and the establishment of order, was in accordance

with the ruler's own search for power; but it corresponded with the general interest. Similarly with Elizabeth: "everything that the people had most at heart, the monarch had at heart too" – and yet there was no responsibility. "Had Peter the Great, or the rugged savages whom he began to civilize, the truest inclination towards the things which were for the real interest of those savages?"

Such were the mistakes of his teachers, Mill says, but he adds that mere criticism does not constitute political theory. Much of their argument had a direct relevance to the state of affairs in England at the beginning of the nineteenth century; their mistakes were in form, but their aims, like the abuses they attacked, were substantial. Here is Mill's best defence of his father's political theory, and when one reads it, one is aware that by 1843, when it was written, most of the ghosts of his early years had been laid. The mistake of the school, he says,

consisted in presenting in a systematic shape, and as the scientific treatment of a great philosophical question, what should have passed for that which it really was, the mere polemics of the day. Although the actions of rulers are by no means wholly determined by their selfish interests, it is chiefly as a security against those selfish interests that constitutional checks are required; and for that purpose such checks, in England, and the other nations of modern Europe, can in no manner be dispensed with. It is likewise true, that in these same nations, and in the present age, responsibility to the governed is the only means practically available to create a feeling of identity of interest, in the cases, and on the points, where that feeling does not sufficiently exist. To all this, and to the arguments which may be founded on it in favour of measures for the correction of our representative system, I have nothing to object; but I confess my regret, that the small though highly important portion of the philosophy of government, which was wanted for the immediate purpose of serving the cause of parliamentary reform, should have been held forth by thinkers of such eminence as a complete theory.

Mill hastens to add that their practice is not a true measure of their worth, for they "were too highly instructed, of too comprehensive intellect, and some of them of too sober and practical a character, for such an error," and they were ready to make allowances in applying their doctrines.[46] But allowances are not enough: "There is little chance of making due amends in the superstructure of a theory for the want of sufficient breadth in its foundations. It is unphilosophical to construct a science out of a few of the agencies by which the phenomena are

---

[46] From one point of view, the argument of Joseph Hamburger's *James Mill and the Art of Revolution* is an explanation of this readiness.

determined, and leave the rest to the routine of practice or the sagacity of conjecture." In social science, all laws of nature, however apparently insignificant, must play a role in rational theory. "The whole of the qualities of human nature influence those phenomena" of society, Mill comments, "and there is not one which influences them in a small degree. There is not one, the removal or any great alteration of which would not materially affect the whole aspect of society, and change more or less the sequences of social phenomena generally." [47]

As usual, Mill does not isolate his father when criticizing the Philosophic Radicals, but in effect he is showing the weak spots in James Mill's political writings that he himself, as is shown in Part II below, tried to overcome. To begin with, James Mill's foundations were too narrow – not in themselves mistaken, but insufficient. The younger Mill always retained a note of respect for the wisdom of his elders; in "Aphorisms" he argues, for example, with his father undoubtedly in mind: "A scientific system is often spun out of a few original assumptions, without any intercourse with nature at all; but he who has generalized copiously and variously from actual experience, must have thrown aside so many of his first generalizations as he went on, that the residuum can hardly be altogether worthless." [48] His father had, in spite of the evidence of his *Essay on Government*, been too much in and of the world not to have used his wide experience; his assumptions, therefore, narrow as they appear to the casual reader, actually are those left over from a vast number tried and found wanting. The correction is to be made not by throwing away everything, but by rescuing the baby from the bath water. The younger Mill's acceptance of Carlyle, Coleridge, and Comte as mentors was in part due, as many critics have seen, to his desire to repair the deficiencies in the teachings of Bentham and James Mill, but the process was neither that of putting new wine in old bottles, as some have thought, nor that of off with the old, on with the new, as others have held. The shortest statement that has any claim to accuracy is rather trite: he retained much learned from Bentham and James Mill, but made it his own; any inconsistencies are his own responsibility, not his elders'.

More needs to be said, however, about their failings, for the younger Mill saw further weaknesses in their application of theories. His own education had been directed too much towards "knowing that" and too

[47] The preceding quotations are all from *Logic*, II, 481–7 (VI, viii, 3).
[48] *Dissertations and Discussions*, I, 209.

little to "knowing how." Many times he tried to characterize the error of his father, sometimes naming him, but more often referring generally to "geometrical" speculators. One of the direct references is in a note to James Mill's *Analysis of the Phenomena of the Human Mind*, where he mentions his father's "impatience of detail." "The bent of his mind was towards that, in which also his greatest strength lay; in seizing the larger features of a subject – the commanding laws which govern and connect many phenomena." [49] This criticism appears in the *Autobiography* (16) thus: "A defect running through his otherwise admirable modes of instruction, as it did through all his modes of thought, was that of trusting too much to the intelligibleness of the abstract, when not embodied in the concrete." An example is to be seen in the opening remarks of James Mill's article advocating the ballot. The only possible objection to his argument, he says, is that it is too complete. (In fact the argument is based, as usual, on "the principles of human nature.") "People who have their reasons for not liking a conclusion to which demonstration leads," he says, echoing the Hobbsian argument against Macaulay attributed to him in the *Autobiography*, "have nothing for it but to decry demonstration." [50] Only the demonstration is important; correctness of the deductions being accepted, the matter is proved. But as John Mill, prompted by Macaulay's attack,[51] argues in "On the Definition of Political Economy":

We are . . . in great danger of adverting to a portion only of the causes which are actually at work. And if we are in this predicament, the more accurate our deductions and the more certain our conclusions in the abstract, (that is, making abstraction of all circumstances except those which form part of the hypothesis,) the less we are likely to suspect that we are in error: for no one can have looked closely into the sources of fallacious thinking without being deeply conscious that the coherence, and neat concatenation of our philosophical systems, is more apt than we are commonly aware to pass with us as evidence of their truth.[52]

So the error of abstraction compounds the error of incompleteness. The mind becomes "the slave of its own hypotheses"; limiting the problem arbitrarily to suit our purposes, we forget the limitations, and assume

[49] *Analysis*, ed. J. S. Mill (London, 1869), I, xix.
[50] "The Ballot," *Westminster Review*, 13 (1830), 15.
[51] Cf. R. P. Anschutz, *The Philosophy of J. S. Mill* (Oxford, 1953), 81.
[52] *Works*, IV, 332.

that the conclusions are universally applicable.[53] By 1831 Mill was echoing some criticisms of the Utilitarians that his opponents had been making for several years. He intends Bentham, as well as his father, when he says that those "who build their philosophy of politics upon what they term the universal principles of human nature . . . often form their judgments, in particular cases, as if, because there are universal principles of human nature, they imagined that all are such which they find to be true universally of the people of their own age and country."[54]

Bentham's Constitutional Codes for all comers were just the sort of abstract documents to invite such criticism. Even in the work best designed to meet objections to his habit of abstraction, *The Influence of Time and Place in Matters of Legislation*, Bentham leaves himself open:

> Legislators who, having freed themselves from the shackles of authority, have learnt to soar above the mists of prejudice, know as well how to make laws for one country as for another: all they need is to be possessed fully of the facts; to be informed of the local situation, the climate, the bodily constitution; the manners, the legal customs, the religion, of those with whom they have to deal. These are the data they require: possessed of these data, all places are alike. If they are more at home in their own country than elsewhere, it is only because the requisite stock of facts in the former situation is already possessed by them, without their being obliged to wait the time which, in a foreign country, it would require to seek them out.[55]

This is substantially the same argument used by James Mill in his *History of India* to assert his competence to deal with Indian affairs while lacking personal acquaintance with them; indeed he claims a superiority because of the resultant lack of bias! As Bentham argues in *The Influence of Time and Place* (172), pleasures and pains are the same in different countries, and only their different local causes need concern the legislator. Human nature, that is, is everywhere the same; certain accidental and external features vary, but they may easily be catalogued. The basic syllogism is: an Englishman may be controlled by such and such manipulations of reward and punishment; all men are like Englishmen; therefore all men may be so manipulated. The flaw in the argument is obvious: neither premise is true, as John Mill was constantly to indicate.

[53] "Miss Martineau's Summary of Political Economy," *Works*, IV, 226. Cf. his comment on French "geometrical" thinkers in *Examination of Sir William Hamilton's Philosophy* (London, 1872), 627–8.
[54] *Spirit of the Age*, ed. F. A. Hayek (University of Chicago Press, 1942), 47.
[55] *Works*, I, 180–1.

Furthermore, Bentham makes a difficult problem appear easy when he implies that all the data on local situation, climate, bodily constitution, manners, customs, and religion may be gathered by the legislator. And "the requisite stock of facts" about one's own country is extremely hard to come by. Bentham believed, of course, that he was looking at all times and places for facts, and not spinning theories out of his own substance. Bowring remarks:

Mr Bentham has mentioned, that, in all his pursuits and inquiries, one idea was constantly operating on his mind. If Bacon, with his 'Experimentalize!' was justly honored for doing more than any man who had preceded him, for the diffusion of the philosophy of physics, Bentham, with his ever-present maxim – 'Observe!' – is intitled to the first rank among those who have successfully labored for the advancement of the philosophy of morals.[56]

John Mill, however, had a question for Bacon: is your experimental method adequate? and he has one for Bentham: is your observation complete? Even overlooking its flaws in this respect, *The Influence of Time and Place* is not fully typical of Bentham's attitude. The best defence of his habit of confining a discussion to the few principles that he considered important appears in the introduction to his *Works*, in terms reminiscent of Mill's defence of his father. Bentham's political pronouncements, it is there asserted, fall into two classes. In the first "he lays down those principles and rules of action which ought to guide a people, supposed to have thrown off all trammels of prejudice and established custom, and to be in search of the very best form of government which a practical philosopher would dictate to persons ready implicitly to adopt his arrangements." Such an ideal society, wholly guided by reason, is the target for most of Bentham's works. In the second class, in which Bentham had "immediate practical ends in view, his endeavour was to mould the existing machinery of established institutions and opinions to the production of the best practical results." The defence is a fair one, but it certainly needs to be stated. A man may, in polemical writing, overlook the conditions within which his argument is confined, to gain argumentative advantage. In so doing, however, he foregoes his claim to the title of philosopher. The first class mentioned above is composed of plans for the ideal society; the second, it may be said, is composed of means to it. The writer is probably correct in his admonition:

[56] *Deontology*, I, 316.

The reader, therefore, must not take it for granted that the principles and institutions which are developed in the former class of works, are such as their Author would recommend to a practical statesman, connected with an established government, to put into immediate operation, however much he might wish to establish in the statesman's mind a leaning to such opinions as an ultimate end of gradual change.[57]

This admonition bore fruit in the younger Mill's thought, as is shown in detail below; he was never tempted to forget the ideal in the crush of present circumstances, but equally he never forgot the circumstances when advocating practical policies.

In view of his considered and thorough criticism of his elders' sociological methods, it must appear surprising that Mill isolates for special praise Bentham's "method of detail" in his great review article. Bentham had great facility at, and took great enjoyment in, drawing up tables which broke down complex problems, such as providing for all kinds of indigence, into their component parts. In isolation, each showed itself as manageable, and a comprehensive programme could be devised by including all the separate items. From the standpoint of John Mill, it is obvious that these tables too often depended on ingenuity rather than facts; when a class proved resistant to "bifurcation" into smaller units, often the word which characterized the class was not so recalcitrant, and symmetry replaced evidence as the reformer's guide. Whatever the merits of this method, however, John Mill does not examine it carefully, and it appears more realistic to explain his praise in another context. He connects Bentham's method with the dialectic of Plato, the questioning of nature by Aristotle and Bacon, the 'negative" philosophy of the eighteenth-century sceptics and empiricists, and with the normal activity of those periods of history which he, following the Saint-Simonians, Comte, and Coleridge, calls "critical," "transitional," and "progressive." What he was praising was not the intimate workings of Bentham's method, or its universal applicability, but the very use of method by Bentham in ethics, politics, and sociology.

This account of Mill's reassessment of the work of his father and Bentham is of course incomplete;[58] it should be clear, however, that the

[57] Works, "Introduction," I, 47.

[58] The account may be filled out by a close examination (not here offered) of the following pattern, starting with the obituary of Bentham in 1832. In the next year his unsympathetic "Remarks on Bentham's Philosophy" appeared as an anonymous appendix to Bulwer's England and the English (referred to in the text above). Two

reassessment was as important to him as his new awareness of the need for personal cultivation in the resolution of his mental distress. But much has been anticipated, and it is time to look back at the crucial years to see how others aided him in the resolution, and directed him towards his mature position.

———

years later, in his own *London Review* he published his review of Sedgwick, a defence of utilitarianism which does not deal with Bentham (his father forced him "to omit two or three pages of comment" on utilitarianism which James Mill "considered as an attack on Bentham & on him" [*Early Draft*, 158n]). In these years Mill was obviously personally withdrawn from his father, enough so to have earned the epithet "mysterious" from him; in 1836 James Mill died, and his son took over his position as head of the family. In 1838 appeared John Mill's review article on Bentham's *Works*, which gave offence to more rigid Benthamites, but is much less critical than the Bulwer Appendix; in "Coleridge," two years later, he attempted to redress the balance further without yet jumping on the Benthamite scale; in Book VI of his *Logic* (1843) he delivers his verdict on the shortcomings of the school's method. In a letter to the Editor of the *Edinburgh Review* in 1844 he objects strongly to Bentham's ill-considered remarks about James Mill. Eight years later, reviewing Whewell, he is much more firmly committed to Benthamism, and finally in 1854, working on both the *Autobiography* and the essay later published as *Utilitarianism*, he gives his favourable mature judgment of both, which is of a piece with that in "Whewell." Having recognized (and I think gone beyond) his seesaw (see the Preface to *Dissertations and Discussions*, I, iv–v), he was confident in his final warm tributes, both in the ultimate version of the *Autobiography* and, for James Mill, in the Introduction and Notes to the second edition of the *Analysis* (1869), which was published as an act of filial piety as well as of public utility. In the case of both men, he felt that his earlier criticism had been too soon and too strong, and he did his best to amend the damage he thought he had done.

There are of course many references to both in Mill's writings which I have not mentioned at all, and some anecdotal material about his relations with them. More important, I have not touched on some important areas which deserve at least cursory mention. John Mill remained his father's disciple in associationism, without contributing much to the school's thought. The contributions of James Mill and Bentham to political economy were recognized by him, but recognized as outranked in importance by those of Adam Smith, Malthus, and Ricardo, as well as by those of McCulloch, Senior, and himself. Throughout his life he praised Bentham for inspiring legal reform and for his practical and theoretical grasp of the law, and he correctly saw that Bentham's main contribution as well as his main interest was in law. But while he devoted a good deal of his criticism of Bentham to eulogy of these reforms, the activity held only an abstract charm for him. Lastly, he perhaps over-estimated the part played by his father through personal influence in aiding the cause of reform.

3

Harriet Taylor

IF MILL's final tributes to his father and Bentham are warm, judged by his usual standards, his tributes to Harriet Taylor throughout his life are hot by any standards. She exemplified for him the best in human nature, combining in herself the highest poetic with the highest rational powers; quick and yet subtle, she was devoted always to the betterment of mankind. She was for him, in fact, the perfect utilitarian. No one else has ever been able to agree with him.

Their life together, seen from the outside, may be summarized briefly. Mill met her in 1830, in the early years of his attempt to find a new way of life for himself; he was then discovering the Saint-Simonians, and was soon to meet Carlyle, but at the time the only important new influence on him was that of Coleridge, whose thought he had encountered through the closest of his new friends, John Sterling. More important, however, was the influence of Romantic poetry, which had taught him to sympathize, and also to aspire and admire. Outside his own family he had almost literally known no woman of his own age, and it is hardly surprising that he was drawn to the attractive wife of John Taylor. On her part there was an unfulfilled longing for intellectual achievement and appreciation, and she found in the young Mill (at twenty-four, her senior by less than two years) a willing mentor and admirer. Within a few years their attraction strained its Platonic bounds, and Mill tried to persuade her to run away with him to the Continent. Held by her duty to her husband and three children, she refused, but they established a lasting liaison as unusual in its form as it was unexampled in its carnal innocence. She lived for the most part away from her husband, and Mill spent much time with her, in her country home, on the Continent, and even in her husband's house. In the early 'thirties Mill paraded their relation, annoying his family, alienating those of his friends who tried to interfere, and amusing society. Gradually he became more of a recluse, devoting his life to his work and to Harriet, and justifying his seclusion by attacks on English society for its petty narrowness.

The relation continued in this way until John Taylor's death in 1849; two years later they married, and for the next seven years, until her death in Avignon in 1858, they lived a quiet life about which comparatively little is known. Even less would be known had not ill-health enforced frequent separations, during which they corresponded at great length. Her death was an enormous shock to him; he found consolation in posthumous worship of her, in an increased devotion to writing, and in the continued companionship of her daughter Helen, who came to occupy an almost equal place in his estimation. From the time of Harriet's death until his own in 1873, he spent about half of each year in Avignon, having bought a house near the cemetery in which she is buried, and he himself died there and is buried with her.

This account is in no way new or controversial; the tale is well told in Professor F. A. Hayek's *John Stuart Mill and Harriet Taylor*, and retold with some embellishment in Michael St J. Packe's *The Life of John Stuart Mill*. There the matter might well rest, had Mill not praised her in such extreme terms. With the revival of interest in Mill in the last twenty years, however, it has seemed important to assess his judgment of his wife as part of the general attempt to assess his own importance.

Mill and Harriet worried, not without reason, about people's reactions to their unconventional friendship, but so far as posterity is concerned, they worried for the wrong reasons. During the writing of the early draft of the *Autobiography*, Mill suggested to Harriet that telling their story "simply & without reserve" would be advisable if publication were delayed for a century, but that they must be careful now "not to put arms into the hands of the enemy." Harriet replied, arguing that the relation should be presented "in its genuine truth and simplicity – strong affection – intimacy of friendship – & no impropriety. It seems to me," she says, "an edifying picture for those poor wretches who cannot conceive friendship but in sex – nor believe that expediency & consideration

for the feelings of others can conquer sensuality." This, she adds, is of
course not her reason for wishing Mill to describe their life together: "It
is that every ground should be occupied by ourselves on our own
subject."[1]

It cannot be argued that prurient curiosity and malicious gossip have
decreased in popularity in the last century, but even those "poor
wretches" who confuse sex and friendship have felt more pity than rage
about Harriet and Mill. What has caused controversy and continued
interest has not been the nature of Mill's relation with, but the extent of
his claims for, his companion and wife. His hyperbolic statements about
her powers have offended successive generations, and not least the present
one which, if it has no living memory of her, has more literary evidence.
The most notorious of Mill's encomiums of her appear in the *Autobiography*; less objectionable to most tastes are those in the dedications
of the *Principles of Political Economy* and *On Liberty*, in her epitaph,
and in the prefatory remarks to her "Enfranchisement of Women." Most
of these are well known, and so a passage from the last named, less
quoted than the others, will suffice as illustration. In the "Enfranchisement" not "even the faintest image can be found," says Mill,

of a mind and heart which in their union of the rarest, and what are deemed
the most conflicting excellences, were unparalleled in any human being that I
have known or read of. While she was the light, life, and grace of every society
in which she took part, the foundation of her character was a deep seriousness,
resulting from the combination of the strongest and most sensitive feelings
with the highest principles. All that excites admiration when found separately
in others, seemed brought together in her: a conscience at once healthy and
tender; a generosity, bounded only by a sense of justice which often forgot its
own claims, but never those of others; a heart so large and loving, that whoever was capable of making the smallest return of sympathy, always received
tenfold; and in the intellectual department, a vigour and truth of imagination,
a delicacy of perception, an accuracy and nicety of observation, only equalled
by her profundity of speculative thought, and by a practical judgment and
discernment next to infallible. So elevated was the general level of her faculties,
that the highest poetry, philosophy, oratory, or art, seemed trivial by the side
of her, and equal only to expressing some small part of her mind. And there is
no one of those modes of manifestation in which she could not easily have
taken the highest rank, had not her inclination led her for the most part to

[1] British Library of Political and Economic Science (London School of Economics),
Mill-Taylor Collection, L, #40 (10/2/54 and 14–15/2/54). Cf. Stillinger, *Early Draft*,
6–9.

content herself with being the inspirer, prompter, and unavowed coadjutor of others.[2]

Here and elsewhere it is clear that he believed her to be the best example of a utilitarian who ever lived, combining in herself the intellectual powers of James Mill with the poetic powers of Shelley and Carlyle; she always looked to the good of the species, and her proposals for moral and intellectual reform were based on a superb understanding of practical difficulties and of human nature. As he says on her tombstone: "Were there even a few hearts and intellects like hers, this earth would already become the hoped-for heaven."[3]

Concerning her importance, there have recently been two schools of thought: that of the 1950s and that of the 1960s. Following on the reve-latory work of Professor Hayek, in the 1950s Mr. Packe and Dr. Ruth Borchard tended to accept Mill's estimate of Harriet's importance to him, and even went beyond to assert her complete dominance over him. Pro-fessor von Hayek was himself more cautious, not discussing the question at length, but saying that Harriet's influence was quite as great as Mill asserted, although it did not work as is generally believed; he surprisingly recorded his agreement with Knut Hagberg that she made Mill into a "Radical rationalist."

In the 1960s this attitude has been often challenged, most effectively by Professor Jack Stillinger in his edition of the *Early Draft* of Mill's *Autobiography*, by H. O. Pappé in his *John Stuart Mill and the Harriet Taylor Myth*, and by Professor Francis Mineka in "The *Autobiography* and the Lady," a review article dealing with the two books just men-tioned. The new view is that whatever Harriet may have meant to Mill emotionally, her intellectual contribution was far slighter than he thought it. In Professor Mineka's words (306): "Neither he nor his recent bio-graphers have convinced us that she was the originating mind behind his work, but no one can doubt her importance in Mill's inner life, the well-springs of which had been threatened by drought."

Once this distinction is made, the air of unreality which has gathered

---

[2] *Dissertations and Discussions*, II, 411–12.

[3] It should be noted that when discussing his father's epitaph, Mill remarks that it is not "a fault in an epitaph to be pretentious . . . provided it does not pretend to more than is thought just by friends & admirers. People expect that an epitaph shall contain what a man's admirers think of him — not what is thought by all the world." (*Earlier Letters*, XII, 334.)

around the problem begins to clear. Mill loved and cherished his wife, feeling that she complimented and completed his qualities. He was given to excessive praise of those he admired, and she was almost the only person whom he continued to admire through life, and in whom he found an open emotional response adequate to his needs. What she was to him, however, she was and has been to no one else. Judging her personality by the responses of her contemporaries and by the written record, it is hard to share Mill's enthusiasm. If pressed, I, like many others, would call her vain and vituperative, proud and petulant – but such comments are not relevant in estimating her place in his life. He did not find her so.

In examining the evidence, we may begin with a hypothesis based on the views of Mineka, Stillinger, and Pappé. The relation between Mill and Harriet, it seems likely, was that common, if not invariable, in marriages between members of the *intelligentsia*: frequent discussion, mutual enlightenment, considerable independence in thought, and – the pattern is now changing – subordination of the wife's ambitions to the husband's. It can be argued that Mill could not have written any of his works subsequent to the *Logic* without her; it can equally well be argued (as by Mr. Pappé) that he could have written any of them without her. In point of fact, he did not write them without her; she was his closest companion and confidante both before and after their marriage, and his work was discussed frequently by them. This much can be assumed; the most important question then is: in what ways did she contribute significantly to his work?

The judgments of contemporaries on this matter are of little worth, both because of the personal feelings involved, and because of the seclusion of the Mills' life. The best judgment, though inconclusive, may stand for all; Mill's brother George, who knew Harriet well, said that she was a "clever and remarkable woman, but nothing like what John took her to be." [4]

The other direct evidence is of two kinds: Harriet's known writings and Mill's assessments. First, her writings. She published only one substantial essay, and a few notices, reviews, and poems, and her literary remains are slight – a handful of letters, a few early manuscripts, and some fragments. Little can be established by such tenuous evidence, but at least negatively it is suggestive. Early in their acquaintance, at Mill's suggestion, Harriet put down on paper her views on the relation between

[4] Alexander Bain, *John Stuart Mill* (London, 1882), 166. Cf. Stillinger, *Early Draft*, 25.

the sexes and on toleration. These interesting documents, published by Hayek, can be seen as forerunners of Mill's *Subjection of Women* and *On Liberty*. Her essay, "The Enfranchisement of Women," written just before their marriage, appeared in the *Westminster Review* in 1851, and was reprinted by Mill in his *Dissertations and Discussions* after her death; it too bears upon both these works. The manuscript fragments, with the exception of personal notes, are mainly on these same topics, especially as seen in relation to personal conduct and the improvement (generally through strong criticism) of social morality; there is also more than a hint of Romantic sensibility. For example, one finds a brief lecture, probably directed to Mill, on the necessity of neatness; there is a stray comment: "*equal* high respect for oneself and others – That is my democracy." In an early note advising Mill to see Italy she remarks, "it is the *people* that are the charm of Italy – as they are the curse of England," and follows this by remarking: "I never saw but in one head of Titian an *ideal* Christ except my boatman on Como."[5] Her poems are slight lyric effusions which combine pre-Romantic diction with Romantic mood.

The conclusion from an examination of this material is simply this: Harriet, like Mill, considered questions of toleration and sexual equality important, especially in their ethical implications, and she employed a method of argument different in quality and intensity from Mill's. There is no strong indication of influence, but what there is suggests that, particularly in the early years when she was Mill's pupil, he influenced her more than she influenced him. He states quite firmly, and there is independent evidence to support his assertion,[6] that he was concerned about the inequality of the sexes before he met her. Certainly his interest in toleration and liberty antedated his acquaintance with her. She undoubtedly quickened and sustained his interest in these matters, but she did not initiate it, and cannot be said to have controlled his thought. His *Subjection of Women*, written after her death, is a stronger, more coherent, and broader plea for sexual equality that her "Enfranchisement of Women,"[7] and the manuscript fragments, as might be expected from

[5] Mill-Taylor Collection, Box III, #101.
[6] See, e.g., his "Periodical Literature," *Westminster Review*, 1 (1824), 526.
[7] In the preface to the reprint in *Dissertations and Discussions* rather than simply saying that the "Enfranchisement of Women" is Harriet's, Mill says that it differs from their other "joint productions" (here he refers to "the more recent" articles in *Dissertations*) in that for it he was "little more than an editor and amanuensis." He goes on to say that the essay does not represent her at her best; one may agree,

their inchoate form, are inferior to his writings on their topics.[8]

When one moves on to Mill's comments, leaving the correspondence aside for the moment, one is overwhelmed by the manifest exaggeration. George Grote is reported to have said that only Mill's reputation could survive such exhibitions.[9] One theme running through the encomiums is, however, of major importance : Mill's direct acknowledgment of her part in his writings. In the *Autobiography* he comments generally that she was the joint author of all his works from the *Principles of Political Economy* to *On Liberty*, and in so far as those two works are concerned, he repeats the assertion in dedicating them to her. In the bibliography of his published writings which he prepared, however, the general assertion is considerably weakened. There he again comments that the *Principles* was a work of joint authorship, and identifies in particular those other writings in which she played a part.[10] With one exception, these are newspaper leaders and letters, all dealing with cases of domestic cruelty. Why, it must be asked, did he specially annotate these items unless their composition differed in some way from that of his other works? The conclusion would seem to be that in these cases she actually *wrote* at least a draft of the article. Another possible conclusion is that she was in fact the sole author of these pieces, but Mill's eagerness to ascribe to her not only God's portion but Rome's as well would seem to negate this. Is it not reasonable to suppose that these small pieces were prepared jointly, from notes or drafts prepared by Harriet?

This suggestion is not so innocent as it may seem, if it is joined with the previous one that these articles differ in some way from Mill's other writings. The test becomes crucial when one recalls that during the 1850s, especially from the end of 1854 on, manuscripts were either written or

---

without going the length of Francis Palgrave in reviewing Mill's *Autobiography* in the *Quarterly Review*, 136 (1874), 174, who says : "The most that can be said [of the "Essay"], is that it is a respectable parody of Mill's worst style. Feebler arguments and more pompous words have rarely come together."

[8] The preceding argument parallels Pappé's extended discussion of some of the published material; his conclusions are borne out by what he did not examine.

[9] Bain, *John Stuart Mill*, cf. Stillinger, *Early Draft*, 24.

[10] See Ney MacMinn, *et al.*, *Bibliography of the Published Writings of J. S. Mill* (Northwestern University Press, 1945), x, 59–60, 62–3, 66, 71–6, 79. The one item which did not appear in a newspaper is the pamphlet on Fitzroy's Bill "for the more effectual prevention of assaults on women and children." Mill's annotation here is similar to that in the Preface to the "Enfranchisement of Women" : "In this I acted chiefly as amanuensis to my wife." (MacMinn, 79.)

drafted containing material later published as *On Liberty*, the *Autobio-graphy*, *Utilitarianism*, and two of the *Three Essays on Religion*. In the absence of a detailed contemporary account of their collaboration, the best evidence would be manuscripts in either or both of their hands, show-ing emendations and suggestions as well as continued argument. Of the works named, unfortunately, apparently only one has survived in manu-script, the early draft of the *Autobiography*, and we are forced back on it for evidence. Of course there is no guarantee that there was not another manuscript, prepared by Harriet, but there is no evidence to suggest that there was, and from her comments in letters at the time, it would seem that Mill was responsible for the only draft. In any case, the manuscript that has survived is in his hand. She supplied marginal comments, some cancellations and additions, but no sustained narrative. Her demonstrable contribution was largely improvement of wording, adjustment of sense, and suppression of information tending to belittlement of the author. If it is argued that the work is after all the account of Mill's life, it may be said in partial rebuttal that the shape of the work as a whole, and again the contemporary correspondence, indicate that the draft of the *Auto-biography* was intended, *inter alia*, to justify their life together,[11] and Mill could here more than anywhere else rely on her for the description. On what evidence there is, then, one is justified in assuming that Mill wrote the only draft, Harriet criticized it carefully, and it was left for Mill to finish.

There is no reason to suspect that *On Liberty* should come under another category, though her part was probably larger. Mill was in the habit, from early manhood, of preparing (as Bentham also did) two inde-pendent versions of a work, and then combining them. He comments in the *Autobiography* (176) that *On Liberty* "was more directly and literally our joint production than anything else which bears my name, for there was not a sentence of it that was not several times gone through by us together, turned over in many ways, and carefully weeded of any faults, either in thought or expression, that we detected in it." So, he continues, "although it never underwent her final revision, it far surpasses, as a mere specimen of composition, anything which has proceeded from me either before or since." In the face of the other evidence, this retains more than it gives away. The implication is strong that once more Mill wrote a

[11] Cf. Mineka, "The *Autobiography* and the Lady," *University of Toronto Quarterly*, 32 (1963), 303.

draft, and then went through it with Harriet; the process may have been repeated; but eventually the final manuscript emerged, *again* composed in full by Mill, and Harriet's death prevented her criticism of it.

One may infer an even stronger case for the other works written first in this period, for their final versions were, without doubt, written after her death. The case is a presumptive one, but there is no other, and it is supported by common experience of the way husband and wife collaborate. Furthermore, it does not deny that Harriet may have played a large part in formulating a projected work, and also in discussing its contents. But again common experience suggests that discussion before, and even during, the composition of a work plays a smaller part in its final form than the actual day-by-day composition; the interplay of mind and hand is finally what determines the direction and effect, and to a major extent the content, of an argument.

The most interesting case of all is the *Principles of Political Economy*, which Mill emphatically describes as a "joint production." Here there is incontrovertible evidence of her participation, and Mill is particular in ascribing part of the work to her. He says that the chapter on the probable futurity of the labouring classes (Book IV, chap. vii) "is entirely due to her: in the first draft of the book, that chapter did not exist. She pointed out the need of such a chapter, and the extreme imperfection of the book without it: she was the cause of my writing it; and the more general part of the chapter, the statement and discussion of the two opposite theories respecting the proper condition of the labouring classes, was wholly an exposition of her thoughts, often in words taken from her own lips." [12] Furthermore, when Mill was revising the work for the second and third editions, Harriet suggested and in part insisted upon modifications in the chapter on property (II, i) which gave a much more favourable impression of socialism than had the first edition. Mill also says, in a passage difficult to interpret exactly, that she was responsible for the "general tone" of the work that is given by the distinction between the laws of distribution and production, a distinction which allows for greater hope for mankind's economic improvement through modification of the former.[13]

[12] *Autobiography*, 174. It should be noted that even here, in his strongest statement, Mill admits by implication that he not only held the pen, but largely guided it.

[13] The passage in question is heavily rewritten in the MS of the press copy, the only MS known, but there is no direct trace of Harriet's hand. This passage has, it may be added, given much difficulty to interpreters of Mill. For a full record of the evidence, see Appendix G to Mill's *Principles* in *Collected Works*, III (1965), 1026–37.

On the basis of content and style, it is also not unreasonable to see her influence in a few other places, such as the concluding section of Book IV, chapter vi, and in certain discussions of population, and there is one short passage in the manuscript probably in her hand.

Now granting all this, are we justified in accepting the work as a "joint production"? The impression given by Packe and Hayek is that we are, and recently Gertrude Himmelfarb has implied that we need no more evidence of the part she played.[14] It seems to me that we could do with much more, if we are to accept the work as a "joint production." The *Principles* consists of five Books and seventy-three Chapters; we know that Harriet had a place in two important chapters, and can assume that she helped with perhaps four more. Mill himself says, between the two passages last referred to from the *Autobiography*, that he "did not learn" the "purely scientific part of the Political Economy" from her, and the statement cannot be denied. It is hard to believe that in this case the absence of evidence is not significant. It might also be relevant to remark that Mill quotes or cites over one hundred authors in the *Principles*, some at great length, and yet no one has suggested that, for example, Ricardo and Cairnes were joint authors of Mill's *Principles*; the point is not entirely facetious, for Mill's debt to them is manifest and detailed. Only if the importance of the *Principles* is seen as lying mainly in the passages and revisions which give it a socialist cast can it be argued that Harriet's role was a major one, and then one is left, as Gertrude Himmelfarb argues, with apparently irreconcilable contradictions between the Mill who remained an ardent champion of free enterprise and the Mill who was reluctantly dragged by Harriet into support for socialism. Such a view, while interesting, is hardly just to the *Principles* or to either of its authors.

There is, fortunately, a way out of this difficulty, and one which does justice to both Harriet and Mill. Another passage in the *Autobiography*, which looks at first sight like another piece of extravagance, provides the clue.

With those who, like all the best and wisest of mankind, are dissatisfied with human life as it is, and whose feelings are wholly identified with its radical amendment, there are two main regions of thought. One is the region of ultimate aims; the constituent elements of the highest realizable ideal of human life. The other is that of the immediately useful and practically attainable. In both these departments, I have acquired more from her teaching, than from all

14 "The Two Mills," a review of the *Principles* in *The New Leader*, 10 May, 1965, 29.

other sources taken together. And, to say truth, it is in these two extremes principally, that real certainty lies. My own strength lay wholly in the uncertain and slippery intermediate region, that of theory, or moral and political science: respecting the conclusions of which, in any of the forms in which I have received or originated them, whether as political economy, analytic psychology, logic, philosophy of history, or anything else, it is not the least of my intellectual obligations to her that I have derived from her a wise scepticism, which, while it has not hindered me from following out the honest exercise of my thinking faculties to whatever conclusions might result from it, has put me on my guard against holding or announcing these conclusions with a degree of confidence which the nature of such speculations does not warrant, and has kept my mind not only open to admit, but prompt to welcome and eager to seek, even on the questions on which I have most meditated, any prospect of clearer perceptions and better evidence. I have often received praise, which in my own right I only partially deserve, for the greater practicality which is supposed to be found in my writings, compared with those of most thinkers who have been equally addicted to large generalizations. The writings in which this quality has been observed, were not the work of one mind, but of the fusion of two, one of them as pre-eminently practical in its judgments and perceptions of things present, as it was high and bold in its anticipations for a remote futurity. (132–3; cf. 171–2.)

The division of labour is rather unusual, at least in its description. There are two "main regions of thought" for the reformer, and one apparently "minor." In typically self-deprecatory fashion, Mill limits his competence to the "uncertain and slippery intermediate region . . . of theory, or moral and political science," which is found between the two areas of "real certainty," where Harriet found scope for her ranging talents. These are the "region of ultimate aims" and that of "the immediately useful and practically attainable," and her mind was "as pre-eminently practical in its judgments and perceptions of things present, as it was high and bold in its anticipations for a remote futurity."

The passage is in fact revealing: in what we have of her writings, Harriet constantly has her eye on the future, even when criticizing the present; she was a woman of dreams and aspirations, and she must constantly have breathed into Mill a more hopeful and expansive view of human possibilities. This function is the one she performed in the *Principles*, on what evidence we have; her contributions have to do with the ideal and the future, and it can be demonstrated that Mill's praise for socialism is throughout based on enthusiasm concerning its possibilities, not on its theoretical symmetry or its consonance with abstract principles. Similarly with *On Liberty*, which Mill thought of as hers in a special sense; it was written more for the future than for the present, and while its warnings are urgent, it has an inspirational basis, embodying "the highest realizable ideal of human life." While he was not, as has been said of Fontenelle, born a hundred years old in caution and circumspection, he did not have a deep fund of enthusiasm, and he relied on her to replenish his hope. As he remarked to Bain, "stimulation is what people never sufficiently allow for." [15]

In describing this first area of Harriet's competence as one of "real certainty," Mill appears to have in mind not only the debilitating effect of incessant qualification, but also the absolute nature of moral ideals which are not themselves amenable to proof. But his description of the area of "the immediately useful and practically attainable" as also one of "real certainty," is less easily explicable. Perhaps he means nothing more unusual than that one can quickly see whether one's actions fulfill one's intentions in the daily concerns of life. He may also be merely referring to his pronounced inability to manage such practical matters as ordering groceries and dealing with difficult neighbours, even tieing his shoes, for here his reliance on her was unusual, and will become notorious with the publication of their later correspondence.[16] Certainly he was envious of the ability of the man of action to assume certainty, and his acknowledged lack of "intuition" into solutions of practical problems may have softened his judgment of its practical value.

Here it is necessary to mention the epistolary evidence which, from the point of view of Mill's admirers, is unfortunate, and only slightly less so from the point of view of Harriet's supporters. "It is notable," Professor Stillinger remarks (*Early Draft*, 26), "in the correspondence of these two self-styled reformers of the world's opinions, who worried whether there would be any thinkers after them, how seldom *ideas* are touched on." In general, few of Harriet's letters are extant, but Mill's letters to her will fill a large volume. Apart from her suggestions concerning the *Principles*, which are dealt with in Mill's side of the correspondence, there is good evidence of her encouragement; she entered fully into his plans for

---

[15] Bain, *John Stuart Mill*, 149. Cf. Packe, 316, where in his major assessment of Harriet's influence he makes sensible judgments, spoiled only by his insistence that "her predominance was even more complete" than Mill admitted. The comment might be thought fair in relation to their personal affairs, but referring as it does to her contribution to his works, it is gross exaggeration.

[16] Cf. Stillinger, *Early Draft*, 18, 25–8.

the writing done in the 1850s, and unquestionably gave enthusiastic help when she was with him. But we simply cannot say that she was the author of these works on the basis of the letters. They are mostly concerned with the mundane trivia of life; health, weather, and domestic problems occupy as much place here as in Harriet's extant correspondence with her first husband, John Taylor, whom she found unequal to her aspirations. What is revealed, however, is Mill's extraordinary dependence on Harriet in practical matters. His reliance on her for the smallest decision about household matters is foolish at the very least, and indicates that she was not only a father substitute for him, but a mother substitute as well, if one can accept his and Harriet Grote's comments on his mother.[17] He very much needed someone to look after him.

But this personal practicability is not the primary issue; the practicability on which Mill insisted in matters of policy depended on an intimate knowledge of men and of social change. If this is the quality he is claiming for her in the *Autobiography*, one must again question the accuracy of his judgment. In all the writings which can safely be accepted as strongly influenced by her, the exhortations to reform are based on moral principles and disgust at injustice and brutality, not on considerations of practicability in particular situations. But even in the newspaper articles attacking the law for permitting domestic brutality, which in their low view of human (especially male) nature suggest that there is as little hope as there is great need for reform, she is concerned with *practice*, and this is the vital issue. Mill saw in Harriet the qualities which he found lacking in himself and in his education. Sensing his inability to forecast greater happiness than seemed presently attainable, he also felt that he was unable to keep his eye sufficiently on the immediate situation. Here Mill, as so often, probably sees his father's faults in himself. James Mill's ability to live in abstractions and generalizations seemed to his son to have been inherited by him. He, however, became aware of the fault, and while his father's dogmatism allowed him to march on hob-nailed propositions from the "slippery intermediate region" of theory over the

[17] See *ibid.*, 13, 36, 56n, 184, and Bertrand and Patricia Russell, eds., *The Amberley Papers*, I, 421. The worthy Francis Place should also be heard, whispering to Lady Romilly at Ford Abbey in 1817: "Mrs. Mill has six children here but they won't trouble you, you'll never see them. As for her you need not trouble yourself about her, she is a very worthy excellent woman, as good a creature as ever lived, but poor thing she has no mind in her body." (*Romilly-Edgeworth Letters, 1813–1818*. London: Murray, 1936, 176.)

treacherous bogs of practice, John Mill was one of the chief begetters of the present age of qualification.

His belief that Harriet brought practice into the foreground at least indicates that he thought it should be there, and her influence reinforced the lesson he learned in his professional career in the India House. His occupation, he says in the *Autobiography* (60), gave him opportunities to see and meet difficulties and objections, to examine means and failures, and to work with others. He had to learn to persuade, to satisfy "various persons very unlike" himself that "the thing was fit to be done," and he "became practically conversant with the difficulties of moving bodies of men, the necessities of compromise, the art of sacrificing the non-essential to preserve the essential." He learned not to be "indignant or dispirited" when he could not have his own way, and "to bear with complete equanimity the being overruled altogether." And, demonstrating the connection between personal ethics and general philosophic approach that marks his thought, Mill says: "I have found, through life, these acquisitions to be of the greatest possible importance for personal happiness, and they are also a very necessary condition for enabling any one, either as theorist or as practical man, to effect the greatest amount of good compatible with his opportunities."

The persuasion of others and the practicability of programmes both derive from experience and habitual recognition of conflicts and contingencies, and Mill's own happiness depended on the same awareness. He retained respect for those who were able to use their accumulated experience of human reactions and technical difficulties in applying plans to actual situations, although he also retained a disrespect for those who were so concerned with practical details that they refused to see the value of theory. The disrespect he shared with his elders, who had castigated "merely practical men"; Mill's complex new awareness of methodological and ethical problems, as well as his experience in the India House, undoubtedly contributed to his revaluation of practice, and there is no reason to doubt that Harriet Taylor, whose approach as poet and prophetess was more concrete than abstract, also influenced him in this direction.

Here, in fact, one can properly begin a final estimate of her influence. Harriet was for Mill the perfection of the poetic temperament: she began with the highly sensitive physical constitution typified by Shelley, and went on to develop her philosophic powers until she became the outstanding (if non-productive) example of the cultivated poet. Hers was "a character preeminently of feeling," combined as Mill had not in any other case known it to be, "with a vigorous & bold speculative intellect. Hers was not only all this but the perfection of a poetic & artistic nature." [18] The practical is here left far below, and the hyperbole must again be discounted, but the area from which the hyperbole springs should not be overlooked, for again not the truth of the description but the nature of her influence is in question. In the early years of his acquaintance with her he discovered the power of poetry to give him moral inspiration, and explained that discovery in his theory of poetry. It is not then surprising to find him saying: "the first years of my friendship with her were, in respect of my own development, mainly years of poetic culture." Appreciation was involved, but the "real poetic culture was, that my faculties, such as they were, became more & more attuned to the beautiful & elevated, in all kinds, & especially in human feeling & character & more capable of vibrating in unison with it." [19] The ethical relevance of this remark is apparent enough, and its equal relevance to his release from despair can be demonstrated.

The complex picture reveals its pattern when one recalls that his awakening to poetry accompanied his assessment of his own powers as a "Logician" and the initiation of the studies which lead to his *Logic*, and when one places in this context the passage describing Harriet's powers in the regions of "ultimate aims" and the "immediately useful and practically attainable."

Harriet was to him the "Artist" who is described in the essential prolegomena to an understanding of Mill's thought, the concluding chapter of his *Logic*. In his correspondence with Carlyle in 1832–34, it will be recalled, Mill distinguishes between the Artist and the Logician, and gives Carlyle the laurel, himself the rule. This distinction appears in his "On the Definition of Political Economy" (written perhaps as early as 1831, though not published until 1836), where he introduces the more formal terms which he uses in the *Logic*, generalizing the function of the artist and seeing the logician as scientist. In the last chapter of the *Logic*, "Of the Logic of Practice, or Art; including Morality and Policy," Mill connects "art" and "science" together in the groundplan for reform. Art differs

[18] Stillinger, 199 (the passage occurs in the "Rejected Leaves" of the *Early Draft*).
[19] *Ibid.*

from science in being concerned with ends and practice, not with "inquiries into the course of nature." Further, "the imperative mood is the characteristic of art, as distinguished from science. Whatever speaks in rules, or precepts, not in assertions respecting matters of fact, is art. . . ." Because the "Artist" decides on an end, the distinction between his activities and those of the "Scientist" is not simply that between practice and theory, although the analogy is close at times.

The art proposes to itself an end to be attained, defines the end, and hands it over to the science. The science receives it, considers it as a phenomenon or effect to be studied, and having investigated its causes and conditions, sends it back to art with a theorem of the combination of circumstances by which it could be produced. Art then examines these combinations of circumstances, and according as any of them are or are not in human power, pronounces the end attainable or not. The only one of the premises, therefore, which Art supplies, is the original major premise, which asserts that the attainment of the given end is desirable. Science then lends to Art the proposition (obtained by a series of inductions or of deductions) that the performance of certain actions will attain the end. From these premises Art concludes that the performance of these actions is desirable, and finding it also practicable, converts the theorem into a rule or precept.[20]

Such rules are neither perfect nor complete, because, from the conditions of human existence and reason, the theorems on which they are based are necessarily imperfect. Moreover, the rules must be worded as short moral maxims, inevitably limited in use, for if they were too cumbersome they could not be remembered and applied in ordinary circumstances by ordinary people. When complications arise, reference must be made to the end, and to the theorems on which the rules are based. A "wise practitioner" will treat the rules as provisional: "Being made for the most numerous cases, or for those of most ordinary occurrence, they point out the manner in which it will be least perilous to act, where time or means do not exist for analysing the actual circumstances of the case, or where we cannot trust our judgment in estimating them." [21] The very presence and prevalence of such rules indicate that men have found them helpful in everyday life, the arena of ordinary morality. Common formulas do not excuse us from the search for perfection, however, and

[20] *Logic*, II, 546–8 (VI, xii, 1–2). For an account of some Saint-Simonian ideas that may have influenced Mill's thought on the role of the Artist, see Dwight Lindley, "The Saint-Simonians, Carlyle, and Mill" (Ph.D. thesis, Columbia, 1958), 70, 355–6.

[21] *Logic*, II, 549 (VI, xii, 3).

ignorance of scientific truth, even in the "moral" area, cannot be pleaded indefinitely. When "circumstances permit," Mill argues, we must turn to the data to correct and limit our rules. The connection between Art and Science, if not obvious, is morally necessary. ". . . Art in general, consists of the truths of Science, arranged in the most convenient order for practice, instead of the order which is the most convenient for thought." [22] Science aims at thoroughness and truth; art at practice and utility. Art, then, concerns itself only with such of the details of the theoretical problem as lead to practical rules.

But though most of the material comprised by an art comes from the corresponding science, the most important part, the end desired, is the business solely of the art. It supplies the major premise, and supplies it in a language foreign to science :

Propositions of science assert a matter of fact : an existence, a coexistence, a succession, or a resemblance. The propositions now spoken of do not assert that anything is, but enjoin or recommend that something should be. They are a class by themselves. A proposition of which the predicate is expressed by the words *ought* or *should be*, is generically different from one which is expressed by *is*, or *will be*. [23]

Mill here indicates his awareness of the difference, often ignored by Bentham, and pounced on by critics of naturalistic utilitarianism, between descriptive and normative judgments. The only "fact" expressed in the propositions of art, Mill says, is that the person expressing them approves of the end, and of conduct appropriate to that end. But no one can expect others to adopt rules merely because he approves of them, and the reformer must be prepared in practising the final stage of his "Art" to seek implementation through persuasion and defence. If he has done his preparatory work carefully, he will have formidable weapons, for his art will be based on the "laws of nature disclosed by science" and "the general principles of what has been called Teleology, or the Doctrine of Ends," or, "borrowing the language of the German metaphysicians," the "principles of Practical Reason." [24]

In summary, the reformer has to consider three activities, two of which are properly considered as art, one as science. Initially the art decides on and defines the end to be pursued in any particular endeavour. Science then studies this end as an effect to be achieved; it inquires into the causes, and hands the problem back to Art with a description of the

[22] *Ibid., 551* (VI, xii, 5).   [23] *Ibid., 553* (VI, xii, 6).   [24] *Ibid.*

means by which the end may be reached. These means are then examined and, if they are found practicable and moral, the Artist proclaims the end as the object of immediate action, and makes the theorem of its attainment, formulated by Science, into a rule or precept for practical guidance, and attempts to obtain general agreement so that the end may be attained. (The whole plan is posited on a democratic society where persuasion and not single command is effective.) In the form of dialogue, the procedure might be seen as follows: the Artist says to the Scientist: "How can I achieve end X, which I believe to be of great importance?" The Scientist, after studying the problem, replies: "X can be achieved by plans A, B, or C." These plans are then tested to see if their implementation is possible and not destructive of X. Say A is ruled out on the first grounds, and B on the second, but C passes both tests. The Artist then turns to society generally, and says: "If you, like me, wish to achieve X, do C." And he tries to persuade them to his view.

The explanation of the reformer's programme is in fact the unifying element in Mill's thought, and while it cannot be pretended that it can be seen in every detail of each of his works, those details can best be brought together for a comprehensive view by its application throughout. Its connection with the account of Harriet's abilities will be obvious: she represented the Artist in both his activities; he was the Scientist, dealing with "the uncertain and slippery intermediate region, that of theory, or moral and political science." Even here, in his estimation, in "political economy, analytic psychology, logic, philosophy of history, or anything else," she was responsible for the "wise scepticism" and characteristic openness to persuasion which gave his works a "greater practicality" than that found in other authors "equally addicted to large generalizations." The area he modestly allows himself might be thought large enough for most ambitions, and it is the one on which his fame largely has rested; it may seem ungenerous, then, to suggest that one can enlarge Mill's estimate of himself without depreciating Harriet's powers. But the end, after all, in each of his works, is utility, and she is not a major figure in the utilitarian tradition, as he most certainly is. She contributed to the personal growth, the "many-sidedness," which is reflected in his enlarged view of human happiness, and she constantly renewed his enthusiasm for reform. The Scientist's contribution, he says, was his. Where Science meets Art, in the validation of means, she may have taught him much, but except perhaps in *On Liberty* there is no evidence that she had any part in actually working on the problem. There is, partly because of their secluded life, equally little evidence that, in spite of her hypothetical understanding of human nature and her practical knowledge, she was instrumental in forwarding plans for reform (most of Mill's work in this area, it might be remarked, came after her death). And finally, the theoretical groundwork is Mill's.

This mighty labour, then, only brings into view the mouse with which it began. The conclusion, in Pappé's words (vii), is that "Harriet assisted Mill in his work and took an understanding and active interest in it." As might have been assumed, she helped him with his writings, making suggestions, alterations, and corrections; more important, she gave him confidence and inspiration, coupled with an admiring affection he found nowhere else. Without her, one may guess, he might not have written *On Liberty* and the *Autobiography* – but she was not their author. Also, it is likely that without her, *Utilitarianism*, the *Principles of Political Economy*, and the essays on Nature and the Utility of Religion would not have been quite what they are. To speculate on possible gains had he never met her is fruitless. She was in and of his intellectual and emotional life in an unusual degree, but not in an unexampled way, and she was not, in any meaningful sense, the "joint author" of his works.

4

Other Influences

THE MOST SIGNIFICANT influences on Mill in his formative years were those of his father, Jeremy Bentham, and Harriet Taylor, but other important influences need examination. Even before he met Harriet, as we have seen, Mill began to stray from the fold, and his first encounters with the wolves took place in the debates which began in 1825.[1] His first opponents, on formal grounds, were the Owenites, but from the speeches which remain we can conclude that their arguments had little effect on him. In the London Debating Society, however, he met John Sterling and Frederick Maurice, the former of whom soon replaced in his affection such earlier friends as John Roebuck and George John Graham. Sterling and Maurice introduced him to the work of Coleridge, and eventually he met the poet in person. As his range of acquaintance grew, he even came to meet and breakfast with such, to the Benthamites, strange creatures as Wordsworth, Greville, and Southey.[2] He met the Unitarian Fox, and his rather eccentric circle, including the Flower sisters and the Taylor family. He met Gustave d'Eichthal, and through him became acquainted with the leading Saint-Simonians, Bazard and Enfantin, and with the writings of the sect, including Auguste Comte's earliest work. In turn, this interest led to his correspondence and meeting with Carlyle. From the time of the

[1] Earlier debates in the Utilitarian and Mutual Improvement Societies did not, so far as is known, include non-Benthamites.

[2] See Anna J. Mill, "J. S. Mill's Visit to Wordsworth, 1831," *passim*; Henry Taylor, *Autobiography* (London, 1885), I, 160; *Greville Memoirs* (London, 1938), II, 57, 122, IV, 428; and BM Add. MS. 39,179A, ff.65, 73.

French Revolution of 1830 he took an absorbing interest in French political life, and at the same time – no matter how little we know of his part in the movement – he must have been engaged in the Radical attempt to win passage of the Reform Bill. These years, between 1826 and 1832, especially the last two, were a time of intense activity for Mill. The retrospective account in the *Autobiography* is condensed and slightly confused, and it is likely that he was too busy at the time to see where he was being led by his new friends and new thoughts.

Some of the new directions, especially the poetic one discussed above, were fruitful, and the benefits remained with Mill through life. Others were so ephemeral that they may here be dismissed. Still others, in varying degrees, had a strong influence that was later rejected, or a strong influence, in one area, that remained. In this last group, which merits comment, are Coleridge, Carlyle, the Saint-Simonians, Comte, and de Tocqueville.

Coleridge

Although Mill met Coleridge it is perhaps best to say that he knew him through his disciples Sterling and Maurice, and through his works, especially *On the Constitution of Church and State*.[3] He certainly read the poetry, and he quotes from "Dejection: an Ode" and "Work without Hope" in the *Autobiography* to express his condition; it is interesting that Coleridge should best reveal Mill's distress, and Wordsworth lead him out of it. The despairing mood of much Romantic poetry is touched on by Mill in a few passages, as connected with brooding self-analysis; this is the rejected Byronism. In the Wordsworth of mountains and also of duty is found the wider reference that releases self-contained tension.[4] Mill eschewed transcendentalism, ignored the specifically religious aspect of Coleridge's thought, and could look only with scorn upon his attempts to expound political economy (where Toryism and not Conservatism was at stake).[5] The new attempt at a philosophic basis for conservatism in ecclesiastical and political matters impressed Mill, no matter how he argued against it in the London Debating Society, and he was led by it to look at

[3] See *Earlier Letters*, XII, 221, and XIII, 408–9. Cf. *Autobiography*. 107–9. Somewhat surprisingly, the religious sections of Coleridge's *Literary Remains* provide the most extensive quotations in Mill's "Coleridge."   [4] Cf. Matthew Arnold.
[5] "Coleridge," *Dissertations and Discussions*, I, 452.

institutions in a new way. The Benthamites, he came to feel, by overlooking some aspects of human nature and experience, remained ignorant of important social facts. As he says in 1840, Coleridge "saw so much farther [than Bentham] into the complexities of the human intellect and feelings" that he was able to gain a large measure of insight into social structures.[6] Looking at the society which he hoped to alter, Mill became aware that some of the institutions criticized by the Benthamate group are not retained through the malign power of sinister interests,[7] but rather because they fulfill social needs. Standing outside received opinions, he and his colleagues mistook accidents for essences, while Coleridge, within the tradition, was able to "discover by what apparent facts [received opinion] was at first suggested, and by what appearances it has ever since been rendered continually credible – has seemed, to a succession of persons, to be a faithful interpretation of their experience." [8]

So while Mill continued, with Bentham, to question the validity of institutions, he also became, with Coleridge, concerned about their meanings. From this time, partly through the influence of Coleridge, and partly through that of the Saint-Simonians, Mill's examination of the past became more careful. His study of history, already wide in scope, changed in direction : history became for him less a field in which to find isolated and remote examples to demonstrate the impracticability and inutility of institutions, and the glory of change, and more and more a record of the various and continuous means by which institutions have been moulded by man to satisfy his needs. He did not, of course, see what for Coleridge and Burke was essential, the Divine plan behind institutions; he moved instead towards a philosophy of history, without accepting Coleridge's attempt to delineate one.

For example, he was attracted by the belief expressed in *On the Constitution of Church and State* that temporal social forms are but manifestations of an ever-unfolding Idea which is itself both origin and end of the institutions which embody it. Shorn of transcendental implications, the notion appears in *Representative Government* more than twenty-five years afer Coleridge's death : "In treating of representative government, it

---

[6] *Ibid.*, 394.

[7] It is a mistake to say that the Coleridgean school "cunningly pander to the interests of hierarchies and aristocracies, by manufacturing superfine new arguments in favour of old prejudices" (*ibid.*, 405–6).   [8] *Ibid.*, 394. Cf. "Bentham," 331–2.

is above all necessary to keep in view the distinction between its idea or essence, and the particular forms in which the idea has been clothed by accidental historical developments, or by the notions current at some particular period" (86). And the article on Bentham which appeared in 1833 contains hints of a new evaluation of institutions which as a Benthamite he should have reviled, an evaluation better expressed seven years later in "Coleridge": "an enlightened Radical or Liberal . . . must know, that the Constitution and Church of England . . . are not mere frauds, or sheer nonsense – have not been got up orginally, and all along maintained, for the sole purpose of picking people's pockets; without aiming at, or being found conducive to, any honest end during the whole process" (437).

Actually the part of Coleridge's work most interesting to Mill was the assessment and criticism of the Church of England – though the criticism stayed longer with him. In estimating the importance of the function Coleridge sees for the Church, it is necessary to see that this function was not only a possible one, but one dear to Mill's heart. According to Coleridge, the National Church is the guardian of the "Nationalty" (the portion of the wealth of the nation not personally owned), and its guardianship includes the duty of employing that wealth to the nation's advantage. This duty involves an attempt "to secure to the subjects of the realm generally, the hope, the chance, of bettering their own or their children's conditions . . ., [and] to develope, in every native of the country, those faculties, and to provide for every native that knowledge and those attainments, which are necessary to qualify him for a member of the state, the free subject of a civilized realm." [9] In other words, the "Clerisy" (a term put forward by Coleridge, and seized upon by modern commentators) has as its function the education of the nation. This concept appealed to Mill so much that whereas in 1828 he says: "I am an enemy to church establishments because an established clergy must be enemies to the progressiveness of the human mind," five years later he says that Church property is "held in trust, for the spiritual culture of the people of England." And further: "A national clerisy or clergy, as Mr. Coleridge conceives it, would be a grand institution for the education of the whole people: not their school education merely, though that would be included in the scheme; but for training and rearing them, by

[9] On the Constitution of Church and State (London, 1830), 76–7. Cf. ibid., 51ff., "Coleridge," 438; and J. H. Muirhead, Coleridge as Philosopher (London 1930), 192.

systematic culture continued throughout life, to the highest perfection of their mental and spiritual nature." [10]

The realization that the end of the Clerisy is an exalted rather than a mean one does not prevent Mill from attacking the clerics of the actual Church as Established, of course, and in his attack he claims Coleridge as an ally. The conservative philosopher, he says, has set "in a clear light what a national church establishment ought to be, and what, by the very fact of its existence, it must be held to pretend to be," and so has "pronounced the severest satire upon what in fact it is." [11] But while the abuses of the Church call forth strictures from Coleridge, the reforms which he envisages are not as unqualifiedly secular as Mill's, whatever the latter may think. The difference is fundamental: for Coleridge Theology must be "root and trunk" of all education, while for Mill national education should be secular; again, while Mill asserts that education should work for the highest mental and spiritual perfection, "spiritual" for him, and certainly not for Coleridge, means "moral." [12] In short, he treats Coleridge's argument as he tends to treat all others, in utilitarian terms: "To every argument tending to prove the *utility* of the Church Establishment, or any other endowed public institution, unprejudiced attention is due." [13] Finally, Mill (like most of us) makes Coleridge mean what he wants him to mean, and his support for church education in his later years was on totally different grounds, in as much as it provided an alternative to government education, and thus ensured a necessary variety. The state's right to see that endowments are employed to useful purposes connected with the donor's wishes was also interpreted in wide terms by Mill, and he could not see that the religious element in the endowments was essential to social utility.

Coleridge's historical attitude to the division of political power within the state contributed more basically to Mill's mature thought, for, com-

[10] "Speech on the Church" (date corrected from 1829) in *Autobiography*, ed. Laski, 319 (the argument is, of course, the standard Benthamite one); "Corporation and Church Property," in *Collected Works*, IV, 220.

[11] "Coleridge," 444. Cf. "Corporation and Church Property," 220–1.

[12] *On the Constitution of Church and State*, 49; "Corporation and Church Property," 219–20, where Mill uses "spiritual culture" to mean "the culture of the inward man – his moral and intellectual well-being, as distinguished from the mere supply of his bodily wants."

[13] "Corporation and Church Property," 200–1. Cf. Britton's discussion, *John Stuart Mill*, 110.

bined with other influences, it helped him towards a new view of representation. To Coleridge, the constitution embodies the balance between the powers of permanence and the powers of progression, the former being realized in the landed proprietors, and the latter in the industrial and commercial classes.[14] Political institutions must take into account the essential social basis of these powers, and the opposition between them. In effect, they are the material embodiment of the Idea of the State, and therefore of the Idea of Government, which is but the State in the political sphere. Parliament, then, must be composed of representatives of the two interests, and Coleridge's interpretation of English history supports his thesis that parliament has always been so composed. Mill saw much of value in this description, and though for him landowners tended to be cancerous elements in the body politic, he was able to see that a conservative element in the legislature is desirable.[15] He also agreed with Coleridge that if landed property came to be held as a trust rather than merely a support of hereditary dilettantes, then its representation would accord with utility.[16] The "progressive" interest offers no difficulty to Mill, for it is, in effect, that advanced by the Benthamites, and he never questions the utility of its representation. Mill did not accept Coleridge's division as such, however, but it can be seen mixed with the dominant Saint-Simonian flavour of the "Spirit of the Age": "Worldly power . . . belonged to two classes, but to them exclusively, the landed gentry, and the monied class; and in their hands it still remains" (44). Later he gives the distinction a characteristic twist, saying that the antithesis "is rather between the contented classes & the aspiring – wealth & hopeful poverty – age & youth – hereditary importance & personal endowments."[17] In accordance with his mature belief in the necessity of conflicting social forces, he willingly accepts the clash of interests. In On Liberty, for example, once again clothed in Saint-Simonian garb, Coleridge's view appears: "In politics . . . it is almost a commonplace, that a party of order or stability, and a party of progress or reform, are both necessary elements of a healthy state of political life" – but the sentence is completed by Mill's modification – "until the one or the other shall have so enlarged its mental grasp as to be a party equally of order and of progress, knowing and distinguishing what is fit to be preserved

[14] On the Constitution of Church and State, 18–20. Cf. "Coleridge," 455ff.
[15] Earlier Letters, XII, 75.   [16] "Coleridge," 455.   [17] Earlier Letters, XIII, 409.

from what ought to be swept away." [18] What remained with Mill, it will be seen, is less the specific content of Coleridge's argument than the general perspective. He learned, that is, to look for hidden rather than surface meanings in the history of institutions. As a result he gained a new conception of the division of political power; the Whigs and Tories seemed more reasonable to him than they had to his father; and he learned to look in a new way upon representation in a democratic government.

History demonstrates, as Coleridge pointed out, that a purely negative attitude towards government, as preached by the Philosophic Radicals is not in accordance with the facts of human experience. Political laissez-faire, unmodified and unqualified, is not a true instrument of social organization.[19] So the Tories, in their fight against the least-government principle, were not merely protecting their own selfish interests, but were putting into political form their belief "that it is good for man to be ruled; to submit both his body & mind to the guidance of a higher intelligence & virtue." [20] His quarrel subsequently was not with this doctrine, but with its justification of specifically Tory principles – he could not see that the desirable leadership was to be found in the Tory party and in hereditary landowners, as Carlyle came to believe. He also perceived more clearly in later years that the true function of such leadership is to advance the commonweal, not to preserve the *status quo*. Nonetheless Mill was impressed by Coleridge's description of the central government as a unifying, preserving, and stabilizing force, and as an intellectual and moral educator. This modification of political laissez-faire stayed with Mill longer than any other of Coleridge's ideas, and the well-known comment which he makes in his "Coleridge" is typical of his attitude towards the positive function of the state throughout his life : "government can do something directly, and very much indirectly, to promote even the physical comfort of the people; and . . . if, besides making a proper use of its own powers, it would exert itself to teach the people what is in theirs, indigence would soon disappear from the face of the earth" (455).

Mill retained this opinion, then, but except in so far as he adopted an historical attitude to political problems (and here Saint-Simon and Comte influenced him more than Coleridge), and in so far as he continued what he took to be Coleridge's attack on the abused functions of the National

---

[18] *On Liberty* (London, 1859), 85–6.   [19] "Coleridge," 453ff.
[20] *Earlier Letters*, XII, 84.

Church, the influence of Coleridge was mainly confined to the decade 1830–40, and the article on Coleridge which closed that decade is less a criticism of Coleridge, or a reassessment of Bentham, than a declaration of assured and well-founded independence. "On the whole," he wrote to Nichol in 1837, "there is more food for thought – and the best kind of thought – in Coleridge than in all other contemporary writers. . . ." [21] He continued to believe so, but the food he selected was carefully chosen to suit his palate, and he rejected as indigestible most of what others took for sustenance.

The Saint-Simonians

Almost contemporary with the influence of Coleridge was that of the Saint-Simonians. In 1828 Gustave d'Eichthal, an ardent disciple and missionary of Saint-Simon, heard Mill speak in the London Debating Society, was struck by his mental powers, and after being introduced to him by Eyton Tooke, endeavoured to enlist the young Utilitarian in the Saint-Simonian army. He showered Mill with the literature of the sect (including Comte's early *Système de politique positive*), and in a lengthy correspondence continually pressed the new message of social liberation. Although Mill was in a receptive mood at the time, he was reluctant to become sectarian again [22] – after the heady draught of mother church, he refused all watered-down liquids. Furthermore, he was critical from the first of the single-mindedness of the sect, their desire to channel all human activity behind their beliefs, their ignoring of conflicting desires and needs in their rush to reorganize society. (Any view of Mill as a doctrinaire overlooks even this early manifestation of his desire for flexibility.) Still, he was deeply affected by the ardent proselytizers, even more deeply than the generous account in the *Autobiography* (114ff.) indicates.

As in the cases of Coleridge and Carlyle, the contribution was less in specific detail than in the manner of regarding history and social experience. The Saint-Simonians had a philosophy of history: the progress of human development, they held, involves an alternation of critical and organic periods. (This belief, like Comte's concept of the "three stages" owes a major debt to such Continental thinkers as Herder and Turgot.) Organic periods, in which people are united by a positive creed which

[21] *Ibid.*, 221.

[22] See, e.g., *ibid.*, 34–8, where he criticizes the Saint-Simonians for their sectarian activities, which only result in the substitution of one partial view for another.

binds them in sympathy and hence in effort, gives way to critical periods when the creed in question has led to all the progress inherent in it. Critical periods are characterized by negative criticism, scepticism, and selfishness. Mill seized upon this analysis of history to explain contemporary problems. The lack of unified purpose, the negative philosophy, the social unrest typical of his time were to be seen as manifestations of a transitional critical period, which was destined to give birth to a new organic period. In his Saint-Simonian series of articles, "The Spirit of the Age," which have been used to prove much more than they can, Mill shows how he uses this notion: "The first of the leading peculiarities of the present age is, that it is an age of transition. Mankind have outgrown old institutions and old doctrines, and have not yet acquired new ones" (6). One must remember that these remarks were made in 1831, between the French Revolution of the previous year in which his sympathies were much engaged, and just before the old English institutions were supposed to disappear with the passing of the Reform Bill. But even in his early flush of enthusiasm, the form that the idea was to take in his later thought is indicated, for he holds that in the exercise of private judgment, which is proper to a transitional period, man is able to improve upon the beliefs and institutions of his forefathers (18). Thus the intellectual anarchy decried by the Saint-Simonians, in as much as it is essential to the age, is almost an equivalent term for freedom of inquiry. The order of the organic period is essential to the preservation of the social union, but advance is only to be achieved through diversity, and so Mill comes to hold that the best condition is that in which the beneficial features of the critical period are provided for within the framework of the organic state.[23]

For Mill, a more important facet of the Saint-Simonian philosophy of history is its recognition of the relativity of forms and institutions. Each element of social organization must be seen in its historical context. Society is progressive, and in its development it sheds successively its institutional skins. Old forms are not to be despised, neither are they to be revered, but they must be studied to reveal their significance as manifestations of stages of human progress. Here one is reminded of the Saint-Simonian influence on Carlyle, and also of Mill's later attitude towards Bentham and Coleridge: what is the meaning *and* the use of an

[23] His later discussions of historic periodicity, as in *On Liberty* (63), bear almost no resemblance to Saint-Simonian periodicity.

institution? Henceforth a difference is to be observed in Mill's treatment of historical bodies, most strikingly, for example, in his discussion of the Catholic Church and mediæval society in his articles on the French historians.

The social organization prophesied by the Saint-Simonians also influenced the direction of Mill's thought. While he objected to the sect's kind of socialism on the grounds both of desirability and practicability,[24] he was led to reconsider his attitude to socialist plans for the reorganization of economic relations, for here the sect had something to offer. He recognized that there was a hope of modifying the undesirable elements in economic machinery to fulfill social desires and needs. He also was attracted by the Saint-Simonian plans for the reward of industry and merit, their sympathy with the poor, their recognition of the value of mental labour, and their demand for the emancipation of women. But other features repelled him, such as the attack on private property, the attention to social rather than individual moral renovation, the emphasis on woman's spiritual nature, and most emphatically, the tendency to mental despotism and the suppression of individual opinion. In spite of Mill's assertions in these years of the need for moral and spiritual leadership in the community, he did not accept the Saint-Simonian desire to establish immediately a supreme power, modelled on the Catholic hierarchy. Later, in his *Political Economy*, he rejects Saint-Simonian socialism for this very reason, pointing out that by no stretch of the imagination can one conceive of a few or one determining, in a pontifical manner, the material, moral, and mental needs of each and every member of the community (II.i.4). It need not be denied, of course, that in the first flush of enthusiasm Mill was attracted by the promised benefits of organized intellectual leadership. The value of such leadership is a tenet of his mature political philosophy, but in 1831 he was willing to give much more power to rulers than he later considered desirable.[25]

This later caution is shown in his reaction to another facet of the Saint-Simonian programme. In considering the changes necessary for the implementation of ideal communism, he writes to d'Eichthal, they put the cart before the horse:

[24] See, e.g., *Autobiography*, 117; *Earlier Letters*, XII, 47–8.
[25] See, e.g., *Spirit of the Age*, 17, 19–21, 25–6, 31, 35–6, and the contemporary letter to d'Eichthal, *Earlier Letters*, XII, 26–8.

you imagine that you can accomplish the perfection of mankind by teaching them St Simonism, whereas it appears to me that their adoption of St Simonism, if that doctrine be true, will be the natural result and effect of a high state of moral and intellectual culture previously received: that it should not be presented to the minds of any who have not already attained a high degree of improvement, since if presented to any others it will either be rejected by them, or received only as Christianity is at present received by the majority, that is, in such a manner as to be perfectly inefficacious.[26]

Their emphasis is too much on the power of *amour*.[27] Writing again to d'Eichthal, he says:

I chiefly differ from you in thinking that it will require many, or at least several, ages, to bring mankind into a state in which they will be capable of it; & that in the mean time they are only capable of approximating to it by that gradual series of changes which are so admirably indicated and discussed in the writings of your body, and every one of which independently of what it may afterwards lead to, has the advantage of being in itself a great positive good.[28]

One final aspect of Mill's later thought is discernible in his reaction to the Saint-Simonian attempts to put their ideals into action. He wrote to d'Eichthal in 1831: "I watch the experiment; and watch it with all the solicitude and anxiety of one, all whose hopes of the very rapid and early improvement of human society are wrapt up in its success." About the same time he wrote to Carlyle that the Saint-Simonians were trying to "preach to the world by their example, which, they are beginning to find out, is after all the most impressive and in every way profitable aspect of the life even of those whose vocation it is to be the Speakers of the Word." [29] He recommends and tolerates experiment so that the truth of a theory may be tried. Only experience, and wide experience, gives validity to schemes; deduction is relatively worthless until supported or corrected by experimental verification. The Saint-Simonians should, in the interests of social development, have the freedom to implement their doctrines – a freedom which they might well deny to others. It was thus, as one among many systems, that Mill viewed the sect's programme: "St Simonism is all in all to you, St Simonians; but to me it is only *one* among a variety of interesting and important features in the time we live in. . . ." [30] Apart from the very important impetus given to his search for

26 *Earlier Letters*, XII, 49.
27 See *Correspondence inédite avec Gustave d'Eichthal*, 144 (d'Eichthal to Mill).
28 *Earlier Letters*, XII, 88-9.   29 *Ibid.*, 89, 106.   30 *Ibid.*, 108.

a philosophy of history, the equally important insight into the nature of socialist doctrines, and their introduction of Comte and Carlyle to him, any significance which the sect had for Mill disappeared with its dissolution under practical and legal pressure early in the 1830's. Their doctrines appear henceforth in his writings as examples of unworkable socialist plans.

Carlyle

As indicated above, one of the most important effects of Saint-Simonianism on Mill was its indirect introduction of him to Thomas Carlyle. Looking back on his articles of 1831 on "The Spirit of the Age," Mill says in his *Autobiography* (122): "The only effect which I know to have been produced by them, was that Carlyle, then living in a secluded part of Scotland, read them in his solitude, and saying to himself (as he afterwards told me) 'here is a new Mystic,' inquired on coming to London that autumn respecting their authorship; an inquiry which was the immediate cause of our becoming personally acquainted."

Much has and will be written about this strange friendship, but the most important fact is that it did not, as it could not well, endure. It began in misconception by Carlyle, was continued only through Mill's failure to present and defend his beliefs, and ended when Mill finally could hold back no longer and one by one introduced qualifications which Carlyle could not admit in a disciple. Or rather, it seems not actually to have ended, although close comradeship did not survive the early 1830's, but limped along at least into the 1840's. After that time the differences between the two make it pointless to talk of friendship, but some contact was inevitable, and it was publicly marked by acerbity only in print. It is likely that Carlyle, on his part, would never have broken off the friendship, for all the evidence seems to indicate that he saw no difficulty in reserving judgment upon his acquaintances until they were out of earshot. Admittedly, we should be worse off without some of his comments on Mill, but Mill was worse off with them.

The gleanings from Saint-Simonianism presented by the "new Mystic" in his articles appealed to Carlyle in more than one way. The criticism of the present age seemed apt, although it is doubtful whether he ever placed as much emphasis as Mill on the alternation of "critical" and "organic" periods – except in a figurative sense. The Saint-Simonian belief in the organization of social power accorded well with Carlyle's conviction that men in the mass are morally unable to govern themselves; the conception of strong leadership is evident in his thought even at this time, and was to become dominant. Being older by a decade, more worldly-wise, and less willing to follow others, Carlyle saw sooner than Mill the extravagances in the Saint-Simonian position, but the genuine enthusiasm felt by both during the early development of the sect carried them far into each other's confidence. Many of their early letters are concerned with Saint-Simonian affairs, particularly with the legal and schismatic difficulties in which the group were soon embroiled. Both were sympathetic, but the sympathy was touched more and more with criticism as the sect's antics became more and more fantastic.

Mill had not yet developed the extreme reserve that marks most of his correspondence as well as his published works, and his letters to Carlyle, especially in 1832 and 1833, go beyond even his letters to d'Eichthal in exposing enthusiasm. For this reason the correspondence has a greater interest for the student of Mill than it would have merely as a record of his early relations with Carlyle.

Carlyle's mistaken assumption that Mill was or would soon become his disciple can be easily understood when one reads Mill's letters, some of which reflect not only the thought, but even dimly the style of the prophet of Ecclefechan. In July, 1832, for example, Mill writes:

For although the task which we undertake is, to speak a certain portion of precious Truth, and instead of speaking any Truth at all, it is possible our light may be nothing but a *feu follet*, and we may leave ourselves and others no wiser than we found them; still, that one sincere mind, doing all it can to gain insight into a thing, and endeavouring to declare truthfully all it sees, declares *this* (be it what it may), is itself a truth; no inconsiderable one; which at least it depends upon ourselves to be fully assured of, and which is often not less, sometimes perhaps more, profitable to the hearer or reader, than much sounder doctrine delivered without intensity of conviction. And this is one eternal and inestimable preeminence (even in the productions of pure Intellect) which the doings of an honest heart possess over those even of the strongest and most cultivated powers of mind when directed to any other end in preference to, or even in conjunction with, Truth.[31]

Further on in the same letter the associate of the founders of the Society for the Diffusion of Useful Knowledge is faithless enough to refer to 1832

[31] *Ibid.*, 111; Professor Mineka reads "men of the strongest" where I have "even of the strongest".

as a time when "every body is cackling about the progress of intelligence and the spread of knowledge." [32]

Apart from their shared interest in the Saint-Simonians (and their mutual acquaintance with such men as Charles Buller), the two found a bond in Carlyle's constant, and Mill's growing, dissatisfaction with the new "Reformed" Parliament. Carlyle was always sure that mere manipulation of the franchise could do little to improve a nation of "twenty-seven millions, mostly fools," and Mill was gradually learning the same lesson, if he expressed it in less forceful terms. The hopes of the reformers had been very high, and their disillusionment and dissolution as an effective force proceeded apace in the months following the opening of the new Parliament. In May, 1832, Mill, flushed with the victory, wrote to Carlyle that the Tory party, "at least the *present* Tory party,"

is now utterly annihilated. Peace be with it. All its elevated character had long gone out of it, and instead of a Falkland it had but a Croker, instead of a Johnson nothing better than a Philpotts. Wellington himself found that if he meant to be a minister he must be a Whig; and the rest of his party though in the main Whigs already, did not chuse that particular phasis of Whiggery & determined to be nothing at all; & truly they had no very great step to make into absolute non-entity. There is nothing definite and determinate in politics except radicalism; & we shall have nothing but radicals and whigs for a long time to come, until society shall have worked itself into some new shape, not to be exactly foreseen and described now.[33]

By February of 1833, however, his enthusiasm had cooled somewhat, and he wrote to Carlyle of "this strange Wittenagemote," the Reformed Parliament: "all that seems certain is, that it is to reform the Church – heaven bless the mark! where, I wonder, will they find a Church to reform." [34] And in his next letter all his illusions are gone, gone so completely that he forgets he ever had them:

the Reformed Parliament has not disappointed me any more than you; it is (as Miss Martineau, I understand, says of Brougham) so ridiculously like what I

[32] *Ibid.*, 112; cf. 33.

[33] *Ibid.*, 106–7. This effusion is mostly enthusiasm, of course; writing to d'Eichthal three years earlier, on the occasion of Catholic Emancipation, Mill announced that "the Tory party . . . is broken; – it is entirely gone. It placed all on this stake, & it has lost it." (*Ibid.*, 28.)

[34] *Ibid.*, 141. This letter, contemporary with "Corporation and Church Property," shows like that article the influence of Coleridge, which can also be seen in Mill's admission, in the letter last quoted, of greatness in at least earlier Tories.

expected : but some of our Utilitarian Radicals are downcast enough, having deemed that the nation had in it more of wisdom and virtue than they now see it has, and that the vicious state of the representation kept this wisdom & virtue out of parliament. At least this good will come out of their disappointment, that they will no longer rely upon the infallibility of Constitution-mongering : they admit that we have as good a House of Commons as *any* mode of election would have given us, in the present state of cultivation of our people. They are digging a little nearer to the root of the evil now, though they have not got to the *tap*-root. . . .

In true Carlylean fashion, he raises our expectations only to confound them, for we never find out what the "*tap*-root" of evil is; instead Mill goes on to remark that he is tired of politics, and even if he were in the House of Commons he could do no good :

what sort of voice must it be which could be heard through all this din : what were a single nightingale amidst the cawing and chattering of 657 rooks and magpies and jackdaws? Truly if there were not in the world two or three persons who seem placed here only to shew that *all* is not hollow and empty and insufficient, one would despair utterly. It is only the knowledge that such persons have an actual existence on the same globe with us, which keeps alive any interest in anything besides oneself, or even could I but *believe* that the good I see in a few comes not from any peculiarity of nature, but from the more perfect developement of capacities and powers common to us all – and that the whole race were destined, at however remote a period either of individual or collective existence, to resemble the best specimens of it whom I have myself known – I verily believe, with that faith, I could be content to remain to eternity the solitary exception.[35]

In fact, this is just the belief that Mill was coming to have, at least initially under the influence of Harriet Taylor and the Unitarian circle. The tone of this part of the letter, which is consonant with the written (and undoubtedly spoken) exchanges between Harriet and Mill at this time, might have disturbed Carlyle, who preferred flights from rocky crags to soft landings. But the next letter is a return to the Carlylean mode : in fact, it represents Mill at his most Carlylean, implicitly expressing such distinctive marks as the gospel of work and the doctrine of the hero, and allowing for only a little hope.

Though I am sick of politics myself, I do not despair of improvement that way; *you* hear the cackle of the noisy geese who surround the building, *I* see a

[35] *Ibid.*, 145–6 (9/3/33). In the final sentence, Professor Mineka reads "specimen" where I have "specimens".

little of what is going on inside. I can perfectly sympathize in Bonaparte's contempt of the government of *bavards:* talking is one thing and *doing* another : but while every corner of the land has sent forth its noisy blockhead to talk, over head I am near enough to see the real men of *work*, and of head for work, who are quietly getting the working part of the machine into their hands, and will be masters of it as far as anybody can be with that meddling and ignorant assembly lawfully empowered to be *their* masters. After that let even *one* man come, who with honesty, & intellect to appreciate these *working* men, has the power of leading a mob, – no rare combination formerly, though a very rare one now; and there will be as good a government as there *can* be until there shall be a better people. .... *A chacun selon sa capacité* is far enough from being realised, to be sure, but the *real* deviation great as it is, falls far short of the *apparent*. It is much more in their apparent than in their real power that such men as Brougham and Althorp are exalted above their proper station. ....

How long is this dreary work [in Parliament] to last; before a *man* appears?

Finally, speaking of Harriet Martineau, about whom he is never enthusiastic, Mill writes that in her *Illustrations of Political Economy* she

reduces the *laissez faire* system to absurdity as far as the *principle* goes, by merely carrying it out to all its consequences. In the meantime that principle like other negative ones has work to do yet, work, namely, of a destroying kind, & I am glad to think it has strength left to finish that, after which it must soon expire : peace be with its ashes when it does expire, for I doubt much if it will reach the resurrection. I wish you could see something I have written lately about Bentham & Benthamism – but you can't.[36]

The last sentence refers to his "Remarks on Bentham's Philosophy," the anonymous appendix to Bulwer's *England and the English*, an apostate work that he was not willing to reveal to be his. But Mill's criticism in this piece is, while strong, not damning, and his next letter to Carlyle shows a desire to re-trench. His sincerity in the earlier letters derives mainly from his desire to please and learn, and the frequent italics, more appropriate to a teen-age diary, are a measure of his straining. Mill expresses thoughts which are to be seen again in his later works, but thoughts which, shorn of their Carlylean phraseology and orientation, appear as part of his reasoned criticism of egalitarian democracy and "negative" philosophy.

[36] *Ibid.*, 151–2. For a later opinion of *"bavardage,"* see *Representative Government*, 105.

But this is to anticipate: Mill's withdrawal from the role of Carlyle's scholar began with an embarrassed reluctance to express objections to his "teacher's" tenets. In a passage which should be borne in mind by critics of Mill's later remarks on truth, especially in *On Liberty*, he says:

I have not any great notion of the advantage of what the 'free discussion' men, call the 'collision of opinions,' it being my creed that Truth is *sown* and germinates in the mind itself, and is not to be struck *out* suddenly like fire from a flint by knocking another hard body against it: so I accustomed myself [recently] to *learn* by inducing others to deliver their thoughts, and to teach by scattering my own, and I eschewed occasions of controversy (except occasionally with some of my old Utilitarian associates).[37]

And, he adds, he still holds that this was a good practice, but he carried it too far.

The important part of the passage is that in which he emphasizes the inner and organic nature of what he calls "Truth." He is, of course, referring to belief or conviction, and his terminology is the result of his association with Carlyle, to whom intense conviction was truth. It may also be recalled that the faith in the clear light of reason to persuade, held by James Mill and Bentham, also can lead to a confusion between conviction and truth. John Mill suffered from this confusion, but less than most of us do, because the two sources from which it arose, Carlyle and his father, partly counteracted each other. The vagueness in Carlyle's attacks upon the false, and his failure to define, were not attractive to Mill, as he had from his youth been taught to consider imprecision in word and thought as one of the cardinal sins. On the other hand, the tendency to hold by the immediately clear as true, regardless of others' opinions and observations, the tendency that weakens much of James Mill's work, was partially neutralized in his son by the lessons he learned from Carlyle and others (such as Coleridge, and in some degree, Goethe), that truth is many-sided, and not to be apprehended at one glance and for all time. Mill became quite chary of declaring this or that opinion to be true, and one of the most characteristic features of his work, and yet one that has not been sufficiently noted, is the caution which underlies his recommendations of policies (with the possible exception of female emancipation), and the constant demand which he makes for an unceasing play of thought about ideas and institutions.[38]

[37] *Ibid.*, 153 (18/5/33).

[38] The comparison with Arnold here implied is brought out in Edward Alexander, *Arnold and Mill* (New York, 1965), and in my "John Stuart Mill and Matthew Arnold," *Humanities Association Bulletin*, 34 (1961), 20–32.

For Mill furthermore, truth is not mathematical in demonstration, to be reached by the addition and subtraction of elements. It is, in the sense of belief, though not of proof, a growth, as the metaphors in the letter to Carlyle indicate. It is "*sown* and germinates in the mind," he says, and he never ceased to hold this view. As will be shown later,[39] the organic and personal nature of truth (and conviction) is the unexpressed background to his demand in *On Liberty* for discussion of established beliefs, and support, even if casuistic, for unpopular or discarded tenets. It is not that truth results from the artificial or natural juxtaposition of conflicting beliefs "like fire from a flint by knocking another hard body against it," but that difficulties and strengths made evident by argument are brought home with striking immediacy to the individual. No belief or truth which has not been known as one's own can have life and vigour, as Mill testifies more than once from his own experience.

His habitual mode of expression, however, is not appropriate to the presentation of such matters; his style, controlled and measured, often cloaks more than it reveals the strength of his personal attachment to beliefs. His reasons and reasonings often leave the impression that nothing more than addition, subtraction, and cancellation lie beneath the argumentative surface. An example is to be found in the distinction between the "Artist" and the "Logician" discussed above. In the correspondence with Carlyle, the distinction serves as a tactical instrument for defining their differences in approach; he uses it to soften their disagreements. But it also, as has been seen, reflects his growing confidence in his own usefulness, and as it is developed in the letters, Mill's independence is increasingly seen. Logic, "the antithesis of Poetry or Art," he explains, is valuable, for just as all men can walk, so all men can reason, but nonetheless a cure for lameness is useful.[40] In March, 1834, by which time his tone has become more impatient and sure, he remarks that although some of the Philosophic Radicals are narrow, they are not, as Carlyle thinks, empty. "Have not all things," he asks, "two aspects, an Artistic and a Scientific; to the former of which the language of mysticism is the most appropriate, to the latter that of Logic?"[41] At the time, it should be remembered, Mill was working out a scientific methodology for the social and moral sciences, and the introduction of the word "Scientific" shows that his distinction between two areas of human endeavour was taking a firmer

[39] See below, pp. 184ff.   [40] *Earlier Letters*, XII, 173 (2/8/33).   [41] *Ibid.*, 219.

shape.[42] Increasing self-confidence is the mark of the years 1834 to 1840, as is shown in the discussion of his reassessment of his early teachers' strengths, as well as in his explanations to Carlyle.

The approaching coolness in their relations can, by hindsight, be seen when he mentions in 1833 his willingness to learn from others with whom he is far from agreeing completely. He comments: "most of those whom I at all esteem and respect, though they may know that I do not agree with them *wholly*, yet, I am afraid, think, each in their several ways, that I am considerably *nearer* to agreeing with them than I actually am." [43] Carlyle, not wishing to lose a promising disciple, refused to admit that any real difference separated them, and so Mill, as a preface to his expression of new strength, writes in his next letter: ". . . I had persuaded myself for a long time that the difference [between us] was next to nothing; was such as counted for little in *my* estimation at least, being rather in some few of our speculative premises than in any of our practical conclusions." [44] As usual, Mill is more interested in agreement concerning practice than concerning theory, and in the next letters he enters upon a justification of their respective roles. He even begins to interject a little criticism, suggesting that Carlyle's "mode of writing between sarcasm or irony and earnest," as exhibited in *Sartor Resartus* and " Cagliostro," should be used less often.[45] There is also a hint of the subject which led, in large measure, to the breakdown of the other correspondence carried on by Mill in a deceptive fashion, that with Comte; Mill knows, he says, what Carlyle means by saying that Mme. Roland is more a man than a woman, "but *is* there really," he adds, "any distinction between the highest masculine & the highest feminine character?" [46] One is reminded immediately of the presence in the background of Harriet Taylor – and Jane Carlyle. The bait was ignored, perhaps because Carlyle felt a little less sure of a man who could advance such arrant nonsense. Mill also mentions, as examples of disagreements which he had not fully indicated before, his inability to accept more than a hypothetical God, and his continued adherence to a utilitarian ethic.[47]

To this point the course of their friendship is easy to trace, for after their first meeting in London Carlyle hastened off to the remote fastnesses of Dumfriesshire for his battle with the elements, his wife, and

---

[42] See pp. 64–7 above.   [43] *Earlier Letters*, XII, 153 (18/5/33).
[44] *Ibid.*, 161 (5/7/33).   [45] *Ibid.*, 176 (5/9/33).   [46] *Ibid.*, 184 (5/10/33).
[47] *Ibid.*, 206–8 (12/1/34).

himself, and carried on the extensive correspondence quoted from above. After Carlyle's return to London in May, 1834, in search of a more extensive livelihood and fame, there is little documentation of his meetings with Mill, although there can be little doubt that they met frequently. In 1835 occurred the oft-discussed incident of the burning of the manuscript of the first volume of Carlyle's *French Revolution*, while it was in Mill's possession. Little need be added to the story of shock and (initially) mutual generosity except to point out that Mill wrote to Carlyle in March, 1835, immediately after the episode, to say that if Carlyle had misgivings about Mill's ability to preserve fragile papers, he could entrust his next manuscript to Harriet. Mill can hardly have been disingenuous enough to make this suggestion had she indeed been responsible. Whatever the vagaries of Carlyle's memory in later years, there is no reason to doubt that a servant of the Mills used the pages as fire-lighters, mistaking them for discarded notes.

The conflagration placed a strain on the friendship, however, for in spite of the noble attitude adopted by each, Carlyle's real sense of loss and Mill's acute sense of guilt could not but persist. Mill's best atonement was not his gift of money to keep the household together while the volume was rewritten, but his review of Carlyle's second version. Mill had, of course, a genuine interest in the French Revolution, and had contemplated writing a history of it for some years. He supplied Carlyle with many of the books used for his research, and probably engaged in long discussions concerning it. One can be grateful, in most ways, that Mill left the writing to Carlyle.

Mill's review article, in 1837, bestows praise on Carlyle's work liberally. In particular its epic quality, its vivid presentation, the scope of Carlyle's vision, and his ability to give life to historical persons are cited by Mill. He notes also Carlyle's freedom from narrow political bias in treating this, the most divisive event of modern history: "We should say that he has appropriated and made part of his own frame of thought, nearly all that is good in all these several modes of thinking," Tory, Whig, and Democrat.[48] Carlyle's prose style is given qualified approval:

although a few dicta about the 'mystery' and the 'infinitude' which are in the universe and in man, and such like topics, are repeated in varied phrases greatly too often for our taste, this must be borne with, proceeding, as one cannot but see, from feelings the most solemn, and the most deeply rooted

[48] *London and Westminster Review*, 5 & 27 (1837), 43.

which can lie in the heart of a human being. These transcendentalisms, and the accidental mannerisms excepted, we pronounce the style of this book to be not only good, but of surpassing excellence. . . . (17–8)

In summation, Mill finds the work to be a superlative and "true" history – its truth, in this case, undoubtedly deriving from Carlyle's ability to breathe life into men and events.

One criticism which might be considered of little importance takes on significance when placed in the contexts of their correspondence and of Mill's work on logic and method. Carlyle is much opposed to "formulae," preconceived and inculcated attitudes towards events, institutions, and human existence in general. Mill's sees some wisdom in this position:

> Doubtless, in the infinite complexities of human affairs, any general theorem which a wise man will form concerning them, must be regarded as a mere approximation to truth; an approximation obtained by striking an average of many cases, and consequently not exactly fitting any one case. No wise man, therefore, will stand upon his theorem only – neglecting to look into the specialties of the case in hand, and see what features *that* may present which may take it out of any theorem, or bring it within the compass of more theorems than one. But the far greater number of people – when they have got a formula by rote, when they can bring the matter in hand within some maxim 'in that case made and provided' by the traditions of the vulgar, by the doctrines of their sect or school, or by some generalization of their own – do not think it necessary to let their mind's eye rest upon the thing itself at all; but deliberate and act, not upon knowledge of the thing, but upon a hearsay of it; being (to use a frequent illustration of our author) provided with spectacles, they fancy it not needful to use their eyes. It should be understood that general principles are not intended to dispense with thinking and examining, but to help us to think and examine.

So far Mill goes with Carlyle but, knowing the direction of Mill's thought on these matters, and with his assessment of the abilities of his recently deceased father in mind, the reader is not surprised at the divergence. General principles must be given their due, as making the past available for guidance in the present. "The essence of past experience lies embodied in those logical, abstract propositions, which our author makes so light of: – there, and no where else. From them we learn what has ordinarily been found true, or even recal what we ourselves have found true, in innumerable unnamed and unremembered cases, more or less resembling the present."

The point at issue, it should be said, is one of not much interest to

Carlyle. He objects to cant, his enemy as much as Mill's (and Mill's teachers'), and tends to define dogmatism as other people's opinions. But Mill was much interested in these questions, for personal as well as theoretical reasons, and this criticism should be seen as connected with his ethical position as well as his logical one. At the time, he needed to make his defence of theorems and hypotheses whether attacked directly or obliquely, and here he hints at a necessary asset of the social scientist by making a point about the historian of society. A method is necessary, involving not empirical wool-gathering, but planned organization of problem and material, so that carding and weaving may lead to a fabric.

Without a hypothesis to commence with, we do not even know what end to begin at, what points to enquire into. Nearly every thing that has ever been ascertained by scientific observers, was brought to light in the attempt to test and verify some theory. To start from a theory, but not to see the object through the theory; to bring light with us, but also to receive other light from whencesoever it comes; such is the part of the philosopher, of the true practical *seer* or person of insight.[49]

Such a "scientific" history as Mill here and elsewhere presages took over the field, and led to some peculiar and dull passages – even some would say, to dangerous interpretations. But Carlyle, in any case, could not be expected to receive such criticism in a repentant mood.

The review as a whole was most favourable, however, and it cannot but have checked, if it did not stop, the growing discontent. Mill was at this time also using Carlyle as an occasional reviewer in the *London and Westminster*, and the two continued to meet on friendly terms at least up to the time of Carlyle's lectures in 1840, *On Heroes, Hero-Worship, and the Heroic in History*. Mill subscribed to the series of lectures, and according to Richard Garnett, was so outraged by Carlyle's comment on Bentham in his lecture "On the Hero as Prophet" that he shouted out his disapproval.[50] This story has the ring of probability, but it is questionable. Eleven days later Caroline Fox, after hearing Carlyle's lecture "On the Hero as Man of Letters" (which contains a second attack on Benthamism) with Mill's sister Harriet, went back to the Mills' house where, she says, "Several busts of Bentham were shown, and some remark being made about him, John Mill said, 'No one need feel any delicacy in canvassing his opinions in my presence;' this indeed his review [of Bentham in 1838]

[49] This and previous two quotations from *ibid.*, 47–8.
[50] *Life of Carlyle* (London, 1887), 171.

sufficiently proves. Mrs. Mill gave us Bentham's favourite pudding at dinner!" And two weeks later, on 3 June, 1840, she found the Carlyles chatting brilliantly at the Mills'.[51]

The story is plausible, however, just because there is so much in Carlyle's definition of heroes and heroic action which would distress Mill, and the anecdote at least expresses what was implicit in their cooling relations. Mill began to use Carlyle's ideas and phrases as examples of a retrograde social philosophy, and they came into conflict over the Irish and colonial question in the *Examiner*.[52]

As their views developed (or hardened) a more overt clash became inevitable, and it occurred when Carlyle wrote his "Occasional Discourse on the Negro Question" for *Fraser's Magazine* in 1849. In it he castigated "Exeter Hall Philanthropy" and "The Dismal Science" of political economy as the two villainous defenders of "Black Quashee," the ignorant, indolent "Nigger" who was causing disorder in the British West Indies. Mill, stung into protest, replied in the next issue of *Fraser's* with "The Negro Question." Carlyle preaches, he says, the law of the strongest, of force and cunning. In opposing the best tendencies in human history and human nature, he is wrong in his facts, and hopelessly wrong in principle. Far from the age being too humane, it is not humane enough; pain is being diminished, and if it cannot be abolished, at least pain-causing tyranny can. Carlyle is appealing to the worst instincts in man, and is harming immeasurably the progress of the species. The aspect of Carlyle's doctrine which receives fullest analysis by Mill is the "Gospel of Work," and the attack is indicative of the degree in which Mill had become aware of the vagueness and indirection of Carlyle's exhortations.

[51] *Memories*, I, 188–9, 203.
[52] See "Claims of Labour," *Collected Works*, V, 370, and *Principles of Political Economy, ibid.*, III, 759 (IV, vii, 1), for references to *Past and Present*. It should also be noted that in 1859 Mill excluded his review of Carlyle's *French Revolution* from his *Dissertations and Discussions*. Carlyle's "Repeal of the Union" appeared in the Examiner, 29 Apr., 1848, and was answered by Mill's "England and Ireland," 13 May, 1848. Mill points to a change in Carlyle, for instead "of telling of the sins and errors of England, and warning her of 'wrath to come,' as he has been wont to do, he preaches the divine Messiahship of England, proclaims her the prime minister of Omnipotence on this earth, commissioned to reduce it all (or as much of it as is convenient to herself) into order and harmony, or at all events, under that pretext, into submission, even into 'slavery,' under her own power — will it or will it not" (307).

Work, I imagine, is not a good in itself. There is nothing laudable in work for work's sake. To work voluntarily for a worthy object is laudable; but what constitutes a worthy object? On this matter, the oracle of which your contributor [Carlyle] is the prophet has never yet been prevailed on to declare itself. He revolves in an eternal circle around the idea of work, as if turning up the earth, or driving a shuttle or a quill, were ends in themselves, and the ends of human existence.[53]

Mill was apparently never aware of the importance of the gospel of work to Carlyle's "anti-self-consciousness" theory; and in fact their views, though Mill thought them similar (*Autobiography*, 100), were divergent. They both objected to individual self-centredness, but Carlyle denied the validity of introspective psychology of any sort, and advocated a drowning of the individual in extra-personal moral purposes, known and accepted through intuition; Mill, on the other hand, decried only a self-centred search for happiness and, far from denying the validity of introspection, defended it, for example, against Comte. Work, for Mill, is apt to interfere with moral purposes, which are seen by him in terms of individual, conscious, internal development. "In opposition to the 'gospel of work,'" he says, "I would assert the gospel of leisure, and maintain that human beings *cannot* rise to the finer attributes of their nature compatibly with a life filled with labour." Not, of course, that work is unnecessary:

There is a portion of work rendered necessary by the fact of each person's existence: no one could exist unless work, to a certain amount, were done either by or for him. Of this each person is bound, in justice, to perform his share; and society has an incontestable right to declare to every one, that if he work not, at this work of necessity, neither shall he eat. Society has not enforced this right, having in so far postponed the rule of justice to other considerations. But there is an ever-growing demand that it be enforced, so soon as any endurable plan can be devised for the purpose.[54]

And the whites, he adds, have just as much "right to work" as the blacks; if they do not avail themselves of it, they must suffer the consequences.

Carlyle's reaction was predictable: he purported to be surprised to learn that the "shrill attack" was by Mill, and when he revised the article for separate publication he enlarged it without softening a single judgment, and altered the title to *The Nigger Question*. Their final public clash, the most serious of all, occurred sixteen years later over the same

[53] *Fraser's Magazine*, 41 (1850), 27.   [54] *Ibid.*, 28.

problem of the rights of the coloured population of the West Indies. The controversy over Governor Eyre was extremely bitter, with Mill leading the attempts to bring him to trial for authoritarian cruelty beyond the law, and Carlyle lending the full weight of his reputation to the defenders of Eyre's actions.[55] By this time there was really no common ground left; their opinions had diverged from the beginning of their acquaintance, and real friendship could not last. Still their correspondence seems to have continued fitfully, and when Mill received reports of Carlyle's inaugural address as Rector of Edinburgh University, he wrote to say: "Please thank Mrs. Carlyle for her remembrance of me. I have been sorry to hear a rather poor account of her health, and to see by your Edinb. address that your own is not quite satisfactory."[56] Had Harriet been alive to pen this last comment, there would be little doubt about its tone; as it is, it must – regrettably – be accepted as innocent.

It is difficult to assess Carlyle's part in Mill's intellectual development, in view of their wide differences. Mill is little help, for he contents himself with general statements and judgments. An undated manuscript fragment, probably written by Harriet, describes what must have been Mill's feelings as he emerged from Carlyle's influence: "Young people feel about Carlyle's writings as they regard the clouds which seem to hide paradise – & to our feelings while the illusion lasts they create the paradise which they seem to hide."[57] Mill's mature judgments are generous, but unenthusiastic. To W. T. Thornton he wrote in 1869: "It is only at a particular stage in one's mental development that one benefits much by [Carlyle] (to me he was of great use at that stage), but one continues to read his best things with little, if any, diminution of pleasure after one has ceased to learn anything from him."[58] His longest account, in the *Autobiography* (122–3), mentions Carlyle's early writings as having, though not by themselves alone, helped to enlarge his "early narrow creed." Speaking of these writings, he says:

[55] See Bernard Semmel, *The Governor Eyre Controversy* (London, 1962), for a full and easy account, which would be better if Mill was not described as an advocate of "universal manhood suffrage" (63), and as a "handsome, white-haired old man" (71) in 1866.

[56] National Library of Scotland, MS 618, #81. Jane Carlyle died almost immediately thereafter.   [57] Mill-Taylor Collection, Box III, #154.

[58] *Letters*, ed. H. S. R. Elliot (2 vols. London, 1910), II, 220–1 (23/10/69).

What truths they contained, though of the very kind which I was already receiving from other quarters, were presented in a form and vesture less suited than any other to give them access to a mind trained as mine had been. They seemed a haze of poetry and German metaphysics, in which almost the only clear thing was a strong animosity to most of the opinions which were the basis of my mode of thought; religious scepticism, utilitarianism, the doctrine of circumstances, and the attaching any importance to democracy, logic, or political economy. Instead of my having been taught anything, in the first instance, by Carlyle, it was only in proportion as I came to see the same truths through media more suited to my mental constitution, that I recognized them in his writings. Then, indeed, the wonderful power with which he put them forth made a deep impression upon me, and I was during a long period one of his most fervent admirers; but the good his writings did me, was not as philosophy to instruct, but as poetry to animate.

The judgment is a just one, except perhaps for the "long period" of admiration which Mill recalls. Carlyle introduced Mill to, rather than supplied, new modes of thought. His articles on Goethe seem to have been Mill's first introduction (and perhaps his only one) to the German poet and philosopher, and his articles on French thinkers, such as his "Diderot," while Mill did not accept them fully, must have shown him new ways to regard the Continental thinkers. Mill was learning from his own experience as well as from the Coleridgeans (Sterling was a close friend of both) and Saint-Simonians, at the same time that he was most intimate with Carlyle, and so it is not surprising that he should give Carlyle a small place in his retrospective account. Criticisms of utilitarianism coming from the Coleridgeans were easier for him to accept, for in his view they had a better insight into the limitations of Benthamism, and their criticisms were less bombastic than Carlyle's.

Carlyle's constructive work was not fully developed in the early 1830's,[59] and in any event its elements had little appeal for Mill, or were of no use to him. His early flush of enthusiasm for heroes soon paled; as a personal exhortation, the gospel of work was not needed, and as a social doctrine it was pernicious. The rejection of sham and pretense was a Benthamite as well as a Carlylean tenet, and Mill was learning from Coleridge that much which appears sham to destructive criticism holds a real and important meaning for one interested in construction and re-

---

[59] His triumph began with the publication of the *French Revolution* in 1837, which was quickly followed by the first general publication in England of *Sartor Resartus*, and then by *Chartism, Heroes, Hero-Worship, and the Heroic in History, Miscellaneous and Critical Essays,* and *Past and Present.*

construction. Perhaps some weight may be attached to Carlyle's rejection of easy solutions to social, political, and economic problems, in favour of long-term moral development, for Mill definitely came to agree with him. But, as with the abandonment of self-preference, they attached different meanings to the terms. It seems fair, in summation, to say that Carlyle may well have gained more from Mill than Mill from Carlyle, although the intellectual exchange amounted to very little. Carlyle was helped to a literary reputation by Mill, both by review and by personal influence, and he had the use of Mill's library at a very important time. Mill found in Carlyle a receptive (if possibly too retentive) ear, and from him gained a measure of verve and colour in his prose style which, unfortunately, weakened over the years. The discussion may be closed with a passage in which this last influence may be seen at what must have been the height of its effect; here Mill deals with a theme which he may have borrowed from Carlyle, but which was his own as much as any Victorian's. When death approaches, he writes,

the whole of life will appear but as a day, & the only question of any moment to us then will be, Has that day been wasted. Wasted it has not been by those who have been, for however short a time, a source of happiness & of moral good even to the narrowest circle. But there is only one plain rule of life eternally binding, & independent of all variations in creeds & in the interpretations of creeds & embracing equally the greatest moralities & the smallest – it is this – try thyself unweariedly till thou findest the highest thing thou art capable of doing, faculties & outward circumstances being both duly considered – and then DO IT.[60]

Comte

An influence of a totally other kind was that of Auguste Comte. Although Mill did not correspond with him until 1841, the effect of the "Father of Sociology" was operating on Mill much earlier. In 1828 d'Eichthal introduced him to Comte's thought by sending him the latter's *Système de politique positive*, but this document, Saint-Simonian in origin and tone, failed to leave a distinct impression on Mill's mind. When he read the first two volumes of Comte's *Cours de philosophie positive* in 1837, however, he realized the strength of Comte's approach. The exact extent of the debt

[60] *Earlier Letters*, XIII, 425–6 (16/4/40). There are other passages in Carlyle which would repay further attention concerning his influence on Mill; see, for example, his comments on truth and error in "Novalis," and on Johnson and Hume as "half-men" whose qualities should be combined, in "Boswell's Life of Johnson" (*Miscellaneous and Critical Essays* [London 1872], II, 185–6; IV, 130).

is difficult to establish because of the shared beliefs and frequent agreement: both aimed at a scientific reorganization of society, and therefore directed their minds to problems of method; both believed in the limitation of inquiry to phenomena, and recommended a recognition of this limitation to reformers; both held that moral progress was possible and probable, if not inevitable. Within this large area of agreement – for them it was large – their debts and differences are to be seen.

Mill's account of his relations with Comte is conditioned to a major extent by the trend of their separate speculations, and is therefore perhaps less reliable than any other portion of the *Autobiography*, with the exception of the sections describing Harriet and Helen Taylor. The principal topics touched on are the material borrowed from Comte to be added to his own independently conceived theory of induction; the taking over whole of the "inverse deductive or historical" method; and in social and political philosophy the recognition given by Comte to strong and organized leadership, the value of the positivist separation of spiritual and temporal power, and the great need for a "Religion of Humanity." [61] The account is in some ways less than generous, for it was only with the passing years that Mill came to treat Comte as an enemy rather than as a teacher and ally. (For example, in his *Logic* the many references to Comte were gradually reduced from edition to edition.) It was, furthermore, as the exponent of a philosophy of history that Comte first came into Mill's ken,[62] and the logical method which supported this philosophy, although Mill came to regard it as the most important aspect of Comte's thought, was not initially its sole recommendation.

Comte concurred in the Saint-Simonian belief in the existence of critical and organic periods, and indeed played a part in the concept's development, but in later years he concentrated on a different pattern. He proposed a philosophy based on the necessary and successive progress of history, society, even the individual, from a Theological through a Metaphysical to a Positive state. Mill gives an extensive analysis of the first two of these stages in the opening chapter of *Auguste Comte and Positivism*, but they played a very minor role in his own thinking. The Positive state, however, as the end product of historical forces, has an important bearing on the scientific and sociological parts of Mill's work.

[61] *Autobiography*, 146ff. Cf. *Utilitarianism* (London, 1867), 48–50; *Letters* (Elliot), I, 183; "Diary," *ibid.*, II, 362. For the Religion of Humanity, see pp. 137–9 below.
[62] *Auguste Comte and Positivism*, 2nd ed. (London, 1866), 86.

In the last and most perfect stage, the mind no longer searches for absolute notions and final causes, but looks only for the laws of phenomenal events; the positivist willingly admits the limitations of human knowledge to phenomena, and also admits the relativity of that knowledge. These concepts were familiar to Mill; as he says, the "same great truth formed the groundwork of all the speculative philosophy of Bentham, and pre-eminently of James Mill. . . ." [63] The mode of presentation, the historical analysis, and the breadth of scope were, however, new and enticing.

Two elements of Comte's scientific structure held special charm for Mill: the hierarchy of the sciences, and the division of individual sciences into Statics and Dynamics. The hierarchy demands a recognition of the continuity and interdependence of the sciences. The rate of advance of each science towards the positive state, which rate determines its place in the hierarchy, depends on its generality, simplicity, and independence of other sciences. Comte's hierarchy is arranged on these principles in the following order: Mathematics, Astronomy, Physics, Chemistry, Biology, and Sociology. Mathematics, as the simplest, most general, and most independent, reached the positive stage first; the other sciences reached, or will reach it more slowly; Sociology, as the most complicated, most specific, and most dependent, must reach it last. The more complicated sciences depend on and take account of the laws of simpler ones, yet also react on the simpler ones by modifying their hypotheses. Sociology, or Social Physics as Comte first called it, comprehends in a real manner all other science, while being in a sense derivative from all science. The science of society is thus, Mill agreed, removed from the jurisdiction of *a priori* and intuitional philosophies. The hierarchy, viewed in the light of Saint-Simonian theories of the modifiability of institutions, reinforced Mill's belief that social arrangements could be scientifically reordered. Mill praised, long after he had rejected most of Comte's ideas, his political relativism:

M. Comte is . . . free from the error of considering any practical rule or doctrine that can be laid down in politics as universal and absolute. All political truth he deems strictly relative, implying as its correlative a given state or situation of society. This conviction is now common to him with all thinkers who are on a level with the age, and comes so naturally to any intelligent

---

[63] *Ibid.*, 8. Cf. Mill's discussion of Bentham's moral and political method in "Bentham," 339ff.

reader of history, that the only wonder is how men could have been prevented from reaching it sooner.[64]

A rather more technical point was also important to Mill, as Alexander Bain indicates when discussing his own agreement with Mill: "The improvement effected in the Classification of the Sciences was apparent at a glance; while the carrying out of the Hierarchy, involving the double dependence of each science upon the preceding, first as to Doctrine and next as to Method, raised the scheme above the usual barrenness of science-classifications." [65] This matter occurs again in Mill's *Inaugural Address*, taking its proper place in his mature view of method in the social sciences.

The division of individual sciences into Statics and Dynamics was also prized by Mill for the light which it cast on Sociology. Comte pressed the division through all sciences, but Mill was primarily interested in the highest science, where the distinction gave rise to the principles of Order and Progress. Comte's idea came to reinforce the division already recognized by Mill in Coleridge and the Saint-Simonians, for "Order" and "Progress" correspond closely to the "Permanence" and "Progression" of the former and the "Stationary' and "Progressive" of the latter. It is hardly surprising, then, to find variations of this distinction in Mill's discussion of the social sciences in his *Principles of Political Economy, Representative Government*, and *On Liberty*.

Much as Mill admired this distinction, however, just here he was forced to reject the implications and development of Comte's doctrine. He accepted the division, certainly, but he rejected Comte's analysis of the parts. The Dynamics of Society, that part of sociological theory dealing with the interest of Progress, involving as it does the law of the three stages, for the most part satisfied Mill, although he came to care more for the description than the implications, and criticized the terminology, suggesting that "Personal" or "Volitional" should be substituted for "Theological"; "Abstractional" or "Ontological" for "Metaphysical"; and "Phaenomenal" and "Experiential" for "Positive." [66] The case is otherwise with the Statics of Society, that part of Comte's doctrine dealing with the interest of Order. Contrasting its treatment with that of Dynamics, Mill comments on its summary nature and its weakness, saying that Comte

[64] *Auguste Comte and Positivism*, 115.   [65] Bain, *John Stuart Mill*, 71.
[66] *Auguste Comte and Positivism*, 9–10. See also "Theism," in *Three Essays on Religion* (London, 1874), 157ff.

"can hardly have seemed even to himself to have originated, in the statics of society, anything new, unless his revival of the Catholic idea of a Spiritual Power may be so considered. The remainder, with the exception of detached thoughts, in which even his feeblest productions are always rich, is trite, while in our judgment far from being always true." [67]

To estimate the full disagreement in this area between Mill and Comte is important because of the emphasis Mill gives it. Some discussion of Comte's position is therefore necessary. As he held that Order was characteristic of the Theological stage of human and scientific development, so he held that Progress was characteristic of the Metaphysical stage. The stationary order of the first stage gives way before the critical attack of the progressive second stage, but no satisfactory way of holding society together then develops. But the Positive stage, as the end product of history, evolves a doctrine equally progressive and hierarchical. Order is supplied by the attention paid to the interconnection of past and present, and the relation of Sociology to the hierarchy of sciences; progress is supplied by the recognition of the relativity of knowledge, which ensures that development will proceed from the assimilation of new laws into the system. Order will also profit from a recognition of relativity, which encourages a wise resignation to incurable political evils. Progress, therefore, is "in its essence identical with Order, and may be looked upon as Order made manifest." [68] This union is ultimately based on the intellectual unity resulting from the limitation of investigation to phenomena. Society agrees to agree on the past discoveries of science, thus giving Order, and agrees to agree with the future discoveries of science, thus ensuring Progress. From this unity the formulation of the Comtian doctrine of freedom arises: "true liberty is nothing else than a rational submission to the preponderance of the laws of nature, in release from all arbitrary personal dictation." [69] The individual can be free, then, only in a society which is cognizant of the rule of natural law, that is, in a positivist society.

The social contract among individuals which is necessary for unity is enforced by the moral power of public opinion, and in a sense the contract is the recognition, conscious or not, of this power. To organize this forces there are three requisites: "first, the establishment of fixed principles

[67] *Auguste Comte and Positivism*, 89.
[68] *General View of Positivism* (London, 1908), 116.
[69] *Positive Philosophy* (London, 1875), II, 39.

of social action; secondly, their adoption by the public, and its consent to their application in special cases; and, lastly, a recognized organ to lay down the principles, and to apply them to the conduct of daily life." [70] The principles must, of course, be established by scientists, and can be applied only by them; the scientist, or philosopher in Comte's terminology, must therefore constitute the moral authority in society, with public opinion supplying the authority with force. As religion comes to be identified with positivism, moral and spiritual become one, and thus the moral authority becomes synonymous with the spiritual authority, and the scientist becomes philosopher-priest. Comte provides for the rigid organization of this spiritual power, and eventually came to the point of calculating the number of philosophers necessary for the whole of Europe.[71]

Mill's changes of attitude towards this part of Comte's thought provide an interesting commentary on the growth of his own independent position. At the height of his revolt against Benthamism, Mill ceased to defend freedom of thought and inquiry, thinking it merely a manifestation of a "transitional" state of society, and held, with Comte and the Saint-Simonians, that only those specially qualified on social topics should be allowed not only to express, but even to form, opinions on matters of social importance. A selection of passages from his writings in the early 1830's can easily be made which, taken out of context, presents a picture very different from that typified by both his earlier immature works and his later mature ones. Mill himself, it may be said, was in a "transitional" phase when he wrote the following passages:

We never hear of the right of private judgment in physical science; yet it exists; for what is there to prevent any one from denying every proposition in natural philosophy, if he be so minded? [But] . . . all persons who have studied those subjects have come to a nearly unanimous agreement upon them. . . . The physical sciences, therefore, (speaking of them generally) are continually *growing*, but never *changing*: in every age they receive indeed mighty improvements, but for them the age of transition is past.

It is almost unnecessary to remark in how very different a condition from this, are the sciences which are conversant with the moral nature and social condition of man. In those sciences, this imposing unanimity among all who have studied the subject does not exist; and every dabbler, consequently, thinks his opinion as good as another's. . . . It is rather the person who *has* studied the

[70] *General View of Positivism*, 155.
[71] See the *Catechism of Positivism* (London, 1858), *passim*.

subject systematically that is regarded as disqualified. He is a *theorist*: and the word which expresses the highest and noblest effort of human intelligence is turned into a bye-word of derision.

It is . . . one of the necessary conditions of humanity, that the majority must either have wrong opinions, or no fixed opinions, or must place the degree of reliance warranted by reason, in the authority of those who have made moral and social philosophy their peculiar study.

[I]f the multitude of one age are nearer to the truth than the multitude of another, it is only in so far as they are guided and influenced by the authority of the wisest among them.[72]

Those passages are all from "The Spirit of the Age"; there are others:

It is not necessary that the Many should themselves be perfectly wise; it is sufficient, if they be duly sensible of the value of superior wisdom. It is sufficient if they be aware, that the majority of political questions turn upon considerations of which they, and all persons not trained for the purpose, must necessarily be very imperfect judges; and that their judgment must in general be exercised rather upon the characters and talents of the persons whom they appoint to decide these questions for them, than upon the questions themselves.[73]

But similar as are the sentiments expressed here, the difference between this last passage, written in 1835, and the earlier ones is the assumption in the article from which it is taken that pragmatic authority in the political area is arrived at through democratic processes. The discussion has become political, and so it largely remained for Mill. He limited freedom concerning executive decisions, but left the choice of executives free, and more important, he left thought free to play about and use all experience. As he later says: "It is one of M. Comte's mistakes that he never allows of open questions."[74]

In 1835, while his agreement with the Saint-Simonians and Comte is marked, the argument is as noted expressly political, and both agreement and disagreement may be seen in a passage where Mill asserts an essential condition of good government: "That it be government by a select body, not by the public collectively: That political questions be not decided by an appeal, either direct or indirect, to the judgment or will of an un-

[72] *Spirit of the Age*, 19–21, 31, 16.

[73] "Rationale of Representation," *London Review*, I (1835), 348–9. (Reprinted in "Appendix," *Dissertations and Discussions*, I, 470.)

[74] *Auguste Comte and Positivism*, 14–15.

instructed mass, whether of gentlemen or of clowns; but by the deliber-
ately formed opinions of a comparatively few, specially educated for the
task." [75] Perhaps Mill needed the lesson provided by Comte's major writings to see the dangers, for it should be recalled that when this passage
was written, these had not yet appeared.[76] In any case, as time went on
Mill had more and more reservations on secondary questions, and eventually, in line with his increased insistence on liberty, he became completely antipathetic to the limitation of speculation involved in the
Comtian version of this doctrine. The references to Comte in *On Liberty*,
for example, include the following comment: "M. Comte . . . aims at
establishing (though by moral more than by legal appliances) a despotism
of society over the individual, surpassing anything contemplated in the
political ideal of the most rigid disciplinarian among the ancient philosophers" (29). Again, in *Auguste Comte and Positivism*, he reserves his most
complete condemnation for this aspect of Comte's position: Comte "or-
ganizes an elaborate system for the total suppression of all independent
thought." Mill further comments: "one is appalled at the picture of entire
subjugation and slavery, which is recommended to us as the last and
highest result of the evolution of Humanity. But the conception rises to
the terrific, when we are told the mode in which the single High Priest
of Humanity is intended to use his authority" (168–9).

This is not to say that Mill rejected all of Comte's "Statics": as already
indicated, there were broad areas of agreement both before and after his
reading of Comte. Since he still saw elements of the transitional in his own
time, and continued to believe that (one might say by definition) something better will succeed to the transitional state, there are a few conciliatory remarks concerning even this part of Comte's structure. He
admits that with the "startling . . . amount of positive knowledge of the
most varied kind" which both believe can be the property of all mankind through proper education, the deference shown to men of superior
knowledge would not be the result of ignorant judgment, but on the other
hand would be the reasonable deference of "those who know much, to

[75] "The Rationale of Representation," 348–9. Cf. "De Tocqueville on Democracy
in America," *London Review*, I (1835), 111n–112n. (These passages are reprinted in
"Appendix," 468, 473–4.)
[76] Bain notes (*John Stuart Mill*, 75) that Grote saw and feared the despotic element
in Comte's thought sooner than Mill.

those who know still more." [77] But the time for the institutionalization of such doctrine is, for Mill, still far in the future:

A time such as M. Comte reckoned upon may come; unless something stops the progress of human improvement, it is sure to come: but after an unknown duration of hard thought and violent controversy. The period of decomposition, which has lasted, on his own computation, from the beginning of the fourteenth century to the present, is not yet terminated: the shell of the old edifice will remain standing until there is another ready to replace it; and the new synthesis is barely begun, nor is even the preparatory analysis completely finished. (*Comte*, 120.)

So he believes that representative democracy, "Metaphysical" as it may be for Comte, is the only available method for the attainment of a just and lasting political authority. As it does not depend upon a theory of abstract right, but finds its source in scientific investigation, validated by reference to the utilitarian end, Mill's faith in democracy is not Metaphysical, but rather Positive. In his words: "there is also a Positive doctrine, without any pretension to being absolute, which claims the direct participation of the governed in their own government, not as a natural right, but as a means to important ends, under the conditions and with the limitations which those ends impose." [78]

Once again, then, Mill is seen to reject much of the content of a philosophy which earlier held appeal for him. As he grew older and wiser he saw that Comte's system was unsatisfactory, and worse, dangerous. But Comte, far more than the Saint-Simonians and Coleridge, impressed Mill by his scientific approach to a philosophy of history. Disagreeing with the practices suggested by Comte's conclusions, Mill retained the method he learned from the French thinker, insisting only on more rigid conditions of proof and a reduction of wild generalizations. Society is to be scientifically reordered, but not, Mill thought, in the doctrinaire manner proposed by Comte, for the reordering depends on a moral and intellectual revolution which in turn depends on freedom. Furthermore, while Mill agrees with Comte about the great possibilities of science, he is constantly aware of the limitations of human control of the physical universe and man's moral tendencies. Comte is a scientific humanist; Mill, a humanist using science.

So, even when recognizing agreement about the possibility of achiev-

[77] *Auguste Comte and Positivism*, 76, 98.

[78] *Ibid.*, 79; cf. 155. Mill speaks of the belief in *laissez-faire* in the same way, *ibid.*, 77–8.

ing social amelioration through a scientific study of phenomena, and about happiness as the end, Mill saw a danger when he first read Comte. In 1829, writing to d'Eichthal, he criticizes the abstractness of French thought, which in Comte leads to a concentration on social improvement narrowly conceived. Government and the social union, Mill says, do not "exist for the purpose of concentrating and directing all the forces of society to some one end," but "for all purposes whatever that are for man's good: and the highest & most important of these purposes is the improvement of man himself as a moral and intelligent being, which is an end not included in M. Comte's category at all." He continues, clearly recalling his experience of three years earlier: "The united forces of society never were, nor can be, directed to one single end, nor is there, so far as I can perceive, any reason for desiring that they should. Men do not come into the world to fulfil one single end, and there is no single end which if fulfilled even in the most complete manner would make them happy." [79] Comte, Mill had realized even then, was so much concerned with society that he had no time for the individual, and as Mill's ethic of progress depends on the individual, full agreement was never possible.

Again, however, it must be admitted that there are similarities in the ethical positions: both see moral development as the triumph of specifically human qualities over animal instincts, and altruism over egoism. Mill's growing impatience with simple progressivist beliefs was reinforced, if not initiated, by his study of Comte, and his interest turned to an inductive examination of social and historical trends. Here he was able to see Comte's value, saying that if "it cannot be said of him that he has created a science, it may be said truly that he has, for the first time, made the creation possible" (Comte, 124). Perhaps his failure to create Sociology was the result of his lack of objectivity towards his own theory; he, like Bentham, failed to make use of other's minds, and erected his arrogance into a course of "cerebral hygene," during which he refused to read any works but his own. (He broke the rule to read Mill's Logic.) He retained, as Mill saw in his first work, more respect for a unified theory than for evidence.

A detailed treatment of their discussion of method, which may be seen in their extensive correspondence,[80] is not appropriate here, but one

[79] Earlier Letters, XII, 36 (8/10/29).
[80] See ibid., XIII, and Lettres inédites de John Stuart Mill à Auguste Comte, ed. L. Lévy-Bruhl (Paris, 1899).

matter must be mentioned. Mill willingly acknowledges his debt in borrowing the "inverse deductive or historical" method, which is crucial to an understanding of his social philosophy. Comte's tendency towards absolutism, in Mill's estimate an aberration, is not inherent in the method, but results from misapplication of it. Comte also has an inadequate conception of proof, especially after his adoption of his "subjective" method in his writings after the *Cours*, and so his conclusions are not as valuable as they might be made.[81] With the earlier method itself Mill finds no quarrel. In 1854, at a time when the sociological programme of Comte had become anathema to him, he wrote to Barbot de Chément: "J'admets en général la partie logique de ses doctrines, ou en d'autres mots, tout ce qui se rapporte à la méthode et à la philosophie des sciences."[82]

The discussion of Mill's method in Chapter VI will make clear just how important the "inverse deductive" method is for Mill; his other genuine debts to Comte are not so easily recognized, nor are they admitted by Mill in his later years. One feels it would have been only just of Mill to acknowledge the insight Comte gave him into the organic workings of social institutions, and to admit the worth of Comte's philosophy of history. But once again it is necessary to say that no specific borrowings, apart from logic, are made by Mill, and it is even more difficult for a thinker to describe an influence coming upon him from more than one direction than it is for a student of the thinker's work to do so. Mill's attitude towards history had been altered by Coleridge and the Saint-Simonians before he read Comte's major works, which served to reinforce the earlier influences; when he was reading Comte he was also reading the French historians for whom he had singular respect; and he was far more likely to attribute his debt to any of them than to Comte, for he was "as radically and strenuously opposed as it is possible to be, to nearly the whole of his later tendencies, and to many of his earlier opinions" (*Comte*, 3).

De Tocqueville

The discussion of de Tocqueville in Mill's *Autobiography* stands in pleasant contrast with that of Comte. In 1853–4, when the relevant portions were written, Mill was far more aware of his debt to the former, for with the passing years he had turned more and more towards a con-

---

[81] See *Autobiography*, 146–7, and *Auguste Comte and Positivism*, 59, 62–3.
[82] *Letters* (ed. Elliot), I, 182 (7/8/54).

sideration of practical ways and means to the implementation of a socially valuable and viable democracy, and away from the development of theories of social reorganization. The grand plan was accepted, and the details of reform demanded attention; further alterations in the plan would become possible only when improvement on the present basis was realized. In addition, time had shown that de Tocqueville's warnings referred to imminent dangers, and Mill had exercised his talents to the full, preaching the utility of individualism, while what Leslie Stephen calls the "later vagaries of positivism" [83] had offended Mill's practical sense, and revealed the moral and scientific deficiencies of the positive philosophy.

Mill's relations with de Tocqueville, while always cordial, were not intimate. They met in 1835 and corresponded, with varying frequency, until 1859. Early and late, their letters indicate their shared interests: the correspondence begins with a discussion of the first volumes of de Tocqueville's *Democracy in America*, and ends with a letter in which de Tocqueville, too close to death even to read the work, thanks Mill for a copy of *On Liberty*. It is easy to underestimate the impact of de Tocqueville's thought on Mill; to indicate its strength it may be sufficient to note that after reading *Democracy in America* his political opinions, formerly fluctuating and uncertain, became sure and, except with reference to means, did not thereafter alter.

Mill states in the *Autobiography* (134) that the modification of his democratic views dated from his reading of *Democracy in America*, and continues:

In that remarkable work, the excellences of Democracy were pointed out in a more conclusive, because a more specific manner than I had ever known them to be, even by the most enthusiastic democrats; while the specific dangers which beset Democracy, considered as the government of the numerical majority, were brought into equally strong light, and subjected to a masterly analysis, not as reasons for resisting what the author considered as an inevitable result of human progress, but as indications of the weak points of popular government, the defences by which it needs to be guarded, and the correctives which must be added to it in order that while full play is given to its beneficial tendencies, those which are of a different nature may be neutralized or mitigated. I was now well prepared for speculations of this character, and from this time onward my own thoughts moved more and more in the same channel,

[83] *The English Utilitarians*, III, 368.

though the consequent modifications in my practical political creed were spread over many years. . . .

The role here outlined, that of the sincere but critical friend of democracy, was just that played by Mill. His practical modifications took some years to develop because he in effect practiced the theoretical programme he devised for the Scientist and Artist in the moral sciences. Mill accepted the results of de Tocqueville's scientific investigation into social trends, and attempted, in view of these results, to devise means to the great utilitarian end. The means have to be practical, moral, and in accordance with the known laws of social development. The discovery of means is therefore not a quick and easy task, and usually follows at a distance the first insight into social laws. Mill did not himself attempt to discover these laws, except by simple observation, but, accepting those which he believed to be valid, concentrated his attention on means. The contribution of de Tocqueville to his thought is in truth unique, for Mill accepted the main conclusions and adopted them into his own system. He never saw reason to discard them, and the modifications he proposed were slight. His tribute is spontaneous and forthright – and was not withdrawn. Writing to de Tocqueville after reading the completing volumes of *Democracy in America*, he says:

although my own thoughts have been accustomed (especially since I read your First Part) to run very much in the same direction, you have so far outrun me that I am lost in the distance, & it will require much thought & study to appropriate your ideas so completely as to be qualified to say what portion of them I shall at last feel to be demonstrated & what, if any, may seem to require further confirmation. In any case you have accomplished a great achievement: you have changed the face of political philosophy, you have carried on the discussions respecting the tendencies of modern society, the causes of those tendencies, & the influences of particular forms of polity & social order, into a region both of height & of depth, which no one before you had entered, & all previous argumentation and speculation in such matters appears but child's play now.[84]

Mill's enthusiastic adoption of another's conclusions needs some explanation other than his obvious sympathy with those conclusions: in Mill's view de Tocqueville's great recommendation is his method. As if to finish the revolution in his political thinking initiated by Macaulay's strictures on the *Essay on Government*, carried on by his reading in Cole-

[84] *Earlier Letters*, XIII, 434 (11/5/40).

ridge, the Saint-Simonians, Herschel, and Whewell, and intensified by his study of Comte, de Tocqueville's work came along as a consummate illustration of the proper method in social investigation. De Tocqueville's method, says Mill,

is, as that of a philosopher on such a subject must be – a combination of deduction with induction: his evidences are, laws of human nature, on the one hand; the example of America, and France, and other modern nations, so far as applicable, on the other. His conclusions never rest on either species of evidence alone; whatever he classes as an effect of Democracy, he has both ascertained to exist in those countries in which the state of socicty is democratic, and has also succeeded in connecting with Democracy by deductions à priori, tending to show that such would naturally be its influences upon beings constituted as mankind are, and placed in a world such as we know ours to be.[85]

In short de Tocqueville satisfies, as Comte did not, Mill's demand for proof. By 1840, when the passage last quoted appeared in his second and greater review of Democracy in America, Mill had largely completed his logical speculations, and could hardly have failed to look for support for his views on method in such a work. De Tocqueville was delighted with Mill's analysis of his procedure, remarking in a letter: "Je fais relier votre article avec une exemplaire de mon livre. Ce sont deux choses qui doivent aller ensemble et que je veux toujours pouvoir mettre à la fois sous les yeux." [86] And in 1843, having studied the Logic, he wrote to Mill: "J'ai été particulierement frappé de ce que vous dites de l'application de la logique à l'étude de l'homme. Je crois comme vous qu'en se servant de la méthode que vous indiquez, en s'attachant aux points que vous signalez, on donnerait à cette première de toutes les sciences une physionomie nouvelle et qu'on lui fournirait enfin des bases plus solides que celles sur lesquelles elle s'est appuyée jusqu'ici." [87] Mill, piling tribute on tribute, replied: "J'éprouve un grand plaisir en apprenant que vous partagez mes idées sur le méthode propre à perfectionner la science sociale: les suffrages

[85] "Tocqueville," Dissertations and Discussions, II, 5. In de Tocqueville's work, for the first time, says Mill, democracy is "treated as something which, being a reality in nature, and no mere mathematical or metaphysical abstraction, manifests itself by innumerable properties, not by some one only; and must be looked at in many aspects before it can be made the subject even of that modest and conjectural judgment, which is alone attainable respecting a fact at once so great and so new" (ibid., 4).

[86] Oeuvres complètes, VI, 330 (18/12/40). M. J.-P. Mayer informs me that there is no evidence that de Tocqueville carried out his notion.   [87] Ibid., 344 (17/8/43).

qu'on doit le plus ambitionner en parielle matière sont ceux du très petit nombre des penseurs qui, comme vous, ont rendu des services vraiment importants à cette science." [88]

The scientific basis and orientation of de Tocqueville's investigation of democracy, when revealed by Mill's analysis, appeared as a major step in the creation of this part of the Moral Sciences. There are other reasons for Mill's approval, of lesser importance here only because they represent shared ideas rather than borrowed ones. Mill agreed with de Tocqueville, for example, that in a democracy "the course of legislation and administration tends always in the direction of the interest of the greatest number." [89] De Tocqueville, in a passage partially quoted by Mill in his review, argues that democratically elected officials, as opposed to aristocratic ones, tend to promote the public good. He points out that the private interests of aristocrats (Bentham's "sinister" interests) oppose and combine against the general good, and continues:

There is indeed a secret tendency in democratic institutions to render the exertions of the citizens subservient to the prosperity of the community, notwithstanding their private vices and mistakes; whilst in aristocratic institutions there is a secret propensity, which, notwithstanding the talents and the virtues of those who conduct the government, leads them to contribute to the evils which oppress their fellow-creatures. In aristocratic governments public men may frequently do injuries which they do not intend; and in democratic states they produce advantages which they never thought of.[90]

Another of de Tocqueville's findings had similar appeal for Mill: the tendency of democratic institutions, particularly local ones, to promote "the diffusion of intelligence," and to stimulate "the active faculties of that portion of the community who in other circumstances are the most ignorant, passive, and apathetic. . . . Activity, enterprise, and a respectable amount of information, are not the qualities of a few among the American citizens, nor even of many, but of all." [91] Mill also praises de Tocqueville's discussion of enlightened self-interest, not as a substitute for a "higher principle" of morality, but as an auxiliary to it. In de Tocqueville's view:

The principle of interest rightly understood is not a lofty one, but it is clear and sure. It does not aim at mighty objects, but it attains without excessive exertion all those at which it aims. As it lies within the reach of all capacities, every one can without difficulty apprehend and retain it. By its admirable con-

[88] Earlier Letters, XIII, 612 (3/11/43).   [89] "Tocqueville," 29.
[90] Democracy in America (London, 1862), I, 281.   [91] "Tocqueville," 27.

formity to human weaknesses, it easily obtains great dominion; nor is that dominion precarious, since the principle checks one personal interest by another, and uses, to direct the passions, the very same instrument which excites them.[92]

This surprising confirmation of Bentham's views would not, by 1840, be disturbing to Mill, who did not dispute in his mature years the value of enlightened self-interest, when properly subordinated.

The degree to which Mill incorporated de Tocqueville's conclusions in his mature thought is best indicated by mentioning the three dangers which de Tocqueville saw in the establishment of democratic institutions: the destruction of individuality through the over-riding power of public opinion, the suppression of minority opinion by the increasingly powerful numerical majority, and the loss of initiative and spontaneity through the growing tendency towards centralization. These dangers are, of course, intimately related, but their separation enables one to see their importance for Mill. The first is the central theme of On Liberty; the second lies behind the schemes outlined by Mill in Representative Government; and the third is the main cause of the modifications which Mill demanded of all types of socialism.

Like Mill's, so de Tocqueville's fear of democracy is explicable only when it is seen what democracy means to them. Mill shows that de Tocqueville is discussing not political democracy primarily, but rather social and economic equality, "the absence of all aristocracy, whether constituted by political privileges, or by superiority in individual importance and social power." And it "is towards Democracy in this sense, towards equality between man and man, that he conceives society to be irresistibly tending. Towards Democracy in the other, and more common sense, is may or may not be travelling. Equality of conditions tends naturally to produce a popular government, but not necessarily. Equality may be equal freedom, or equal servitude."[93] Equality in this sense, it is clear, means more than an approximation to an economic and political mean; it is rather a condition of identity of interest, and ultimately of opinion. De Tocqueville notes that as coincidence of opinion advances, opinions themselves become more deeply rooted and less susceptible to change, and therefore the independent thinker becomes not only more rare, but also less able to influence others. The tyranny over the mind thus established is for de Tocqueville the chief danger in democracy. In

[92] Democracy in America, II, 147.   [93] "Tocqueville," 7–8.

Mill's words: "his fear, both in government and in intellect and morals, is not of too great liberty, but of too ready submission; not of anarchy, but of servility; not of too rapid change, but of Chinese stationariness."[94] This common nineteenth-century image is here borrowed from de Tocqueville, who says:

The Chinese, in following the track of their forefathers, had forgotten the reasons by which the latter had been guided. They still used the formula, without asking for its meaning; they retained the instrument, but they no longer possessed the art of altering or renewing it. The Chinese, then, had lost the power of change; for them to improve was impossible. They were compelled, at all times and in all points, to imitate their predecessors, lest they should stray into utter darkness, by deviating for an instant from the path already laid down for them.[95]

This attack on formulae, directed against practice rather than theory, clearly had more appeal for Mill than Carlyle's anti-cant fulminations; its grip on Mill justifies one more quotation, this from a letter to de Tocqueville:

Among so many ideas which are more or less new to me I have found (what I consider a very great compliment to the justness of my own views) that one of your great general conclusions [in Part II of *Democracy in America*] is exactly that which I have been almost alone in standing up for here, and have not as far as I know made a single disciple – namely that the real danger in democracy, the real evil to be struggled against, and which all human resources employed while it is not yet too late are not more than sufficient to fence off – is not anarchy or love of change, but Chinese stagnation & immobility.[96]

The correctives advocated by de Tocqueville are popular education, involving the inculcation of a spirit of liberty and an understanding of its worth, and political freedom, which does not necessarily mean pure political democracy.

It need hardly be said that these opinions coincide with those expressed by Mill in *On Liberty*. Two of the many examples which might be chosen will serve to illustrate the similarity:

As the various social eminences which enabled persons entrenched on them to disregard the opinion of the multitude, gradually become levelled; as the very idea of resisting the will of the public, when it is positively known that they have a will, disappears more and more from the minds of practical politicians; there ceases to be any social support for nonconformity – any substantive

[94] *Ibid.*, 56.   [95] *Democracy in America*, II, 55.
[96] *Earlier Letters*, XIII, 434 (11/5/40).

power in society, which, itself opposed to the ascendancy of numbers, is interested in taking under its protection opinions and tendencies at variance with those of the public.

[T]here is . . . in the world at large an increasing inclination to stretch unduly the powers of society over the individual, both by the force of opinion and even by that of legislation : and as the tendency of all the changes taking place in the world is to strengthen society, and diminish the power of the individual, this encroachment is not one of the evils which tend spontaneously to disappear, but, on the contrary, to grow more and more formidable. The disposition of mankind, whether as rulers or as fellow-citizens, to impose their own opinions and inclinations as a rule of conduct on others, is so energetically supported by some of the best and by some of the worst feelings incident to human nature, that it is hardly ever kept under restraint by anything but want of power. . . .[97]

To the student of British thought the view has been so closely identified with Mill that it is with some surprise that one reads passages in de Tocqueville which parallel Mill's thought so closely as the following :

It would seem as if the rulers of our time sought only to use men in order to make things great; I wish that they would try a little more to make great men; that they would set less value on the work, and more upon the workman; that they would never forget that a nation cannot long remain strong when every man belonging to it is individually weak, and that no form or combination of social polity has yet been devised, to make an energetic people out of a community of pusillanimous and enfeebled citizens.[98]

This opinion, expressed again by Matthew Arnold twenty-five years later, is not borrowed by Mill from de Tocqueville, for it is found in Mill's review of Sedgwick in 1835. But though de Tocqueville is not the source, his empirical observations, and the deductions from them, gave urgency to the discussion, while his argument reinforced Mill's own message. In addition, de Tocqueville and Mill based their warnings on the same principle : the despotism of custom and opinion is not harmful because it contravenes any inherent right the individual has to self-expression, but because it prevents the moral and mental advance of mankind. Only the freedom to develop judgments and to act on them can ensure progress.

The second danger inherent in democracy, the stifling of minority opinion by the majority, is also indicated by apathetic behaviour. The remedy is perhaps simpler, however, for although the only real cure is a

[97] On Liberty, 132, 29. Cf. ibid., 13, 109–10, 126–7, and below 182ff.
[98] Democracy in America, II, 394.

moral regeneration, political measures (such as those advocated in *Representative Government*) can in Mill's estimation preserve minority opinion. He says, in reviewing *Democracy in America*: "Now, as ever, the great problem in government is to prevent the strongest from becoming the only power; and repress the natural tendency of the instincts and passions of the ruling body, to sweep away all barriers which are capable of resisting, even for a moment, their own tendencies." [99] De Tocqueville, believing in both the utility and inevitability of democracy, and being himself an advocate of the popular cause, saw the principal danger of democratic institutions not in the power of the majority to make coercive laws, but in its ability to establish what Mill calls a "dispensing power over all laws." [100] The threat is not that the minorities will be violently suppressed, but that they will have no opportunity to give effect, or even voice, to their opinions. It is necessary, therefore, that there "should exist somewhere a great social support for opinions and sentiments different from those of the mass." [101] To this end are designed Mill's devices in *Representative Government* and elsewhere.[102]

The final danger noted by de Tocqueville, the loss of initiative and spontaneity consequent upon the growth of central authority in the state, must be recognized as a vital element in Mill's political speculations. In the *Autobiography* (134–5) he acknowledges de Tocqueville's contribution:

A . . . subject on which . . . I derived great benefit from the study of Tocqueville, was the fundamental question of Centralization. The powerful philosophic analysis which he applied to American and to French experience, led him to attach the utmost importance to the performance of as much of the collective business of society, as can safely be so performed, by the people themselves, without any intervention of the executive government, either to supersede their agency, or to dictate the manner of its exercise. He viewed this practical political activity of the individual citizen, not only as one of the most effectual means of training the social feelings and practical intelligence of the people, so important in themselves and so indispensable to good government, but also as the specific counteractive to some of the characteristic infirmities of Democracy, and a necessary protection against its degenerating into the only despotism of which, in the modern world, there is real danger – the absolute rule of the head of the executive over a congregation of isolated individuals, all equals but all slaves.

[99] "Tocqueville," 77.   [100] *Ibid.*, 38. Cf. *On Liberty*, 12–13.
[101] "Tocqueville," 73.   [102] See below, 228ff.

In each of these areas, then, Mill is one with de Tocqueville, and when these areas are added together, they cover most of the ground occupied by Mill's democratic beliefs. De Tocqueville initiated or shared almost all his thought on these subjects, and so appears, in proper perspective, to have been, excepting Harriet Taylor, the most influential of all those with whom Mill came in contact during his great developmental decade. The way in which de Tocqueville reinforced Mill's attitude towards sociological method has been mentioned, and is treated again in Chapter VI. The more important question of Mill's handling of de Tocqueville's findings is also treated below, in Chapter VII, where the conditions of sociological advance are discussed. But at this point it is possible to see just how much their essential thought was shared. One of the most outstanding of their joint characteristics is their fine impartiality. Although starting from opposite sides of the question, de Tocqueville from the aristocratic and Mill from the radical, they both looked on democracy as a reality to be analyzed, and bestowed praise and blame according to the results of the analysis, not according to preconceived notions. Their similarity in temper, as well as in thought, marks off the Frenchman from the others who influenced Mill, for his humble, but thorough and moral approach to sociological questions was more congenial to Mill than the ruminations of Coleridge, the rhapsodies of the Saint-Simonians, the explosions of Carlyle, and the decrees of Comte.

II

Mill in Maturity

5

Moralist

MILL'S MATURE and autonomous attitude towards moral and social phenomena was developed finally in his *Logic*, and from the time of its publication in 1843 no significant change of opinion affecting the total structure of his thought is to be found in his works. Some changes are evident within specific areas, especially in politics, but these changes reinforce rather than disrupt his position. In the *Logic* he settled the main lines of his method, involving the relation between the two controlling features of his thought, his desire for social advance and his sense of the practical, the first the impelling force behind his work, the second the limiting condition on it.

Viewed in this way, he remained a representative of the school of Bentham and James Mill. John Mill says of his father, in words more applicable to himself, that he had a "deeply rooted trust in the general progress of the human race, joined with a good sense which made him never build unreasonable or exaggerated hopes on any one event or contingency. . . ."[1] The younger Mill never for long loses sight of social improvement, and consequently his work is never fundamentally pessimistic – he can always find a way out of difficulties. Although he understood better than his father the difficulties of relating theory and practice, he too seems occasionally to forget about practicability in his vision of the future. Here, as has been seen, his hopes were encouraged by his wife's high dreams and were in accord with the proper optimism of the "Artist." In general Mill is incautious only in dealing with the distant future, the

[1] *Analysis*, I, xvi.

future in which society will be perfect, the future that got further and further away from Mill as he grew older. No matter how distant the goal, however, he did not despair, for his temper, like Browning's, was that of the strenuous optimist. Life is earnest, but life is good; in the struggle lies happiness.

No matter what the source, happiness is for the utilitarian the prime consideration – and Mill is once and for all a utilitarian. Almost twenty years separate his *Logic* from the "Teleology" or "Doctrine of Ends" which he mentions therein, but when his *Utilitarianism* was published he added a footnote to the last chapter of the *Logic* to indicate that the later work contains his account of the ultimate standard by which all human activity is to be judged. But – and here lies the reason for some mistaken views of Mill's position – while *Utilitarianism* is the most complete account of his ethical theory, he had been developing and giving exposition to that theory for some thirty years. Furthermore, *Utilitarianism* was initially designed as a series of periodical articles, and its form controlled its rhetoric and some of its content. Mill condensed some of the most characteristic parts of his theory, and presented a lengthy and popular defence of Utilitarianism which has attracted more attention than its polemical purpose warrants. Though *Utilitarianism* cannot be denied a large place in his thought, it does not contain either a full or a totally accurate account of Mill's moral philosophy, and it cannot be properly understood without reference to his other writings.

As explained in the *Logic*, the first task of the moral Artist is to define and describe the end. From Bentham, of course, Mill learned the chief tenets of Utilitarianism: the general formulation of the end as "the greatest happiness of the greatest number," and the definition of happiness in terms of pleasure and pain. Their agreement goes little further than this. Such a remark would not be worth making, if definition by opposition were not a useful tool. Bentham's prime interests were law, legislation, and the mechanics of administration; the prime moral question for him was: how can citizens be made to contribute to the general well-being of the state? This can hardly be considered as the central question in ethical theory, and Bentham wrote little on central moral questions. The extra-personal quality of his ethics may derive in part from the apparent ease with which he found personal happiness. Similarly, the close relation between Mill's system and his own life may well be taken to reflect the difficulty he had in finding personal happiness. In any case, his own account forces reference to his personal experience. After his mental crisis, he felt obliged to consider the relation of personal to general happiness. The "anti-self-consciousness" theory which he took as a guide allowed him to retain his belief in happiness as the "test of all rules of conduct, and the end of life," [2] but he had found that he could not himself achieve happiness by conscious striving after the bits of pleasure which make up happiness. Only by a concentration on secondary ends, treated for the time as primary, could happiness be found "by the way."

The enjoyments of life . . . are sufficient to make it a pleasant thing, when they are taken *en passant*, without being made a principal object. Once make them so, and they are immediately felt to be insufficient. They will not bear a scrutinizing examination. Ask yourself whether you are happy, and you cease to be so. The only chance is to treat, not happiness, but some end external to it, as the purpose of life. Let your self-consciousness, your scrutiny, your self-interrogation, exhaust themselves on that; and if otherwise fortunately circumstanced you will inhale happiness with the air you breathe, without dwelling on it or thinking about it, without either forestalling it in imagination, or putting it to flight by fatal questioning.[3]

Utility may still be defined in analytic terms, but for Mill, it is clear, the greatest happiness for the individual cannot be reached through a selfish calculation of pleasures and pains. The deficiencies in Bentham's account of human nature may be explained as the result of his apparent assumption that an aura of achieved happiness surrounds all or most men without personal effort. Mill, however, had become unhappy, and, as has been shown above, found a way out. Along this way, as sign posts and places of refreshment, were the secondary ends which made the journey possible and pleasant in itself.

His crisis also, it will be recalled, made him realize the necessity of internal culture for both individual and social progress. "I ceased," he says, "to attach almost exclusive importance to the ordering of outward circumstances, and the training of the human being for speculation and for action." [4] He was led to his theory of poetry by his experience and his needs, and that theory led him in turn to a satisfying ethical position. The implications of that theory may now be seen. As expressed in the early 1830s, it involved the belief that the poet is one who speaks *truth*, who deals in *realities*; later Mill was to be more chary of such Carlyleanisms, but the poet remained for him one who represents a scene and

[2] *Autobiography*, 99ff.   [3] *Ibid.*, 100.   [4] *Ibid.*

characters so representative of valid human feelings as to be morally didactive to all his readers. He teaches men to share the feelings of others, and only on such empathy can genuine and enduring morality rest. The importance of this sharing is touched on in a passage in which Mill praises Alexander Bain for separating "Tender Affections" from "Sympathy," and for treating the latter not "as an emotion, but as the capacity of taking on the emotions, or mental states generally, of others. A character may possess tenderness without being at all sympathetic, as is the case with many selfish sentimentalists; and the converse, though not equally common, is equally in human nature."[5]

Ideally, the moral initiate (and all are initiates before the poet-teacher) does not stop at sympathy with actual models, but goes further into a contemplation of perfection beyond that portrayed in literature and history. This Platonic echo is heard in an interesting commendation of the discussion of Beauty in Ruskin's *Modern Painters*, where Mill says that all the elements which Ruskin finds in the idea of Beauty, except those like Moderation,

represent to us some valuable or delightful attribute, in a completeness and perfection of which our experience presents us with no example, and which therefore stimulates the active power of the imagination to rise above known reality, into a more attractive or a more majestic world. This does not happen with what we call our lower pleasures. To them there is a fixed limit at which they stop: or if, in any particular case, they do acquire, by association, a power of stirring up ideas greater than themselves, and stimulate the imagination to enlarge its conceptions to the dimensions of those ideas, we then feel that the lower pleasure has, exceptionally, risen into the region of the aesthetic, and has superadded to itself an element of pleasure of a character and quality not belonging to its own nature.[6]

The highest pleasures for Mill, of course, are those mental pleasures of sympathy which guide the actions of the good man. So the poet, speaking "the word . . . with truthful intent," lets his audience "know one human soul"; the greatest poets, living in accord with their word, reveal nobility through beauty, and lead the audience to emulation. So Milton[7] and

[5] "Bain's Psychology," *Dissertations and Discussions*, III, 134.

[6] *Analysis*, II, 255n.

[7] Later, in a letter to Lalor (c. 20 June, 1852) Mill, probably having heard Harriet on the subject, says: "it is not agreeable to me to be praised in the words of a man whom I so wholly disrespect as Milton, who with all his republicanism had the soul of a fanatic, a despot, and a tyrant." (Mill-Taylor Collection, I, #22, 64r.)

Plato have given us works which are evidence of their lives; more important, the Gospel is the record of Christ's life as much as of his doctrines. [8] The usual attitude towards Jesus is mistaken : he has been "likened to a logician, framing a rule to meet all cases, and provide against all possible evasions, instead of a poet, orator, and *vates*, whose object was to purify and spiritualize the mind, so that, under the guidance of its purity, its own lights might suffice to find the law of which he only supplied the spirit, and suggested the general scope." [9]

Mill's last word on the ethical value of poetry is found in his *Inaugural Address at St. Andrews* which, in this as in other respects, is almost as good a guide to his thought as the *Autobiography*. Here he argues, in terms reminiscent of both his "Bentham" and his *Logic*,[10] that while the two most important parts of education are the intellectual and the moral, the third part, the aesthetic, is also essential. Aesthetic education involves the education of the feelings and the cultivation of the beautiful. The moderns, inferior in poetic control to the ancients, are superior in their choice of subject because they pay more heed to the depths of human experience, having the habit of "meditative self-consciousness" and "brooding and self-conscious minds." Because the proper study of mankind is man, the modern concentration upon inner feelings rather than outer circumstances produces more interesting, more useful, and more moral literature.

In this context the important modification (really no more than an intensification) of one aspect of his poetic theory becomes significant. The cultivation of the beautiful which Mill desiderates is in truth for him primarily a cultivation of beautiful character; the most beautiful nature is human nature. His passion for Wordsworth, continued throughout his life,[11] is most easily explained by his agreement with the poet's belief in the power of nature to moralize man as it moralizes the poet's song. Now the ethical value of the poet becomes apparent : he presents scenes and characters which play upon the feelings of his readers in such a way as to

[8] "Writings of Junius Redivivus," *Monthly Repository*, 7 (1833), 263.

[9] "On Genius," 657.   [10] "Bentham," 387; *Logic*, II, 553 (VI, xii, 6).

[11] See Hayek, *John Stuart Mill and Harriet Taylor* (London, 1951), 221 : "You can I dare say imagine how I enjoy the beauty when I am *not* looking at it – now in this bedroom by candlelight I am in a complete nervous state from the sensation of the beauty I am living among – while I look at it I only seem to be gathering honey which I savour the whole time afterwards." (JSM to HTM, from Naples, 9/2/55.)

pattern out for them a standard of beautiful conduct. If fully communicated, the standard becomes a model permitting of imitation. And imitation is at the root of Mill's ethic. Lacking the supernatural sanctions, he supports his form of the Religion of Humanity with natural sanctions. The test of action, ultimately utilitarian, practically and immediately is the actual or imagined approbation of some revered figure. The "passion for ideal excellence," as he remarks in "The Utility of Religion," [12] can be made into a powerful motive; the individual must ask himself whether Socrates, Howard, Washington, Antoninus, or Christ,[13] or even "ideal perfection embodied in a Divine Being" [14] would approve his conduct, and then model his behaviour according to the answer of his conscience.

The literary presentation of great men dedicated to altruism and duty supports and aids conscience which, as will be seen below, is cultivated in other ways. As conscience is a restraining force, preventing evil actions, so cultivated sentiment is active, leading a man to dedicate himself to love of his country, human improvement, freedom, and virtue. The self must be felt to be insignificant; devotion to others must be all. And the great source of this "elevated tone of mind . . . is poetry, and all literature so far as it is poetical and artistic." All other arts, as their content too is "feeling," tend to the same end, as does natural beauty, especially of the sublime order, for there is affinity between the cultivation of the good and the cultivation of the beautiful. The virtuous man who has learned to appreciate beauty will try to realize it in his own life, "will keep before himself a type of perfect beauty in human character, to light his attempts at self-culture." Mill even goes so far as to say that there is truth in Goethe's remark that the Beautiful is greater than the Good, for it includes the Good, and adds perfection to it.[15] As always with him, then, art centres upon humanity and is dedicated to morality.

This conclusion has a grim sound, reinforcing, as it does, common views about Victorian denigration of enjoyment in art. One needs to be reminded that Mill found a genuine emotional release in poetry, a release which he found otherwise only in his relations with his wife. His retired life and reserved manner precluded any public display of aroused emotion,

[12] *Three Essays on Religion*, 108. [13] *Ibid.*, 109.

[14] *Inaugural Address* (London, 1867), 92. Bain reports, without noticeable sympathy, that Mill "seemed to look upon Poetry as a Religion, or rather as Religion and Philosophy in one" (*J. S. Mill*, 154).

[15] The preceding passages are in *ibid.*, 89–96.

but we have one glimpse in Kate Amberley's Journal which is as suggestive as it is brief. In 1870 he read aloud Wordsworth and Shelley to an intimate circle, and Lady Amberley records that while intoning the latter's "Ode to Liberty" "he got quite excited & moved over it rocking backwards & forwards & nearly choking with emotion; he said himself: 'it is almost too much for one.' " [16]

This is a long way from the youth who, according to Mrs. Grote, wrote (and later destroyed) an essay against all feeling.[17] That youth had been a good disciple, but his straying in this regard is an enlargement of utilitarianism rather than a departure from it. Not only all men, but each part of every man must be accounted for in moral philosophy. A psychology based on selfishness and an ethic devised for and applied to social problems alone are not adequate. Mill continued to think them important, and not to be overlooked, and so is accused of destroying the consistency of the utilitarian belief by introducing anomalous elements. In fact, by shifting the basis of morality to the whole man, he provided a wider ethical unity which met, at the very least, his own needs.

This unity, he felt, as it was derived from the whole of life, was applicable to the whole of life. He argues for the necessity of a single end in moral questions, for the acceptance of several ends guarantees conflict and confusion in complicated questions.[18] There are cases in which it is important to assert the final authority of judgments based on utility.[19] But other ends, as he had found for himself, are given validity by human experience, and must not be discarded by the utilitarian.[20] Unlike his teachers and his opponents, Mill does not sneer at, but attempts to account for, moral theories differing from his own. Allowing various ends proposed by other systems to have a place, he denies to them only the first place.[21] Furthermore, as happiness is not to be pursued for its own sake, such a search being self-defeating, other ends are not only ad-

[16] *Amberley Papers*, II, 375.   [17] *Ibid.*, I, 421.

[18] "Bentham," 385; *Utilitarianism*, 4–5, 33, 37.

[19] *Letters* (ed. Elliot), II, 88 (19/10/67); *On Liberty*, 24; "Newman's Political Economy," *Works*, V, 443; *Utilitarianism*, 25, 38; "Thornton on Labour and its Claims," *Works*, V, 650-1, 655.   [20] *Utilitarianism*, 53.

[21] See, e.g., "Thornton on Labour and its Claims," *Works*, V, 650ff. A more primitive form of this idea may be seen in James Mill's grouping of Prudence, Fortitude, Justice, and Beneficence (the first two individual, the second two social) under the general heading of virtue. He does not develop the idea in John Mill's way. (*Analysis*, II, 288; *Fragment*, 250ff.)

mitted into theory, but are, in practice, seen as valid in particular situations. Conflict alone makes it necessary to assert the primacy of utility.

In practice, then, there is little or no reason for moral thinkers of most shades of opinion to quarrel with utilitarians. Nothing is more characteristic of Mill than this belief, which is best expressed in his review of Blakey's *History of Moral Science*:

The grand consideration is, not what any person regards as the ultimate end of human conduct, but through what intermediate ends he holds that his ultimate end is attainable, and should be pursued: and in these there is a nearer agreement between some who differ, than between some who agree, in their conception of the ultimate end. When disputes arise as to any of the secondary maxims, they can be decided, it is true, only by an appeal to first principles; but the necessity of this appeal may be avoided far oftener than is commonly believed; it is surprising how few, in comparison, of the disputed questions of practical morals, require for their determination any premises but such as are common to all philosophic sects.[22]

While in matters of everyday practice there is little reason for quarrel, in the sphere of moral reform there is. A very great issue is at stake in the battle between utilitarianism and systems based only on subjective feelings: this issue is the improvement of the human condition. If utility be the true doctrine, then morality is not stationary, but advancing; closer and closer approximation is made to the objective ideal of the greatest happiness of the greatest number. Furthermore, as man advances, his conception of the end alters in accordance with his increased vision; utility is a relative ethic in this respect. Believing as he does, with the Saint-Simonians and Comte, that historical periods condition belief, Mill needs a moral system which, through its recognition of the relativity of judgments and ideals, allows for progression. Finally, as it is based upon objective judgments, utility permits of examination and not merely of statement.

An appreciation of the importance of the war against intuitive and subjective moral systems was part of his lasting legacy from Bentham, and, as the earlier discussion has shown (see 33 above), it is perhaps the most important part. His continued advocacy of the cause may be seen throughout his works, but is most obvious in his specifically ethical writings. For example, in his review of Sedgwick (1835), he says:

[22] "Blakey's History of Moral Science," *Monthly Repository*, 7 (1833), 669ff. Cf. "Bentham," 384; "Remarks on Bentham's Philosophy," 344n.

Moral doctrines are no more to be received without evidence, nor to be sifted less carefully, than any other doctrines. An appeal lies, as on all other subjects, from a received opinion, however generally entertained, to the decisions of cultivated reason. The weakness of human intellect, and all the other infirmities of our nature, are considered to interfere as much with the rectitude of our judgments on morality, as on any other of our concerns; and changes as great are anticipated in our opinions on that subject, as on every other, both from the progress of intelligence, from more authentic and enlarged experience, and from alterations in the condition of the human race, requiring altered rules of conduct.[23]

Again, reviewing Whewell (1852), he returns to the same theme:

The contest between the morality which appeals to an external standard, and that which grounds itself on internal conviction, is the contest of progressive morality against stationary – of reason and argument against the deification of mere opinion and habit. The doctrine that the existing order of things is the natural order, and that, being natural, all innovation upon it is criminal, is as vicious in morals, as it is now at last admitted to be in physics, and in society and government.[24]

So Mill always makes a clear-cut distinction between the intuitionists and the utilitarians as the supporters, respectively, of immobility and advance, of conservatism and liberalism, of, in short, evil and good.

Dealing with progress, Mill talks, in the passage cited, as if intellect were the only progressive element in man's nature and therefore the controller of man's progress as well as the judge of experience. His earlier writings often give this impression, just as they also give the impression that man is rapidly approaching the millennium.[25] Experience tempered both these beliefs, as Mill came to see that institutional alterations, which were expected by Bentham to produce socially beneficial changes in the behaviour of rational and self-seeking individuals, were actually doing little to advance human well-being. The only change which would guarantee real advance would be an improvement in the moral state as well as the intellectual state of mankind – and they are not the same. By 1833, when concerned with the cultivation of emotion through poetry, Mill could say that one must not fall into

[23] *Dissertations and Discussions*, I, 158–9.

[24] *Ibid.*, II, 472–3. An earlier passage supporting this position, and also attacking feeling, is in *Westminster Review*, I, 540.

[25] "Speech on the Utility of Knowledge," in *Autobiography*, 268ff.; "Speech on the Church," *ibid.*, 319, 321–2; *Spirit of the Age*, 24.

the error of expecting that the regeneration of mankind, if practicable at all, is to be brought about exclusively by the cultivation of what [many of our social reformers] somewhat loosely term the *reasoning* faculty; forgetting that reasoning must be supplied with *premises*, complete as well as correct, if it is to arrive at any conclusions, and that it cannot furnish any test of the principles or facts from which it sets out; forgetting too that, even supposing perfect knowledge to be attained, no good will come of it, unless the *ends*, to which the means have been pointed out, are first *desired*.[26]

There must be radical changes in the condition of man's desires before any large increase in happiness can be achieved. Any reform which does not take into account the state of national morality must fail in its role as an instrument of social utility, particularly, as the Saint-Simonians have pointed out, in an age of transition.[27] History must be viewed in this light: the French Revolution, for instance, is an "outward manifestation" of a moral revolution dating from the Renaissance. "All political revolutions," in fact, "not effected by foreign conquest, originate in moral revolutions. The subversion of established institutions is merely one consequence of the previous subversion of established opinions." The reformer who learns this lesson from the historian will moderate his proposals in accordance with the dictates of practical experience.

Unquestionably it is possible to do mischief by striving for a larger measure of political reform than the national mind is ripe for; and so forcing on prematurely a struggle between elements, which, by a more gradual progress, might have been brought to harmonize. And every honest and considerate person, before he engages in the career of a political reformer, will inquire whether the moral state and intellectual culture of the people are such as to render any great improvement in the management of public affairs possible.[28]

There is always the possibility, as Mill points out in the same place, that institutions are actively preventing moral and intellectual improvement, in which case the reformer will still strive for beneficial alterations. Here again Mill brings Coleridge and Bentham together.

Just because he brings them together, however, one would expect to find a difference between his position and Bentham's. It occurs in consideration of the pre-eminence of individual or institutional reform. Both

[26] "Writings of Junius Redivivus," *Monthly Repository*, 269. Intellect is, however, the controlling element; see pp. 151-2, 167-8 below.

[27] *Spirit of the Age*, 6ff.

[28] "A Few Observations on the French Revolution," *Dissertations and Discussions*, I, 56-7, 59.

work for social utility, but Mill argues that social ends cannot be understood, much less achieved, except by individuals. Here is the central import of *On Liberty*. As Sterling said, Mill believed "that individual reform must be the groundwork of social progress."[29] The individual must not be shut up within a controlled and restrictive system of social morality; he must be free to choose his own destiny in the light of his moral views – consideration always being given to the happiness and equal development of others. In a restrictive system, society cannot advance, for moral attitudes and practices remain stagnant. The rulers may, of course, change their decrees, but unless the rules are felt by individuals as a living internal force, as duty and conscience, no real improvement can result. A necessity for social advance and freedom of thought is, therefore, such freedom of action as makes freedom of thought more than a phrase.[30] That this notion, at least, cannot be attributed to Harriet alone is seen in "The Spirit of the Age," where Mill says, "in an age of transition the source of all improvement is the exercise of private judgment . . ." (18). And in forecasting an organic age, Mill in his later writings saw the necessity for encouraging private judgment all the more as public opinion hardens.

Mill is clearly concerned primarily with the individual and not with society, and yet he is a utilitarian; that is, he believes the supreme moral end to be the greatest happiness of the greatest number. He, like Bentham, then must reconcile individual with social ends. But for Mill the abstract problem became a personal one, and he discarded the selfish basis of earlier utilitarian thought, and tied the individual's happiness to his sympathy for others. Still his solution is not logically satisfying, any more than is Bentham's; but Mill's approach is more fruitful for ethics, just as Bentham's is for law. Concentration on either side of the happiness equation, social and individual, curiously enables one to maintain at least a superficial consistency. Bentham, working directly for social happiness, attempts to limit the activity of the individual by imposing painful checks on anti-social acts, and offering pleasurable rewards for socially beneficial ones.[31] As harmful acts by individuals decrease, the total pleasure in-

[29] Fox, *Memories*, II, 9. See *Autobiography*, 166–8.

[30] Reference should be made not only to *On Liberty*, *passim*, but also to "Notes on the Newspapers," *Monthly Repository*, 8 (1834), 370, 175–6; "Notes on Some of the More Popular Dialogues of Plato," *ibid.*, 841; "Whewell," *Dissertations and Discussions*, II, 503–4; "Grote's History of Greece," *ibid.*, 526; and *Auguste Comte and Positivism*, 143.   [31] See, e.g., *Principles of Morals and Legislation, Works*, I, 83.

creases, and more happiness is available for individuals. Mill, working for social happiness through individual happiness, is concerned with those activities of society which, by stifling individual development, prevent social utility. Individuals find their happiness in promoting social ends, and society is moved onwards towards its goal.[32] So, starting from the opposite end of the problem, Mill reaches the same apparent result as Bentham by the use of multiplication rather than division. Writing to Carlyle in 1834, he says: "Though I hold the good of the species (or rather of its several units) to be the *ultimate* end, (which is the alpha & omega of my utilitarianism) I believe with the fullest Belief that this end can in no other way be forwarded but by the means you speak of, namely by each taking for his exclusive aim the developement of what is best in *himself*." [33]

This belief never varied. The individual in Mill's ethic advances social utility primarily by concentration on his own perfection. Reference to the ultimate end, it will be remembered, is not for Mill necessary in most situations. He objects to Bentham's belief that "all right thinking on the *details* of morals" depends upon the express assertion of the greatest-happiness principle.[34] Comte is even more mistaken in his attempt to channel all human desires into one path, even if that path leads in theory to social utility:

May it not be the fact that mankind, who after all are made up of single human beings, obtain a greater sum of happiness when each pursues his own, under the rules and conditions required by the good of the rest, than when each makes

---

[32] While Mill's devotion to the utilitarian end in *On Liberty* is clear, and only a recognition of the over-riding importance of general happiness can allow one to see the proper dimensions of liberty, it must be admitted that Mill attaches more importance to liberty than utility demands. He seldom ventures into the hazy land between ontology and physiology, but when he does, it is clear that he sees the desire for liberty as a basic element in the human constitution. When this belief is seen in conjunction with his attitude towards individual development, it is possible to discern a meld of Aristotelian and Platonic elements in his thought. He would seem to hold, on the one hand, that there is a specific teleology built into the human constitution, which transforms itself from potency to act in fulfilling itself. On the other hand, he seems to be searching for what might (with Coleridge more than Newman in mind) be called "The Idea of an Individual." The second, more Platonic notion, is better suited to the general cast of Mill's ethical thought, for it allows for the incessent search after perfection, the search in which perfection lies.

[33] *Earlier Letters*, XII, 207–8.   [34] "Bentham," 384; my italics.

the good of the rest his only object, and allows himself no personal pleasures not indispensable to the preservation of his faculties? [35]

The multifarious aspects of life are too valuable to be seen *only* as means to the single social end. In any case, uniformity of character and behaviour is not part of this end; on the contrary, it prevents its realization.

It is not by wearing down into uniformity all that is individual in themselves, but by cultivating it and calling it forth, within the limits imposed by the rights and interests of others, that human beings become a noble and beautiful object of contemplation; and as the works partake the character of those who do them, by the same process human life also becomes rich, diversified, and animating, furnishing more abundant aliment to high thoughts and elevating feelings, and strengthening the tie which binds every individual to the race, by making the race infinitely better worth belonging to.[36]

Since social utility is always seen by Mill in terms of the individuals who will enjoy it, his moral goal has more vitality and complexity than Bentham's. For Mill the end of morality is a state of being, not an abstract formula. The perfect community will be permeated with morality; its institutions, customs, and ways of life will be the conditions of happiness. Morality is essentially an individual and human, not a logical problem. Thus, while logically it may be difficult to establish the proper relation between the supreme end, the greatest happiness of the greatest number, and subordinate ends, such as liberty and equality, if the problem is seen as involving the ways in which, say, liberty of speech and equal economic opportunity aid in the establishment of a society in which individual happiness will be most probable, Mill's ethic becomes more clear.

This view of morality helps solve the problem in earlier utilitarianism signalled by the word "maximization." The total pleasure may be increased while particular individuals are left miserable, even if, as Bentham says, each is to count for one in estimating pleasure. But Mill, seeing happiness as a by-product of (even if also the impulse behind) the perfect state, holds that properly understood, equality of opportunity to achieve happiness is part of the principle itself. In other words, the perfect society will provide not only for the greatest possible production of happiness, but also for its equitable distribution.

An indication of the way in which Mill developed an individualistic

[35] *Auguste Comte and Positivism*, 141–2; "object" reads "subject" in the 1st ed.
[36] *On Liberty*, 113.

utilitarianism without losing either the principle's larger reference or its practicability may be seen in the introductory remarks of his *Inaugural Address*. He proposes to speak, he says, of the way in which the departments of general culture "all conspire to the common end, the strengthening, exalting, purifying, and beautifying of our common nature, and the fitting out of mankind with the necessary mental implements for the work they have to perform through life" (24). Social manipulation will not of itself produce this end, for institutions and political forms must not be treated as mere machinery, as they are by James Mill and Bentham; they are rather organic means of "carrying forward the members of the community towards perfection, or preserving them from degeneracy." [37]

Each person must concentrate on what he can vizualize, and not expend his efforts in useless attempts to advance an end which he cannot even clearly formulate. He must be ready, if opportunity occurs, to be guided by public utility, but his moral function is better as well as more easily fulfilled by attention to his immediate surroundings. "The great majority of good actions are intended, not for the benefit of the world, but for that of individuals, of which the good of the world is made up . . ." – and so they should be.

The multiplication of happiness is, according to the utilitarian ethics, the object of virtue: the occasions on which any person (except one in a thousand) has it in his power to do this on an extended scale, in other words, to be a public benefactor, are but exceptional; and on these occasions alone is he called on to consider public utility; in every other case, private utility, the interest or happiness of some few persons, is all he has to attend to.[38]

Increasingly it becomes apparent that Mill believes individuals should, as they will, look most frequently to the good of "some few persons," their immediate associates, husbands and wives, and children. By cultivating sympathy where it "naturally" occurs, we learn to extend its operation. He is, in other words, departing from the selfish psychology underlying Bentham's moral theory. This psychology admittedly would recognize and explain the same facts, but would derive the impulse towards care of others from the ultimate impulse to look after oneself.

One of Mill's criticisms of his father's system of ethics that bears upon his discarding of enlightened egotism also illuminates another area of his thought. James Mill, in his *Fragment* (249), distinguishes between moral

[37] "Remarks on Bentham's Philosophy," 328–9.   [38] *Utilitarianism*, 27–8.

and immoral acts on the following basis : there are two sorts of action in which other persons than the agent have an interest, "those to which the actor was led by a natural interest of his own; [and] those to which the actor was not led by any interest of his own." The acts which others wish the agent to perform, but to which his own interest would not lead him, are moral acts, and society recognizes them by rewarding the agent in order to control his behaviour. On the other hand, the acts to which the agent is led by his own interest, and which are harmful to society, are immoral, and must be prevented by society through punishment. There are, of course, cases in which society's desires coincide with those of the individual, either as to the performance or non-performance of actions.

John Mill remarks that this distinction boils down to a belief that moral feelings can be induced in an individual through his preknowledge of the good and evil opinions of society produced by his actions. He therefore refuses the explanation offered by his father, saying :

It seems to me to explain everything about the moral feelings, except the feelings themselves. It explains praise and blame, because these may be administered with the express design of influencing conduct. It explains reward and punishment, and every other distinction which we make in our behaviour between what we desire to encourage, and what we are anxious to check. But these things we might do from a deliberate policy, without having any moral feeling in our minds at all.[39]

In short, probity, prudence, design, personal calculation, the foundations of Benthamite ethics, are denied moral significance by Mill. When we observe actions which we like or admire because they are moral, we praise or blame them not from policy, but because we already have a moral feeling. Praise and blame are merely the external expression of that feeling. If we are only trying to produce an effect salutary to ourselves or society, we may praise and blame from policy, but our actions are not moral for that reason.

An interesting moral situation is found in those acts, performed at times by all people, in which the individual's own interest is sufficient to benefit society without reward or punishment. When we see others performing such actions, there is no feeling of moral approbation specifically centring on the agents concerned, but a pleasant association which spreads over the whole of life. (The economic doctrine of the "hidden hand" produces, it may be remarked, just this kind of pleasant mental glow.) When,

[39] *Analysis*, II, 323n.

however, an individual performs beneficial acts not through his own interest, acts which not everyone in his situation would perform, then the pleasure we experience is associated directly with the agent. And so with the opposite case, in which harmful acts are performed from no individual interest.

Some acts result in favourable or unfavourable sentiments without exciting the particular feelings connected with the performance or non-performance of obligations. Unless association theory is more fully presented than in James Mill's account, it is open to the charge that it does not fully explain such feelings. John Mill's attempt at explanation in associationist terms is found in the last chapter of *Utilitarianism*, on justice, where, as he says in a note to his father's *Analysis* (II, 324n–325n), he tries "to shew what the association is, which exists in the case of what we regard as a duty, but does not exist in the case of what we merely regard as useful, and which gives to the feeling in the former case the strength, the gravity, and pungency, which in the other case it has not." He goes on in this note to give roughly the same argument as in the chapter on justice. The particularly strong feelings associated with justice, duty, and obligation arise, Mill argues, from the belief that punishment of some sort should be attached to actions. The original source of this belief is the animal desire for retaliation, not moral in itself, but moralized "when it is united with a conviction that the infliction of punishment in such a case is conformable to the general good, and when the impulse is not allowed to carry us beyond the point at which that conviction ends." [40]

Mill needs this explanation, being particularly susceptible himself to appeals based on justice. His acceptance of the equal worth of individuals, for example, which conditions his social as well as his ethical thought, is really the result of a belief in justice. [41] But as his adherence to Bentham's attack on such concepts indicates, he could not accept "natural justice" or "natural right" as basic elements of consciousness or of conscience. Hence

[40] *Analysis*, II, 326n. Cf. *Utilitarianism*, 95–6: the sentiment attached to justice is "simply the natural feeling of resentment, moralized by being made coextensive with the demands of social good. . . ." In his *Logic* (II, 443n; VI, iv, 3) he says, echoing one of his father's weak arguments more closely than usual, that this explanation is founded on "historical experience," as direct experimentation is not possible.

[41] See, e.g., *Utilitarianism*, 92–5; *Subjection of Women* (London, 1869), 1–3 and *passim*; Mill-Taylor Collection, Box III, 110.

he has to explain justice in terms of utility, through association theory. Such an explanation, without weakening the sentiment itself, places the force of the feeling of justice behind utilitarianism.

In Mill's analysis, a selfish feeling (here one of retaliation) is not initially moral, but becomes moral when connected with utility. The connection could be made through a rational, Benthamic calculation of interests, or through sympathetic elements in man's makeup. The relation between these two kinds of explanation in Mill's thought is complicated. For him, the individual is not only self-seeking but also altruistic, although his sympathy at least originally does not extend beyond a small number of others.[42] Social utility begins, therefore, not in a careful calculation of motives and deterrents, though such a calculation is useful, but finds its origin in sympathy. Although there is difficulty in wording, Mill's intention seems clear.[43] Moral excellence, he argues, "must have a deeper foundation that either the calculations of self-interest, or the emotions of self-flattery." [44] It is founded (as has been seen in the discussion of poetry) on sympathy, although sympathy itself is related to individual pleasures and pains.

[42] "Nature," *Three Essays on Religion*, 49–50.

[43] The difficulty arises over the "naturalness" of sympathy. For example, in "Whewell" (481n), does he mean, in saying, "the good of others becomes our pleasure because he have learnt to find pleasure in it," that moral feelings are not "natural"? Compare *ibid.*, 481, and Mill-Taylor Collection, Box III, #110, where one finds : "Regard for the feelings of others is not a natural but an artificial feeling, the result of education and circumstances, the principal circumstance being mutual dependence." The question takes on less importance for Mill than it might, as his theory depends upon results and not upon origins (see 146ff. below). Compare also the discussion in *Analysis* (II, 309n) : "it is undoubtedly true that the *foundation* of the moral feeling is the adoption of the pleasures and pains of others as our own: whether this takes place by the natural force of sympathy, or by the association which has grown up in our mind between our own good or evil and theirs. The moral feeling rests upon this identification of the feelings of others with our own, but is not the same thing with it. To constitute the moral feeling, not only must the good of others have become in itself a pleasure to us, and their suffering a pain, but this pleasure or pain must be associated with our own acts as producing it, and must in this manner have become a motive, prompting us to the one sort of acts, and restraining us from the other sort." This theory, Mill says, is his father's, but it appears likely that the clause beginning "whether this takes . . ." is the son's modification. Notice that morality is connected with motivation to action; none of the utilitarians was apt to adopt a sentimental theory which ended in good feeling alone.

[44] "Tocqueville," 51. Cf. the remarks on Paley in "Whewell," 455.

The idea of the pain of another is naturally painful; the idea of the pleasure of another is naturally pleasurable. From this fact in our natural constitution, all our affections both of love and aversion towards human beings, in so far as they are different from those we entertain towards mere inanimate objects which are pleasant or disagreeable to us, are held, by the best teachers of the theory of utility, to originate. In this, the unselfish part of our nature, lies a foundation, even independently of inculcation from without, for the generation of moral feelings.[45]

The problem is further entered into in another note to his father's *Analysis* (II, 217n–218n):

That the pleasures or pains of another person can only be pleasurable or painful to us through the association of our own pleasures or pains with them, is true in one sense, which is probably that intended by the author, but not true in another, against which he has not sufficiently guarded his mode of expression. It is evident, that the only pleasures or pains of which we have direct experience being those felt by ourselves, it is from them that our very notions of pleasure and pain are derived. It is also obvious that the pleasure or pain with which we contemplate the pleasure or pain felt by somebody else, is itself a pleasure or pain of our own. But if it be meant that in such cases the pleasure or pain is consciously referred to self, I take this to be a mistake. By the acts or other signs exhibited by another person, the idea of a pleasure (which is a pleasurable idea) or the idea of a pain (which is a painful idea) are recalled, sometimes with considerable intensity, but in association with the other person as feeling them, not with one's self as feeling them. The idea of one's Self is, no doubt, closely associated with all our experiences, pleasurable, painful, or indifferent; but this association does not necessarily act in all cases because it exists in all cases. If the mind, when pleasurably or painfully affected by the evidences of pleasure or pain in another person, goes off on a different thread of association, as for instance, to the idea of the means of giving the pleasure or relieving the pain, or even if it dismisses the subject and relapses into the ordinary course of its thoughts, the association with its own self may be, at the time, defeated, or reduced to something so evenescent that we cannot tell whether it was momentarily present or not.

The problem of the moral Artist, then, is one of stimulating the propensity to sympathy which, although weaker than self-love, is still natural and hence available for reform. "The pains of others, though naturally painful to us, are not so until we have realized them by an act of imagination, implying voluntary attention. . . ."[46] "The strongest propensities of uncultivated or half-cultivated human beings (being the purely selfish ones, and those of a sympathetic character which partake most of the

[45] "Sedgwick," 137.   [46] "Sedgwick," 138. Cf. "Whewell," 480n–481n.

nature of selfishness)" must be controlled in a moral state; and Mill views the problem as less desperate than it first appears. On sympathy rests the possibility of the cultivation of goodness and nobility, and the weak natural bent can be developed into a controlling factor.[47] Fortunately, the progress of civilization works with the moralist to produce this result.

The social state is at once so natural, so necessary, and so habitual to man, that, except in some unusual circumstances or by an effort of voluntary abstraction, he never conceives himself otherwise than as a member of a body; and this association is riveted more and more, as mankind are further removed from the state of savage independence. And condition, therefore, which is essential to a state of society, becomes more and more an inseparable part of every person's conception of the state of things which he is born into, and which is the destiny of a human being.[48]

Education will finally unite desires, so that conflict between individual and social interests will almost disappear.[49] Here John Mill may appear closer to his teachers than he is, for although they would agree with the conclusion, they founded their educational schemes on the clarity of reason which unites self-interest to social ends by a prudent calculation.

Another statement by the younger Mill about the silent moralization of man indicates the same sort of agreement and disagreement with his father and Bentham. The mere process of growing up in society, he argues, forwards morality. "As soon as a child has the idea of voluntarily producing pleasure or pain to any one person, he has an accurate notion of utility. When he afterwards gradually rises to the very complex idea of 'society,' and learns in what manner his actions may affect the interests of other persons than those who are present to his sight, his conceptions of utility, and of right and wrong founded on utility, undergo a corresponding enlargement, but receive no new element."[50]

In summary, Mill's position is this: man has sympathetic as well as selfish feelings, and morality depends upon the former, not as Bentham and James Mill thought, upon the latter. Sympathy is weak, but even children try in some measure to moderate the pain and increase the pleasure of their parents, siblings, and friends. As they grow older, more and more associations widen the scope of their altruistic feelings,[51] and reason enters in to aid the moral process. "Mankind are capable of a far

[47] See *Logic*, II, 525ff. (VI, x, 7).   [48] *Utilitarianism*, 46–7.   [49] *Ibid.*, 41.
[50] "Sedgwick," 136.
[51] Cf. James Mill, *Analysis*, II, 286–9 and JSM's note to 308.

greater amount of public spirit than the present age is accustomed to suppose possible," Mill says in his *Political Economy*,[52] adding that through association the improvement will be made. The close bonds of the social union are effective in increasing the power of sympathetic feeling, and the gain is a moral one (here the position needs qualification because of the stultifying power of public opinion). The strong feelings of selfishness do not have a greater sanction because of their original superiority in strength; the ultimate victory of altruism will be moral, for it will make the greatest happiness of the greatest number the normal, even if acquired, end of behaviour in civilized man. Acquired traits, its must again be realized, are at least equally valid for Mill with natural traits.[53]

The moralization of man is a gradual process, however, and its completion is a matter of long years if not centuries.[54] The importance of Mill's gradualism will be seen in the discussion of his social thought, but may be adumbrated here by reference to his attitude to socialism. For the foreseeable future, he thinks, man's selfish tendencies will remain stronger,

[52] *Political Economy*, II, 205 (II, i, 3).
[53] In a note to his father's *Analysis* (II, 233n–234n) he argues: "The two preceding subsections are almost perfect as expositions and exemplifications of the mode in which, by the natural course of life, we acquire attachments to persons, things, and positions, which are the causes or habitual concomitants of pleasurable sensations to us, or of relief from pains: in other words, those persons, things, and positions become in themselves pleasant to us by association; and, through the multitude and variety of the pleasurable ideas associated with them, become pleasures of greater constancy and even intensity, and altogether more valuable to us, than any of the primitive pleasures of our constitution. This portion of the laws of human nature is the more important to psychology, as they show how it is possible that the moral sentiments, the feelings of duty, and of moral approbation and disapprobation, may be no original elements of our nature, and may yet be capable of being not only more intense and powerful than any of the elements out of which they may have been formed, but may also, in their maturity, be perfectly disinterested: nothing more being necessary for this, than that the acquired pleasure and pain should have become as independent of the native elements from which they are formed, as the love of wealth and of power not only often but generally become, of the bodily pleasures, and relief from bodily pains, for the sake of which, and of which alone, power and wealth must have been originally valued. No one thinks it necessary to suppose an original and inherent love of money or of power; yet these are the objects of two of the strongest, most general, and most persistent passions of human nature; passions which often have quite as little reference to pleasure or pain, beyond the mere consciousness of possession, and are in that sense of the word quite as disinterested, as the mortal feelings of the most virtuous human being."
[54] Harriet was more sanguine about the length of time necessary.

and as they cannot be overpowered, they can only gradually be over-
taken and surpassed by altruism. For the time being, then, selfishness cannot be overlooked in social planning.[55] The sceptical position he learned,
partly from his father and partly from Harriet, about the "present imperfect state of human nature" – or feelings, or morals, or education – led
him to moderate his hopes.

His general position can be seen when he discusses the practicability
of socialism in the *Autobiography* :

Education, habit, and the cultivation of the sentiments, will make a common
man dig or weave for his country, as readily as fight for his country. True
enough, it is only by slow degrees, and a system of culture prolonged through
successive generations, that men in general can be brought up to this point. But
the hindrance is not in the essential constitution of human nature. Interest in
the common good is at present so weak a motive in the generality, not because
it can never be otherwise, but because the mind is not accustomed to dwell on
it as it dwells from morning till night on things which tend only to personal
advantage. When called into activity, as only self-interest now is, by the daily
course of life, and spurred from behind by the love of distinction and the fear
of shame, it is capable of producing, even in common men, the most strenuous
exertions as well as the most heroic sacrifices. The deep-rooted selfishness
which forms the general character of the existing state of society, is *so* deeply
rooted, only because the whole course of existing institutions tends to foster it;
modern institutions in some respects more than ancient, since the occasions on
which the individual is called on to do anything for the public without receiving its pay, are far less frequent in modern life, than in the smaller commonwealths of antiquity.[56]

The alteration of institutions is only preliminary to or concurrent
with the moral revolution; not institutions, but "education, habit, and
the cultivation of the sentiments" are the means by which the revolution
will succeed. Already there are superior beings in whom the moral elevation necessary for the fulfilment is present, and they can lead the way
through precept and example. The process could be aided by the formation of a "Religion of Humanity" that would make altruism concrete.
Mill's best passage on this subject is in *Utilitarianism* :

In an improving state of the human mind, the influences are constantly on the
increase, which tend to generate in each individual a feeling of unity with all
the rest; which feeling, if perfect, would make him never think of, or desire,
any beneficial condition for himself, in the benefits of which they are not in-

[55] "Speech on Land Tenure Reform," *Dissertations and Discussions*, IV, 290; *Chapters on Socialism*, Works, V, 740.   [56] *Autobiography*, 163.

cluded. If we now suppose this feeling of unity to be taught as a religion, and the whole force of education, of institutions, and of opinion, directed, as it once was in the case of religion, to make every person grow up from infancy surrounded on all sides both by the profession and by the practice of it, I think that no one, who can realize this conception, will feel any misgiving about the sufficiency of the ultimate sanction for the Happiness morality.[57]

The influence and the danger of Comte's thought are obvious here, and Mill goes on to warn the reader against Comte's system. He argues, however, that even the danger of the Frenchman's thought shows its potential practicability; he has

superabundantly shown the possibility of giving to the service of humanity, even without the aid of belief in a Providence, both the psychical power and the social efficacy of a religion; making it take hold of human life, and colour all thought, feeling, and action, in a manner of which the greatest ascendancy ever exercised by any religion may be but a type and foretaste; and of which the danger is, not that it should be insufficient, but that it should be so excessive as to interfere unduly with human freedom and individuality.[58]

Comte's scheme is self-defeating, in Mill's view, because of its excessive organization and lack of attention to human needs, and because it is based on an incomplete moral theory. Any Religion of Humanity which Mill would support would be a voluntary body, entered into through intellectual and moral persuasion, and not an imposed institution for social control, defined and operated by a hierarchy of officials with state support. Moral power should not be reinforced with temporal power, and in fact need not be. Comte's passion for a secular ritual, discipline, habit of life, and even a calendar based on the practices of the Roman Catholic Church, held, it need hardly be said, no charm for Mill. The coincidence between the two thinkers is no more than a recognition of the vital importance of the feelings which make such a religion possible, and of the tremendous social power made available to morality by a concentration on these feelings. As Mill describes it, the Religion of Humanity need have no institutional basis whatsoever. It is a substitute for supernatural religions only in so far as Mill valued them, and his evaluation did not reach to an appreciation of the benefits gained through organization. His Religion of Humanity is of an extreme Protestant type; its content is conditioned throughout by an insistence on individual freedom of conscience.

---

[57] *Utilitarianism*, 48–9. See also, e.g., *Earlier Letters*, XIII, 738–9, and *Letters* (ed. Elliot), II, 362 (Diary for 24/1/54). [58] *Utilitarianism*, 49.

The only society in which the Religion of Humanity could be practised in an organized form would be the ideal society, the one which automatically protects individual manifestations of will and desire through the internal conviction in each member of the society that freedom is part of the greatest happiness of the greatest number. In the meantime and for all practical purposes, since the perfect society is a goal and not a fact, the Religion of Humanity is a matter of personal attachment to moral aims and practices, a form of individual moral improvement. Behind Mill's description of the Religion of Humanity lies his concept of utility; their connection through the development of ideals of behaviour and feeling (the work, it will be recalled, of the poet) is best revealed in a long and crucial passage in "The Utility of Religion":

A morality grounded on large and wise views of the good of the whole, neither sacrificing the individual to the aggregate nor the aggregate to the individual, but giving to duty on the one hand and to freedom and spontaneity on the other their proper province, would derive its power in the superior natures from sympathy and benevolence and the passion for ideal excellence: in the inferior, from the same feelings cultivated up to the measure of their capacity, with the superadded force of shame. This exalted morality would not depend for its ascendancy on any hope of reward; but the reward which might be looked for, and the thought of which would be a consolation in suffering, and a support in moments of weakness, would not be a problematical future existence, but the approbation, in this, of those whom we respect, and ideally of all those, dead or living, whom we admire or venerate. For, the thought that our dead parents or friends would have approved our conduct is a scarcely less powerful motive than the knowledge that our living ones do approve it: and the idea that Socrates, or Howard or Washington, or Antoninus, or Christ, would have sympathized with us, or that we are attempting to do our part in the spirit in which they did theirs, has operated on the very best minds, as a strong incentive to act up to their highest feelings and convictions.

To call these sentiments by the name morality, exclusively of any other title, is claiming too little for them. They are a real religion; of which, as of other religions, outward good works (the utmost meaning usually suggested by the word morality) are only a part, and are indeed rather the fruits of the religion than the religion itself. The essence of religion is the strong and earnest direction of the emotions and desires towards an ideal object, recognized as of the highest excellence, and as rightly paramount over all selfish objects of desire. This condition is fulfilled by the Religion of Humanity in as eminent a degree, and in as high a sense, as by the supernatural religions even in their best manifestations, and far more so than in any of their others.[59]

[59] "Utility of Religion," *Three Essays on Religion*, 108–9.

The distance between Mill and Bentham is nowhere better illustrated than in this passage. "Outward good actions" are all that are, indeed all that can and should be, expected of the moral citizen in the Benthamic calculation. For Mill, such actions are of course important, as society cannot function without them, but the state of mind which leads to outward good actions cannot be forced on citizens through a set of external rewards and punishments. Internal reform must precede its visible signs. Bentham's scheme is given the important, but subordinate job – the job indeed for which it was designed by Bentham – of improving the legal and part of the legislative systems.

What has been said will make it apparent that Mill's ethic has a concept of development at its core. He is not, as Bentham is, concerned to describe and prescribe a set of rules for society as it exists, because society is progressive, and with its progress come alterations in ends and, therefore, in means. Only someone of strong ironic habit could suggest that man, imperfect as he now is, should make rules for the conduct of man as he is to become. One of Mill's strongest reasons for adhering to utility, indeed, is its amenability to social and individual moral progress. Not only does his doctrine provide for social improvement through accretive development, but also, as the individual is the prime mover in social change, it provides for individual development in life and throughout time. Each generation does not start afresh on the same old problems in morality, but moves onward from the position gained by its forefathers: morality is progressive. Not that Mill believes that morality is inheritable, and accretive genetically; he suggests that there is a body of knowledge which increases with each generation, and is available to the individual, who must, however, develop his own moral autonomy.

Mill criticizes Bentham for not having "a thoughtful regard for previous thinkers, and for the collective mind of the human race"; Bentham, he says, in dismissing "vague generalities," did not see that "these generalities contained the whole unanalysed experience of the human race." [60] This Burke-like insight lies behind Mill's appraisal of Coleridge as one who tried to "discover by what apparent facts [received opinion] was at first suggested, and by what appearances it has ever since been rendered continually credible – has seemed, to a succession of persons, to be a

[60] "Bentham," 351; in 1838 "a thoughtful regard" read "reverence".

faithful interpretation of their experience." [61] The philosopher, attending to all human experience, must take into account such variations in human constitutions as lead to different and more complete records of experience. Philosophers have usually dismissed many sources of information as trivial or worthless. Many observations, Mill says, "have never yet found their way into the writings of philosophers; but are to be gathered, on the one hand, from actual observers of mankind; on the other, from those autobiographers, and from those poets or novelists, who have spoken out unreservedly, from their own experience, any true human feeling. To collect together these materials, and to add to them, will be a labour for successive generations." [62]

Another important source of information is the body of traditional maxims and proverbs. In a casual comment in his *Political Economy* (II, 137), Mill remarks, "experience shows, and proverbs, the expression of popular experience, attest" – and so indicates the cross-fire of evidence operating here that he demands elsewhere (see below, 168ff.). Moral improvement depends, in large measure, on these neglected sources. "There would be great uncertainty" in moral questions and behaviour "if each individual had all to do for himself, and only his own experience to guide him. But we are not so situated. Every one directs himself in morality, as in all his conduct, not by his own unaided foresight, but by the accumulated wisdom of all former ages, embodied in traditional aphorisms." [63] Mill did not pursue this interesting speculation, which probably would have formed part of his abortive "Ethology." It deserves some consideration, however, as it again puts him in the Baconian tradition, in which aphorisms grow into moral essays, and shows him also in defence of utilitarianism, in arguing that calculation is not necessary in normal moral situations. (He looks briefly at the question in his "Aphorisms," and there

[61] "Coleridge," 394.

[62] "Sedgwick," 131. So many of Mill's notions have become commonplaces that to indicate parallels is otiose; this one, however, has found few direct adherents, and it may be worth quoting a modern psychologist who, without evidently knowing of Mill's statement, says: "The student of human nature is nowadays too apt to forget that most of what we know about the mind of man is to be learnt from the writings not of scientists but of men of letters – the poets and the philosophers, the biographers and the historians, the novelists and the literary critics." (Sir Cyril Burt, "Foreword" to Arthur Koestler, *The Act of Creation* [London, 1964], 18.)

[63] "Sedgwick," 145–6.

is a note among his manuscripts, consisting of a list of parallel proverbs in different languages, showing his and his wife's interest.)

He did not intend, however, to set up as a cracker-barrel philosopher, for he saw that the blessings of traditional folk wisdom are mixed with the curse of man's strong tendency to submit to the authority of tradition. His willingness to listen to the accumulated wisdom of the past does not lead him to forego his teachers' criticism of it. Furthermore, such "wisdom" is, by its nature and origin, not precise at best. But then all general propositions, by reason of their formulation and the variety of human experience, are somewhat inaccurate.[64]

When organized, aphoristic wisdom may serve the function of empirical generalizations, as checks against deductions from the laws of human nature and society. In any case their organization permits them to be used as intermediate guides to action in cases of moral choice. Mill is anxious, it may be repeated, to prove that utilitarianism, in so far as it involves calculation, is not impracticable. Its opponents have always held that it is impossible for a man, before acting, to look to the furthest reaches of time and place in order to foresee the exact consequences of an action. But, says Mill, some of the results of behaviour are accidental, and for these a person cannot be held responsible.[65] Other results are, for the most part, foreseeable because of the accumulated experience of the race.[66] This experience may be used by moralists of all shades of opinion, and here, in the area of middle principles and rules for practical guidance, there is almost always agreement amongst moralists. Arguing that there must be a unique first principle in ethics does not entail the making, by utilitarians, of weird and sinful judgments in everyday matters. Secondary principles are as much a part of utilitarianism as of any other ethic:

Whatever we adopt as the fundamental principle of morality, we require subordinate principles to apply it by: the impossibility of doing without them, being common to all systems, can afford no argument against any one in particular: but gravely to argue as if no such secondary principles could be had, and as if mankind had remained till now, and always must remain, without drawing any general conclusions from the experience of human life, is as high a pitch, I think, as absurdity has ever reached in philosophical controversy.[67]

The moralist does not allow these generalizations to go unchecked, but if his own experience can confirm them, and they correspond to the pre-

[64] "Aphorisms," 207–8.   [65] Analysis, II, 401n–402n.
[66] "Sedgwick," 142; Utilitarianism, 34.   [67] Utilitarianism, 36.

dictions of deductive science, there is no reason for him to deny their validity as guides to conduct.

Again one is led to Mill's most important modification of utilitarian ethics, his concentration on the individual. Perhaps the greatest charm which utility held for Bentham was that it permitted of calculation. Acts could be objectively classified according to their beneficial or harmful consequences, and a ready and easy way to the best of all commonwealths could be thus descried. Mill alters the whole scheme by insisting that individual development is the only and difficult way. For Bentham, the legislator or moralist is only "better" in being wiser than the person for whom he is legislating. He merely foresees the weighing of motives, and so loads the scales that the balance must tip in favour of social utility. Mill sees the problem in another way : most action does not, in fact, proceed from careful calculation of consequences, but from habit and custom. The legislator (not the moralist) is perfectly right to calculate consequences, but he cannot presume that individuals will automatically repeat his ratiocinations, and adjust their conduct according to his will. He can, however, by a wider view of motivation, achieve a workable set of laws which will forward social utility or, at the very least, not impede its progress. On the other hand, the moralist must look to the effects of actions not only on society, but also on the individual who performs them, and on all other individuals.[68] The legislator's function is much easier than the moralist's, for the former is concerned only with society, whereas the latter must deal with the relations between individuals and society, as well as with individuals. On Liberty is then the work of a moralist, for it attempts to provide a criterion by which the relative claims of social and individual utility may be judged. It does not lay down a law, but attempts to inculcate a habit of mind.

While, therefore, the legislator may work through the pleasure-pain calculus, the moralist must heed conflicting utilities, and take habit and custom into account. He still may calculate, of course, for he is properly busy about the task of introducing the ideal society, but the individual in his moral actions has no business with calculation of his own private advantage.[69] When criticizing Bentham in 1833, Mill says "the man as

[68] "Sedgwick," 130–1.

[69] See, for example, "Sedgwick," 155, where Mill objects strenuously to the lumping together of egoistic psychology and utility, and "A Few Words on Non-Intervention," Dissertations and Discussions, III, 158, where he repudiates those English

well as 'the woman who deliberates,' is in imminent danger of being lost," [70] and he never leads his readers to suspect any other outcome. He is introducing into utilitarianism consideration of the motives lying behind actions, not in terms of control, for Bentham's treatment of sanctions bears upon this aspect of morals, as does James Mill's treatment of motives,[71] but as important in evaluation and judgment. As is often the case, he projects his own idea of utility onto other unnamed utilitarian theorists who, he says, "have gone beyond almost all others in affirming that the motive has nothing to do with the morality of the action, though much with the worth of the agent." [72] The main assertion is quite true, but the last clause really represents Mill's own modification. The worth of the agent is of absolutely no concern to the pure utilitarian of the Benthamite school (of which, it might be said, Bentham was not a member), who must maintain that morality is a matter of social manipulation and objective calculation. Mill's criticism of the master is again relevant. Bentham intimates, in his discussion of interests and motives, not only that all actions are determined by pleasure and pain, a correct belief in Mill's estimation, but also that they are determined by pleasures and pains in prospect, that is, as consequences of impending actions, in Mill's view a false and dangerous belief.[73] While all actions are judged to be moral or not on their consequential pleasure and pain,[74] agents should

---

public men who present England's actions as based on a rule "which no one, not utterly base, could endure to be accused of as the maxim by which he guides his private life; not to move a finger for others unless he sees his private advantage in it."

[70] "Remarks on Bentham's Philosophy," 334-5.   [71] Analysis, II, 292ff.

[72] Utilitarianism, 26. Cf. Autobiography, 35, where he attributes this belief to his father. Then, in Analysis, I, xvi, he says his father's habit was to estimate men "according to their real worth as sources of good in their fellow-creatures" – a belief which could place him on either side of the argument, or on both. In view of James Mill's remarks in his Fragment, 389-90, regarding motive as pleasure-seeking, it seems proper to regard his son's judgment as based more on observation than on published word. John Mill often tries to exculpate his father from what he thinks to be Bentham's mistakes. It is at least true that following his father's steps in association theory led the younger Mill to speculations which widened his ethical theory.

[73] "Remarks on Bentham's Philosophy," 334. James Mill would seem to be guilty here. Although he recognizes that men cannot be held responsible for all the consequences of their actions, but only those that are foreseeable, he still thinks in terms of consequential calculation. See Fragment, 378. But also see 147n below.

[74] "Bentham," 386.

not be so judged. "Human beings can control their own acts, but not the consequences of their acts either to themselves or to others." [75] It is reasonable to maintain, then, with Paley, that merit should be judged "by the balance, not of our good and evil deeds, which depend upon opportunity and temptation, but of our good and evil dispositions; by the intensity and continuity of our *will* to do good; by the strength with which we have *struggled* to be virtuous; not by our accidental lapses, or by the unintended good or evil which has followed from our actions." [76] Character is still to be rated by utilitarian standards, but not by a *post hoc* examination of results. A good disposition, from which good acts will flow, is worth more in terms of social utility than a few random actions which happen to have good consequences. [77]

The most important task of the practical moralist is to encourage the growth of beneficial habits in individuals. Harmful acts are prevented more frequently by a habitual revulsion than by calculation, and the practice of virtue is itself a powerful instrument ensuring future performance of good deeds. [78] Even in political speculations, where interest is properly taken into account, the scientist cannot forecast on the assumptions that consequential calculations will govern actions, and that motives can be analyzed by pleasure-pain arithmetic. Mill acknowledges a debt to one of his "seminal minds" : "As Coleridge observes, the man makes the

[75] *Principles*, II, 200 (II, i, 1); until 1852 the sentence, after "their acts", read "even on their own minds." Cf. *Analysis*, II, 401n–402n; *Logic*, II, 532–3 (VI, xi, 1).

[76] "Sedgwick," 153.

[77] In this context it is pertinent to ask a question which probably cannot be answered definitely or strongly : how great was John Sterling's influence on Mill? In 1835 (the year of the review of Sedgwick), Sterling writes to Mill about "the most difficult question of practical morality – that of the necessity and limits of compromise," and says : "Now I see by your letter [not known] & the Appendix to Bulwer how much farther you have gone towards my conclusions than I had supposed – I can explain to you in a few words the main point in which I differ from you. The well being of man depends in my belief on a certain state of the Affections & the Will – which when it exists will produce corresponding actions, guided *generally* by the received rules of morals, & will also give rise to the only desirable cultivation of the faculties. I value a man only in proportion as he endeavours to realize this state of mind in himself and to enforce its necessity by example & instruction on others. . . . The question is not one between conservation & movement – but between Right and Wrong. – There are many members of what might be called the movement body with whom I could more cheerfully cooperate than with most conservatives – but they are not general-consequence men." (Mill-Taylor Collection, I, #10 [15/5/35], ff26–7.)

[78] "Remarks on Bentham's Philosophy," 325–34.

motive, not the motive the man. What it is the man's interest to do or refrain from, depends less on any outward circumstances, than upon what sort of man he is. If you wish to know what is practically a man's interest, you must know the cast of his habitual feelings and thoughts." [79]

The present situation, as consciously seen by the individual agent, Mill considers crucial. A rigorous analysis, based on psychological laws, may result in the reduction of motives to their original elements, the seeking of pleasure and the avoidance of pain. But Mill is suspicious of the effects of analysis, and adopts an attitude analogous to the common-sense recognition that salt, while it may be composed of sodium and chlorine, is nonetheless a seasoning. [80] If one admits the power of association to

[79] *Representative Government*, 3rd ed. (London, 1865), 123.

[80] See, for example, *Utilitarianism*, 45–6; *Analysis*, II, 252n, 295n. The last reads : "The case [of desire of posthumous fame] is merely one of many others, in which something not originally pleasurable (the praise and admiration of our fellow-creatures) has become so closely associated with pleasure as to be at last pleasurable in itself. When it has become a pleasure in itself, it is desired for itself, and not for its consequences; and the most confirmed knowledge that it can produce no ulterior pleasurable consequences to ourselves will not interfere with the pleasure given by the mere consciousness of possessing it, nor hinder that pleasure from becoming, by its association with the acts which produce it, a powerful motive."

James Mill recognizes the fact, but his argument is different : "Gratitude remains gratitude, resentment remains resentment, generosity, generosity in the mind of him who feels them, after analysis, the same as before. The man who can trace them to their elements does not cease to feel them, as much as the man who never thought about the matter. And whatever effects they produce, as motives, in the mind of the man who never thought about the matter, they produce equally, in the minds of those who have analysed them the most minutely.

They are constituent parts of human nature. How we are actuated, when we feel them, is matter of experience, which every one knows within himself. Their action is what it is, whether they are simple or compound. Does a complex motive cease to be a motive whenever it is discovered to be complex? The analysis of the active principles leaves the nature of them untouched. To be able to assert, that a philosopher, who finds some of the active principles of human nature to be compound and traces them to their origin, does on that account exclude them from human nature, and deny their efficiency as constituent parts of that nature, discovers a total incapacity [like that of Mackintosh] of thinking upon these subjects. When Newton discovered that a white ray of light is not simple but compound, did he for that reason exclude it from the denomination of light, and deny that it produced its effects, with respect to our perception, as if it were of the same nature with the elementary rays of which it is composed?" (*Fragment*, 51–2.)

John Mill was closer to the Romantic sensibility which worried about Newton's anatomizing, but he commends this passage (*Analysis*, II, 320n) when defending his father. He presumably had forgotten what he had remembered when writing his *Autobiography*, that while analysis is beneficial to prudence and clear-sightedness, it

build up complex ideas, why base the validity of the complex idea on the validity of its sources? Mill shows his pragmatic concern in the *Logic*:

When the will is said to be determined by motives, a motive does not mean always, or solely, the anticipation of a pleasure or of a pain. I shall not here inquire whether it be true that, in the commencement, all our voluntary actions are mere means consciously employed to obtain some pleasure, or avoid some pain. It is at least certain that we gradually, through the influence of association, come to desire the means without thinking of the end: the action itself becomes an object of desire, and is performed without reference to any motive beyond itself. Thus far, it may still be objected, that, the action having through association become pleasurable, we are, as much as before, moved to act by the anticipation of a pleasure, namely, the pleasure of the action itself. But granting this, the matter does not end here. As we proceed in the formation of habits, and become accustomed to will a particular act or a particular course of conduct because it is pleasurable, we at last continue to will it without any reference to its being pleasurable.[81]

And, he notes in his father's *Analysis*, "there is nothing at variance with reason in the associations which make us value for themselves, things which we at first cared for only as means to other ends; associations to which we are indebted for nearly the whole both of our virtues, and of our enjoyments." [82]

An action is found pleasurable; the idea of the action becomes associated in the mind with the idea of pleasure; soon the action is performed without reference to the original pleasure, yet it is still pleasurable if the association has become strong. So, as Mill phrases it in *Utilitarianism*: "Will is the child of desire, and passes out of the dominion of its parent

---

worked on him in 1826-7 as "a perpetual worm at the root both of the passions and of the virtues; and, above all, fearfully undermine[d] all desires, and all pleasures, which are the effects of association, that is, according to the theory [James Mill's] I held, all except the purely physical and organic . . ." (97). This is a more extreme statement than he thinks justified, but he remained throughout the rest of his life preoccupied with the present state of feelings and desires rather than their sources.

[81] *Logic*, II, 428 (VI, ii, 4).

[82] *Analysis*, II, 296n. The idea is found in James Mill, for example, in the section to which this quotation is a note, where James Mill says: "In some instances, the Association rises to that remarkable case, which we have had frequent occasions of observing; when the means become a more important object than the end, the cause, than the effect." His reference is always, however, to painful *consequences*; he does not rise (as his son points out in a note to II, 297) to the conception of the association producing such a strong feeling that from habit, and not from calculation, a particular course of action is adhered to, or a particular act performed.

only to come under that of habit." [83] In so doing, it loses none of its virtue, nor does the man who has developed a habit of virtue become less virtuous (though, as *On Liberty* makes clear, the moral pump must be kept primed).

It may be wise to show that this is not only a theoretical position by citing a few analogous cases in which Mill argues for the developed state of feeling, and for social obligation, as against their original components. Criticizing Thornton's rejection of utility, Mill says that prescriptive rights in property can be defended only on the basis of utility, and not on the basis of natural justice, because the interaction of events and general concourse of social development have rendered the present distribution of property more conducive to utility than a radical adjustment according to original rights would be.[84] Another example is the "natural inclination" which Mill was most concerned to control, sexual desire. The only method of eradicating poverty finally is through limiting the growth of the population; the moral person voluntarily checks his desires to further social utility. The brute or natural instinct is definitely immoral for Mill; the cultivated, civilized devaluation of the natural instinct is moral.[85] Again, criticizing his father's view of the effect of "times of great excitement" in raising patriotic feeling, Mill points out that the expectation of public reward for the exhibition of politically desirable sentiments is not sufficient to explain the strength of the effect. Reference must be made to the accumulative results of sympathy with others, and association of the individual's well-being with that of the country. One simple and original element cannot account for the final feeling.[86] So also with the great horror of the evil opinion of others which may lead men to suicide, although in killing themselves they lose all chance of happiness. Such premonitions of evil opinion may have been the "crude matter" from which

[83] *Utilitarianism*, 60–1. James Mill, of course, also recognized the strong force of habit, and indeed emphasized its importance for utility, through the proper sort of moral education. But his analytical bias always turns him away from the actual state to the origins, as, for example, in *Fragment*, 255: "Since moral acts are not performed first by habit, but each upon the consideration which recommends it; upon what considerations, we may be asked, do moral acts begin to be performed?" John Mill would be more likely to say: "Since moral acts *come to be* performed by habit. . . ."

[84] "Thornton on Labour and its Claims," 652ff.

[85] See, e.g., *Principles*, II, 367–8 (II, xiii, 1).   [86] *Analysis*, II, 274n–275n.

the horror first grew, "but, once formed, it loses its connexion with its original source." [87]

Mill is arguing, in effect, for a conscience. In *Utilitarianism* he insists that utility has, like all other moral systems, both external and internal sanctions. The internal sanction is a feeling in one's mind, painful, for example, when duty is violated. When this feeling is disinterested, and connected with the pure idea of duty, it is the essence of conscience, but "in that complex phenomenon as it actually exists, the simple fact is in general all encrusted over with collateral associations, derived from sympathy, from love, and still more from fear; from all the forms of religious feeling; from the recollections of childhood and of all our past life; from self-esteem, desire of the esteem of others, and occasionally even self-abasement." Conscience is accretive, growing through association into a complicated set of feelings which, just because complicated, appears mysterious. Whether it is innate or acquired is irrelevant to its moral power, which is tested only by the strength of the subjective feelings and their ability to move to action, which do not depend on their origin. Mill states that the feeling is acquired, of course – but it is not, for that reason, the less "natural." He points out that it "is natural to man to speak, to reason, to build cities, to cultivate the ground, though these are acquired faculties." There is a basis of sympathy on which conscience can be built, the "regard to the pleasures and pains of others." [88] In any event, utilitarians have as much claim to the sanctions of conscience as any other moralists.

As morality is progressive, it cannot be explained by its primitive sources. Existence is itself a sanction. Mill is not charmed by the idea of "nature," or of "natural sanctions." As he says in *Utilitarianism*: "In the case of [Justice], as of our other moral sentiments, there is no necessary connexion between the question of its origin, and that of its binding force. That a feeling is bestowed on us by Nature, does not necessarily legitimate all its promptings." [89] And in his essay "Nature" he indicates, in a well known passage, a conflict of meanings: "Nature," he says, "either denotes the entire system of things, with the aggregate of all their properties, or it denotes things as they would be, apart from human intervention." If the first meaning be accepted, then morality, immorality, and amorality are all natural, and no support is attached to any doctrine,

[87] *Ibid.*, 297n.   [88] *Utilitarianism*, 40–5.   [89] *Ibid.*, 62.

practice, or element by its attribution to nature. Any sanction derived from "Nature" in its second meaning, moreover, is both immoral and irrational:

> Irrational, because all human action whatever, consists in altering, and all useful action in improving, the spontaneous course of nature:
> Immoral, because the course of natural phenomena being replete with everything which when committed by human beings is most worthy of abhorrence, any one who endeavoured in his actions to imitate the natural course of things would be universally seen and acknowledged to be the wickedest of men.[90]

Humanity is the reference line for all morality, and the good of the species (or of all sentient creatures) is the end of all moral action. "Nature," in the second meaning, is specifically divorced from such a reference or end.

> The scheme of Nature regarded in its whole extent, cannot have had, for its sole or even principal object, the good of human or other sentient beings. What good it brings to them, is mostly the result of their own exertions. Whatsoever, in nature, gives indication of beneficent design, proves this beneficence to be armed only with limited power; and the duty of man is to co-operate with the beneficent powers, not by imitating but by perpetually striving to amend the course of nature – and bringing that part of it over which we can exercise control, more nearly into conformity with a high standard of justice and goodness.[91]

(The reference to "beneficent powers" relates to Mill's imperfectly formulated Manicheanism, which may be seen throughout his *Three Essays on Religion*.)

> To transgress against the natural is in fact moral, to comply with it, immoral, in the specifically human sciences and arts. "If the artificial is not better than the natural, to what end are all the arts of life? To dig, to plough, to build, to wear clothes, are direct infringements of the injunction to follow nature."[92] Mankind not being perfect, there may be improvement; if nature is the original starting point, then subsequent stages, if closer to an ideal, are morally better. In "Theism" Mill brings in one phase of the current speculations on development and evolution to support this argument, and also, incidentally, to support his demand for experiential checks on ratiocination.

[90] *Three Essays on Religion*, 64–5.   [91] *Ibid.*, 65.
[92] *Ibid.*, 20. Cf. *Utilitarianism*, 45.

From what, except from experience, can we know what can produce what – what causes are adequate to what effects? That nothing can *consciously* produce Mind but Mind, is self-evident, being involved in the meaning of the words; but that there cannot be unconscious production must not be assumed, for it is the very point to be proved. Apart from experience, and arguing on what is called reason, that is upon supposed self-evidence, the notion seems to be, that no causes can give rise to products of a more precious or elevated kind than themselves. But this is at variance with the known analogies of Nature. How vastly nobler and more precious, for instance, are the higher vegetables and animals than the soil and manure out of which, and by the properties of which they are raised up! The tendency of all recent speculation is towards the opinion that the development of inferior orders of existence into superior, the substitution of greater elaboration and higher organization for lower, is the general rule of Nature. Whether it is so or not, there are at least in Nature a multitude of facts bearing that character, and this is sufficient for the argument.[93]

Mill does not, of course, abandon "Nature," and adopt a transcendental ethic. Man is bound by the world; he must work within the limits of, and through, physical laws. If he attempts to ignore nature he can only damage or destroy himself. But he need not feel obliged to bend beneath non-prescriptive laws; that part of nature which is amenable to alteration *should* be altered in accordance with man's moral desires.

Nature is, furthermore, irrational, and man's reason is his great moral tool. The form which the discussion has taken in this chapter may have suggested that Mill is renegade to this part of his inheritance as well. He admits feeling into the discussion, as an essential fact of experience which cannot and should not be overlooked, at peril of loss of will and high desire, but he nonetheless depends on reason. Social advance comes only through the clear and reasoned perception of means to the end, and while the improvement of feeling and sentiment may be part of that end, and essential to its discovery as a living force, only reason can formulate means. Feeling, it is true, persuades, but persuasion based on feeling alone will end in disaster, at best encouraging habitual obedience to commands only randomly moral.

The whole movement of humanity towards happiness is controlled by intellect. Mill's dialectic of history is idealistic to this extent. *On Liberty* is imbued with this belief, and Mill gives expression to it in many places throughout his works, notably in his second review of de Tocqueville's *Democracy in America*, in discussing Guizot when reviewing Michelet's

[93] *Three Essays on Religion*, 152–3.

History of France, and in *Representative Government*,[94] but his fullest statements are in the *Logic*. He rests the whole possibility of the foundation of social science and of a scientific history upon the isolation of a dominant element in the record of experience, an element which may, through its manifestations, reveal a pattern upon which a philosophy of development may build. Among the agents of social progress, one element is shown by history and human nature to be predominant: "This is, the state of the speculative faculties of mankind; including the nature of the beliefs which by any means they have arrived at concerning themselves and the world by which they are surrounded." This element is the "central chain, to each successive link of which, the corresponding links of all the other progressions" may be joined. Just as sympathy, though finally triumphant over selfishness, is originally weak by its side, so the "speculative faculties" do not conquer through their basic strength.

It would be a great error, and one very little likely to be committed, to assert that speculation, intellectual activity, the pursuit of truth, is among the more powerful propensities of human nature, or holds a predominating place in the lives of any, save decidedly exceptional, individuals. But, notwithstanding the relative weakness of this principle among other sociological agents, its influence is the main determining cause of the social progress; all the other dispositions of our nature which contribute to that progress, being dependent on it for the means of accomplishing their share of the work.

At this point he foreshadows the message of *On Liberty*: "The weakness of the speculative propensity in mankind generally, has not, therefore, prevented the progress of speculation from governing that of society at large; it has only, and too often, prevented progress altogether, where the intellectual progression has come to an early stand for want of sufficiently favourable circumstances."[95] The stronger emotional propensities, which tend unguided to disrupt society and prevent advance, give way before the united and uniting force of the speculative faculties. The gauge of progress is, then, the state of the intellect: "Every considerable advance in material civilization has been preceded by an advance in knowledge; and when any great social change has come to pass, either in the way of gradual development or of sudden conflict, it has had for its precursor a great change in the opinions and modes of thinking of society."[96]

In this respect Mill carries on the tradition of the Philosophic Radi-

[94] *Dissertations and Discussions*, II, 72-3; *ibid.*, 135.
[95] *Logic*, II, 525-7 (VI, x, 7). Cf. *ibid.*, 536-7 (VI, xi, 2).   [96] *Ibid.*, 527 (VI, x, 7).

cals; his position is more carefully prepared than theirs, but in practice he is fully as much an advocate of the "March of Mind" as they were. As has been noted, variations on one of their themes, "the present imperfect state of human nature, morality, education," appear time and again in his discussions of the progress of society, and insist as he will upon the necessity of a revolution in "modes of feeling," he equally insists on a concomitant – or perhaps even previous – improvement in "modes of thought."

The role of the intellect is the pursuit of truth. Truth for Mill (however he might capitalize it in his early correspondence with Carlyle) lies not in the realm of the absolute and transcendental, but in the everyday relation between opinion (or belief) and experience. When opinion agrees with observation, there is truth. (Facts by themselves, therefore, cannot be "true.") A belief or opinion, he argues in "Grote's Plato," "is relative not only to the believing mind, but to something else – namely, the matter of fact which the belief is about. The truth of the belief is its agreement with that fact. . . . No one means anything by truth, but the agreement of a belief with the fact which it purports to represent."[97] In associationist terms, "belief in the existence of a physical object, is belief in the occurrence of certain sensations, contingently on certain previous conditions." If the sensations actually occur, then the belief is true.[98]

It is important to note that the agreement is not between belief and objective reality. As an empiricist, Mill will not look beyond experience, and his discussion of matter ("the permanent possibility of sensation") shows that for him the objective world cannot be known to have been known. The passage quoted above from "Grote's Plato" continues: "We grant that, according to the philosophy which we hold in common with Mr. Grote, the fact itself, if knowable by us, is relative to our perceptions – to our senses or our internal consciousness; and our opinion about the fact is so too; but the truth of the opinion is a question of relation between these two relatives, one of which is an objective standard for the other."

This attitude towards truth is not paralyzing, although it abandons all hope of certainty. Fundamentally all beliefs are hypothetical in so far as they assume a correspondence between "reality" and observed fact, but a pragmatic man who is accustomed to basing action on less than

[97] *Dissertations and Discussions*, III, 357–8.   [98] *Analysis*, I, 414n.

perfect certainty will not baulk at this leap. Still, a certain measure of success in the fulfilment of expectations is necessary for utility, and for even approximately accurate predictions men need ever truer beliefs. And the search for truth is a matter of evidence and proof. As Mill says in one of his early speeches, the "good of mankind requires that nothing should be believed until the question be first asked, what evidence there is for it." [99] And, modified by time and for the occasion, the same idea appears late in his life, in the *Inaugural Address*: "The most incessant occupation of the human intellect throughout life is the ascertainment of truth. We are always needing to know what is actually true about something or other." [100] No advance is possible unless opinion is made conformable to experienced fact, and Mill means nothing more when he speaks of truth. He argues, for example, that received opinion must be checked against experience, putting his case in the following form: "There is no philosophy possible where fear of consequences is a stronger principle than love of truth. . . ." [101] Again, he criticizes Comte for not being as solicitous about proof as becomes a positivist, meaning that Comte's passion for system led him away from truth. That he intended his *Logic* to be a treatise on truth in his sense of the word is shown by the subtitle, "A Connected View of the Principles of Evidence and the Methods of Scientific Investigation," and his view is shown also in a note to his father's *Analysis*: "to shew what it is that gives . . . belief its validity, we must fall back on logical laws, the laws of evidence." [102]

There is no seeming limit to the range of human belief and opinion; history and experience point out that no two generations or individuals would draw up the same list of universally believed propositions: "One age or nation believes implicitly what to another seems incredible and inconceivable; one individual has not a vestige of a belief which another deems to be absolutely inherent in humanity." [103] So opinion must be free, and not encompassed within the limits imposed by one society and one generation. Truth cannot be achieved merely by a compilation of varying shades of opinion, or a synthesis of beliefs, but any belief may have within it some truth – that is, it may be conformable to a part of experience. Proof, the comparison of opinion with experience, is the only road to such truth as man can obtain.

[99] "Speech on the Church," 322.   [100] *Inaugural Address*, 43.
[101] "Coleridge," 461.   [102] *Analysis*, I, 427n.   [103] *Logic*, II, 98 (III, xxi, 1).

Evidence is not that which the mind does or must yield to, but that which it ought to yield to, namely, that, by yielding to which, its belief is kept conformable to fact. There is no appeal from the human faculties generally, but there is an appeal from one human faculty to another; from the judging faculty, to those which take cognizance of fact, the faculties of sense and consciousness. The legitimacy of this appeal is admitted whenever it is allowed that our judgments ought to be conformable to fact. To say that belief suffices for its own justification is making opinion the test of opinion; it is denying the existence of any outward standard, the conformity of an opinion to which constitutes its truth.[104]

One cannot leave the discussion of Mill's ethic without at least glancing at the problems, suggested by this quotation, which have most exercised critics of *Utilitarianism*. Unquestionably, more careful attention has been devoted to Mill's attitude in that work towards proof, to his introduction of qualitative judgments into utilitarian theory, and to his loose use of "desirable," than to any other part of his ethical thought. There can be no question that these matters are important in ethics, and there can be equally little question that Mill did not appreciate the difficulties of his wording – having admitted thus much, I would still argue that a disproportionate amount of attention has been given to these problems.

From the outset it must be admitted that Mill does not, in his own meaning of the word, especially as used in his *Logic*, prove that utility is the end of life, individual and social. He admits in *Utilitarianism* that such proof is as impossible for a utilitarian as for the supporter of any other ethical system: "Questions of ultimate ends are not amenable to direct proof." Having already said that some proof most be offered to induce belief, however, he commits himself, as in the title of Chapter IV, to examine "Of What Sort of Proof the Principle of Utility is Susceptible." "Considerations may be presented," he says, "capable of determining the intellect either to give or withhold its assent to the doctrine; and this is equivalent to proof."[105] But when treating evidence and proof in the *Logic* and elsewhere,[106] he never for a moment considers that the acceptance of a belief is equivalent to its proof. He is substituting a psychological for a logical explanation, depending on the presence of a

[104] *Ibid.*, 97 (III, xxi, 1); the third sentence was added in 1862. Cf. *Analysis*, I, 435n.
[105] *Utilitarianism*, 6.
[106] Cf. Levi's remarks on "convictionism" in "A Study in the Social Philosophy of John Stuart Mill" (Ph.D. thesis, Chicago, 1940), 16.

belief rather than upon its correspondence to fact. His usual attitude is to regard the prevalence of a belief as an index to the probability of its truth, but not to regard it as proof. Conviction is of the essence of moral creeds, but is not objective proof.

The problem is ultimately one of descriptive as against normative judgments. Mill recognized the difference between them, but could not abandon the first as the basis of objectivity, although he needed the second as the *raison d'être* of his system. His analysis of justice, for example, traces back a moral feeling to its elements, and finds the essence of such feelings to be an animal desire for retaliation. The basis is then descriptive, for the feeling is founded, as he says, upon "historical experience." The desire for retaliation is moralized, however, by being connected with the good of one's fellow creatures. Now the feeling is normative. But how nas its sanction been changed? Whether by rational calculation or by sympathy (and Mill favours the latter), there must be an alteration in the judgment radical enough to permit the elucidation of a moral code. In fact, Mill smuggles in the specifically normative element, in much the same way that Hobbes smuggles obligation into his contract theory.

Similar comment is appropriate concerning Mill's apparent introduction of a qualitative judgment between kinds of pleasures. Mill really makes no addition to or significant alteration in utilitarian ethics in recognizing qualitative differences, for Bentham points to them only to analyze them away in terms of bodily organization, thus denying them any special sanction,[107] and the form in which Mill presents his case permits of an easy reduction to quantitative terms.[108] Mental pleasures, he believes, are more conducive to utility than physical pleasures. But why? Because they are more lasting, less mixed with pain, and more easily related to others. In other words, a present mental pleasure, as compared

[107] Chapter vi, "Of Circumstances Influencing Sensibility," *Principles of Morals and Legislation, Works*, I, 21ff.

[108] The admission of qualitative distinctions by James Mill (see *Autobiography*, 34) undoubtedly influenced his son. In the form there presented, there is, as John Mill says, no reason why a utilitarian should deny them. As early as his debating society days he was saying: "It is sufficiently notorious that the kind of writing which is preferred by instructed & cultivated minds, is not that which pleases the half-instructed & pseudo-refined; & altho' whatever gives pleasure to any body is so far good, our standard of taste if we have one, must be founded on what it is incident to the minds of the highest degree of cultivation to approve & admire." ("Speech on the Present State of Literature" [1827], *Adelphi*, 1 [1924], 688; corrected from the MS.)

with a present physical pleasure, is more productive of future pleasure, especially for society. More pleasure is the result: the qualitative distinction has become a quantitative one. Mill might have said, but did not, that the quantitative difference is so great and so constant that it can pragmatically be considered to be qualitative.

The test of qualitative pleasures, as of quantitative, is the opinion of experienced men. It is, then, a descriptive test. Only the experience of the judges has made them more capable of moral judgments than a pig. They have known more, and can therefore cast up the differences in consequences of various pleasures, and so come to a rational decision. But such a decision is not moral merely because it is rational; it is moral because Mill (an experienced man) believes it to be conducive to general utility. (For Bentham it would be moral just because it is rational, but his ethic is descriptive only.) The circularity of Mill's argument further weakens it. Men prefer their higher (non-animal) faculties, and are unwilling to sink to a "lower" state, because they have a feeling which may be called pride, a love of liberty and personal independence, or a love of power and excitement, but which should be called a sense of dignity. All human beings possess this sense of dignity, but to a varying degree, in proportion as they possess higher faculties. That is, a man prefers higher faculties because he has them, exercises them, and prefers them. A man who prefers higher pleasures should be asked to judge whether they are higher.

The final problem which has led to extended comment arises in Chapter iv of *Utilitarianism*, where Mill, having said that ultimate ends cannot be proved in the usual sense, offers what proof is available. In doing so, he says:

The only proof capable of being given that an object is visible, is that people actually see it. The only proof that a sound is audible, is that people hear it: and so of the other sources of our experience. In like manner, I apprehend, the sole evidence it is possible to produce that anything is desirable, is that people do actually desire it. If the end which the utilitarian doctrine proposes to itself were not, in theory and in practice, acknowledged to be an end, nothing could ever convince any person that it was so. No reason can be given why the general happiness is desirable, except that each person, so far as he believes it to be attainable, desires his own happiness. This, however, being a fact, we have not only all the proof which the case admits of, but all which it is possible to require, that happiness is a good: that each person's happiness is a good to that person, and the general happiness, therefore, a good to the aggregate of all persons.[109]

That each person desires his own happiness does not ensure that each person will desire the general happiness, of course, and Mill is probably not intending to suggest that simple multiplication of personal desires will give a utilitarian sum, but his language leaves him open to the accusation, just as Bentham was. The main problem, however, is found in the identity Mill seems to be establishing between the kind of proof given by the senses and the kind of proof necessary in ethics. "Visible" and "audible" are descriptive; "desirable" is normative. The caveat introduced in the title of the chapter – that only this kind of proof is possible – is not defence enough against the charge that what is and what should be are here confused. This flaw was pointed out to Mill by his German translator, Theodor Gomperz, but Mill shrugged it off, saying that the passage could be altered in translation if Gomperz wished.[110] It is hard to believe that he did not understand the objection; it appears more likely that he did not consider the question important. Why, we cannot say, but one can at least surmise that *Utilitarianism* was not, in his view, a major work (he hardly mentions it in the *Autobiography*, although the neglect may result from the piecemeal writing of the section in which it is mentioned).

Mill did not advance this part of utilitarian theory beyond Bentham, and it might be argued that there is no advance possible, on Mill's own grounds. He uses association theory to introduce developmental concepts, and includes all aspects of conduct in moral theory in a way foreign to Bentham's thought, but while he denies any moral sanction to natural traits he ultimately has a naturalistic basis for his theory. Because he himself accepts the greatest-happiness principle as guide, associations which promote its fulfilment can be seen as moral; thus the movement away from nature is an ethical process. The normative element, however, is as it must be, assumed and not proved.[111] Its analysis, as in the case of justice, may not destroy it, but neither does it explain it.

[109] *Utilitarianism*, 52–3.

[110] See Adelaide Weinberg, *Theodor Gomperz and John Stuart Mill* (Geneva, 1963), 51–3.

[111] Whether or not a pleasure is desired must be decided, he argues (*Utilitarianism*, 58), "like all similar questions, upon evidence. It can only be determined by practised self-consciousness and self-observation, assisted by observation of others." It is a matter of description, in other words. But should such a pleasure be desired?

As has been suggested, these considerations, important as they are in evaluating Mill as an ethical theorist, and in evaluating utilitarianism itself, are not of great importance in a study of his application of ethics in social and political thought. Before this application is discussed, however, a glance at method is necessary. At this point we have seen how he sets forth the end of society, the greatest happiness of the greatest number, in view of individual happiness and internal development. With increasing approximations to truth, and with the increased sympathy which will apply truth to man's condition, the utilitarian ideal will be approached. The truth may not make men free, as the exigencies of existence limit freedom, but it will make men happier. The devising of means for the discovery of truth and its organization into a useful body of knowledge is the work of the "Scientist" and not of the "Artist," and this work must be briefly considered.

6

Method:

Scientist and Artist

IN HIS GENERAL approach to the theory of reform Mill is clearly in the mainstream of British empiricism. He wished to introduce into the study of human behaviour the scientific approach that had demonstrated its fruitfulness elsewhere. Like Huxley, for example, he was convinced, and worked to convince others that, properly considered, the law of cause and effect is exhibited in individual and social behaviour. The panorama of history and of contemporary society can and should be studied in an attempt to discover causal sequences, with the ultimate aim of prediction and control through understanding. Such a belief can, of course, lead to an abandonment of moral imperatives, but it should be unnecessary to say that Mill agreed with Emerson and Arnold that there is a law for man and a law for thing. To recognize this distinction, however, is not to deny that man is subject to the law of nature as well as moral law. The "Scientist" does not make normative decisions, but his findings enable the "Artist" to avoid futile and foolish proposals. Mill's purpose was the amelioration of mankind's lot through the Artist's application of the Scientist's findings.

This purpose should be borne in mind throughout the following discussion, for not the similarities, but the differences, between Mill's view and that of, say, Comte, are the hallmarks of his sociological thought. In spite of his enthusiasm, in spite of the glorious possibilities he saw in the distant future, in spite of his faith in science to reveal useful laws, he is sceptical. Man cannot penetrate beyond the phenomenal level; his inductions can never be complete; his generalizations can never be fully proved. Investigations into human nature produce at best empirical laws, mere graspings after a description of phenomenal relations, not at all explanatory. Even when connected by deduction with previously established and more basic "laws" they are of uncertain validity, to be recognized as approximations to the order of an unknowable and perhaps non-existent substratum. The mind of man abstracts and selects; reason can formulate "natural laws," but cannot comprehend nature; a law does not correspond to a process. As Mill points out, sciences can be "exact," that is, deal in "real laws" rather than "approximate generalizations," only by treating "tendencies" and not "facts." The scientist, and particularly the Moral Scientist, who is deprived of the experimental and observational techniques of his brother scientists, must not expect to find more than provisional truths, and if he thinks he is finding absolute truths he must not be allowed to persuade society of his omniscience. Mill is no worshipper of science; he sees it as a good servant but a ruinous master. Passages could easily be collected from his *Logic* to show that the Moral Scientist cannot unconditionally predict the future. Without certainty, complete faith must not be placed in the would-be controller. Science is, however – and here Mill is insistent – useful in the moral area, since knowledge insufficient for prediction is valuable for guidance. Men aware of the limitations of scientific knowlege are best prepared to use science's findings to promote utility.

This view, as much as anything else, prevented Mill from outlining a complete sociology. Compared to Comte's, his hierarchy of sciences is fragmentary and inconclusive, for he did not know enough, and felt he could not know enough, to fix finally its shape. He described limits and interconnections, but did not attempt to force organization on provisional materials. Here, it may be said, is his failure as a theorist, but the failure itself refutes any attempt to characterize him as a pure ideologue. His humility arises from the inductive basis of his theory of knowledge, and his awareness of the complexity of human affairs. Ratiocination, the great weapon of the dogmatist, cannot in his view discover new truths, being bound in its own closed system. The syllogism is a shorthand expression of thought, a tool useful for understanding, expression, and conviction, but not for revelation. Formal logic merely shuffles the cards given in experience. Since induction is always uncertain, the dogmatic social scientist is an unnatural hybrid not to be entrusted with political power. Science, it must be asserted again, is not normative; it needs Art's directional commands.

One can wish that Mill had brought his distinction between "Artist" and "Scientist" to bear with more emphasis on political thought. A few reasonable guesses, as a preliminary to a general discussion of his view of the Scientist, are justified. No matter what his early enthusiasm for the "Clerisy" and intellectual authority, it is clear that in Mill's mature thought there is no provision for the Scientist as political ruler. He works at the command of the Artist, for the Artist's ends, somewhat as a civil servant provides material for his Minister regardless of his political persuasion. If this analogy is sound, one can see how the work of at least some Scientists could be supported. But it is doubtful whether Mill thinks of the Artist in his primary role, as the fashioner of ends, in a political context. In his final role, as a persuader, it can be argued that the Artist is presenting a platform for election. However, Mill does not seem to have seen the question in such terms: no candidate (not even Mill himself) stands for election on the express basis of his conception of the *summum bonum*. Still the Artist, as translator of the Scientist's theorems into rules of conduct, can be seen as a democratic legislator. He also can be seen as Educator, free-lance Moralist, Preacher, and Writer. It is probably most accurate to think that Mill conceived of him as a private citizen, devoted to social amelioration, but devoid of special powers. Most of his work would be done in his own community, for example through local politics, private associations, and school boards. On the larger scale one may, perhaps, indulge one's fancy, and visualize university departments of Teleology, with professors advancing rival ends to be accepted or rejected by the public at large. Mill was, however, not an academic, and he probably believed that there is an effective public belief in utility sufficient, at least in the political area, to ensure that in a democracy the greatest happiness of the greatest number will be sought by all parties, provided that the representatives' responsibility be constitutionally guaranteed.

As already indicated, although Mill's position is not clearly stated, there would in this case be provision for public support of some scientists dedicated to the study and solution of social problems. They might be civil servants, or, as is more likely for Mill, they might work in universities and other privately controlled institutions, making their findings readily available for practical application by the Artist as legislator and educator. This view at least allows one to interpret Mill's non-systematic sociology in practical political terms in a democratic society. The Scientist, so important to Mill, is not accorded authority to implement his findings; he serves rather than controls the country; devises means, not ends. The Artist draws out the social significance of the Scientist's theorems, and applies them, with public consent, using persuasion in a democratic way. He does, however, depend for his practical plans on the Scientist's work.

In the final book of his *Logic* Mill provides the outline of method necessary to make the Scientist's work useful, and sketches in the proper scientific questions in the moral sciences. In tracing out his hierarchy of social sciences, he places the linked disciplines of Psychology and "Ethology" in the fundamental position; in the derivative and final position is Sociology proper, which is divided into Social Statics and Social Dynamics. This final division is not, he indicates, all-inclusive, for Political Economy and Political Ethology must also be considered. His outline, which need not be summarized here, centres on the distinct problems of method encountered in each area. These lead finally to the assertion of the proper method for Sociology itself, in its attempt to answer the questions posed by man's needs.

In Sociology the principal question for the Scientist is: What are the laws which determine the general circumstances of society? Or, what are the causes which produce, and the phenomena which characterize, states of society generally? All the great social facts enter into a consideration of the "state of society": for example, the intellectual and moral development of the people, the condition of economic relations, class divisions, common beliefs, tastes and aesthetic development, and institutional forms. The natural correlation between these elements must not be forgotten, nor must it be forgotten "that not every variety of combination of these general social facts is possible, but only certain combinations; that, in short, there exist Uniformities of Coexistence between the states of the various social phenomena." These uniformities are corollaries of the laws of causation by which these elements are really determined. "The mutual correlation between the different elements of each state of society, is therefore a derivative law, resulting from the laws which regulate the succession between one state of society and another; for the proximate cause of every state of society is the state of society

immediately preceding it." [1] The great problem of social science is therefore to find the laws according to which one state of society succeeds
to another.

There being change, the vexed question of human progressiveness must
be faced. Mill, in indicating that there is a choice only between a cycle
and a progress, not only ignores such diagrammatic schemes as the
Christian and "chaos" theories, but also interjects a consideration which
is disturbing in the total context of his thought. He asks the question
so incessantly put in more recent years: is progress synonymous with
improvement? Is the history of man a story of constant and inevitable
movement towards (no matter what the definition) perfection? Many
Victorians seem, in retrospect, not even to have considered the question,
but to have unhesitatingly and eagerly made the identification. Mill
realizes that it is not necessary: "The words Progress and Progressiveness are not here to be understood as synonymous with improvement
and tendency to improvement. It is conceivable that the laws of human
nature might determine, and even necessitate, a certain series of changes
in man and society, which might not in every case, or which might not on
the whole, be improvements." [2] The interesting implications of this statement for Mill's social theory are, however, forestalled by the following
comment: "It is my belief indeed that the general tendency is, and will
continue to be, saving occasional and temporary exceptions, one of improvement; a tendency towards a better and happier state." This belief,
he adds, is not a matter of method, but a theorem of the science of society;
it cannot be doubted however that the theorem had taken a firm hold on
his mind before he began to consider method, and to assume his impartiality on the question or human progressiveness would be sadly to
err. Mill rejected Comte's outline of Social Statics because he saw that
Comte would allow no real conflict of opinion, thought, and individual
development, and therefore, as Mill's ethic makes clear, no progress, no
movement towards the ethical end. His valid objections to Comte's
neglect of the conditions of proof are not enough to persuade one that
only method is in question. Even a cursory glance at *Auguste Comte and
Positivism* reveals that the fire and passion of Mill's argument is expended
in the great cause of human improvement, and not in the service, im-

[1] *Logic*, II, 509–10 (VI, x, 2).

[2] *Ibid.*, 511 (VI, x, 3). Cf. *ibid.*, 365–7 (V, v, 4), where he argues that the evidences for
progress support at best an empirical law.

portant as it may be, of method. Although Mill's method is not the result of his ethical convictions, there is at least a pleasing coincidence in recommendations.

In his *Logic*, however, Mill is concerned at this point merely with constant historical change (rather than cyclical repetition). Continental philosophers, he says, having recognized this pattern, have adopted a useful historical method. Through careful consideration and analysis they attempt to find the law of progress which will, when found, permit the prediction of future developments, on the analogy of an extrapolated series. Unfortunately, a fundamental misconception vitiates many of their findings, for they suppose that such a law of the succession of social states is a law of nature, whereas it is at best an empirical law. "The succession of states of the human mind and of human society cannot have an independent law of its own; it must depend on the psychological and ethological laws which govern the action of circumstances on men and of men on circumstances."[3] As Comte alone has realized, an empirical law needs verification; it must be connected with the psychological laws upon which it ultimately depends. If the deduction *a priori* agrees with the historical evidence, then the empirical law is converted into a scientific law. Only then can it be depended on for prediction beyond merely adjacent cases.

The necessity of deductive checks does not mean, of course, that predictions *a priori* have any validity, or that purely *a priori* considerations are capable of describing the order in which human development must have taken place – that is, of predicting past history (as, for example, in contract theories). The possible success with one or two terms of the series would soon be overwhelmed by the necessary failure when the great and carrying weight of the influence of succeeding generations comes into effect. So, if empirical laws are not derivable from the phenomena, no proper sociology is possible; only the secondary considerations which are concerned with the introduction of new causes can be established. History, fortunately, reveals regularities; the points of agreement among societies are more important than the differences (such as natural varieties and original diversities of local circumstances); there is, therefore, an increasing uniformity exhibited in the progressive development of the species. The uniformity is increasing because the

[3] *Ibid.*, 512 (VI, x, 3).

originally disparate developments are coming more and more under one another's influence. Empirical laws exist, and "the problem of general sociology is to ascertain these, and connect them with the laws of human nature, by deductions showing that such were the derivative laws naturally to be expected as the consequences of those ultimate ones."[4] Even with such an agreement it is not possible to demonstrate that the actual development was the only one possible, but only to show that it was the most likely or, even less, that it was possible. The consilience is necessary, though, for the limited nature of the data and their complexity lead to the formulation of incorrect empirical laws, "not only in this country, where history cannot yet be said to be at all cultivated as a science," says Mill, "but in other countries, where it is so cultivated, and by persons well versed in it."[5]

Still, then, Mill continues the attack on such thinkers as Comte and the Saint-Simonians, whose orderings of events into patterns appealed to him so strongly earlier in his career. He is not objecting to conceptual treatments as such; in fact he agrees in part at least with those advanced by the French philosophers; but he is insisting that the patterns be subjected to proof. An empirical law may be found in history to justify, for example, a belief in the alternation of critical and organic periods, but this law is not a law of nature. Our view of the past and of the present may be enriched by an understanding of the ramifications of such a law, but it is not correct to predict the future on the basis of it. Still less proper is it to devise a social system for the future by extrapolation. Empirical laws may be a guide and an admonition to the social reformer, but they cannot provide a gospel. The revelation is not complete.

By such paths Mill arrives at his account of the proper method for sociology, the "Inverse Deductive, or Historical Method." There are two branches of the social science, it will be recalled, Social Statics, which deals with the laws of co-existences, and Social Dynamics, which deals with the laws of successions. The first is concerned with order; the second with progress. So much of the discussion is borrowed from Comte that it is gratifying to record Mill's praise for him. In Social Statics (concerning which, it will be remembered, they differed so widely) Mill admits that Comte had indicated the necessary connection between the contemporary state of civilization and the form of government, and thus

---

[4] *Ibid.*, 514 (VI, x, 4).   [5] *Ibid.*, 515 (VI, x, 4).

made clear the danger of considering government in the abstract, except as a preliminary gathering of material later to be used in a social philosophy. So, Mill must have felt, his father and Bentham had erred, and just here is Coleridge's superiority over them evident. Indeed, in his article on Coleridge Mill takes on one of the tasks of Social Statics, the delineation of the requisites of a stable political union.

In Social Dynamics it must be realized that each state of society produces the whole of the next state, and that one part of the first does not produce one part of the second, and so on. "Little progress, therefore, can be made in establishing the filiation, directly from laws of human nature, without having first ascertained the immediate or derivative laws according to which social states generate one another as society advances; the *axiomata media* of General Sociology." [6] Here again his early mentors had erred. Even going beyond them, and looking to such empirical social laws as the tendency of mental to prevail over bodily qualities, and masses over individuals, is not adequate, for such laws are only evidence towards the establishment of middle principles, and are not themselves the necessary middle principles.

To obtain better empirical laws the statical view of society must by combined with the dynamical view, so that not only the progressive changes of the various elements, but also their contemporaneous states, will be considered. Then the empirical law of correspondences, including both simultaneous states and simultaneous changes of the elements, may be found, and will become when verified *a priori* a truly scientific law of the development of society.

If one element could be revealed as the prime mover in social development, the problem of describing that development scientifically would obviously be greatly simplified, for, says Mill, if that element be treated as a central chain, "to each successive link of which, the corresponding links of all the other progressions" are appended, "the succession of the facts would by this alone be presented in a kind of spontaneous order, far more nearly approaching to the real order of their filiation than could be obtained by any other merely empirical process." [7] Fortunately, such a central chain does exist: the state of the speculative faculties of mankind, including their beliefs concerning themselves and the world by which they are surrounded. As has already been seen in the

[6] *Ibid.*, 523–4 (VI, x, 6).   [7] *Ibid.*, 525 (VI, x, 7).

discussion of Mill's ethic, intellect is the controlling force in social advance, and again there is a pleasing agreement between conviction and methodology.

Here once more he has Comte to support him. For Mill the main problem in sociology is the establishment of the law of intellectual progression in mankind, through finding it in history as an empirical law, and then converting it into a scientific theorem by connecting it deductively with the principles of human nature. Comte is the only person to have attempted this task, and his law of the three stages has "that high degree of scientific evidence, which is derived from the concurrence of the indications of history with the probabilities derived from the constitution of the human mind." [8] But regardless of the value of Comte's speculations or any similar ones, Mill says, the method now described is the only one by which the derivative laws of social order and social progress can be discovered. By means of it man can penetrate the mists of the future, and determine what artificial means may be used, and to what extent, to help the natural progress in so far as it is beneficial, to compensate for inherent inconveniences and disadvantages, and to guard against dangers and accidents. "Such practical instructions, founded on the highest branch of speculative sociology, will form the noblest and most beneficial portion of the Political Art." [9] Again Science is to provide theorems for conversion by Art into practical rules.

The principal feature of Mill's methodology for the Moral Sciences is his insistence on verification by comparison. This reflects his greatest contribution to logic, the dual treatment of induction and deduction. His *Logic* was written, as he says in the *Autobiography* (158), to support the doctrine "which derives all knowledge from experience, and all moral and intellectual qualities principally from the direction given to the associations" – but support for this doctrine does not entail a denigration of deduction, as James Mill bears ample witness. It is not in arguing deductively that the *a priori* school err, but in accepting "intuitive truths" as premises for deductions, and in expecting deductions to lead to new truths. Premises, Mill insists, must be obtained originally by induction, and so must unfortunately be incomplete; furthermore, novelty in idea can come only through induction. So induction is essential and basic, though not to be used without caution.

[8] *Ibid.*, 528 (VI, x, 8).   [9] *Ibid.*, 529 (VI, x, 8).

METHOD: SCIENTIST AND ARTIST 169

On the other side of the logical fence, he is far from denying the merits of pure ratiocination merely because his education had suffered from an excess of it. In fact, he insists on the study of formal logic, pointing out that it is less likely than induction to result in error when used by unskilled persons. As he argues in his *Inaugural Address*, great benefits derive from the study of logic if it includes as it should "the principles and rules of Induction as well as of Ratiocination."

As the one logic guards us against bad deduction, so does the other against bad generalization, which is a still more universal error. If men easily err in arguing from one general proposition to another, still more easily do they go wrong in interpreting the observations made by themselves and others. There is nothing in which an untrained mind shows itself more hopelessly incapable, than in drawing the proper general conclusions from its own experience. And even trained minds, when all their training is on a special subject, and does not extend to the general principles of induction, are only kept right when there are ready opportunities of verifying their inferences by facts.[10]

The mistakes resulting from too complete a reliance on deduction have already been discussed, but the mistakes resulting from an insufficient grasp of the principles of induction need further mention, for Mill's canons of method are designed to prevent this sort of error specifically, one may guess, because of the tension he felt between theory and practice. He was never content to allow induction to be confused with a simple empiricism, as his criticism of Macaulay shows. Macaulay was over-willing to accept superficial and unorganized observation for Baconian induction, and Baconian induction is not itself sufficient. An early attack on "practical men," immoderate and polemical, shows the position from which he began:

A reasoner must be hard pressed, when he is driven to quote practical men in aid of his conclusions. There cannot be a worse authority, in any branch of political science, than that of merely practical men. They are always the most obstinate and presumptuous of all theorists. Their theories, which they call practice, and affirm to be the legitimate results of experience, are built upon a superficial view of the small number of facts which come within the narrow circle of their immediate observation; and are usually in direct contradiction to those principles which are deduced from a general and enlarged experience. Such men are the most unsafe of all guides, even in matters of fact. More bigotted to their own theories than the most visionary speculator, because they believe them to have the warrant of past experience; they have their eyes open

[10] *Inaugural Address*, 57–8. Cf. *ibid.*, 53. Some of the dangers inherent in simple inductions are discussed in the *Logic*, I, 526–7 (III, x, 8).

to such facts alone as square with those theories. They are constantly confounding facts with inferences, and when they see a little, supply the remainder from their own imaginations.[11]

This attitude Mill learned from his father, and within a few years his view altered, as he came to see that the principles he had accepted as "deduced from a general and enlarged experience" needed examination. Henceforth his attack was not on "practical men," but on "*merely* practical men." Practical men and theorists should work together, so that experience can be subjected to logical criticism and made methodical, before its validity as a guide can be asserted.[12] Whether the specific facts serve as the basis of induction or as a check against deductive laws based on the "laws of human nature," they must be organized; "a preliminary work of preparation" must be performed on them, "to fit them for being rapidly and accurately collated . . . with the conclusions of theory. This preparatory treatment consists in finding general propositions which express concisely what is common to large classes of observed facts; and these are called the empirical laws of the phenomena." Mill's definition of an empirical law indicates that caution is necessary, for they are not truly scientific laws. Only the causal laws which lie behind and explain empirical laws can lay claim to this elevated description. The correct organization of experience must be attempted, however, and so the combination of induction and deduction is imperative. Here in part is found the justification of Karl Britton's assertion: "It is the great achievement of John Stuart Mill to have found logic deductive and to have left it both inductive and deductive."[13]

In his discussion of the five experimental methods used in induction,[14] Mill makes it clear that although these methods are all that are available to the student of society, they are not sufficient of themselves to produce certainty. Deduction is necessary, so that one process can check the other and produce, not absolute certainty (which cannot be obtained in human speculations and examinations) but as close an approach to it as

<hr/>

[11] "War Expenditure," *Collected Works*, IV, 19. One can trace the gradual change in Mill's views by comparing this with such passages as those found in "The Silk Trade," *ibid.*, 127, 130; "The Currency Jungle"; *ibid.*, 190; and "The Definition of Political Economy," *ibid.*, 324–5, 334.

[12] See, e.g., "On the Definition of Political Economy," *ibid.*, 324–5; "The Income and Property Tax," *ibid.*, V, 562ff.; and "Duveyrier's Political Views of French Affairs," *Edinburgh Review*, 83 (1846), 471.

[13] *John Stuart Mill*, 147.   [14] *Logic* (III, viii, 1–6).

is possible, and as is required for social action. The first essentials of the would-be student, then, are humility, wonder at the vastness and complexity of the material, and a healthy scepticism as to the instruments,[15] as well as a passion for well-doing. In "Grote's Plato" he comments on man's experience of the world:

Multiplied failures have taught us the unwelcome lesson, that man can only arrive at an understanding of nature by a very circuitous route; that the great questions are not accessible directly, but through a multitude of smaller ones, which in the first ardour of their investigations men overlooked and despised – though they are the only questions sufficiently simple and near at hand, to disclose the real laws and processes of nature, with which as keys we are afterwards enabled to unlock such of her greater mysteries as are really within our reach. This process, which human impatience was late in thinking of, and slow in learning to endure, is an eminently artificial one; and the mind which has been trained to it has become, happily for mankind, so highly artificialized, that it has forgotten its own natural mode of procedure.[16]

In the same vein he points out in "Theism" that "the canons of scientific evidence" have been established by the "successes and failures of two thousand years."[17] Here again, as in his ethical theory, Mill is acknowledging the value of accumulated human experience, initially unorganized, but amenable to organization.

This conclusion can be seen even in his arrangement of the hierarchy of moral sciences. In the Science of Society "the elementary facts are feelings and actions, and the laws of these are the laws of human nature, social facts being the results of human acts and situations." Comte has pointed out, though, that the only conclusions, drawn deductively from the laws of human nature, that have any validity for sociology are those which concern the earliest stages of human development, of which there are very scanty traces left to serve as either elementary material or checks. Mill himself feels that even here such conclusions are of doubtful worth. The process of history, as seen by the scientist, reveals that the phenomena of society are determined less and less by the "simple tendencies of universal human nature," and more and more by the "accumulated influence of past generations over the present." The human beings who provide the data are not abstract but historical, and are what they are as a result of the action of society upon them. What then of the universal

[15] See *Inaugural Address*, 41ff.   [16] *Dissertations and Discussions*, III, 278–9.
[17] *Three Essays on Religion*, 129.

laws of human nature? For Comte, their place in sociology is the inverse of that held by laws in the deductive physical sciences: the latter serve as the basis of the deduction, which is verified by specific experience; the former themselves furnish the verification of laws determined on the basis of specific experience. The check is essential. Mill agrees, and adopts Comte's method.

If a sociological theory, collected from historical evidence, contradicts the established general laws of human nature; if (to use M. Comte's instances) it implies, in the mass of mankind, any very decided natural bent, either in a good or in a bad direction; if it supposes that the reason, in average human beings, predominates over the desires, or the disinterested desires over the personal; we may know that history has been misinterpreted, and that the theory is false. On the other hand, if laws of social phaenomena, empirically generalized from history, can when once suggested be affiliated to the known laws of human nature; if the direction actually taken by the developments and changes of human society, can be seen to be such as the properties of man and of his dwelling-place made antecedently probable, the empirical generalizations are raised into positive laws, and Sociology becomes a science.[18]

While in this context the main point is that neither induction nor deduction can stand alone, and that neither has a peculiar and definite superiority, it can also be said that here Mill brings together two other "seminal" influences on his thought, James Mill and Macaulay, and that the dialectic of his argument bears out the dialectic of his life. This substratum to his methodology can be seen also in his best account of the interdependence of the two kinds of logic, in his *Examination of Sir William Hamilton's Philosophy*:

To have an inadequate conception of one of the two instruments by which we acquire our knowledge of nature, and consequently an imperfect comprehension even of the other in its higher forms, is not all. He [who is not conversant with scientific deduction] is almost necessarily without any sufficient conception of human knowledge itself as an organic whole. He can have no clear perception of science as a system of truths flowing out of, and confirming and corroborating, one another; in which one truth sums up a multitude of others, and explains them, special truths being merely general ones modified by specialities of circumstance. He can but imperfectly understand the absorption of concrete truths into abstract, and the additional certainty given to theorems drawn from specific experience, when they can be affiliated as corollaries on general laws of nature – a certainty more entire than any direct observation can give. Neither, therefore, can he perceive how the larger inductions reflect

18 This and the previous quotations from *Auguste Comte and Positivism*, 84–6.

an increase of certainty even upon those narrower ones from which they were themselves generalized, by reconciling superficial inconsistencies, and converting apparent exceptions into real confirmations.[19]

In view of the importance of the meeting of theory and practice in Mill, one more methodological consideration must be given place: the role of hypothesis.[20] It is necessary to begin any investigation with a plan, a preconceived idea, or informed guess, as to the outcome. "Neither induction nor deduction would enable us to understand even the simplest phaenomena" seen in nature, if, as Comte has pointed out, we did not begin by anticipating on the results with a provisional supposition as to their disposition.[21] Hypotheses, which by definition do not permit of initial proof, are assumed "as premises for the purposes of deducing from them the known laws of concrete phaenomena." But the matter is not left there:

To entitle an hypothesis to be received as one of the truths of nature, and not as a mere technical help to the human faculties, it must be capable of being tested by the canons of legitimate induction, and must actually have been submitted to that test. When this shall have been done, and done successfully, premises will have been obtained from which all the other propositions of the science will thenceforth be presented as conclusions, and the science will, by means of a new and unexpected Induction, be rendered Deductive.[22]

Mill is not of course suggesting the existence of a body of self-evident truths; he is suggesting the utility, indeed the necessity, of having an aim when attacking scientific problems. His criticism of Whewell makes his position clear:

That the theory itself preceded the proof of its truth – that it had to be conceived before it could be proved, and in order that it might be proved – does not imply that it was self-evident, and did not need proof. Otherwise all the true theories in the sciences are necessary and self-evident; for no one knows better than Dr. Whewell that they all began by being assumed, for the purpose of connecting them by deductions with those facts of experience on which, as evidence, they now confessedly rest.[23]

The full comprehension of Mill's view of these problems requires a careful study of his *Logic,* and no summary can replace that study, but this brief account makes possible an understanding of the task of the

[19] *Examination,* 622–3. Cf. *Inaugural Address,* 53.
[20] See also Appendix, 273–4 below.   [21] *Logic,* II, 18 (III, xiv, 5).
[22] *Ibid.,* I, 562–3 (III, xiii, 7).   [23] *Ibid.,* I, 286–7 (II, v, 6).

scientist in the moral disciplines. He must carefully consider phenomena to discover such laws as are discoverable, in order to predict conditionally the future course of human events. He must discover the laws of social change, by noting the facts given in contemporary and historical experience, converting them into empirical laws, and then verifying them by deducing them from the known laws of human nature. This work being done, the Scientist is still busy; he must formulate theorems describing how, in the light of the laws of sociology, the ethical end proposed by the Artist may be achieved. It is here that Mill's reputation has mainly been founded.

Although the work of the Scientist, in Mill's account, is directed by the Artist, and so cannot be called "pure," it is clear that the primary activity is not related to practice. The study of phenomena which leads to the elucidation of laws, which can then give birth to theorems, is itself initially disinterested. Mill outlines the methods of procedure in this area, but does not himself work in it. Karl Britton has remarked that he can find little or no evidence that Mill used the "inverse deductive" method, and suggests that the conclusions had more effect on the method than the method on the conclusions.[24] The suggestion seems to me wrong, for when Mill adopts the Scientist's role it is as a devisor of means, and here the inverse deductive method has no relevance. Mill does not attempt to discover laws; he works out theorems on the basis of others' findings. He is neither ant nor spider, but bee.

One other question is not easily resolved. In the translation of theorems into rules for behaviour, both Artist and Scientist are involved. Not only must the theorems be desirable; they must also be practicable. To ascertain the former is the work of the Artist, for he alone is able to apply normative tests. But tests for practicability would appear to be within the Scientist's area of competence, although Mill does not make the point. Only if one considers Mill's account as in itself important does this omission cause concern; it is more important to see that Mill's own work was in the area where the two overlap. He attempts primarily to convert theorems into rules for practical guidance, and he applies both tests: practicability and utility. These are the keynotes of his sociology.

Though Mill did not himself work out the laws of social change, he recognized their importance in designing means, for they, with the laws

[24] *John Stuart Mill*, 89.

of nature, are limiting conditions on moral reform. They are also for Mill unlike physical laws in being partially modifiable by human desires and actions. Not that Mill is able to indicate to what extent man has power to control his own destiny, but he always asserts that the power is there. Each action, he argues in the *Logic*, is the result of a concatenation of causes, some individual, some social, some physical. Experience shows what logic cannot reveal, that exceptional individuals have had an effect on social development not explicable by known physical and social laws. Further knowledge may force a revision of this view, and reconsideration of the free-will and determinism antinomy, but there is no immediate necessity for such revision and reconsideration. Experience argues for free-will, and the Scientist should be guided by experience. In devising means he must see himself as capable of producing effects, even though he does not ignore physical and social developments that may frustrate his intentions. Mill's sense of practicability enters in to temper his enthusiasm and to make dogmatism impossible. But not to destroy confidence, for the careful establishment of social laws will aid mankind "not only in looking far forward into the future history of the human race, but in determining what artificial means may be used, and to what extent, to accelerate the natural progress in so far as it is beneficial; to compensate for whatever may be its inherent inconveniences or disadvantages; and to guard against the dangers or accidents to which our species is exposed from the necessary incidents of its progression." [25]

What social laws must be borne in mind by the social engineer? Nowhere does Mill isolate them and give them careful definition, and so caution must be exercised when describing them as integral elements in his thought. The outlines may, however, be traced. If the distinction between Social Dynamics and Social Statics is to be maintained, it is clear that the former occupies the larger place in Mill's work. But the latter cannot be ignored, for Mill insists that correspondences must be established between simultaneous changes of parts, as well as between their simultaneous states. It will be recalled that the laws most easily obtained, from historical generalization, are empirical laws, which can only with immense difficulty be converted into "middle principles" by ratiocinative verification. This verification must be attempted, and will in all likelihood finally be achieved; then predictions may properly be made, and means

[25] *Logic*, II, 529 (VI, x, 8).

properly devised. But Mill cannot wait for a full answer, and so anticipates the "Positive" state of knowledge.

As has already been stated, Mill did not apply his methodology to arrive at the laws; he borrowed results from others, sometimes without either insisting on proof or supplying it himself. One of his criticisms of de Tocqueville is here apposite: in *Democracy in America*, Mill says, insufficient examples are given, so that conclusions actually founded on observation appear to be "mere abstract speculations." [26] He might himself have remembered this criticism, for he seldom includes sufficient examples when talking of social laws. The brevity of most comments on society and politics, crammed as they are into articles, speeches, and pamphlets, makes necessary the omission of many of the facts on which the conclusions depend. Even James Mill can be defended on this ground. But the criticism is really damaging only when it represents an appeal to experience in cases where facts stand out stubbornly against theory. Though Science, like Art, is long, and life is short, polemical concision is not excuse enough for incomplete investigation. (It might be added, however, when the Age of Humdrum has replaced the Age of Humbug, that complete investigation is not excuse enough for polemical naivety – or boredom.)

One law accepted by Mill came to him through his studies in the philosophy of history. He learned from the Saint-Simonians to see in history the record of a series of alternating periods, differentiated as eras of order and eras of progress. The latter, it will be recalled, involve critical analysis and conflict; the former, constructive synthesis and agreement. Mill held that one final period of order will probably ensue, in which all previous progress will be caught up, but in which freedom will be unrestricted. When the Positive state of knowledge is attained in Sociology, he says, "no important branch of human affairs will be any longer abandoned to empiricism and unscientific surmise: the circle of human knowledge will be complete, and it can only thereafter receive further enlargement by perpetual expansion from within." [27] In joining other prophets of a final completion, Mill is at least wise in not giving a date to the time when the present "transitional" phase will give way to a "stationary" state.

His interpretation of these concepts is not as strict as the Saint-

[26] "Tocqueville," 36.   [27] *Logic*, II, 530 (VI, x, 8).

Simonians', and he similarly accepts loosely from Comte the view of
history as an overall movement from a Theological through a Metaphysical to a Positive state of knowledge and society. It is not surprising
that the ideas blend in Mill's thought, for Comte began as a Saint-
Simonian, and there are clear resemblances between the Positive state and
the periods of "Order," although the importance of the positive system
of knowledge for Comte leads to different emphasis. As we have seen,
Mill treasures Comte's "law" because it involves the predominance of
intellectual elements. The manner in which the speculative elements lead
the advance of society is shown, says Mill, "by a striking instance of consilience" between "the evidence of history and that of human
nature . . ." [28] He says that Comte has supplied proof for his generalization: the law of the three stages appears "to have that high degree of
scientific evidence, which is derived from the concurrence of the indications of history with the probabilities derived from the constitution of
the human mind." [29]

Here again the notion of progress is important. Mill, although not
sure enough of the evidence to call the law of progress, in so far as it
involves improvement, a scientific law, holds it to be an empirical law,
on which man must, in the absence of a better foundation, base tentative
predictions. If the Positive state of knowledge is better, no matter by what
standard (Mill as usual refers to utility), than the Metaphysical, and
society with the individual is moving towards the Positive state, then
society is progressive. Mill's language betrays his beliefs, no matter how
cautious his argument. He says, for example, in the *Logic*: "Every considerable advance in material civilization has been preceded by an advance in knowledge: and when any great social change has come to
pass, either in the way of gradual development or of sudden conflict, it
has had for its precursor a great change in the opinions and modes of
thinking of society." [30] The last half of the sentence is careful, but the
first is unmistakably progressivist.

Mill believed, then, that society progresses through a series of states,[31]

---

[28] *Ibid.*, 525 (VI, x, 7).   [29] *Ibid.*, 528 (VI, x, 8).   [30] *Ibid.*, 527 (VI, x, 7).

[31] His definition of a "State of Society" is broad: "What is called a state of society,
is the simultaneous state of all the greater social facts or phenomena. Such are, the
degree of knowledge, and of intellectual and moral culture, existing in the community, and in every class of it; the state of industry, of wealth and its distribution;
the habitual occupations of the community; their division into classes, and the

led in its advance by the speculative faculties. At this level of generalization, one other law, with its derivatives, really concludes Mill's list of social laws: the development of civilization results in a gradual equalization of social conditions, involving the disappearance of economic, political, and class-hierarchical differences. One result of this tendency is political democracy; another is the increasing power of masses over individuals; yet another is the spread of literacy over the whole population. A further important consequence is the alienation of property from the traditional landowning class; the growth of socialism and the breakdown of the class system are products of the same laws that result in democracy. The intimate connection between all these effects should be stressed, for Mill insists, as has been seen, that one state of society leads to the succeeding state, not one element of one state to one element of the next.

Here Mill owes a debt to de Tocqueville as well as to Comte, as can be seen in his criticism of the former for not making plain the meaning of "democracy" in his great work. Mill indicates in his review that in context the term refers not to popular government, but to equality of social conditions, and goes on to say that de Tocqueville has confounded the effects of democracy (in the larger sense) with the effects of civilization. "He has bound up in one abstract idea the whole of the tendencies of modern commercial society, and given them one name – Democracy; thereby letting it be supposed that he ascribes to equality of conditions, several of the effects naturally arising from the mere progress of national prosperity, in the form in which that progress manifests itself in modern times." [32]

The fertile field of sociological investigation here entered by Mill is, however, little cultivated by him. When writing on civilization in the *London Review* in 1836, one year after de Tocqueville had stimulated his interest in the problem, he fails to define civilization, relying instead on a circular explanation, and really treats civilization as the cause of

relations of those classes to one another; the common beliefs which they entertain on all the subjects most important to mankind, and the degree of assurance with which those beliefs are held; their tastes, and the character and degree of their aesthetic development; their form of government, and the more important of their laws and customs. The condition of all these things, and of many more which will readily suggest themselves, constitute the state of society or the state of civilization at any given time." (*Ibid.*, 508–9 [VI, x, 2].)

[32] "Tocqueville," 62–3.

which social democracy is the effect. He introduces many elements into the discussion, it is true, but does not follow them up. Civilization involves dense populations living in fixed habitations, flourishing commerce and manufactories, the pleasures of social intercourse, peace through the protection of person and property, and diminished reliance on individual strength and courage. The principal consequence of increasing civilization is "that power passes more and more from individuals, and small knots of individuals, to masses: that the importance of the masses becomes constantly greater, that of individuals less." [33] This "law of human affairs" appears elsewhere in Mill's writings on society, and he seems generally to consider civilization as the cause, and democracy as the result. His interest was concentrated, however, on social democracy, and the discussion of civilization occupies little place in his writings after 1840. But the larger context was never absent from his mind, and it is best to understand "democracy" in his writings as referring to social democracy, equality between man and man, and not, unless specifically indicated, as political democracy, popular control of government. Political institutions, he always maintained, must reflect social facts, and therefore political democracy must follow social democracy: "whatever is the growing power in society will force its way into the government, by fair means or foul. The distribution of constitutional power cannot long continue very different from that of real power, without a convulsion." [34]

De Tocqueville's failure to define his terms did not lead Mill to discard his findings, of course, which had more than temporary validity because they were based on the "historical method," and so had the status of "middle principles." Such validated conclusions are combined by Mill with generalizations drawn from unorganized experience and "empirical laws," and the only defence is the rather sophistic one mentioned above in connection with de Tocqueville: he does not give all his data, or his methodological argument, and therefore, while not guilty of drawing conclusions illegitimately from insufficient material, he may appear to do so. An example will illustrate: Mill believed that socialism will dominate economic relations in the future, and he worked on methods to aid its beneficial effects and to moderate its harmful consequences, but he nowhere gives what amounts to proof that socialism is in fact coming – that the evidence of history agrees with the known laws

[33] "Civilization," *Dissertations and Discussions*, I, 163.   [34] *Ibid.*, 173.

of human nature in describing social changes which will lead to socialism. It is probable that Mill made no attempt to satisfy his own rigid conditions of proof in this investigation, but if he did, he so compressed his account that his conclusions stand as almost stark affirmations.

The laws mentioned above are those that must be taken into account by the Scientist when drawing up theorems in accordance with the end designated by the Artist. The actual state of a given society is thus and so, and the planner must consider to what extent he can work with these trends, and how, when necessary and expedient, he may counteract them.

The final test, though, is reserved for the Artist: the examination of the means in terms of the end to establish their validity. The scientific theorems are not fully translated into rules of conduct until they are seen not only to be possible, in view of their relation to the known laws of social development, and practicable, in view of their adaptability to the exigencies of the contemporary human situation, but also desirable, in view of their general utility.

The whole scheme is dedicated to the improvement of man's condition. Writing to Pasquale Villari in 1872, Mill says that his own task is less explanation of the past than anticipation of the future.[35] He saw himself, in this respect, as a prophet, warning and admonishing as well as foretelling. He sympathized with the tendencies he observed in nineteenth-century society, in so far as they worked towards the ethical end he desired. He perceived, however, that some elements in the development were less desirable than others, and some positively harmful. Thus, though a democrat, he held that the suppression of minority opinion resulting from democratic developments was inimicable to the utilitarian end. Similarly, he approved of socialism (in his own definition), but wished to prevent such of its accompanying tendencies as might limit individual freedom. His father and Bentham were so obsessed with their opponents' faults that they had no time to examine the dangers in the reforms they were so strenuously advocating; John Mill, studying social change and approving its general direction, was better able to relax and look for imperfections in a movement that appeared to him, on the whole, to be beneficial. To A. C. Cummings he writes, in 1863:

[35] *Letters* (ed. Elliot), II, 333 (28/2/72).

I do not, as you seem to think, take a gloomy view of human prospects. Few persons look forward to the future career of humanity with more brilliant hopes than I do. I see, however, many perils ahead, which unless successfully avoided would blast these prospects, and I am more specially in a position to give warning of them, since, being in strong sympathy with the general tendencies of which we are all feeling the effects, I am more likely to be listened to than those who may be suspected of disliking them.[36]

[36] *Ibid.*, I, 289–90 (23/2/63).

7

Mill's Views
on Society and
Politics

❋

THE RESOLUTION of methodological problems launched Mill into his mature career, where his most characteristic and best-known work was done as a Scientist proposing means, and as an Artist validating them. His main effort was expended on the conflicts between society and the individual resulting from the growth of civilization. He was most interested in Britain, where increasing social equality was changing the points of reference in all sociological discussions.

Mill isolates two elements which exert an influential effect on social affairs: property, and powers and acquirements of mind. Both of these he sees spreading more widely through society, as they should, but the result of spreading is a thinner and more even layer.[1] As privileged status becomes more rare, exceptional individuals tend to disappear, and society presents a more and more uniform face to experience. Furthermore – and of maximum importance to Mill's social and political thought – as the majority becomes more powerful and coherent, less and less place is given to minorities and individuals. While majority power is constantly growing, minority influence is constantly dwindling.

What can a reformer do to counteract this tendency? Whether or not one feels that Mill established the theoretical foundations of his position, the position is clear: while equalization cannot and should not be prevented, the harmful tendencies which accompany it or result from it can and should be prevented. Talking of, and agreeing with, de Tocque-

[1] "Civilization," 163ff.

ville, he says: "The progress and ultimate ascendancy of the democratic principle has in his eyes the character of a law of nature. . . . Like other great powers of nature, the tendency, though it cannot be counteracted, may be guided to good. Man cannot turn back the rivers to their source; but it rests with himself whether they shall fertilize or lay waste his fields." [2] While "great results . . . are daily shaping themselves forth under the plastic power of that irresistible Necessity, wrought by the natural laws of human civilization," there is still a task for public-spirited reformers.[3] The increased intercourse amongst men and the diffusion of knowledge will produce social democracy, do or threaten what conservatives will, but the process may be hastened, delayed, or redirected. Action to these ends will follow from one of two opinions: either the people are ready for social democracy, or they are not. Are they, that is, able and willing by themselves and in the mass to provide securities against the harmful effects of egalitarian social conditions? Mill plainly answers, No. In the present intellectual and moral condition of the people social democracy cannot but delay the realization of the best possible state.

Social democracy, he holds, means the government of public opinion. Bentham, it will be recalled, exalts public opinion as a great check on immoral actions. Mill sees difficulty in this position; public opinion is a great check on what society sees as immoral actions, but it cannot be assumed, indeed experience denies, that society, especially as it now is, can determine with any accuracy what its true interest is. The rule of public opinion is the rule of the majority, and the majority is intolerant of any view but its own.[4] The most frequently repeated idea in Mill's work is the import of his message in *On Liberty*: "stagnation [is] the greatest of our dangers, and the primary source of almost all social evils"; only the Civil War could bring an end to "the intellectual and moral stagnation that previously prevailed" in the United States; the "danger of American democracy was stagnation – a general settling into a dead level of low morality and feeling"; "the real ultimate danger of democracy" is "intellectual stagnation"; "the greatest danger of a settled state of society" is "intellectual stagnation"; one result of the fear of

[2] "Tocqueville," 6–7.
[3] "Postscript: The Close of the Session," *London and Westminster Review*, 2 & 31 (1835), 273.
[4] See, e.g., "Bentham," 377–9; *Representative Government*, 127–8.

public opinion is "a general torpidity and imbecility"; there is "a relaxation of individual energy" in such a state; "the most serious danger is that the national mind should go to sleep." [5] If society stagnates, if it repels change, it cannot attain happiness.

Mill does not uphold the rights of minorities and of individuals because of an abstract principle of justice; he refers all questions of conflicting utilities to the ultimate principle. Equality is a good, but only a relative good; justice is also a relative good; and in spite of critics such as the two Stephens, so is liberty.

Liberty, however, has in most cases for Mill (that is, in the English society with which he is concerned) a greater utility than either justice or equality. He holds this belief because, as he emphasizes in the *Logic*, all advance depends on the intellectual apprehension and practical application of truth – in other words, on the ever closer approximation of belief to experience. Any society has but a partial glimpse of truth, and egalitarian democracy tends, through its deification of public opinion, to perpetuate the error which is mingled with its partial truth. Though his grounds are made more apparent, and his position is better prepared, Mill is fighting the same battle as did his father and George Grote for freedom of expression and conduct, and so may be held to be continuing the tradition. Like them, he holds that the despotism of custom and opinion is harmful not because it contravenes inherent individual rights to self-expression, but because it is opposed to utility. He goes beyond them, however, when he bases his hope for utility on the moral as well as the mental advance of mankind. Only the freedom to develop judgments and to act upon them can ensure progress: "the peculiar evil of silencing the expression of an opinion is, that it is robbing the human race; posterity as well as the existing generation; those who dissent from the opinion, still more than those who hold it." [6]

A proper understanding of *On Liberty*, and in particular of the rule concerning intervention in individual affairs, is impossible without reference to the principle of utility, and is extremely difficult without reference to the rest of Mill's social thought. The rule or principle, it must be remembered, is a practical one, and therefore is to be interpreted

---

[5] *Amberley Papers*, II, 64 (also *Letters*, ed. Elliot, II, 87); Mill-Taylor Collection, XLV, #25; *ibid.*, LV, #14; *Letters* (ed. Elliot), I, 302; Mill-Taylor Collection, XLV, #32; *Principles of Political Economy*, III, 935 (V, x, 6); "Civilization," 177; Mill-Taylor Collection, XLV, #2.   [6] *On Liberty*, 33.

according to an actual situation. Mill is providing a guide to action and, as always for him, such guides should be tested by the ultimate principle when subordinate utilities conflict. The principle is,

that the sole end for which mankind are warranted, individually or collectively, in interfering with the liberty of action of any of their number, is self-protection. That the only purpose for which power can be rightfully exercised over any member of a civilized community, against his will, is to prevent harm to others. His own good, either physical or moral, is not a sufficient warrant.[7]

Mill is not preaching anarchy, but a rational approach to individual rights. Private actions are not amoral for him, as they often seem to be for Bentham; Mill knows full well that opinion will intrude upon and affect men's personal conduct. Only persons well acquainted with the exact circumstances of any situation are competent to judge, however, and Mill wishes to exclude ignorant public opinion from governing where it has but a small interest.[8]

A utilitarian justification of individual liberty is not simple for Mill, for he includes the full development of each and every human being in the ethical end. Morality is dynamic for him, not static as it is for Bentham, and the elements of happiness are seen in terms of the possessors of happiness, individual citizens. There is a trace in Mill of the belief often associated with his defence of liberty, a belief that a feeling of freedom is a necessary accompaniment of happiness, but the whole concept is more complex.

If it were felt that the free development of individuality is one of the leading essentials of well-being; that it is not only a co-ordinate element with all that is designated by the terms civilization, instruction, education, culture, but is itself a necessary part and condition of all those things; there would be no danger that liberty should be undervalued, and the adjustment of the boundaries between it and social control would present no extraordinary difficulty. But the evil is, that individual spontaneity is hardly recognized by the common modes of thinking, as having any intrinsic worth, or deserving any regard on its own account.[9]

Here Mill develops his case, indicating the inter-relations of individuality and other means to the social end, and also pointing to the leading role it plays in the achievement of that end, and as an element in that end.

The second sentence quoted, however, opens the door for accusations

[7] *Ibid.*, 21–2. Cf. "On Punishment," *Monthly Repository*, 8 (1834), 736; *Auguste Comte and Positivism*, 143; "Grote's History of Greece," 526.
[8] "Notes on the Newspapers," 176, 589.   [9] *On Liberty*, 102.

of inconsistency, by suggesting that individuality is an end in itself. There is in fact here a tension between two justifications of individual liberty: first, it is conducive, indeed essential, to utility; second, it is a basic human need. But though one may censure Mill for his wording, the tension does not destroy his position. There are other basic human needs, and recognition of them does not challenge the *summum bonum*. Taking Mill's position as a whole, there is no room for any other "end in itself" than utility, and if one wishes to defend Mill on all points, one can even point out that in this context the overall position is maintained. In the first sentence of the passage quoted he refers to the development of individuality as "one of the leading essentials of well-being," and the passage occurs in the chapter entitled "Of Individuality, as One of the Elements of Well-being." The saving word "one" is present, if not always stressed. A parallel case is his argument in answer to Spencer's criticism, where he says that, rightly understood, the utilitarian end includes an acceptance of individuals as equal in the determination of happiness. This equality is not an end in itself, though it is an important part of the end. So with individual freedom.

Once the relation Mill finds between utility and liberty is seen, the place of *On Liberty* in his thought becomes clear. Only a man free from improper social control is truly self-dependent, for only through the battle of existence can one learn the conditions of the strife, one's own strength, and the way to victory.[10] Only the self-dependent can solve the problems lying between the present imperfect and the future perfect state of man. Just as the rich should loose the guiding reins on the poor, and allow them freedom to win their destiny, so should the public, in its corporate form, allow the individual freedom for his own concerns. A "tolerable amount of common sense and experience" is required before a man can be trusted to look after his own affairs, but granting this tolerable amount, "his own mode of laying out his existence is the best, not because it is the best in itself, but because it is his own mode."[11] This statement might be misinterpreted as an argument from natural right and justice, but its background makes clear Mill's meaning: if one has no control over one's affairs, one never becomes a first-class citizen, and always becomes a social liability. The social end demands a full realization of all individual potentials.

[10] See, e.g., "Tocqueville," 57.   [11] *On Liberty*, 121.

This point is related to another even more important one: the individual must be mentally and morally alert in his responses to experience. One of Mill's arguments for free discussion rests upon the need to make all beliefs and opinions immediately real and living to the individual. Except as instruments of coercion, dead dogmas are valueless, and therefore opposed to utility. By allowing a free play of thought on all manner of subjects, society ensures that its members will have the vital kind of belief required for stability as well as progress. Here Mill is again generalizing from his own experience. While developing his independent position, he thought on a "host of subjects":

Much of this, it is true, consisted in rediscovering things known to all the world, which I had previously disbelieved, or disregarded. But the rediscovery was to me a discovery, giving me plenary possession of the truths, not as traditional platitudes, but fresh from their source: and it seldom failed to place them in some new light, by which they were reconciled with, and seemed to confirm while they modified, the truths less generally known which lay in my early opinions, and in no essential part of which I at any time wavered.[12]

This is the way of all truths; they must be renewed to each inhabitant of the world through his own discovery of them. Not that each fact need be sought out anew, but each person must puzzle over his own experience by himself, guided but not controlled by older and wiser teachers. It is impossible to learn vicariously, Mill says in "On Genius," once more remembering his own experience:

Every one, I suppose, of adult years, who has any capacity of knowledge, can remember the impression which he experienced when he *discovered* some truths which he thought he had known for years before. He had only believed them; they were not the fruits of his own consciousness, or of his own observation; he had taken them upon trust, or he had taken upon trust the premises from which they were inferred. If he had happened to forget them, they had been lost altogether; whereas the truths which we *know* we can discover again and again *ad libitum*.[13]

The previous passages give a record of his meeting with new or rejected material, such as the thought of Coleridge and the Saint-Simonians; this passage relates to his first understanding of the beliefs of his father and Bentham. Neither new nor old truths, Mill holds, have any grip and influence until the individual has experienced the events or felt the force of the arguments on which belief is based:

[12] *Autobiography*, 118.   [13] "On Genius," 652.

the traditional maxims of old experience, though seldom questioned, have often so little effect on the conduct of life; because their meaning is never, by most persons, really felt, until personal experience has brought it home. And thus also it is that so many doctrines of religion, ethics, and even politics, so full of meaning and reality to first converts, have manifested (after the association of that meaning with the verbal formulas has ceased to be kept up by the controversies which accompanied their first introduction) a tendency to degenerate rapidly into lifeless dogmas; which tendency, all the efforts of an education expressly and skilfully directed to keeping the meaning alive, are barely sufficient to counteract.[14]

The individual, in short, must have freedom to develop his own intellect, and society, through its institutions, must provide that freedom and not attempt to control individual activity. "Knowledge comes only from within; all that comes from without is but *questioning*, or else it is mere *authority*."[15]

Mill is not arguing only for the man of great intellect, the discoverer of new truths, but for all men. Freedom, he says in *On Liberty* (62), is as essential, or more so, "to enable average human beings to attain the mental stature which they are capable of. There have been, and may again be, great individual thinkers, in a general atmosphere of mental slavery. But there never has been, nor ever will be, in that atmosphere, an intellectually active people." Not advance only, but the securing of the present position, depends on active, vital, and free opinion.[16] Behind these arguments lies social utility, the end and test of all subordinate ends, of which, for Mill, freedom is the most important, surpassing even equality.[17]

Important as these considerations are, they are in the main relevant to the conditions of social improvement; they are not themselves the instruments of it. Free discussion also ensures the advance. The original thinker, the genius, as Mill often calls him, is absolutely essential for social progress.[18] All new truths must, in the first instance, be discovered by individuals, and even in making their way must long be the property of minorities.[19] There are "as many possible independent centres of im-

---

[14] *Logic*, II, 233–4 (IV, iv, 6).   [15] "On Genius," 652.

[16] Mill-Taylor Collection, XLV, #32.

[17] "Centralisation," *Edinburgh Review*, 115 (1862), 326.

[18] *On Liberty*, 115–16. On the place of the individual in history, see *Logic*, II, 537–42 (VI, xi, 3).

[19] "Corporation and Church Property," *Collected Works*, IV, 217.

provement as there are individuals." [20] In "On Genius" (652), explaining his attitude towards the leading individual, he says, for example: "the capacity of extracting the knowledge of general truth from our own consciousness, whether it be by simple *observation*, by that kind of self-observation which is called *imagination*, or by a more complicated process of analysis and induction, is *originality*; and where truth is the result, whoever says Originality says Genius."

Mill's concern that original thought should have free play, like his concern for individuality in general, leads him into excessive statements of his position. In a passage quoted above, he says that there may be "great individual thinkers in an atmosphere of slavery," while elsewhere he appears to deny experience to emphasize his point:

Originality is not always genius, but genius is always originality; and a society which looks jealously and distrustfully on original people – which imposes its common level of opinion, feeling, and conduct, on all its individual members – may have the satisfaction of thinking itself very moral and respectable, but it must do without genius. It may have persons of talent, who bring a larger than usual measure of commonplace ability into the service of the common notions of the time; but genius, in such a soil, is either fatally stunted in its growth, or if its native strength forbids this, it usually retires into itself, and dies without a sign.[21]

"Genius," he says again, "can only breathe freely in an *atmosphere* of freedom." [22] In fact, Mill is arguing that any society which suppresses free discussion must itself do without the genius; he is not saying that the benefits that society denies itself may not be known in succeeding generations. Over-assiduous control of individuals limits freedom of inquiry and freedom to propagate truths (and errors), but genius cannot be totally prevented from exerting itself, unless all exceptional individuals are killed. Mill does not fear that genius will be destroyed, for original thinkers will always appear; he does fear that progress will be slowed or prevented if genius cannot disseminate and implement its findings.

Civilization, with its *laissez-aller* and its *laissez-faire* which it calls tolerance, has, in two thousand years, done thus much for the moral hero, that he now runs little risk of drinking hemlock like Socrates, or like Christ, of dying on the cross. The worst that can well happen to him is to be everywhere ill spoken of,

[20] *On Liberty*, 126.
[21] "Grote's History of Greece," 528–9. Cf. "Civilization," 197.
[22] *On Liberty*, 116.

and to fail in all his worldly concerns: and if he be unusually fortunate, he may, perhaps, be so well treated by the rest of mankind, as to be allowed to be honest in peace.[23]

It is unfortunately an "eternal law" that persons of "distinguished originality" must "themselves create the tastes or the habits of thought by means of which they will afterwards be appreciated." [24] The proponents of worthy reforms must expect to be long disregarded, to be vilified and rejected, before the effective social power (in a democracy, public opinion) achieves with their help their elevated viewpoint.[25]

It will now be obvious why, in such works as *On Liberty*, *Thoughts on Parliamentary Reform*, *Representative Government*, and *Principles of Political Economy*, Mill attaches so much importance to the individual's freedom from social control. Individual and minority opinion must be cherished by society, much as the public may object to particular tenets and beliefs. The great mass of people must be allowed to follow freely the lead provided by exceptional individuals. Repudiating both the Carlylean and Comtean versions of leadership, Mill nonetheless pleads for reverence:

The initiation of all wise or noble things, comes and must come from individuals; generally at first from some one individual. The honour and glory of the average man is that he is capable of following that initiative; that he can respond internally to wise and noble things, and be led to them with his eyes open. I am not countenancing the sort of 'hero-worship' which applauds the strong man of genius for forcibly seizing on the government of the world and making it do his bidding in spite of itself. All he can claim is, freedom to point out the way.[26]

The means outlined in Mill's political writings, such as personal representation, plural voting, legislative commissions, and competitive civil service examinations, are designed to aid the wise leader, and of course Mill's educational schemes provide for reverence towards the moral and intellectual teacher. His plan for the social reward of the "genius" falls into the same pattern. "Honours" are not sufficient; many a man of exceptional ability is lost to the world through lack of the small provision which would

[23] "Notes on Some of the More Popular Dialogues of Plato," 841.

[24] "Alfred de Vigny," *Dissertations and Discussions*, I, 321–2.

[25] See "Radical Party in Canada," *London and Westminster Review*, 6 & 28 (1838), 510; "Postscript," *London and Westminster Review*, 1 & 30 (1835), 255.

[26] *On Liberty*, 119–20.

keep him free from the necessity of "mechanical drudgery." Professor-ships and fellowships should be supplied, because "every person of dis-tinguished intellectual powers, whom society has not sense enough to place in the situation in which he can be of the greatest use to it, is a reproach to society, and to the age in which he lives." [27] The Clerisy is too important to be ignored.

Mill's support of antagonism is an outgrowth of his demand for truth and bears an intimate relation to his belief in the individual origin of new ideas. His dialectic does not depend, as sometimes appears,[28] upon a union and reconciliation of half-truths, for "half-truths" is a misleading term. That is, truth residing in a correspondence between opinion and fact, half-truths are really approximations to truth, resulting from incomplete and partial views. Opinions are based on experience, and particular experience may be insufficient for a correct generalization. Everywhere but in mathe-matics, says Mill, truth "is not a single but a double question; not what can be said for an opinion, but whether more can be said for it than against it." [29] One cannot simply add half-truths together, but one can combine the inductive generalizations on which partial views are founded, thus permitting a more complete induction and a closer approximation to truth. Absolute knowledge being impossible, what might be called "empiri-cal opinions" (on the analogy of "empirical laws") may be used as the basis of action, although their incompleteness should be recognized. Can-dour and honesty demand an admission that opinions may be erroneous, and the only healthy society is one in which provision is made for the correction of errors. Antagonism is therefore necessary, for differences of opinion bring to light ignored and wrongly interpreted experience.

In other words, "no whole truth is possible but by combining the points of view of all the fractional truths. . . ." [30] The "points of view" may be combined, as they contain new material, but even limited human truth is whole. Every system cannot be true, but each system may con-tain truths; it may, in effect, have given recognition to certain corres-pondences between belief and experience; and these lesser truths are necessary for a correct theory, law, or belief.[31] Neither Bentham nor Coleridge, for example, gives a complete picture; Coleridge is ignorant of

[27] "Notes on the Newspapers," 455.
[28] See, e.g., "Bentham," 357; *Spirit of the Age*, 13–15.   [29] "Grote's Plato," 331.
[30] "Bentham," 357.   [31] See *Inaugural Address*, 78–9.

experience lying outside tradition; Bentham, of that within tradition.[32] Conflict between the two philosophies emphasizes the limited view of each, and a closer approximation to truth is achieved not by the mechanical addition of one to the other, but by careful analysis and comparison, with the aim of revealing limitations of experience and errors of generalization.

Mill conceives his own work somewhat in these terms. He says, in "On Genius" (653), "I have sometimes thought that *conceptive* genius is, in certain cases, even a higher faculty than *creative*." He who can, without originating any completely new truth, combine the philosophy of, say again, Coleridge and Bentham, possesses more of the truth than either of them.[33] All traditional experience, all homely maxims, all literature, contain material for the determination of truth, and so they, like new inductions, must be given place. The difficulties of correct induction must not lead, however, to the acceptance of counsels of despair; incomplete truth must be recognized for what it is, and new information must be allowed open circulation.

The free clash of opinions should therefore be provided for in society. The argument of *On Liberty* is well known: liberty of thought and discussion should be allowed because (a) a suppressed opinion may be true, and so of obvious utility; (b) a suppressed opinion may contain some correct views; and (c) even though a new opinion be false, the activity necessary to defend the old true opinion against the false will quicken the true opinion into life, and so make it individually and socially operative. The last possibility is important for Mill, and really counters effectively the criticism that he is carrying his position too far in suggesting that even established truths of science should be constantly questioned. Apart from the obvious observation that the history of science is a record of discarded "truths," even Aristotle, Bacon, and Newton being shouted down by new evidence, Mill contends that truths learned by rote are practically useless. As he argues in "Thornton on Labour and its Claims" (641): "Scientific laws always come to be better understood when able thinkers and acute controversialists stir up difficulties respecting them, and confront them with facts which they had not yet been invoked to explain."

An application of this doctrine may be seen in Mill's "Bailey on Berkeley's Theory of Vision." Berkeley's doctrine, says Mill, has been accepted

---

[32] See "Coleridge," 393–5; "Bentham," 331–2, 356.   [33] "Coleridge," 397.

by thinkers of all shades of opinion, and if it is wrong, there must be some radical error in the method of investigating the phenomena concerned. Bailey's attack, then, is of double worth, for the accepted belief, even if true, should go back to first principles to justify itself, and thus strengthen its foundations; if it is false it should give way to another. "If the result of this re-examination" by Bailey "be unfavourable to the received opinion, science is happily weeded of a prevailing error; if favourable, it is of no less importance that this too should be shown, and the dissentient, if not convinced, at least prevented from making converts." [34] This last point needs emphasis, for here again Mill is continuing his father's tradition in holding that an open discussion will lead men to accept the belief which has the best-established foundations. And in accepting the utility of discussion and debate, he is carrying further the lessons he learned from his own education. "There is no knowledge, and no assurance of right belief, but with him who can both confute the opposite opinion, and successfully defend his own against confutation." [35]

All is not confutation, however; one must in argument retain a spirit of tolerance and reverence. Kate Amberley in her usual erratic way reports Mill as saying that the great thing is "to consider one's opponents as one's allies; as people climbing the hill on the other side. . . . [He said that] even the foolish good things did good in one way as then they were seen & corrected – and that the errors & exagerations of both parties counteract one another & so did good." [36] The glimpses of truth seen by antagonists should not be rejected in proud and silly attempts to reassure oneself, but should be accepted as aids towards a new and better view. "To understand a mode of thought different from our own, is always a valuable acquisition; and on a subject" – such a centralization – "where everything depends on a correct balancing of opposite considerations, there is a peculiar propriety in studying the face of the question with which most of us are least familiar." [37] It ill behooves imperfect men to scorn aid from others, particularly from great thinkers. In a passage perfectly illustrative of his own practice, Mill says that one of the greatest

[34] "Bailey on Berkeley's Theory of Vision," *Dissertations and Discussions*, II, 86. Cf. "Coleridge," 465.
[35] "Grote's Plato," 331. Cf. "Endowments," *Collected Works*, V, 621.
[36] *Amberley Papers*, I, 373.
[37] "Centralisation," 330. Cf. *Spirit of the Age*, 13–15; "Bentham," 357.

assets an investigator can possess is "a slowness to condemn." A man should

look upon all things with a benevolent, but upon great men and their works with a reverential spirit; rather to seek in them for what *he* may learn from *them*, than for opportunities of shewing what they might have learned from him; to give such men the benefit of every possibility of their having spoken with a rational meaning; not easily or hastily to persuade himself that men like Plato, and Locke, and Rousseau, and Bentham, gave themselves a world of trouble in running after something which they thought was a reality, but which he Mr. A. B. can clearly see to be an unsubstantial phantom; to exhaust every other hypothesis, before supposing himself wiser than they; and even then to examine, with good will and without prejudice, if their error do not contain some germ of truth; and if any conclusion, such as a philosopher can adopt, may even yet be built upon the foundation on which they, it may be, have reared nothing but an edifice of sand.[38]

Difficulties arise from the almost invariable conflicts between generations, and the fluctuation of opinion from age to age. A prejudice gives way not to truth, but to an opposite prejudice, and only after a long time does the pendulum pass again through the centre where truth may lie. New beliefs, to vary the metaphor, come to light and are prized, more because they suit the needs of the age than because what they replace is less true. "Spiritual doctrines of any significance," whether true or not, have a varied history:

Their meaning is almost always in a process either of being lost or of being recovered. Whoever has attended to the history of the more serious convictions of mankind – of the opinions by which the general conduct of their lives is, or as they conceive ought to be, more especially regulated – is aware that even when recognising verbally the same doctrines, they attach to them at different periods a greater or less quantity, and even a different kind, of meaning. The words in their original acceptation connoted, and the propositions expressed, a complication of outward facts and inward feelings, to different portions of which the general mind is more particularly alive in different generations of mankind. To common minds, only that portion of the meaning is in each generation suggested, of which that generation possesses the counterpart in its own habitual experience. But the words and propositions lie ready to suggest to any mind duly prepared the remainder of the meaning. Such individual minds are almost always to be found: and the lost meaning, revived by them, again by degrees works its way into the general mind.[39]

[38] "Use and Abuse of Political Terms," *Tait's Edinburgh Magazine*, 1 (1832), 167.
[39] *Logic*, II, 235 (IV, iv, 6). Cf. *On Liberty*, 34–6, 82–4; "Coleridge," 402–3, 425; "Corporation and Church Property," 211.

The periodic alternation, suggested by Saint-Simonian concepts, is translated by Mill into a doctrine of his own, which he conveys in typical language in his message to the students of St. Andrews: "whatever you do, keep, at all risks, your minds open : do not barter away your freedom of thought." [40]

Truth is, in spite of variations in opinion, gradually revealed by man's efforts; generalizations from experience approach more and more closely to the rigorous demands of proof. As man nears the best possible state, more and more opinions will be accepted more and more widely with more and more justification.[41] Teachers, recognizing this process, should not foster an "essentially sceptical eclecticism," [42] but should give all the support they can to opinions which they themselves accept – all the support they can, that is, short of stifling antagonists' opinions. And support includes enlivening discussions of basic principles and evidence so that, to repeat a point made earlier, truth may be renewed to each person born into this world. As man advances, the dangers of truth stagnating becomes greater and greater, for the more evidence supporting a doctrine, the less opposition naturally arises for the necessary functions of questioning and combating.

Mill depends almost completely upon education to remedy this defect. Teachers must preserve within their lessons a spirit of active inquiry, and must never work for an absolute identity of undigested opinion in the pupils. Comte is again wrong, for the crushing force of public opinion is strengthened immeasurably by a uniform and unified educational system. Much of the force of Mill's argument for private education arises from his conviction that divergences both of method and material are essential to the preservation and advancement of the social union.

Another mode of preserving antagonism formed a part of Mill's own education, and he suggests that it too may be included in formal education. This means is debate, both informal and organized. In the Mutual Improvement Society, in the Utilitarian Society, in the early morning meetings at Grote's house, in the Co-operative Society, and most important, in the active struggles in the London Debating Society, Mill learned to thrash out problems and to appreciate alternate views. Remembering his experience, he says :

[40] Inaugural Address, 83–4.   [41] On Liberty, 79.   [42] Inaugural Address, 79.

There would be nothing impracticable in making exercises of this kind a standing element of the course of instruction in the higher branches of knowledge; if the teachers had any perception of the want which such discussions would supply, or thought it any part of their business to form thinkers, instead of 'principling' their pupils (as Locke expresses it) with ready-made knowledge.[43]

Intellectual debates stimulate mental activity, ensure that difficulties on both sides of questions are studied, and thus aid the detection and discrimination of truth and falsehood.[44]

Mill is, of course, remembering more than his own experience; in this advocacy of debate is to be seen one of the most striking examples of the effect of his Greek studies on his thought. The dialectic of Plato and Aristotle provides him with the model of questioning. Both the negative and positive aspects of Plato's dialectic, he says, are useful: the negative attack with its demand that all objections and difficulties be met, and the positive search for common elements and unifying principles.[45] The links in Mill's mind among the Greeks, Bacon, and Bentham are made manifest when he discusses dialectic in his review of Grote's *History of Greece*. He points out that the negative dialectic exposes "the loose, vague, confused, and misleading character of the common notions of mankind on the most familiar subjects." [46] The method is always necessary, for only through the exposure of error can man be led to seek true knowledge. Just as Bacon attacked received notions in science, so Plato and Bentham employed a critical barrage against ill-formulated and ill-conceived beliefs in morals and politics. In this respect Mill may be said to have remained a Benthamite throughout life, but it is better to see both him and Bentham as disciples of Plato.

Even as a young debater Mill argues that all opinions in religion and politics come to be questioned because the

good of mankind requires that it should be so. The good of mankind requires that nothing should be believed until the question be first asked, what evidence there is for it. The very idea of progressiveness implies not indeed the rejection, but the questioning of all established opinions. The human intellect is then only in its right state when it has searched all things, in order that it may hold fast by that which is good.[47]

[43] "Grote's Aristotle," *Dissertations and Discussions*, IV, 228.   [44] *Ibid.*, 226.
[45] "Grote's Plato," 320–1, 284–5; *Inaugural Address*, 32–3.
[46] "Grote's History of Greece," 511n.
[47] "Speech on the Church," 322 (punctuation corrected from MS).

Forty years later his voice is raised again to the same purpose, in his address to St. Andrews University:

To question all things; never to turn away from any difficulty; to accept no doctrine either from ourselves or from other people without a rigid scrutiny by negative criticism, letting no fallacy, or incoherence, or confusion of thought, slip by unperceived; above all, to insist upon having the meaning of a word clearly understood before using it, and the meaning of a proposition before assenting to it; these are the lessons we learn from the ancient dialecticians.[48]

Scepticism, it must again be emphasized, is not the necessary result of this method; only a healthy respect for truth need result. Mill's praise of Bentham's "method of detail" must be understood in reference to negative dialectics, for as has already been indicated, when Mill praises Bentham he is not using "method" in the sense employed in the *Logic*. The scientific spirit which he finds in Bentham's investigation of the moral sciences is the same spirit exhibited by Plato, although Bentham systematizes his proceedings. Both Plato and Bentham look on morals and politics as subjects to be investigated through the operations of reason, and not as subjects the tenets of which are to be accepted on authority;[49] it is this attitude to which Mill refers, not the ordered investigation of experiential data in which he himself follows not Bentham but Bacon. Mill did not find in Bentham an understanding of the conditions of proof or the intricacies of induction. With Plato, he approaches morals and politics in a scientific spirit: he asks questions, some of which are the right ones; he does not, however, know what to do with the answers. Only in the area of investigation does Bentham's method deserve the high praise Mill gives it. But for Mill half the battle is the scientific approach; patience and care are more important than originality after the first bold steps are made. The fostering of this spirit is one of the most important tasks of education in Mill's view, and the dialectic of the laboratory requires the free dialectical debate of the classroom.

In Mill's political thought the dialectic of the classroom, the study, and the debating hall is joined by the dialectic of parliament. One of the main functions of a representative body is the free presentation of opposing opinions. "The House of Commons is not only the most powerful branch of the Legislature; it is also the great council of the nation; the place where the opinions which divide the public on great subjects of

[48] *Inaugural Address*, 32–3.   [49] "Grote's Plato," 284ff.

national interest, meet in a common arena, do battle, and are victorious or vanquished." [50] All shades of opinion, all conflicting passions, all warring interests, meet on common ground, and there is at least a chance that truth will be aired, if it does not immediately triumph. Only in parliament, and to a lesser degree in the courts of law, is the value of debate made manifest, and it is most essential that this aspect of their operation be preserved.[51]

Social antagonisms are naturally realized in the political area, where class and occupational interests are bodied forth as powers and parties. One particular form of political antagonism fascinated Mill, the division between, in Coleridge's words, the interest of permanence and the interest of progression, or in the form their political embodiments took during Mill's lifetime, the Conservative and Liberal parties. While he held that ultimately the true interests of the upholders of order are included in the interests of the proponents of progress (another way of stating the division, learned from the Saint-Simonians), he also believed the antagonism between the two to be inevitable and useful.[52] While he thought of the Conservatives as playing upon selfishness, and the Liberals promoting altruism, he saw pragmatic advantages in both. The one interest works to hold society together, and to preserve the advance thus far made; the other leads and pushes society on towards its goal. Although the representatives of the two parties appear to be opposed on almost all points, in fact their aims are both comprised within the larger purview of utility; their strife promotes the greatest happiness by keeping all necessary considerations alive and in public view. So also with sectional interests; when all have a voice, temporary and accidental power cannot easily become concentrated behind one sectional interest. Each interest, ideally, depends on the strength of its case, for only by persuasion of others can it implement its policies through the parliamentary forum.[53]

The most important function of antagonism in politics is yet to be seen. In every polity there is one supreme power, which tends to become the sole power, but when democracy shall have triumphed, as it must and will, the tendency to eliminate all other forces will be more pronounced

[50] "Recent Writers on Reform," *Dissertations and Discussions*, III, 57.
[51] "Grote's Plato," 331.
[52] See *On Liberty*, 85–7. Cf. Mill's discussion of Toryism and Liberalism in "Coleridge," especially 466.   [53] *Representative Government*, 129–30.

than ever. In words anticipatory of Acton's famous dictum, Mill states his position with force:

It is not the uncontrolled ascendency of popular power, but of any power, which is formidable. There is no one power in society, or capable of being constituted in it, of which the influences do not become mischievous as soon as it reigns uncontrolled – as soon as it becomes exempted from any necessity of being in the right, by being able to make its mere will prevail, without the condition of a previous struggle. To render its ascendency safe, it must be fitted with correctives and counteractives, possessing the qualities opposite to its characteristic defects.[54]

Without a permanent provision for antagonism, no government and no society can remain strong and progressive; only conflict can prevent degeneration and decay.[55]

An exact balance of powers is impossible, as James Mill had pointed out, and, as Whigs had been arguing for a century and more, would not be just or expedient, for the Commons ought to predominate. Other expedients are, however, available. For Mill the greatest of these, as will be shown below, is Thomas Hare's system of Proportional or Personal Representation, which would give a voice to all significant minorities. An extra-parliamentary force might best arise from the instructed classes: "the desired counterbalance to the impulses and will of the comparatively uninstructed many, lies in a strong and independent organization of the class whose special business is the cultivation of knowledge; and will better embody itself in Universities, than in Senates or Houses of Lords." [56] Mill is sceptical of the value of second chambers as checks upon majority rule, partly because of their past history, partly because of the traditional opposition of his teachers to such bodies, partly because he believes that in the event they could not effectively check a popular majority, and partly because he believes that such bodies are, when effective, more obstructive of worthy ends than helpful. Although, then, he calls for the setting up of "several concurrent powers in the State, which are occasionally in conflict and never exactly identical in opinions and interests," [57] he does not formulate a programme to this end, relying rather on the

[54] "Duveyrier's Political Views of French Affairs," 464. Cf. "Tocqueville," 77.
[55] See *Representative Government*, 116, 148ff.; "The French Revolution of 1848," *Dissertations and Discussions*, II, 402; "Guizot's Essays and Lectures on History," *ibid.*, 236ff.   [56] "The French Revolution of 1848," 402.
[57] "Diary" (18/3/54), in *Letters* (ed. Elliot), II, 379.

institutional guarantee of minority representation by talented individuals
though the Hare system, and on the reform of legislative procedure
through the introduction of a "Legislative Committee." Whatever the
means, though, Mill insists that the toleration of unpopular docrines that
are essential to the progress of society be institutionally guaranteed. In
this spirit he praises the royalist element in French political thought, the
efforts of the Jewish prophets against king and priest, and even the Trac-
tarians for their conflict with Church authorities.[58] He also cites the conflicts between primitivists and progressivists and between aristocrats and
democrats as advancing the recognition of truth.[59] Society must come to
see the necessity of "a social support, a *point d'appui*, for individual resistance to the tendencies of the ruling power; a protection, a rallying
point, for opinions and interests which the ascendant public opinion views
with disfavour."[60]

Before turning from this discussion of antagonism, one should recall
again that Mill is not defending perversity and stubbornness for their
own sakes, nor is he praising eccentricity or liberty as ends in themselves.
The "interests of truth require a diversity of opinions,"[61] and utility,
the interest of society, requires truth. Freedom to act in diverse ways is
essential, for truth is not easy to find and is not easy to recognize when
found. A large amount of experience is required for correct inductions,
and a limitation of experience through authoritarian intervention,
whether by monarchical, aristocratic, or democratic government and
opinion, can only result in improper assumptions. "The truth needs re-
asserting," says Mill in a passion of sincerity, "and needs it every day
more and more, that what the improvement of mankind and of all their
works most imperatively demands is variety, not uniformity."[62] This
belief is spread far and wide through his thought, colouring almost every
work from his hand. Freedom of speech and discussion, minority representation, *laissez-faire* economics, least-government politics, free inquiry
in science, toleration for communal experiments, religious toleration, a
free press – all these are connected not loosely but intimately in Mill's
thought with his desire that the truth should make men happy. The doc-

[58] See "Alfred de Vigny," 290ff.; *Representative Government*, 42; Morley, *Life of Gladstone* (London, 1903), I, 163–4.
[59] See "Civilization," *passim*; "Rationale of Representation," 348 (reprinted in "Appendix," 468–9); *Logic*, II, 542–5 (VI, xii, 4).   [60] *Representative Government*, 150.
[61] *On Liberty*, 92.   [62] "Endowments," 617.

trine is usually so simply stated that its importance is overlooked; commentators raise the cry of "eccentricity and anarchy" and fail to see Mill's meaning: "Since trial alone can decide whether any particular experiment is successful, latitude should be given for carrying on the experiment until the trial is complete." [63] Although opposition to error is a good, suppression even of error cannot but impede the discovery of truth. One's opponents are one's allies, and should be attended to in good faith. Mill shows a determination throughout his career to follow the maxim he lays down in the Logic : "It is a rule both of justice and of good sense to grapple not with the absurdest, but with the most reasonable form of a wrong opinion." [64] Even error, it is again clear, can be made to promote utility.

One other point needs to be made, as relevant to Mill's attitude towards liberty, towards socialism, and in the widest sense towards ethics. Mill is preaching more for the future than for the present. On Liberty was attacked in the nineteenth century on the grounds best stated in a remark attributed to Macaulay : Mill is crying "Fire!" in Noah's flood. His era in Britain was by and large one of toleration, although such proponents of unpopular beliefs as Bradlaugh were liable to strenuous treatment at times. But Mill is concerned with trends in society; he is looking specifically to the time when popular opinion, strengthened immensely by the political recognition of the power of numbers, can assume a menacing and restrictive authority, and interfere with the source of social advance, individual freedom. On Liberty is an attempt to keep the latch off the stable door before the horse can be locked in. As he says in the Autobiography (177–8), the fears he and his wife expressed that the inevitable growth of social equality and the government of public opinion would impose on mankind "an oppressive yoke of uniformity in opinion and practice, might easily have appeared chimerical to those who looked more at present facts than at tendencies; for the gradual revolution that is taking place in society and institutions has, thus far, been decidedly favourable to the development of new opinions, and has procured for them a much more unprejudiced hearing than they previously met with." But this state of affairs is entirely the result of transitional opinions; soon the growing single power will gather all social institutions around itself, control all modes of action not conformable to its will, and utilize its

[63] Ibid., 618. Cf. On Liberty, 101–2.   [64] Logic, II, 470 (VI, vii, 1).

educational facilities to reinforce its doctrines: "Whether this noxious power will be exercised, depends on whether mankind have by that time become aware that it cannot be exercised without stunting and dwarfing human nature. It is then that the teachings of the 'Liberty' will have their greatest value. And it is to be feared that they will retain that value a long time."

Government: Amount

While the foregoing account bears upon the most characteristic features of Mill's social thought, his most detailed work on means and rules of conduct was done in the political area. If one sees him here as, in his own terms, a "Scientist," dealing with problems presented by the "Artist," certain questions are central. First, within what area, for the furtherance of utility, is it right and proper for government to operate? Second, in order that government should promote utility in its own sphere, how is it best selected and composed? One of the usual tests imposed by Mill is here so important that it amounts to a third question: do the governmental institutions designed in answering the first two questions accord with the national habit and character of the people? In answering these questions one comes into contact with almost all Mill's opinions on political questions, and gains a further insight into his social opinions.

Although government is for him, as it was for his father, an artificial means to a recognized end, the word "artificial" had different implications for them, and the end is conceived differently. "Artificial" in John Mill's works implies that through men's art a method of dealing with social exigencies has been found, a method sanctioned by use, and developed through practice. James Mill, on the other hand, does not see the problem as organic, but thinks of an instrument constructed on rational principles to deal with a permanent problem. For the younger Mill institutions are the outgrowth of experience and ratiocination, not of ratiocination alone. So also, although for both the end of government is general utility, far more is included in John Mill's conception. In his *Principles of Political Economy*, for example, he says: "The ends of government are as comprehensive as those of the social union. They consist of all the good, and all the immunity from evil, which the existence of government can be made either directly or indirectly to bestow." [65] This statement is actually more limited than at first appears, for government,

[65] *Principles of Political Economy*, III, 807 (V, ii, 2).

Mill holds, cannot bestow all good and prevent all evil. The social union exists to further all good ends; government deals with only a part of them, and only as an instrument. Even in his earliest writings Mill makes this point plain: "Good government is not the end of all human actions. Though a highly important means, it is still only a means, to an end: and that end is happiness."[66]

The science of government lies within the science of sociology; the former cannot be properly constituted without the latter. As may be learned from a study of French writers, "underneath all political philosophy there must be a social philosophy – a study of agencies lying deeper than forms of government, which, working through forms of government, produce in the long run most of what these seem to produce, and which sap and destroy all forms of government that lie across their path."[67] Government is not then a thing apart, but plays its role as part of all social organization, that is, as part of the great march towards such perfection as the human species is capable of. The problem of describing limits to government action cannot therefore be solved simply by reference to hypothetical original contracts. Mill admits the Aristotelian distinction: men come together for mere life, but they remain together for the good life. The business of government is to promote the good life, but not to encompass or contain it. The functions which are rationally ascribed to governments in contract theories remain valid, although the fiction of the contract bestows no validity upon them. The minimal functions of government, that is, can easily be decided on by a preliminary glance at the necessities of social existence. When Mill is dealing merely with these first essentials, his conception of government seems extremely limited, but again the saving word is present. In *Representative Government* (287), for example, he says: "Security of person and property, and equal justice between individuals, are the first needs of society, and the primary ends of government. . . ." Again, in "Centralisation," he comments: "The first and greatest duty of the State, in all stages of society, is to protect the weak against the strong."[68] But these duties are only primary; Hobbes and Locke are right – as far as they go. To confine the operation of government to legal and police action is to ignore the ethical

[66] "Question of Population," *Black Dwarf*, 11 (1823), 752.
[67] "Armand Carrel," *Dissertations and Discussions*, I, 234.
[68] "Centralisation," 332. Cf. "Rationale of Political Representation," *London Review*, I (1835), 343.

orientation of all institutional questions. The proper inquiry is, how can government promote utility? Obviously for Mill, with his insistence on historical, geographical, and institutional relativity, and with his demand for specific verification, no concrete, final, and comprehensive principle can be found to settle once and for all time the correct area of government actions:

the admitted functions of government embrace a much wider field than can easily be included within the ring-fence of any restrictive definition, and . . . it is hardly possible to find any ground of justification common to them all, except the comprehensive one of general expediency; nor to limit the interference of government by any universal rule, save the simple and vague one, that it should never be admitted but when the case of expediency is strong.[69]

A sense of history is essential to the student of political institutions, for the degree to which government regulates life is dependent on the contemporary social and intellectual complex. Once again a combination of the talents of Bentham and Coleridge is necessary, as Mill argues in his commendation of Maine's work on village communities. While the "universal exigencies of man as man" are primarily important, and the "tendency to accept the existing order of things as final – as an indefeasible fact, grounded on eternal social necessities," is pernicious, only a careful study of the origin and development of institutions can reveal whether new or old solutions to social problems are preferable.[70] In less advanced communities more rigid control is necessary. "The government of leading strings," for example, is needed in a community of slaves. They need guidance from those whom they recognize as the possessors of force; they require, to lead them forward,

a parental despotism or aristocracy, resembling the St. Simonian form of socialism; maintaining a general superintendence over all the operations of society,

---

[69] *Principles of Political Economy*, III, 803–4 (V, i, 2). Cf. "Centralisation" (355): "Few Englishmen, we believe, would grudge to the government, for a time, or permanently, the powers necessary to save from serious injury any great national interest; and equally few would claim for it the power of meddling with anything, which it could let alone without touching the public welfare in any vital part. And though the line thus indicated neither is, nor can be, very definitely drawn, a practical compromise of this sort between the State and the individual, and between central and local authority, is, we believe, the result which must issue from all prolonged and enlightened speculation and discussion on this great subject." The line drawn in *On Liberty* should also be regarded in this light; see 184–5 above.

[70] "Maine on Village Communities," *Dissertations and Discussions*, IV, 131, and *passim*.

so as to keep before each the sense of a present force sufficient to compel his obedience to the rule laid down, but which, owing to the impossibility of descending to regulate all the minutiae of industry and life, necessarily leaves and induces individuals to do much of themselves.[71]

The special exigencies of any situation may also affect the amount of interference which is legitimate;[72] thus temporary control may be permitted in cases normally reserved for individual action. In short,

The degree in which political authority can justly and expediently interfere, either to control individuals and voluntary associations, to supersede them by doing their work for them, to guide and assist, or to invoke and draw forth their agency, varies not only with the wants of every country and age, and the capabilities of every people, but with the special requirements of every kind of work to be done.[73]

The work of government includes both Order and Progress and, although the necessities of Order remain fairly constant through stages of development, the place government plays in promoting Progress changes. In an early state of society the government, not being able to repose trust in private individuals, must actively exert itself in many fields later to be relinquished to private authority. In the final state of society, governmental bodies will be content not to impede progress, and will provide assistance to the private institutions and individuals in whose hands utility finally rests. Mill's allegiance is ultimately to the least-government theory, although his reservations about time and place have legitimately led readers to other conclusions.

His reasons for holding this theory are various, although interrelated. He starts from the argument against government interference put forward by his teachers: persons intimately connected with activities are best able to perform the functions associated with those activities, and to decide on the best means of control. The owner-manager of an industrial concern, for example, has more personal interest in its success or failure than a civil servant can possibly have. Thus, arguing from the known principles of human nature, it is apparent that in an advanced state of civilization, when intellectual and moral growth permits a clear perception of ends and means, the consilience of knowledge and interest recommends that the individual should manage his own business. And experience verifies the conclusion, Mill argues, by revealing that govern-

[71] *Representative Government*, 39–40. Cf. *ibid.*, 17.
[72] See "Centralisation," 355.   [73] *Ibid.*, 323.

mental agencies are very seldom able to hold their own in equal competition with individual enterprise, when the individuals concerned have sufficient industry and control over means. "All the facilities which a government enjoys of access to information; all the means which it possesses of remunerating, and therefore of commanding, the best available talent in the market – are not an equivalent for the one great disadvantage of an inferior interest in the result." [74]

Connected with this argument is another: although government may command the best available talent, it cannot command *all* the talent of the community. The total of intelligence in any state is far greater than that in the government's service. Therefore, government should allow a great freedom to individual enterprise. Here one of the most important tenets of Mill's creed again emerges: the need for experiment. All through his social philosophy runs the theme: only from the widest experience can the best be perceived; therefore all individual endeavours which do not jeopardize the social end should not only be permitted but should be encouraged. This is the meaning of *On Liberty* – not that eccentricity is a value in itself, or that originality in conduct and thought should be encouraged for its own sake, but that only through the cultivation of all facets of human ability can the best means to the acknowledged end be perceived. Experiments in living may be indulged in from mere curiosity or for thrills, but they should be permitted by society and not interdicted by government, for when they are harmless to other citizens, they are likely to promote utility. (The same argument is applicable to Mill's toleration for socialist experiments.) Governments are no more able to define the limits of individual capacity than they are to assign the correct employment for each citizen. Once again the individual is a better judge, though certainly not infallible.

A further limitation on government is dictated by the educative value of individual participation in the business of life. Both intellectual and moral horizons are extended by a careful attention to practical affairs, and such attention is bred best by individual interest in the outcome. When one's interests are taken care of by someone else, one is but a child, and the guardian is likely to construe the interest of the ward as his own. Stupidity and immorality are the inevitable outcomes. Under an authoritative regime, with freedom restricted or unrealized, the citizens are

[74] *Principles of Political Economy*, III, 942 (V, xi, 5).

unable to help themselves, and therefore are unable to promote the social good. They tend to become parasitic, living off the body of the host, the social union, without fulfilling any reciprocal function. The whole union is thereby weakened, and the only possible beneficiaries are the sinister interests in control. Stunted mentally and morally, the dependent slaves of an authoritarian society cannot follow the road to the promised land.

The worth of a State, in the long run, is the worth of the individuals composing it; and a State which postpones the interests of *their* mental expansion and elevation, to a little more of administrative skill, or of that semblance of it which practice gives, in the details of business; a State which dwarfs its men, in order that they may be more docile instruments in its hands even for beneficial purposes, will find that with small men no great thing can really be accomplished; and that the perfection of machinery to which it has sacrificed everything, will in the end avail it nothing, for want of the vital power which, in order that the machine might work more smoothly, it has preferred to banish.[75]

A more technical objection to the extension of governmental functions lies in the breeding of expense. The more functions, the more functionaries; the more expense, the more taxation. Heavy taxation tends to lessen a man's interest in production and efficiency, and thus ultimately to diminish the national wealth. Furthermore, compulsory taxation, vexing to the individual, involves "expensive precautions and onerous restrictions, which are indispensable to prevent evasion," and so expense is again increased.[76]

Finally, governments by extending their operations into more and more areas become huge machines, which not only prevent progress by stifling individual initiative, but become laboured and inefficient. The protection of life and property becomes less sure with the mushrooming of laws, commissions and administrative tribunals.

These then are Mill's objections to government interference. They may be summarized: first, most operations are best performed by those who best know them, and have their interest most closely bound up with the success or failure of the operation. The success of the best adapted and the foresight of the individual are better able to give the proper tools to the man who can use them, and to ensure that he will use them, than the most expertly organized government department.[77] Second, as no govern-

[75] On Liberty, 207.   [76] Principles of Political Economy, III, 939 (V, xi, 2).
[77] See ibid., 941–2 (V, xi, 5); Auguste Comte and Positivism, 78–9; On Liberty, 196.

ment combines in itself all the wisdom of the community, individuals should be encouraged to deal themselves with their own concerns.[78] Only an active and self-dependent people, in the third place, can become morally and intellectually capable of advancing the community. Progress depends on originality of mind and individuality of character.[79] Fourth, the business of life, regardless of the individual's pursuits, is the best education possible, and therefore the best developer of character.[80] Fifth, an authoritarian government creates parasites, destroys freedom, and thus weakens the state.[81] Sixth, more interference means more expense and more taxation; the enforcement of taxation means even more expense.[82] Finally, the multiplication of functions renders the government less capable of fulfilling its primary and essential functions.[83] Mill's conclusion is forthright and definite: *"Laisser-faire, in short, should be the general practice: every departure from it, unless required by some great good, is a certain evil."* [84]

This summary, which includes almost every consideration advanced by opponents of bureaucratic growth, places Mill firmly in the anti-centralization camp. But his habit of including saving and qualifying words makes him, as usual, a troublesome and thoughtful ally. He believes, that is, that often "some great good" demands a suspension of the "general practice." A better statement of his position than the one just quoted is found in *Auguste Comte and Positivism* (77–8):

Believing with M. Comte that there are no absolute truths in the political art, nor indeed in any art whatever, we agree with him that the *laisser faire* doctrine, stated without large qualifications, is both unpractical and unscientific; but it does not follow that those who assert it are not, nineteen times out of twenty, practically nearer the truth than those who deny it.

Experience warrants a general adherence to the least-government policy, but practical considerations and utility must be consulted.

Thus far the negative side. But Mill does not ignore the positive aspects

[78] "Corporation and Church Property," 217; *Principles of Political Economy*, III, 941–2 (V, xi, 5).

[79] "Centralisation," 324; *Principles of Political Economy*, III, 943 (V, xi, 6); *On Liberty*, 196–7.

[80] "Centralisation," 324, 353; *Principles of Political Economy*, III, 936–40 (V, xi, 1–3); *On Liberty*, 196–7.

[81] *Principles of Political Economy*, III, 939–40 (V, xi, 3); *On Liberty*, 206–7.

[82] *Principles of Political Economy*, III, 937–9 (V, xi, 2).

[83] *Ibid.*, 940–1 (V, xi, 4).   [84] *Ibid.*, 945 (V, xi, 7).

of government operation. Behind his appreciation of the beneficial effects of some kinds of government activity lies the political thought of Coleridge. In referring to the positive ends of the State outlined in Coleridge's *Second Lay Sermon*, Mill says that these ends, while valid, are better forwarded indirectly than directly.[85] Thus hesitantly does he approach a fuller admission. The business of government is to promote utility, and all his objections to government action can be seen to be based on the probability that such action will impede mankind's development. If the grounds of objection can be avoided, government can fulfil a great function.

Beyond suppressing force and fraud, governments can seldom, without doing more harm than good, attempt to chain up the free agency of individuals. But does it follow from this that government cannot exercise a free agency of its own? – that it cannot beneficially employ its powers, its means of information, and its pecuniary resources . . . in promoting the public welfare by a thousand means which individuals would never think of, would have no sufficient motives to attempt, or no sufficient power to accomplish? . . . [For example,] a State ought to be considered as a great benefit society, or mutual insurance company, for helping . . . that large proportion of its members who cannot help themselves.[86]

His central theme is that a government "should be allowed the greatest possible facilities for what itself deems good; but the smallest for preventing the good which may chance to come from elsewhere." [87] Government, like a schoolmaster, ought not to do all the pupils' work, but it also ought not to fail in giving guidance and aid.[88] The analogy is close, for government is the great agency for national education, in the usual sense as well as in the sense of individual and social moral development. Again, in the early stages of civilization, as in the early stages of education, government must do more than in the later stages when the individuals have graduated, as it were, into almost full control of their lives.[89]

Mill in fact outlines an extensive list of places and circumstances in which government activity is beneficial. Apart from the prevention of force and fraud, about which he has little to say, one of the most important of the legitimate functions of government is education. Universal education is an absolute necessity if mankind is to attain utility, for cul-

[85] "Coleridge," 455.   [86] *Ibid.*, 454. Cf. *ibid.*, 433.
[87] "Corporation and Church Property," 217.
[88] *Representative Government*, 294.   [89] *Ibid.*, 30, 34.

tivation of the intellect and the feelings is fundamental to moralization. A well-cultivated intellect, he says, is seldom unaccompanied by "prudence, temperance, and justice, and generally by the virtues which are of importance in our intercourse with others." [90] The government, therefore, in as much as it represents the community, and is a means towards the social good, can require a certain standard of education from its citizens. [91] The right to vote, indeed, depends on the possession of a minimal education. "If society has neglected to discharge two solemn obligations, the more important and more fundamental of the two must be fulfilled first: universal teaching must precede universal enfranchisement." [92]

The state should therefore require education, but should it supply it? Once again Mill recalls with revulsion Comte's rigid system:

that all education should be in the hands of a centralized authority, whether composed of clergy or of philosophers, and be consequently all framed on the same model, and directed to the perpetuation of the same type, is a state of things which instead of becoming more acceptable, will assuredly be more repugnant to mankind, with every step of their progress in the unfettered exercise of their highest faculties. [93]

Even the ease with which a state could inculcate the elements of the Religion of Humanity cannot compensate for the resulting lack of variety. "A general State education is a mere contrivance for moulding people to be exactly like one another . . ."; the danger of state schools is "that most fatal one of tending to be all alike; to form the same unvarying habits of mind and turn of character." [94] Majority opinion is thus rendered even more powerful. These objections are avoided when the state, while requiring a definite standard of education through examinations, does not control the day-by-day operation of the schools. State institutions may be established to provide an alternative to private institutions, as "example and stimulus, to keep the others up to a certain standard of excellence." [95] Poor children should have their fees paid by the state, but if the difficulties of means tests can be solved, those parents who are able should contribute towards their children's education. [96]

[90] "Papers relating to the Re-organization of the Civil Service," *Parliamentary Papers*, 1854–55, XX, 95.   [91] See, e.g., *On Liberty*, 189.

[92] *Representative Government*, 160. Cf. "Rationale of Political Representation," 357.

[93] *Auguste Comte and Positivism*, 99.   [94] *On Liberty*, 190; "Endowments," 623.

[95] *On Liberty*, 191.   [96] Mill-Taylor Collection, III, f.69 (24/10/69).

The state must also look beyond the generally limited attitudes of parents, who seldom are concerned with genuine progress. Teachers must not restrict themselves to lessons on how "to *get on* in life"; there must be places "where those kinds of knowledge and culture, which have no obvious tendency to better the fortunes of the possessor, but solely to enlarge and exalt his moral and intellectual nature, shall be . . . *obtruded* upon the public." [97] The knowledge which the world requires for business and trade, and even professional knowledge (excluding medical and some other), the world may be trusted to supply; no state provision is needed to teach anyone but the poorest how to earn his daily bread.[98] Mill suggests that competition, demand and supply, can deal successfully with such matters. Where the state should act is where there is no demand (or a very small one), and yet a constant supply is essential to society's well-being: "all instruction which is given, not that we may live, but that we may live well; all which aims at making us wise and good, calls for the care of Government" because "the majority have neither the desire, nor any sufficient notion of the means, of becoming much wiser or better than they are." [99]

The universities should be aided by the government, for they are most likely to suffer from neglect if left to private individuals. Mill's early paper, "Corporation and Church Property," taken with his "Coleridge" and "Endowments," gives a clear indication of his view of university endowments. The state has the right to ensure that all endowments made for the good of the nation are applied so as to forward that end. The aims of the founders and donors should be taken into account, but the primary consideration must be the social good. Mill suggests that the state may appropriate to educational purposes the endowment funds and facilities used, in his opinion, so ineptly by the Church of England and the old universities:

if there were a fund specially set apart, which had never come from the people's pockets at all, which was given to them in trust for the purpose of education, and which it was considered improper to divert to any other employment while it could be usefully devoted to that; the people would prob-

---

[97] "Notes on the Newspapers," 592.
[98] See "Civilization," 193; "Notes on the Newspapers," 442–3; "Sedgwick," 95.
[99] "Notes on the Newspapers," 443. Cf. *Autobiography*, 128; "Corporation and Church Property," 215.

ably be always willing to have it applied to that purpose. There is such a fund, and it consists of the national endowments.[100]

The government has not only the duty of providing facilities for formal education for those who cannot afford it, and ensuring through examinations that all have attained a certain level before certification; it must go beyond the formal educational system in bringing enlightenment. "The instruments of this work are not merely schools and colleges, but every means by which the people can be reached, either through their intellects or their sensibilities: from preaching and popular writing, to national galleries, theatres, and public games."[101] Private individuals who desire the advance of culture may work along with the state, of course, for no monopoly of education is permissible. Private agency will, in Mill's view, actually provide most of the non-formal education, but it must not be forgotten that the interest of the government is the true interest of the people, and cultivation is a principal part of that interest. Mill's position is quite clear: "the very most important end which any persons in public trust can aim at" is "the instruction of the people."[102]

Here, then, the government most properly can act, though not to establish a monopoly. It is for the good of the people that they should be educated; only the government can be trusted to provide proper intellectual education; government, however, cannot provide such an education alone without stifling the diversity of action and thought which is essential to the good of the people. Government, therefore, may ensure that proper education is supplied, but it may not itself control all educational institutions and practices. Who is to pay? The government, Mill says, when the beneficiaries cannot; when they can, they should. What institutions are available? Those already established may be adapted. State education thus understood is a means to intellectual development; intellectual development is a means to utility. Mill is working within the framework he describes for the Moral Sciences.

Apart from education, of course, there is a large field for positive government operation. Many factors are considered by Mill as he modifies the usual rule that individuals know best and can best achieve their

[100] "Corporation and Church Property," 216; in 1833 "probably be always willing" read "be willing enough". See also ibid., 214, and passim; "Coleridge," 438–45.
[101] "Corporation and Church Property," 214.
[102] "Parliamentary Proceedings of the Session," London and Westminster Review, 1 & 30 (1835), 513.

own ends. Seven cases, of varying importance and magnitude, are mentioned by him with more or less elaboration.

The first is that in which binding engagements are entered into by persons not capable of rationally deciding upon their own interest, such as lunatics, idiots, and children (and, Mill adds, animals).[103] Second, the state may control, through legislation, contracts in perpetuity, such as marriage, making provision for termination in cases where the purpose of the contract is not being fulfilled.[104]

A third exception, and the one which is now open to a wider application, concerns government intervention where owners delegate authority to managers who have no personal interest in the success of the enterprise. "Whatever, if left to spontaneous agency, can only be done by joint-stock associations, will often be as well, and sometimes better done, as far as the actual work is concerned, by the state." [105] While government management is proverbially inefficient, jobbing, and careless, so likewise is that of most joint-stock companies. Managers have often more interest in mismanagement than in good management, and while the stock-holders have in theory a control over the directors, which can then be exerted over the managers, this control is very difficult to operate and maintain, and so is in effect seldom exerted. Government affairs, furthermore, in free countries, have the great advantage of being public; they permit, therefore, a more active discussion and criticism of policies than when private interests are in control. Here, however, Mill safeguards his own position: while government agencies might carry on such work more skilfully and profitably, the other reasons for objecting to interference are still operative, and are generally conclusive. The importance of these reasons for Mill warrants yet another listing of them, so that they may be borne in mind while the exceptions are being considered:

the mischief of overloading the chief functionaries of government with demands on their attention, and diverting them from duties which they alone can discharge, to objects which can be sufficiently well attained without them; the danger of unnecessarily swelling the direct power and indirect influence of government, and multiplying occasions of collision between its agents and private citizens; and the inexpediency of concentrating in a dominant bureaucracy, all the skill and experience in the management of large interests, and all the power of organized action, existing in the community; a practice which

---

[103] *Principles of Political Economy*, III, 951–2 (V, xi, 9).
[104] *Ibid.*, 953–4 (V, xi, 10).   [105] *Ibid.*, 954 (V, xi, 11).

keeps the citizens in a relation to the government like that of children to their guardians, and is a main cause of the inferior capacity for political life which has hitherto characterized the over-governed countries of the Continent, whether with or without the forms of representative government.[106]

But these reasons, while they ultimately rule out most cases of government management, do not lead to the conclusion that government should allow a free hand to business concerns. As Mill argues in "Chapters on Socialism,"

businesses which require to be carried on by great joint-stock enterprises cannot be trusted to competition, but, when not reserved by the State to itself, ought to be carried on under conditions prescribed, and, from time to time, varied by the State, for the purpose of insuring to the public a cheaper supply of its wants than would be afforded by private interest in the absence of sufficient competition.[107]

He believes that two or more large companies will engage in price-fixing, to the detriment of the public interest. In the very important class of enterprises involving public service, many operations such as water supply and the paving and cleaning of the streets should be taken over by the state. In other similar cases, such as the operation of railways and canals, when it is best to allow voluntary agency to run the business, "the community needs some other security for the fit performance of the service than the interest of the managers; and it is the part of government, either to subject the business to reasonable conditions for the general advantage, or to retain such power over it, that the profits of the monopoly may at least be obtained for the public."[108] Expediency justifies, at times, the granting of temporary rights (on the analogy of patent rights), with final reversion to the state; at other times control over maximum charges for service will suffice. In other circumstances it may be expedient for the state to own canals and railways outright, and rent them for limited periods to private companies.

A fourth exception to the general rule of *laissez-faire* is that case in which individual judgment settles upon a course of action which cannot be implemented except through concerted action. Here the government should provide legislation allowing legitimate desires to be carried into effect through combinations. When Mill was writing, the important instance was trade-union and co-operative action. How, asks Mill, can

---

[106] *Ibid.*, 955 (V, xi, 11).   [107] *Works*, V, 730.
[108] *Principles of Political Economy*, III, 956 (V, xi, 11). Cf. *ibid.*, II, 141–2 (I, ix, 3).

workmen obtain, say, a nine-hour working day unless they have a legal right to act in concert?

His attitude here is once again typical of his approach to sociological questions. His opinion of the efficacy of workmen's combinations in raising wages changed late in his life when Thornton proved to his satisfaction the fallaciousness of the wage-fund theory as usually enunciated.[109] Mill came to believe that unions could raise real wages without causing higher prices.[110] Both before and after this change of opinion, however, he characteristically supports the formation of trade unions, at the same time objecting to some of their harmful practices.[111] Freedom is essential; laws which prohibit the combination of labourers to raise wages "exhibit the infernal spirit of the slave master, when to retain the working classes in avowed slavery has ceased to be practicable." [112] Yet again, however, freedom is not an end in itself; it provides a fuller experience from which truth may be induced and belief made conformable to fact. "Independently of all considerations of constitutional liberty, the best interests of the human race imperatively require that all economical experiments, voluntarily undertaken, should have the fullest licence, and that force and fraud should be the only means of attempting to benefit themselves, which are interdicted to the less fortunate classes of the community." [113] As with co-operatives, so with unions: even if they fail in their primary purpose, they direct the attention of the working classes towards other solutions of the problem of poverty, especially towards the control of population growth. Being based on principles of co-operation, unions also forward the moral development of their members and, through the unity of effort and means, provide intellectual education as well. Mill further suggests that "General Unions or Amalgamated Societies," working with "Councils of Conciliation," may help check restrictive practices,

[109] See "Thornton on Labour and its Claims," 643ff., and *Principles of Political Economy*, II, xciv.

[110] See Mill-Taylor Collection, III, f.45 (1/1/66); ibid., LV, #89 (4/10/72), ff.189v, 190r; cf. *Principles of Political Economy*, III, 929–34 (V, x, 5); "Thornton on Labour and its Claims," 656–7. Cf. W. L. Courtney, *John Stuart Mill* (London, 1889) 99–100; Stephen, *The English Utilitarians*, III, 216.

[111] "Thornton on Labour and its Claims," 665–6; *Principles of Political Economy*, II, 396–8 (II, xiv, 6); ibid., III, 932–4 (V, x, 5).

[112] *Ibid.*, III, 929 (V, x, 5); cf. "Notes on the Newspapers," 247–8, 435–7.

[113] *Principles of Political Economy*, III, 934 (V, x, 5). Cf. ibid., 931 (V, x, 5); "Notes on the Newspapers," 247–8.

and also, through understanding, bring the interest of union members and the outside community into closer agreement.[114]

Mill's sympathy is with the labouring poor not because their immediate desires are more in accord with utility than those of the middle and upper classes, but because their share of the general interest has received less attention. Declining, mainly on grounds of ill-health, a request by Spencer Walpole that he serve on a Royal Commission of Inquiry into Trade Unions, Mill expresses his hope that the workmen's side of the question will be adequately represented by men such as his young friend Fawcett, who are trusted by the working men, for, he says, "we all know the other side." No one, he concludes, "will more heartily rejoice" than he if the inquiry leads "to more correct opinions and improved legislation on so vital a subject, and no one will join more cordially in applauding the present Government for every step they take in that direction."[115]

A further field in which the state should operate is that in which action is taken for the interest of others, that is, in cases of charity. The government should so act as to make the aid it gives less attractive than the gain which persons obtain when not receiving aid. The Poor Law of 1834 is therefore the model for such action. Government should not leave charity in private hands because, in the first place,

charity almost always does too much or too little: it lavishes its bounty in one place, and leaves people to starve in another. Secondly, since the state must necessarily provide subsistence for the criminal poor while undergoing punishment, not to do the same for the poor who have not offended is to give a premium on crime. And lastly, if the poor are left to individual charity, a vast amount of mendicity is inevitable. What the state may and should abandon to private charity, is the task of distinguishing between one case of real necessity and another. Private charity can give more to the more deserving. The state must act by general rules. It cannot undertake to discriminate between the deserving and the undeserving indigent.[116]

Another legitimate area of intervention also involves the labouring class. In one section of his *Principles* Mill considers the effects of machinery replacing labour, suggesting that if the process is too rapid, and causes unemployment and distress, legislation may properly be introduced to slow it down. Furthermore, as some improvements in

[114] See "Thornton on Labour and its Claims," 662ff.
[115] Mill-Taylor Collection, Add. Mat. 2, M452 (29/1/67).
[116] *Principles of Political Economy*, III, 962 (V, xi, 13).

machinery, while not actually diminishing the necessary labour force, temporarily cause local unemployment, the government should make provision for those in distress. There cannot "be a more legitimate object of the legislator's care than the interests of those who are thus sacrificed to the gains of their fellow-citizens and of posterity." [117]

Other cases, where the actions are performed by individuals for their own benefit, but where the wide effects can be estimated only by government, also are exceptions to the *laissez-faire* rule. Colonization is a good example: new settlements should be conducted with a view to development, not solely with a view to the interests of the first founders.

A final exception covers enterprises in which individuals are either not interested, or which they cannot undertake because of the high expense and low returns. Such are geographical or scientific expeditions, aids to navigation, research involving long periods of time and expensive equipment, and the maintenance of a learned class. With reference to savants, Mill suggests that university fellowships could be adapted to supply the nation with worthy scholars, who would maintain contact with the public through lectures.[118]

The development of civilization presents a complex problem to Mill, for he holds that people become (as they should) better able to handle their own concerns, but he cannot deny that the increasing multiplicity of social interactions makes necessary more and more government activity. In "Centralisation" (335-6) he makes the obvious but seldom-observed point that parliament has been forced, for example, to regulate the hours of labour, to prohibit the employment of young children, to forbid the employment of women in mines, to enforce regulations against accident and unhealthy conditions in factories, and to demand minimum standards from the owners of merchant ships. But, he argues further on, a distinction must be drawn between one mode of interference and another. There must be new laws to deal with new situations – no legislation dealing with railways was necessary before there were railways – but there need be, in most cases, no extension of executive power. The existing administrative bodies should be competent to handle new cases. Of course, some increase in the number of public employees is inevitable, for many "laws which protect collective against individual interest, would remain unexecuted if voluntary agency were solely relied on for carrying

[117] *Ibid.*, II, 99 (I, vi, 3).   [118] *Ibid.*, III, 968-9 (V, xi, 15).

them into effect." But Inspectors and Commissioners for schools, factories, and charities, for example, need not have administrative powers; they need only warn offenders, and see that the law is put into motion against persistent offenders.

Even here there exists a danger, for there may "be over-legislation, as well as over-administration. A legislature, as well as an executive, may take upon itself to prescribe how individuals shall carry on their own business for their own profit." Still the legitimate function remains:

when, instead of protecting individuals against themselves, [the legislature] only protects them against others, from whom it would be either difficult or impossible for them to protect themselves, it is within its province. . . .

It must, then, be granted that new legislation is often necessitated, by the progress of society, to protect from injury either individuals or the public: not only through the rising-up of new economical and social phenomena, each accompanied with its own public and private inconveniences; but also because the more enlarged scale on which operations are carried on, involves evils and dangers which on a smaller scale it was allowable to overlook. . . . As respects such new laws, and as much new agency as is needed to ensure their observance, the function of the State naturally does widen with the advance of civilisation.[119]

Only so much, however, need be granted, and the necessity for justification is always on the side of interference: the residual powers remain with private persons.

A sequence of questions must always be asked: is such and such an activity conducive to utility? Can it, and will it, be performed by private individuals? If the state can perform it as well as, or even better than, private and voluntary agency, is the increase in efficiency and profit sufficient to outweigh all the harmful effects of intervention? And finally, if intervention is justified by all the answers, one more question must be asked: how can the state action be carried on so as to make possible a future withdrawal, leaving the activity in private hands? This last is an important point for Mill:

the mode in which the government can most surely demonstrate the sincerity with which it intends the greatest good of its subjects, is by doing the things which are made incumbent on it by the helplessness of the public, in such a manner as shall tend not to increase and perpetuate, but to correct, that helplessness. A good government will give all its aid in such a shape, as to encourage and nurture any rudiments it may find of a spirit of individual exertion. It will

[119] "Centralisation," 346–7. Cf. ibid., 348.

be assiduous in removing obstacles and discouragements to voluntary enter-prise, and in giving whatever facilities and whatever direction and guidance may be necessary: its pecuniary means will be applied, when practicable, in aid of private efforts rather than in supersession of them, and it will call into play its machinery of rewards and honours to elicit such efforts. Government aid, when given merely in default of private enterprise, should be so given as to be as far as possible a course of education for the people in the art of accom-plishing great objects by individual energy and voluntary co-operation.[120]

General utility is, in fact, the only ultimate justification, as Mill argues even when objecting to the limitation of government action.[121]

So far the discussion has centred on the proper relations between the central government and the citizen; the same considerations enter into the problems of the relations between central and local government. In-deed, as Mill sees them, the situations are similar in a remarkable degree: "Whatever advantages, in promoting the general interest, governments have over individuals, the central government has over any local body; while local bodies stand nearer to the merits as well as the defects which belong to the spontaneous energies of the private citizen." [122] In *On Liberty* (197) the same thought appears: "The management of purely local busi-ness by the localities, and of the great enterprises of industry by the union of those who voluntarily supply the pecuniary means, is . . . recommended by all the advantages which have been set forth in this Essay as belonging to individuality of development, and diversity of modes of action."

Most of the powers set up by legislation are, in fact, local in operation, and only the persons in the particular area can really understand adminis-trative problems.[123] It is true that local despotism is frequently worse than central, because the powers are liable to interpretation and control by narrow and bigoted interests.[124] The central government can, however, check the activities of local bodies.[125] Knowing what is done in the locali-ties and free from their "petty prejudices and narrow views," its voice should carry much authority, but its power should be limited to enforcing

---

[120] *Principles of Political Economy*, III, 970–1 (V, xi, 16).   [121] *Ibid.*, 800 (V, i, 2).

[122] "Centralisation," 342.   [123] *Representative Government*, 289–90.

[124] In his early "Notes on the Newspapers" (452) objecting to the squirearchy, Mill considers this objection serious enough to warrant a large extension of the powers of the central government.

[125] In "Centralisation" Mill is concerned to point out to Dupont-White, whose works he is reviewing, that the Poor Law, while involving a centralisation of know-ledge and experience, is in effect administered locally, under central supervision. The power remains in local hands.

the law. The rules should be laid down by the central legislature, "the central administrative authority only watching over their execution, and if they [are] not properly carried into effect, appealing, according to the nature of the case, to the tribunal to enforce the law, or to the constituencies to dismiss the functionaries who had not executed it according to its spirit." [126] The point is pressed home in the letter printed in *Public Agencies Versus Trading Companies* where Mill argues that, as one of the duties of central government is to hold local government to its duties, "no municipal government" is "complete without an accredited representative on the part of the general government." [127] A proper relation between the two sorts of body would, in fact, be conducive to the general interest in another way, by lightening the load on the central body, and thus allowing it to perform more readily its necessary functions.[128] One of the greatest aids which the central authority can provide to local bodies is advice; it can gather all available information and order it for the use of the local bodies. In *Representative Government* (291) this notion is presented through a Romantic image: "Power may be localized, but knowledge, to be most useful, must be centralized; there must be somewhere a focus at which all its scattered rays are collected, that the broken and coloured lights which exist elsewhere may find there what is necessary to complete and purify them." The same message is found in less metaphorical language in "Tocqueville" (26), and in more scientific form (in Mill's meaning) in *On Liberty* (198): "What the State can usefully do, is to make itself a central depository, and active circulator and diffuser, of the experience resulting from many trials. Its business is to enable each experimentalist to benefit by the experiments of others; instead of tolerating no experiments but its own."

This last approach is typical: if, say, ten local governments are faced with a problem, and attempt solutions diverse in one way or another, the central government can collect the results of all the attempts, organize and publish them, so that other communities can benefit. It operates as a statistical centre. If the central authority were to prescribe one particular solution, not only might bad results be produced but better methods might be lost. The parallel with individual activity is close; in both cases

[126] *On Liberty*, 205–6. Cf. *Political Economy*, III, 941 (V, xi, 4).
[127] "The Regulation of the London Water Supply," *Works*, V, 436.
[128] *Political Economy*, III, 940–1 (V, xi, 4).

to legislate behaviour is to impede advance.[129] So also with voluntary associations; if a group wishes to try a communal experiment it should not be prevented but encouraged, for its experience may provide valuable information leading others onward through improved means.

One of the great advantages of local over central government in Mill's view is its provision of the great ground for people's participation in their own government. De Tocqueville's analysis of American democracy emphasizes the educational value of local institutions, and Mill accepts de Tocqueville's analysis.[130] Municipal institutions, he argues in "Lord Durham's Return," are the best "normal school" to fit a people for representative government.[131] The only democracy which can work, in fact, is one based on a broad inclusion of the people in their own government, whether through municipal institutions or voluntary agencies. Not only are men thus enabled to gain a better knowledge of social and political realities, but as their interests are widened to include the legitimate aims of others they are progressively moralized. Altruism becomes a social fact, and the moral end is brought nearer by just so much as the individual interest approximates to the general interest.

The gathering of authoritative power into the hands of the central government, on the contrary, impedes moral progress not only by removing self-dependence and rational foresight, but by preventing all but the selfish interest from developing.

It is therefore of supreme importance that all classes of the community, down to the lowest, should have much to do for themselves; that as great a demand should be made upon their intelligence and virtue as it is in any respect equal to; that the government should not only leave as far as possible to their own faculties the conduct of whatever concerns themselves alone, but should suffer them, or rather encourage them, to manage as many as possible of their joint concerns by voluntary co-operation; since this discussion and management of collective interests is the great school of that public spirit, and the great source of that intelligence of public affairs, which are always regarded as the distinctive character of the public of free countries.[132]

The prejudice against centralization, while over-active, as Mill points out in *Representative Government*, "Centralisation," and "Tocqueville," to mention only the most obvious sources, is really one of the great

[129] *Ibid.*, 941–2 (V, xi, 5).　　　[130] "Tocqueville," 24ff.
[131] "Lord Durham's Return," *London and Westminster Review*, 32 (1838), 252.
[132] *Political Economy*, III, 944 (V, xi, 6).

sources of the superiority of English over French representative institutions.[133] To underestimate the role of the central government is a mistake, but it is a mistake in the right direction. One's sympathy is with Mill when he writes to J. E. Cairnes: "I have seen M. Millet's article which you mention, and was amused by it. One gets accustomed to strange things, but to find myself held up as an apostle of centralization was indeed something unexpected." [134]

Diversity is his constant demand; his remarks on centralization bear a close relation to his rejection of the systematizing of Comte and the Saint-Simonians:

Unity, indeed, is a phrase, which, as it comes from the lips of a politician, either rhetorical or practical, nurtured in the stifling governmentalism of the Imperial school, is one of the curses of Europe. It stands for the negation of the main determining principle of improvement, and even of the permanence of civilisation, which depends on diversity, not unity. 'One God, one France, one King, one Chamber,' was the exclamation of a member of the first Constituent Assembly. Sir Walter Scott appended to it as an appropriate commentary, 'one mouth, one nose, one ear, and one eye.' And if the jest sets in a strong light the ridiculousness, it does nothing like justice to the mischievousness, of the wretched propensity, which, in order that all the affairs of mankind may be cut after a single pattern, tends irresistibly to subject all of them to a single will.[135]

Government: Selection and Composition

Questions concerning the extent of government operation are closely linked in Mill's thought with questions concerning the choice of governors. In effect he asks: in order that government should promote utility, how is it best selected and composed? In answering this question Mill examines means in terms of national habit and character, practicability, and utility.

The question, it will be seen, contains two parts, each of which may again be divided. Thus it may be asked: by whom should the government be selected? How should it be selected? Then the second part requires treatment: who should be selected? How should the powers and functions of those elected be distributed? Should some functions be per-

[133] See also "Regulation of the London Water Supply," 435; "Duveyrier's Political Views of French Affairs," 474.
[134] Mill-Taylor Collection, LV, #86 (22/4/72), f.184r. Cf. *Letters* (ed. Elliot), II, 341 (to Villari, 19/5/72).   [135] "Centralisation," 358.

formed by persons not selected in the normal way? The question of selection involves the people as a whole; the question of composition is more closely restricted.

When discussing Mill's theory of government it should be borne in mind that the relativity of institutions to the state of society for which they are intended is fundamental to his thought. One of his few commendations of Comte's political theory, cited above, emphasizes this point: "All political truth [Comte] deems strictly relative, implying as its correlative a given state or situation of society. This conviction is now common to him with all thinkers who are on a level with the age, and comes so naturally to any intelligent reader of history, that the only wonder is how men could have been prevented from reaching it sooner." [136] As he writes in 1837 (somewhat more sharply than he would later or publicly): "I myself have always been for a good stout Despotism – for governing Ireland like India. But it cannot be done. The spirit of Democracy has got too much head there, too prematurely." [137] Government must be suited to time and place, and to the particular state of national intellect and custom; furthermore, it must be regarded as a means, and so its forms must be decided upon in terms of social development. Political institutions bear more upon moral and educational questions than upon material ones; they ought, therefore, to be decided on "mainly by the consideration, what great improvement in life and culture stands next in order for the people concerned, as the condition of their further progress. . . ." [138] Finally, the people must be willing to accept the institutions, must be capable of preserving them, and must be able to discharge the duties and functions entailed by them.[139] The reformer as Scientist, in short, must study the history of the community or nation, and must recognize, when outlining the distribution of power, the elements in society which already have economic or intellectual influence, if not political power.[140]

Interesting as these considerations are in Mill's social philosophy, it soon becomes apparent that they have little bearing on his account of political means, as he himself admits in his *Autobiography* (120). The

---

[136] *Auguste Comte and Positivism*, 115.   [137] *Earlier Letters*, XII, 365 (21/12/37).

[138] *Autobiography*, 120. Cf. *Representative Government*, 40. For Mill's approval of the Reform Act of 1832 on these grounds, see "Coleridge," 449; *Thoughts on Parliamentary Reform*, in *Dissertations and Discussions*, III, 2.

[139] *Representative Government*, 70–1.   [140] "Coleridge," 451.

reason is that he holds, all things considered, that representative democracy is the best form for England, and his writings on the subject are mainly confined to English affairs. Other countries provide material for his study, but his reforms are for his native land. His system, as a result, is closely allied to that of his father and Bentham, although he has a deeper appreciation of the problems involved in making representative institutions work for utility. So when the question is asked, by whom should the government be selected? there is no doubt about Mill's answer. He is a democrat. From the time of his earliest sympathy with the Roman populace to his last writings the theme of popular control runs through his thought. His youth was spent in a time when partisanship for democratic beliefs was first effectively expressed in England, and he lived among the men who expressed this partisanship, and for whom democratic reform was the chief instrument in social betterment. Their main tenet, moderated for practical reasons, was universal suffrage. This Bentham advocated in his electoral reform (including even women), and this James Mill intended, even when excluding women and men under forty years of age. Their rationale is that of the younger Mill: only through universal suffrage can the people of a state control their own affairs according to their own interest. There is a difference between the democratic beliefs of the Philosophic Radicals and those of John Mill after the early 1830's, but it is not here. The people as a whole should select that portion of their number who will wield power over them, for only thus can government work for the happiness of all. Mill, however, is more cautious than even his mentors, and insists that a long period must pass before all will be capable of voting intelligently; universal suffrage, therefore, should be gradually achieved. His argument is conducted with the final end in view, but it is not, for that reason, "metaphysical." As he remarks in his criticism of Comte, "there is also a Positive doctrine, without any pretension to being absolute, which claims the direct participation of the governed in their own government, not as a natural right, but as a means to important ends, under the conditions and with the limitations which those ends impose." [141]

Here the dictates of practicability enter: pure democracy, the voice of each speaking in a common forum to decide public affairs, is impossible, for the population is too large, and the distances too vast. The best

[141] *Auguste Comte and Positivism,* 79.

substitute is a representative democracy, in which each person helps to select a portion of the community to stand for the whole. This means being so far practicable, Mill turns to the "middle principles" of sociology to see whether it is in accordance with historical trends. He is delighted to see that society is moving in this direction, and no more need be said.

In this matter, then, Mill adds little to his forerunners' thought, but his particular contributions to the theory of government become evident when the next question is considered: how should the representatives be chosen? As they are to stand for and serve the whole community, they should represent the whole community, and not its separate interests. Although Mill toyed with Coleridge's ideas, his final decision is that the "Progressive" and "Permanent" interests need not be separately provided for: "In this as in every other case, it is not separating classes of persons and organizing them apart, but fusing them with other classes very different from themselves, which eliminates class interests and class feelings." [142] Men of varying personal and occupational interests will always be found in the representative body, and an appreciation of their particular points of view will benefit the nation, but their "sinister interest" should not receive institutional support.

As regards interests in themselves, whenever not identical with the general interest, the less they are represented the better. What is wanted is a representation, not of men's differences of interest, but of the differences in their intellectual points of view. Shipowners are to be desired in Parliament, because they can instruct us about ships, not because they are interested in having protecting duties. We want from a lawyer in Parliament his legal knowledge, not his professional interest in the expensiveness and unintelligibility of the law.[143]

The suffrage, therefore, should not be designed to give power to special interests in the community, although it should, as will be seen, be designed to give voice to separate points of view.

Advocates of universal suffrage face a searching problem: as the real and permanent interest of the community, and not its apparent and transitory interest, should be forwarded by government, it follows that the wisest and best members of the community should be influential in

[142] *Thoughts on Parliamentary Reform*, 24n. As early as his Debating Society days Mill rejects a class-representation theory: "According to our notions the House of Commons should represent only one interest, the general interest" ("Speech on the British Constitution," in *Autobiography*, ed. Laski, 281).

[143] "Recent Writers on Reform," 73.

determining policies. While everyone should be consulted, neither justice not utility is satisfied by the equation of ignorance with knowledge, or stupidity with intelligence.[144] In Coleridge Mill had read: "Men . . . ought to be weighed, not counted. Their worth ought to be the final estimate of their value." [145] In *Representative Government* (340) he echoes this maxim: "opinions may be weighed as well as counted. . . ." Therefore, "a higher figure" should be "assigned to the suffrages of those whose opinion is entitled to greater weight." [146] Mill tried several ways of translating this principle into a practicable rule.

As morality ultimately depends on education, in his view, and as practical action is an important part of education, it appeared to Mill that education, though a rough measure, is the most readily available one for determining a person's ability to perceive the true national interest. In his *Thoughts on Parliamentary Reform* he points out that an electoral system is perfect only when each person has a vote, and the well-educated have more than one vote. The two conditions are mutually dependent; one cannot stand without the other:

if the most numerous class, which (saving honourable exceptions on one side, or disgraceful ones on the other) is the lowest in the educational scale, refuses to recognise a right in the better educated, in virtue of their superior qualifications, to such plurality of votes as may prevent them from being always and hopelessly outvoted by the comparatively incapable, the numerical majority must submit to have the suffrage limited to such portion of their numbers, or to have such a distribution made of the constituencies, as may effect the necessary balance between numbers and education in another manner.[147]

[144] See *Autobiography*, 180–1; *Representative Government*, 168, 181–2.

[145] *Second Lay Sermon*, in *Works* (London, 1894), 429.

[146] *Representative Government*, 174–5. In the Mill-Taylor Collection (XLIX, #17, f.38r.) there is a note bearing on the question of individual worth:
"The mistake of Demagogues & equal-rights-men consists in mistaking the natural or physical equality of men for their mental inequalities – (for superior rank is the reward of superiority of mind, at least in the founder of the enobled race) & in not recognising the social & political necessity of ranks. They are in truth virulent advocates of grades; for they want the ignorant and poor to be uppermost & the better instructed and wealthier to be undermost.
The mistake of the ultra aristocrat on the other hand is to believe in a sort of divine right in him to the possession of what he holds & to grind more out of those under him & to keep them under, as if they had no *right* to rise – not the same right as their own ancestors had to acquire the rank & wealth they themselves gladly [?] possess."
This note has all the marks of a "joint production" with Harriet.

[147] *Thoughts on Parliamentary Reform*, 23. The discussion of plural voting is on 21–8.

He goes on to argue that reading, writing, and a knowledge of the simple rules of arithmetic may properly be demanded of every voter. If the franchise is not to be weighted in favour of education, moreover, the educational qualification for even one vote should be much higher. In short, he is advocating universal suffrage in a modified form: only persons who have proved their rationality are properly qualified for consultation. He insists, of course, that educational opportunities be made available to all, and does not suggest that universal suffrage is justifiable under any other circumstances, any more than a limited suffrage would be justifiable with universal education. Everyone, it is argued, "has an equal interest in being well governed," and everyone therefore "has an equal claim to control over his own government." Mill would agree, "if control over his own government were really the thing in question," but, he adds, "what I am asked to assent to is, that every individual has an equal claim to control over the government of other people." [148] No one, in fact, has a right ("except in a purely legal sense") to rule over others, and such power as anyone has over others is in the nature of a moral trust. As the vote gives one power over others, it cannot be conceived simply as a right; it "is strictly a matter of duty," and the voter "is bound to give it according to his best and most conscientious opinion of the public good." [149] Individuals not being equally capable of so acting, equal voting is only a relative good; circumstances in England actually counteract its potential for good.

In *Representative Government* Mill suggests an alternative to an educational test, based on occupation and experience:

An employer of labour is on the average more intelligent than a labourer; for he must labour with his head, and not solely with his hands. A foreman is generally more intelligent than an ordinary labourer, and a labourer in the skilled trades than in the unskilled. A banker, merchant, or manufacturer, is likely to be more intelligent than a tradesman, because he has larger and more complicated interests to manage. In all these cases it is not the having merely undertaken the superior function, but the successful performance of it, that tests the qualifications; for which reason, as well as to prevent persons from engaging nominally in an occupation for the sake of the vote, it would be

---

[148] *Ibid.*, 18. Cf. *On Liberty*: "The 'people' who exercise the power, are not always the same people with those over whom it is exercised; and the 'self-government' spoken of, is not the government of each by himself, but of each by all the rest" (12).
[149] *Representative Government*, 200.

proper to require that the occupation should have been persevered in for some length of time (say three years).[150]

But though these means to a morally acceptable franchise might be technically practicable, Mill saw that they were unacceptable in England in his time. And he was not sure that they could have passed the most severe test to which he ever subjected his opinions – the approval of Harriet. In the *Autobiography* he sums up his position:

all who desire any sort of inequality in the electoral vote, [desire] it in favour of property and not of intelligence or knowledge. If [plural voting] ever overcomes the strong feeling which exists against it, this will only be after the establishment of a systematic National Education by which the various grades of politically valuable acquirement may be accurately defined and authenticated. Without this it will always remain liable to strong, possibly conclusive, objections; and with this, it would perhaps not be needed.[151]

By the time Mill wrote this, however, his interest in plural voting had lessened, for he had come across a scheme which held much more charm for him, Hare's plan for Personal Representation. Mill's appreciation of the danger of the suppression of minority opinion, indicated in his own experience as well as by de Tocqueville, resulted in modifications of his political as well as his social teachings. That is, it led to the lessons embodied in *Representative Government* as well as in *On Liberty*. In his second review of *Democracy in America* he says: "Now, as ever, the great problem in government is to prevent the strongest from becoming the only power; and repress the natural tendency of the instincts and passions of the ruling body, to sweep away all barriers which are capable of resisting, even for a moment, their own tendencies." [152] Democracy is coming, and the power of the majority will become increasingly tyrannical unless checked. The threat is not that minorities will be violently suppressed, but that they will have no opportunity to give voice, let alone effect, to their opinions. The government of the majority is only an approximation to ideal representative democracy; as the best approximation yet developed, or likely to be developed, it should be put into effect, but not having an absolute utility it should be implemented with such qualifications and modifications as will bring it closer into line with the highest demands of utility.

Mill is constantly reminding his readers that means are only means.

[150] *Ibid.*, 176–7.   [151] *Autobiography*, 180–1. Cf. *Representative Government*, 179.
[152] "Tocqueville," 77.

although when justified by the end, they may be pursued themselves as secondary ends. In the days when he still had hopes of a Radical party, he explained himself thus : "It is utterly false that the Radicals desire organic changes as ends; they desire them as means to other ends, and will be satisfied to renounce them if those ends can be obtained otherwise. To stickle for words and forms instead of substances, is in no case the practice of the English Radicals." [153] Practical results, with utility as the end, are what Mill aims at; the means to the end, in present circumstances, is the giving to every citizen a voice in his own government. "If he is compelled to pay, if he may be compelled to fight, if he is required implicitly to obey, he should be legally entitled to be told what for; to have his consent asked, and his opinion counted at its worth, though not at more than its worth." [154] As every man partakes in the national interest, so every man should be consulted in the determination of that interest.

But, as Mill argues in *Representative Government* (again echoing Coleridge), the "idea" of democracy is far removed from its present manifestations :

The pure idea of democracy, according to its definition, is the government of the whole people by the whole people, equally represented. Democracy as commonly conceived and hitherto practised, is the government of the whole people by a mere majority of the people, exclusively represented. The former is synonymous with the equality of all citizens; the latter, strangely confounded with it, is a government of privilege, in favour of the numerical majority, who alone possess practically any voice in the State. This is the inevitable consequence of the manner in which the votes are now taken, to the complete disenfranchisement of minorities.[155]

The voice of the people commonly heard in a democracy is not the voice of the whole population, but merely that of the majority, or more likely that of "any large number having a strong feeling on the subject." [156] Actually government by majority is a delusion in itself, for it compounds exclusiveness.

A Parliament may be obtained by universal suffrage, which may represent the opinions of a bare majority of the people; and again, when this Parliament

[153] "Parties and the Ministry," *London and Westminster Review*, 6 & 28 (1837), 22–3. Cf. "Notes on the Newspapers," 453–4; "Walsh's Contemporary History," *London and Westminster Review*, 3 & 25 (1836), 290.

[154] *Representative Government*, 167.

[155] *Ibid.*, 132. Cf. *Thoughts on Parliamentary Reform*, 18.

[156] "Whewell on Moral Philosophy," 498. Cf. *On Liberty*, 12.

proceeds to legislate, it may pass laws by a bare majority of itself. The governing body, reduced by this double process of elimination, may represent the opinions or wishes of little more than a fourth of the population. If numbers are to be the rule, a third of the people ought not indeed to have two-thirds of the representation, but every third of the people is entitled to a third of the representation; and though there is no possibility of securing this with any degree of precision, it is better to make some approach to it than to ignore minorities altogether.[157]

Even disregarding this objection, majority rule does not give effect to the true interests of the people; the interest of the majority, which may be at variance in many ways with the total interest, carries all befor it.[158] Suppose, for example, a situation which appears to be unavoidable, "a minority of skilled labourers, a majority of unskilled: the experience of many Trade Unions, unless they are greatly calumniated, justifies the apprehension that equality of earnings might be imposed as an obligation, and that piecework, payment by the hour, and all practices which enable superior industry or abilities to gain a superior reward, might be put down."[159] Furthermore, the course followed by the majority, in their eyes conformable at least to their own interest, if not to the community's as a whole, is often wrong.

It is not what their interest is, but what they suppose it to be, that is the important consideration with respect to their conduct: and it is quite conclusive against any theory of government, that it assumes the numerical majority to do habitually what is never done, nor expected to be done, save in very exceptional cases, by any other depositaries of power – namely, to direct their conduct by their real ultimate interest, in opposition to their immediate and apparent interest.[160]

The minorities, of course, are no more capable than the majority of discerning the true interest of the community, but the inclusion of their opinions in the national councils will at least ensure attention to a wider range of interests, and the mere opposition presented may result in reconsideration of policies, and hence in better legislation.

Political participation, moreover, as an instrument of national education, broadens the horizons of the individual, and takes him away from the narrow bounds of personal business.[161] The optimum state can be

[157] *Thoughts on Parliamentary Reform*, 29.
[158] See *Representative Government*, 117–8, 126–8; "Bentham," 379.
[159] *Representative Government*, 120–1; the phrase "payment by the hour" was added in the 2nd ed. (1861). [160] *Ibid.*, 121–2.
[161] See *ibid.*, 59–69; *Thoughts on Parliamentary Reform*, 17–8.

maintained, in fact reached, only by optimum citizens, men informed on all facets of social life and vitally concerned with legislation. The only real way of inducing interest in political affairs is to give a man "something to do for the public, whether as a vestryman, a juryman, or an elector"; in this way "his ideas and feelings" are taken out of the "narrow circle" of self-seeking.[162] The nearest way to hand is to make him an elector, provided he feels that his vote is effective. Thus he may become 'self-*protecting*" and "self-*dependent*," able to rely on himself and his fellow citizens for results, rather than upon action by an impersonal government.[163]

The scientific study of history reveals, Mill argues, that the form in which representative democracy is developing will result in a tyranny of the majority; utility demands that this result be checked; Mill looks for means. There must be an institutional embodiment of the voice of minorities, "a great social support for opinions and sentiments different from those of the mass."[164] But in spite of long and careful consideration of minority representation, Mill could not himself find a satisfactory answer. In *Thoughts on Parliamentary Reform* (28–32), he mentions two possible ways of enfranchising large minorities, both of them involving three-member constituencies. The first, embodied in the Reform Bill presented by Lord Aberdeen, provides that each elector should be allowed to vote for only two candidates, or perhaps one, although three are to be elected. The second plan, preferred by Mill, is that put forward by J. G. Marshall; under its provisions the elector has three votes, but may give them all to the same candidate. Apart from providing for the expression of minority opinion, this system has the advantage of showing not mere preference, but degree of preference.

But, as already intimated, these plans became unimportant for Mill when he came upon Thomas Hare's scheme for Personal Representation, in which he developed, as Dicey says, a "childlike trust."[165] The relevant passage in the *Autobiography* glows with enthusiasm:

[162] "Tocqueville," 25. [163] *Representative Government, 55.*
[164] "Tocqueville," 73. Cf. "Bentham," 380.
[165] A. V. Dicey, *Lectures on the Relation between Law and Public Opinion* (London, 1905), 425. Dicey's comment at this point is interesting: "The democrat who holds that the majority ought to rule, but that wisdom is to be found mainly in minorities, and that every possible means ought to be adopted to prevent the ignorant majority from abusing its power, has retreated a good way from the clear, the confident, and the dogmatic Radicalism of 1830." "Retreated" might well read "advanced."

I saw in this great practical and philosophical idea, the greatest improvement of which the system of representative government is susceptible; an improvement which, in the most felicitous manner, exactly meets and cures the grand, and what before seemed the inherent, defect of the representative system; that of giving to a numerical majority all power, instead of only a power proportional to its numbers, and enabling the strongest party to exclude all weaker parties from making their opinions heard in the assembly of the nation, except through such opportunity as may be given to them by the accidentally unequal distribution of opinions in different localities. To these great evils nothing more than very imperfect palliatives had seemed possible; but Mr. Hare's system affords a radical cure.[166]

The main outlines of the scheme are easily given.[167] Candidates need not stand for a specific constituency, and so voters may cast their ballots for any candidate. Provision is made for preferential voting, and when a candidate has received sufficient votes to ensure his election, no more votes are counted in his favour, the candidates whose names appear second, on ballots giving elected candidates first place, receiving the votes. Under this system, a minority, no matter how scattered, can elect a candidate representing their opinions, provided their numbers are sufficient, that is, provided their voting members constitute a number equal to the number of the eligible voters divided by the number of seats in parliament. Also, those whose votes serve only to build up an unnecessary margin of victory for a popular candidate, and are thus, in Mill's opinion, disenfranchised, will be able to make their proper influence felt in support of another candidate. Another important effect would be the inclusion of a larger number of independent members in parliament, so that the great parties would be forced in another way to broaden their appeal. The legislature then, "instead of being weeded of individual peculiarities and entirely made up of men who simply represent the creed of great political or religious parties, will comprise a large proportion of the most eminent individual minds in the country, placed there, without reference to party, by voters who appreciate their individual eminence."[168] As truckling to party decreases, so the worth of the representatives will in-

---

[166] *Autobiography*, 181. He believed that Hare's plan might make plural voting unnecessary ("Recent Writers on Reform," 85).

[167] Mill's fullest treatment is in *Representative Government*, 139–62 (pp. 154–61 were added in the 2nd ed., and the long footnote, 161n–162n, in the 3rd). See also "Recent Writers on Reform," and the writings by Hare listed in the Bibliography below.

[168] *Autobiography*, 182.

crease, and parliament will become a true soundingboard for the opinions of the nation.

In the *Autobiography*, it should be noted, Mill commends Hare's plan as "practical," in accordance with his usual demand for attention to the existing state of society. When the scheme was first made public by Hare many objected to it on the grounds of its impracticability, and Mill set to work with Hare and others to meet the objections by argument and revision. At last Mill was satisfied with the details – complex as they appear to some, he defends them as simple [169] – and he continued, from 1860 through his public life, to advocate the plan's inclusion in reform measures. Its great attraction for him is explained by reference to his social philosophy : the plan, while unusual at first glance, is not fundamentally opposed to the existing system in Great Britain, is a valid means to a happier society, and is designed to frustrate effectively one of the most disturbing social tendencies, the increasing dominance of majority opinion.

In all states of civilization, and in all representative systems, personal representation would be a great improvement; but, at present, political power is passing, or is supposed to be in danger of passing, to the side of the most numerous and poorest class. Against this class predominance, as against all other class predominance, the personal representation of every voter, and therefore the full representation of every minority, is the most valuable of all protections. Those who are anxious for safeguards against the evils they expect from democracy should not neglect the safeguard which is to be found in the principles of democracy itself. It is not only the best safeguard, but the surest and most lasting, because it combats the evils and dangers of false democracy by means of the true, and because every democrat who understands his own principles must see and feel its strict and impartial justice.[170]

Mill's change of attitude concerning the secret ballot, one of the great political issues of the nineteenth century, and one of the main planks in the platform of the Philosophic Radicals, may be used to illustrate the sort of criticism to which he subjected means. Originally Mill was as strong an advocate of the ballot as any of his associates, accepting fully his father's argument, expressed in the *Westminster Review*.[171] James Mill argues that rational conviction is replacing force and fraud in political affairs, and that the ballot is the best way of forwarding

[169] See *ibid.*; *Amberley Papers*, I, 372; "Recent Writers on Reform," 79.
[170] *Speech on Personal Representation* (London, 1867), 16.
[171] *Westminster Review*, 13 (1830), 1–39.

this process. It is a great "security," and also a powerful moral force, and, although a moderate reform, makes many other reforms unnecessary. John Mill held so firmly by this measure that in 1835 he argued that the Reform Bill had brought no real improvement because it was not accompanied by the secret ballot.[172] The high hopes of the Radicals were based on the conjunction of the two reforms, and the one without the other proved, as it must have, relatively useless. Pressure could still be exerted on the voter, and so sinister interests could work their will as before, only varying the extent of their bribery and intimidation. So Mill thought until 1835, but thereafter he gradually changed his opinion.[173]

The basic consideration is given in his *Thoughts on Parliamentary Reform*, where he explains that the ballot is, like all other means, not a good in itself, and therefore should be recommended only under certain conditions.

The operation of the Ballot is, that it enables the voter to give full effect to his own private preferences, whether selfish or disinterested, under no inducement to defer to the opinions or wishes of others, except as these may influence his own. It follows, and the friends of the ballot have always said, that secrecy is desirable, in cases in which the motives acting on the voter through the will of others are likely to mislead him, while, if left to his own preferences, he would vote as he ought. It equally follows, and is also the doctrine of the friends of the ballot, that when the voter's own preferences are apt to lead him wrong, but the feeling of responsibility to others may keep him right, not secrecy, but publicity, should be the rule.[174]

James Mill, from whose *History of India* his son borrows the basis of this argument, argued that force and fraud were ceasing to be a force in politics; by 1858, at least, John believed that they were no longer important enough to warrant the introduction of the ballot to counteract them. He writes to Judge Chapman:

. . . I hold that the case is now reversed, and that an elector gives a rascally vote incalculably oftener from his own personal or class interest, or some

---

[172] As background, see "Postscript," 270–7; "Parliamentary Proceedings of the Session," 512–24.

[173] Harriet changed her mind before he did, and probably influenced him (*Autobiography*, 180). In a typically unselfconscious reporting of a dream to Harriet, he writes (13/1/55): "I was disputing about the ballot with Calhoun, the American, of whom in some strange way I had become the brother – & when I said that the ballot was no longer necessary, he answered 'it will not be necessary in heaven, but it will always be necessary on earth.'" (MS, Yale.)

[174] *Thoughts on Parliamentary Reform*, 32–3.

mean feeling of his own, the influence of which would be greater under secret suffrage, than from the prompting of some other person who has power over him. Coercive influences have vastly abated, and are abating every day : a landlord cannot now afford to part with a good tenant because he is not politically subservient. . . .[175]

The working of social laws has done what the ballot promised to do and, designed for a task no longer necessary, it should not be adopted. "At every election the votes are more and more the voters' own. It is their minds, far more than their personal circumstances, that now require to be emancipated." [176] And the casting of a vote in public, openly declaring the state of one's desires and will, is a potent instrument in the emancipation of men's minds.[177] So the secret ballot, originally justified as a means towards the utilitarian end, has been through the operation of social tendencies deprived of its effectiveness, and under the new circumstances it cannot be justified by the end. In fact, it works against that end, and so should not be adopted.[178]

The means of selection are intimately connected with consideration of whom should be selected. The true interest of the people should be expressed and implemented by the government : what sort of men are most likely and most able to understand and implement measures promoting the general interest? The answer for Mill is, of course, the wisest and best in the community. Like the elector, the candidate should not be looking to his own advantage, but the good of the community. Such perfection is ideal, however, and so it is necessary that the elected representatives be responsible to the electors. Here Mill reflects again the beliefs

[175] *Letters* (ed. Elliot), I, 209 (8/7/58).

[176] *Thoughts on Parliamentary Reform*, 36. The substance of Mill's objections may be found here; in "Public Responsibility and the Ballot," *Reader*, 5 (1865); and in chap. x of *Representative Government* (where he quotes his argument in *Thoughts on Parliamentary Reform*).

[177] The celebrated passage which was placed before him by electors during his election address occurs in the passage in *Thoughts on Parliamentary Reform* (44), in which he is discussing the moral consequences of the secret ballot. "There are but few points in which the English, as a people, are entitled to the moral pre-eminence with which they are accustomed to compliment themselves at the expense of other nations : but, of these points, perhaps the one of greatest importance is, that the higher classes do not lie, and the lower, though mostly habitual liars, are ashamed of lying."

[178] In *Thoughts on Parliamentary Reform* (44–6) he goes on, characteristically, to argue the merits of allowing votes to be cast at home, on the grounds of practicability and value.

of his father and Bentham, although his conception of "securities" is far removed from theirs. With them he advocates the claims of the middle class to be leaders of opinion, and therefore to provide the best representatives, but he has a clearer notion of the sort of man who can be elected in an increasingly democratic society.

One who desires to be a legislator should rest on recommendations not addressing themselves to a class, but to feelings and interests common to all classes: the simple as well as the learned should feel him to be their representative; otherwise his words and thoughts will do worse than even fall dead on their minds; will be apt to rouse in them a sentiment of opposition.[179]

Bentham relied on "annuality" of election as the main check on representatives' sinister interests, but Mill, admitting the sense of Bentham's suggestion, once again argues that the course of events has made his argument inappropriate. The representative is no longer isolated from his constituents after election, because the increasing ease of communication, especially through the press, keeps him always before their eyes. Now, Mill says, five years is none too long to establish a sense of continuity, prevent damaging fluctuations in policy, and allow the tendency towards subservience to public opinion (a danger the reverse of what Bentham feared) to be counteracted.[180] A man may act boldly in the correct cause, with some hope of being justified by the event before he can be removed from office by hostile public opinion.[181]

One of the greatest problems which exercised Mill's mind is involved in this discussion. Only a government responsible to the people can be entrusted with the control of public affairs, but a government carried on with the full accord of the people, reflecting their immediate aims and desires, is certain to fall short of excellence.[182] Social progress must be led by the best members of the community, those who by definition do not share the outlook of the average member. It is the duty of the best to offer themselves as public servants; if they do, no great disaster can befall the community: "the aberrations even of a ruling multitude are only fatal when the better instructed have not the virtue or the courage to front them boldly."[183] They must leaven the mass, or, to change the

179 *Ibid.*, 24n.

180 In "Tocqueville" (33) Mill points to the dangers of the American system.

181 See *Representative Government*, chap. xi, *passim*.   182 See, e.g., *ibid.*, 121–2.

183 "Contest in America," *Dissertations and Discussions*, III, 185. Cf. "Endowments," 625–6; "The French Revolution of 1848," 362.

metaphor, they must take the first steps on new roads, speed up and spur on the laggards, and block off false paths. Mill expresses himself strongly on the subject to John Chapman (who has offended him – or Harriet) on his receipt of Chapman's prospectus for a radical review:

by the statement that 'reforms to be salutory must be graduated to the average moral & intellectual growth of society' I presume is meant (though I am by no means sure about the meaning if any) that the measures of a government ought never to be in advance of the average intellect and virtue of the people – according to which doctrine there would neither have been the Reformation, the Commonwealth, nor the Revolution of 1688, & the stupidity & habitual indifference of the mass of mankind would bear down by its own weight all the efforts of the more intelligent & active minded few.[184]

He conceived his own task in the House of Commons along these lines, and planned to expend what reputation he had in the support of unpopular but beneficial measures, such as female suffrage and personal representation. He praised Gladstone, according to Morley, for exhibiting the proper spirit in leadership: " 'If ever there was a statesman' said Mill, about this time [1864], 'in whom the spirit of improvement is incarnate, and in whose career as a minister the characteristic feature has been to seek out things that require or admit of improvement, instead of waiting to be pressed or driven to do them, Mr. Gladstone deserves that signal honour.' " [185]

In the days when he hoped for a Radical Party with strong and capable leadership Mill's belief appears as exhortation:

[184] Mill-Taylor Collection, IX, #1 (9/6/51), ff.2v,3r. Cf. "Notes on the Newspapers," 162.

[185] John Morley, Life of Gladstone, II, 123. Cf. Mill's description of the qualities required in a leader of the Radical Party: "the man we want is the one who can recommend himself not solely by the ability to talk, nor even merely to think, but by the ability to do. We want a man who can wrestle with actual difficulties and subdue them; who can read 'the aim of selfish natures hard to be spelled,' can bend men's stubborn minds to things against which their passions rise in arms; who needs not sacrifice justice to policy, or policy to justice, but who knows how to do justice, and attain the ends of policy by it. We want a man who can sustain himself where the consequences of every error he commits, instead of being left to accumulate for posterity, come back to him the next week or the next month, and throw themselves in his path; where no voting of bystanders can make that success, which is, in truth, failure; where there is a real thing to be done, a positive result to be brought about, to have accomplished which is success – not to have accomplished it, defeat." ("Lord Durham's Return," 243.) Mill mentions as types Washington and Wellington, but it is small wonder that his hopes were not realized. One of Carlyle's "Heroes" at the very least was required.

The people are always eager to follow good guidance, and the sole danger is of their not finding it. Intelligence abounds among the English democracy; but it is not cultivated intelligence. It is mostly of the self-educated sort; and this is commonly more microscopic than comprehensive: it sees one or a few things strongly, and others not at all; it is the parent of narrowness and fanaticism. The coming changes, for come they must and will, are fraught with hope in any case, but also with peril, unless there can be found to lead the van of opinion, to place themselves in the front rank of the popular party, a section of the wisest and most energetic of the instructed classes; men whose education and pursuits have given them a wider range of ideas, and whose leisure has admitted of more systematic study, than will, for a long time to come, be possible, save in occasional rare instances, to those who labour with their hands.[186]

Mill, for polemical reasons, is here pointing to the herd instinct. This passage, written in 1834, shows signs of the Saint-Simonian influence in its emphasis on the necessity of following leaders. In other writings of the same period Mill mentions organization of leadership as a main requisite, along with the vesting of an acknowledged authority in such leadership. For example, he argues, as has been shown, that the complexity of political problems precludes their understanding except by those who have specially studied them: "The multitude will never believe these truths, until tendered to them from an authority in which they have as unlimited confidence as they have in the unanimous voice of astronomers on a question of astronomy."[187] Soon, however, Mill came to see not only that unanimity on political subjects is unlikely, but also that it is undesirable. Moreover, he could no longer, in view of his attitude to moral development, admit the value of sheep-like obedience. Truths merely accepted and not understood are useless; it is better to be wrong for a good reason than to be right for no reason.

Still, then, the problem remains: intelligent and moral leadership is necessary, but difficult to attain in a representative democracy. How can average opinion select better-than-average leaders? The prospect is not a happy one, for even if average opinion is expected only to recognize the best policy, not to produce it, hope will be frustrated.[188] Only the

[186] "Notes on the Newspapers," 164. Cf. "Parties and the Ministry," 24–5; "Tocqueville," 81; "De Tocqueville on Democracy in America" (1835), 111n–112n (reprinted in "Appendix," 473–4); "Guizot's Essays and Lectures on History," 269–70.
[187] "De Tocqueville on Democracy in America" (1835), 111n (reprinted in "Appendix," 474). Cf. the passages mentioned in the previous note.
[188] Mill mentions this hope in "The Rationale of Representation," 348–9 ("Appendix," 470).

best and wisest can know what is best and wisest. Mill being far more interested in practical utility than in theoretical perfection looks for a compromise. His statement of the problem is straightforward and clear:

the grand difficulty in politics will for a long time be, how best to conciliate the two great elements on which good government depends; to combine the greatest amount of the advantage derived from the independent judgment of a specially instructed Few, with the greatest degree of the security for rectitude of purpose derived from rendering those Few responsible to the Many.[189]

The compromise solution he recommends has roots as far back as his adolescence. One of the main tenets of Bentham as well as of the Saint-Simonians and Comte was the need for expert guidance in political affairs. The political technician is as important for social advance as the industrial technician, and unskilled, untrained, and possibly ignorant politicians cannot be entrusted with the detailed care of national affairs.[190] These ideas took deep hold in Mill's mind and, though he rejected the French thinkers' political absolutism, he always appreciated the danger of democracy's falling under the control of incompetent bunglers. He therefore reconsidered the common view of the functions of an elected assembly.

He insisted, first of all, that elected members are not mere delegates; they must be free to act according to their own interpretation of the general interest, and not according to that of their constituents. No pledges should be given by or asked of candidates, who should be chosen not for their willingness to represent local issues and limited interests, but for their ability to serve the general good. That this proposal is not totally impracticable Mill proved by his own election for Westminster in 1865, but he knew its scope to be limited, for its application demands a moral attitude throughout the country which would in itself render the measure unnecessary.

Mill's other proposal is more sweeping, and much more radical. What, he asks, is the function which parliament is expected to perform? Can it perform that function? If not, what other body could perform it? And, finally, what function can an elected assembly perform? Parliament is expected to legislate for the country, to promote the general interest. To do so, Mill argues, remembering Bentham and Plato as well as Saint-

[189] *Ibid.*, 348 ("Appendix," 469). Cf. "De Tocqueville on Democracy in America" (1835), 110 ("Appendix," 471); *Representative Government*, 105–7.
[190] "Recent Writers on Reform," 55–6.

Simon and Comte, it must legislate according to a plan formulated in terms of the end desired, with an eye to practicability.[191] Legislation must, in fact, be developed by the Scientist's method outlined in the *Logic*.[192] Obviously no tyro can perform such duties, for special training is needed. Mill says, therefore:

In proportion as it has been better understood what legislation is, and the unity of plan as well as maturity of deliberation which are essential to it, thinking persons have asked themselves the question – Whether a popular body of 658 or 459 members, not specially educated for the purpose, having served no apprenticeship, and undergone no examination, and who transact business in the forms and very much in the spirit of a debating society, can have as its peculiarly appropriate office to make laws? Whether that is not a work certain to be spoiled by putting such a superfluous number of hands upon it? Whether it is not essentially a business for one, or a very small number, of most carefully prepared and selected individuals? [193]

The questions are rhetorical. Mill proposes, therefore, a "Legislative Commission" or "Commission of Codification," which could be constituted to revise and codify the laws of the nation according to a rational plan (the influence of Bentham is manifest), and which would then continue in existence, drawing up laws as required by parliament at parliament's request, and submitting them for parliament's approval or rejection without amendment. The Commission would be appointed by the Crown, its members being chosen for their special abilities and knowledge, to serve for five years, with the possibility of reappointment. This body would have no power to enact laws, but its existence would ensure that only proper laws could be enacted. As the English national habit of mind is to reject all innovations, no matter how salutary, which entail modifications both in form and substance, but not to reject adaptations of existing institutions, the House of Lords, which is dispensable in its present form, could be altered to perform the new function. Possibly, if life peers were created to design legislation, the Government would allow them to frame all its bills, private members would follow the Government's lead, and so gradually the reform would be realized without any

[191] See "Tocqueville," 34-5, and "Grote's Plato," 371-2, where Mill says that Plato forgot that rulers are not infallible, and that there is intelligence in the multitude.
[192] Cf. "De Tocqueville on Democracy in America" (1835), 111n ("Appendix," 473).
[193] "Duveyrier's Political Views of French Affairs," 465.

dislocation or disruption of the present machinery.[194] After his reading of Coleridge, Mill saw that institutions are organic, and therefore not to be thoughtlessly uprooted in conformity with abstract plans. His is a genuine attempt to combine what he held to be Bentham's merits with Coleridge's; he looked for validity in institutions and also subjected them to searching criticism which would reveal their inutility if they had outlived their original functions.[195] So, while disapproving of both the principle and practice of the House of Lords, he still attempted to find a new function involving a mere adjustment in the existing machinery.

Another means of ensuring that capable men would be available for public service won Mill's energetic support: the reform of the Civil Service through the institution of competitive examinations. His experience at the India House, in addition to his growing prestige as a thinker, made him one of those whose opinion was solicited when the measure was proposed in 1854. Sir Charles Trevelyan asked him for his views, and when Mill complied, Trevelyan wrote back to say of his letter: *"It is the best we have received*, which is no mean compliment." [196] Mill's earnest and careful advocacy of the measure is best seen in his recommendations to the Government, but is found in shorter form in *Representative Government*.[197] The proposed reform, he argues, vindicates the existing social powers by showing that they have no desire to maintain their present pre-eminence without merit; it promises that the country will have the best men for the work; its implementation will encourage the cultivation of the most important branches of mental effort, and will institute a "great and salutary moral revolution, descending to the minds of almost the lowest classes," by ensuring that the Government – "to people in general the most trusted exponent of the ways of the world" – will reward merit and ability. Objections, such as that examinations would admit low persons into government service, and that patronage would be taken from the Crown and disposed on the Commissioners, are briefly dismissed by Mill. He considers at greater length the objection that no examination can test more than a part of the qualities required

---

[194] *Representative Government*, chap. v. 102, and *passim.* Cf. *Autobiography*, 185–6.

[195] See, as well as "Bentham" and "Coleridge," *Representative Government*, 92, and "Parliamentary Proceedings of the Session," 519.

[196] Mill-Taylor Collection, I, #27 (11/5/54), and #28 (24/5/54).

[197] "Papers relating to the Re-organization of the Civil Service," 92–8; *Representative Government*, chap. xiv, *passim*.

in a public servant. The examination, he argues, must be as widely based as possible, taking into account practical knowledge of the work to be performed as well as merely theoretical knowledge. Above all, "it ought to be remembered, that the worth of the examination is as a test of powers and habits of mind, still more than of acquirements; for talent and application will be sure to acquire the positive knowledge found necessary for their profession, but acquirements may be little more than a dead weight if there is not ability to turn them to use." [198] The practicability of the measure is obvious, and while it is designed in accordance with the increasing growth of social equality, it would offset one of the most dangerous potentials of such levelling. The opening of the Civil Service to universal competition, he concludes elsewhere, is a wonderful instance of "unsought concession to the democratic principle" in its "best sense" which "a reformer had imagined even in his dreams." [199]

Provision having been made for the formulation of laws, and the improved implementation of policies through a better government service, the proper functions of the House of Commons can be examined. (Mill clearly has British institutions in mind.) What, first of all, is its relation to the Executive power? A numerous body, Mill holds, is no more fitted to administer laws than to design them. It should, because it is the representative body, select the Executive, for its knowledge is greater than that of the body of electors, and is better able to judge of ability and good will[200] (what Bentham called "appropriate aptitude"). The Executive should, in addition to administering the laws, appoint judges and subordinate officials of all sorts. The body of the House would, through its power to remove from office, have as its task the supervision and control of the Executive. Furthermore, it should publicize the actions of the Executive, and when necessary censure its activities.

The general functions of the House are related to this last task: it should be the country's "Committee on Grievances" and "Congress of Opinions." Members, Mill held – and his practice supported his precept – should accept petitions from their constituents, even if they do not sympathize with the object in view, and even if they are obliged by their conception of the general good to vote against the measure. All shades of opinion in the country should be able to find spokesmen in parliament,

[198] "Papers relating to the Re-organization of the Civil Service," 95.

[199] "Diary" (20/3/54), in *Letters* (ed. Elliot), II, 380. Cf. Morley, *Life of Gladstone*, I, 509.   [200] "Parliamentary Proceedings of the Session," 519.

and all public issues should be discussed fully and from all points of view. These functions a numerous assembly is particularly qualified to perform. In addition, the House of Commons must possess control over expenditures, to guarantee the people's ultimate control over the Executive. The final function of the assembly is the very important one already indicated, the approval or rejection of all legislation put before it by the Legislative Commission at the request either of the Government or of private members.[201]

Throughout the discussion, it will be noted, Mill is giving consideration to practicability in terms of national habits and social trends, and also to the conduciveness of the means to the ultimate end.[202] He never allows, as Bentham sometimes did, his own ingenuity to control his schemes; simplicity and neatness of argument are sacrificed whenever necessary to the exigencies of the situation, and an attempt is made to cover all possibilities. Mill is a gradualist, never asking change to be other than gentle, though as rapid as possible. Violence leads, he thinks, only to the confusion and turmoil which preclude calm and rational choice.[203] One of the best defences of his faith in representative institutions is worthy of quotation in spite of its length; it occurs in his review of Carlyle's *French Revolution*, and begins with Mill taking up Carlyle's remark that constitutions and forms of government really can do little to help man.

Be it admitted once for all, that no form of government will enable you, as our author has elsewhere said, 'given a world of rogues, to produce an honesty by their united action;' nor when a people are wholly without faith either in man or creed, has any representative constitution a charm to render them governable well, or even governable at all. On the other hand, Mr Carlyle must no less admit, that when a nation *has* faith in any men, or any set of principles, representative institutions furnish the only regular and peaceable mode in which that faith can quietly declare itself, and those men, or those principles,

[201] The fullest discussion of these problems is in *Representative Government*, especially 94, 97, 100–1, and 104–5. For other comments see "Tocqueville," 82–3; "The French Revolution of 1848," 365–6, 407–8, 410; "Duveyrier's Political Views of French Affairs," 465–6.

[202] See *Representative Government*, 54; "Rationale of Representation," 347 ("Appendix," 167–8).

[203] "Notes on the Newspapers," 311–2. Cf. "The Currency Juggle," *Works*, IV, 191–2; "State of Politics in 1836," *London and Westminster Review*, 3 & 25 (1836), 271; "The Close of the Session," *Monthly Repository*, 8 (1834), 607.

obtain the predominance. It is surely no trifling matter to have a legalized means whereby the guidance will always be in the hands of the Acknowledged Wisest, who, if not always the really wisest, are at least those whose wisdom, such as it may be, is the most available for the purpose. Doubtless it is the natural law of representative governments that the power is shared, in varying proportions, between the really skilfullest and the skilfullest quacks; with a tendency, in easy times, towards the preponderance of the quacks, in the 'times which try men's souls,' towards that of the true men. Improvements enough may be expected as mankind improve, but that the best and wisest shall always be accounted such, *that* we need not expect; because the quack can always steal, and vend for his own profit, as much of the good ware as is marketable. But is not all this to the full as likely to happen in every other kind of government as in a representative one? with these differences in favour of representative government, which will be found perhaps to be its only real and universal pre-eminence: That it alone is government by consent – government by mutual compromise and compact; while all others are, in one form or another, governments by constraint: That it alone proceeds by quiet muster of opposing strengths, when that which is really weakest sees itself to be such, and peaceably gives way; a benefit never yet realized but in countries inured to a representative government; elsewhere nothing but actual blows can show who is strongest, and every great dissension of opinion must break out into a civil war.[204]

So Mill is still an advocate of representative democracy, as were his father and Bentham, but his modifications are more significant than his allegiance; many men are democrats, but few are thoughtful and careful democrats. The difference between Mill and his mentors appears sharply when reference is made again to a remark of Bentham's: "In truth, representation requires only four things to be perfect – Secrecy, Annuality, Equality, Universality."[205] John Mill eventually modifies or rejects all these provisions.[206] Secrecy gives way to publicity of vote, one-year terms to five-year, equality of voters to plural voting, and universality, which is retained as an ideal, is postponed until the electorate can be properly educated.

[204] "Carlyle's French Revolution," 49. The belief that the best men are called forth in critical times Mill found in de Tocqueville; earlier he had held, with Bentham, that American Presidents are always great men. The explanation given here is the best he can manage in the face of further knowledge.

[205] Bentham, *Works*, X, 587.

[206] Assuming that Bentham intends equality of voters (which he maintained) and not equality of electoral districts, which Mill advocated. James Mill was more cautious than Bentham about the immediate practicability of universal suffrage.

Socialism

As Mill includes politics within sociological studies, questions about political institutions and policies must ultimately be determined by attitudes towards social organization, and related to economic policies. Considerable controversy has arisen over Mill's views of the area where these disciplines meld. He says, in the *Autobiography* (162), that his and Harriet's "ideal of ultimate improvement" would place them "decidedly under the general designation of Socialists." Again (133–4), he describes himself as adhering to a "qualified Socialism"; but his negative approach to the question of government activity – asking, that is, where and when the state may interfere with the individual – puts the "qualified" in a stronger light than the "Socialism." One need not go so far as R. P. Anschutz, who remarks that if Mill's statement concerning the socialist trend of his thought "is examined at all closely, it is plainly an incredible statement," [207] but it does need close examination.

The puzzle is really more a misunderstanding. In this area definitions and distinctions were less clear in Mill's time than they are now, and all kinds of combination and co-operation were described as "Communist" and "Socialist" without (as is often now the case) any intention of confusion. Mill does not use the terms in a way now defensible, but he clearly distinguishes between two types of socialism, and rejects one while approving the other. As his remarks on government indicate, he has no use for the authoritarian desire for efficiency and order through centralization. So he repudiates state socialism. He has little sympathy for those socialists, "more a product of the Continent than of Great Britain," who "may be called the revolutionary Socialists," and who propose to themselves a bold stroke. "Their scheme is the management of the whole productive resources of the country by one central authority, the general government." [208]

On the other hand, his approval goes to such socialist schemes as depend on voluntary organization in small communities, and which look to a national application of their principles only through the self-multiplication of the units.[209] In his *Principles of Political Economy* he defines socialism in what he terms a larger, or Continental sense, not as neces-

[207] *Philosophy of J. S. Mill*, 31.
[208] "Chapters on Socialism," 737, where the other type is also discussed.
[209] *Ibid.*, 746.

sarily implying a total system of equitable rewards, or the abolition of private property, but as meaning "any system which requires that the land and the instruments of production should be the property, not of individuals, but of communities or associations, or of the government." [210] This definition does not square with the other, and Mill's attention to Continental (mainly French) thinkers leads him to look for the sources of both types of socialism outside Britain. To search through the historical and verbal confusion here is interesting and valuable, but not important in determining the main lines of Mill's thought. One point clearly emerges, which will be taken up later: Mill obviously excludes from his socialism the arrogation by the state of private property.

His approach to the question of socialism is, in fact, perhaps the best example of his sociological principles and procedures. All questions must be decided through reference to ethics, and to experience, human nature, and social tendencies. Utility is obviously the main consideration; as early as 1826 he writes: "The end of property, as of all other human institutions, is, or ought to be, no other than the general good." [211] At that time, of course, he viewed the *laissez-faire* policy as the one best suited to the general interest, but the justification allowed for later revision when he became convinced of historical and cultural relativity; since forms of property control and ownership are relative to the general good, they may be altered in accordance with the particular needs of a society. [212] For his time and place, Mill sees the ethical end, which is a way of life, as including equality as a part of itself, not as a separate and abstract metaphysical right. [213] Each person counts for one in the happiness equation; the happiness of every person must be considered when attempts are made to further the general happiness. And although the ingredients of happiness are too many and various to be isolated and mechanically sought after, and their interdependence defeats any separate attack on particular obstructions, one obstacle is so important as to justify direct attack, for it rules out general happiness. That obstacle is poverty. Against it human ingenuity is powerful and, in so far as poverty is equated with suffering, it can be triumphant. [214] While this ideal is being approached, a levelling up can be attempted, so that each person shall at least be free from

[210] *Principles of Political Economy*, II, 203 (II, i, 2), added in the 2nd ed.
[211] "The Game Laws," *Westminster Review*, 5 (1826), 9.
[212] See "Chapters on Socialism," 749ff.
[213] See "The French Revolution of 1848," 395.   [214] *Utilitarianism*, 21.

slavery to elementary needs. No one can be a true citizen who cannot lift his head from his incessant labour, for citizenship demands a striving after the higher perfection dictated by what Matthew Arnold calls "Culture." [215]

The ideal socialist morality, voluntarily followed, is ultimately identical with the utilitarian morality, for self-denying service is the end of each, and the end which paradoxically is most self-satisfying. Each should labour for all without thought of personal gain over others, for the good of the whole is the supreme end. Ideally, "the moral claim of any one in regard to the provision for his personal wants, is not a question of *quid pro quo* in respect of his co-operation, but of how much the circumstances of society permit to be assigned to him, consistently with the just claims of others." [216]

Thus far the utility principle. What of the laws resulting from sociological investigation? The study of history, duly related to the known laws of human nature, shows that social and economic equality is gradually emerging as the product of civilization's growth. Means should therefore be devised by the Scientist in accordance with this development, means validated at each step by the Artist, with his eye always on the overall utility of the resultant policy, and also on its practicability.

The assumption is, of course, that there is something wrong: Mill, with his contemporaries, is questioning the "Condition of England." He admits the accuracy of the socialist criticisms of that condition in several places, one of which will illustrate:

It appears to us that nothing valid can be said against socialism in principle; and that the attempts to assail it, or to defend private property, on the ground of justice, must inevitably fail. The distinction between rich and poor, so slightly connected as it is with merit and demerit, or even with exertion and want of exertion in the individual, is obviously unjust; such a feature could not be put into the rudest imaginings of a perfectly just state of society; the present capricious distribution of the means of life and enjoyment, could only be defended as an admitted imperfection, submitted to as an effect of causes in other respects beneficial. Again, the moral objection to competition, as arming one human being against another, making the good of each depend upon evil to others, making all who have anything to gain or lose, live as in the midst

[215] See Edward Alexander, *Arnold and Mill* (New York, 1965) and my "Mill and Arnold: Liberty and Culture," *Humanities Association Bulletin* (Canada), 24 (1961), 20–32.

[216] *Auguste Comte and Positivism*, 148–9.

of enemies, by no means deserves the disdain with which it is treated by some of the adversaries of socialism. . . .[217]

Justice, an extremely important part of utility, is not then a possible ground for objection to socialism; objections must be based elsewhere, on expedience and practicability.[218] Once this point has been made, the importance of Harriet Taylor in this area of Mill's thought is clearer. As the discussion above has indicated, her influence was important, but not by any means revolutionary. Mill's sympathy with the poor had been evident long before 1848, when the *Principles of Political Economy* first appeared. His alterations for the 2nd and 3rd editions (1849 and 1852) did not result from a change of sympathy, or from abstract considerations. In 1848, the year of revolutions, men with socialist beliefs gained power in Paris for a brief period, and Mill, as he himself says, read more widely on the subject, and observed more carefully the practical effects of socialist schemes and the less visionary plans of some socialist writers.[219] Harriet was as interested as he in the course of events, and contributed largely to the altered discussion of socialism, but the extent of the inconsistencies between the editions has been over-estimated. Given Mill's methodology, which of course does not excuse failure to make his position perfectly plain, the inconsistencies even in phrasing can be understood. The change is simply this: Mill became more convinced of the practicability of certain socialist plans and, as he felt the balance between socialism and free enterprise to be roughly level, he shifted from being an opponent of socialism to being a qualified supporter. The major inconsistencies in phrasing occur in passages which are known, or may reasonably be assumed, to have been suggested by Harriet, and they refer – the point is crucial – to hopes for the future and criticisms of the present, the proper area of operation for the Artist, which as has been shown Mill considered her to be.

For Mill – and the constant revisions of the chapter on "The Probable Futurity of the Labouring Class" that were made by Mill himself show this unequivocally – the qquestion is one of ends and means, and the prac-

---

[217] "Newman's Political Economy," V, 444. Cf. "Coleridge," 456; "Chapters on Socialism," 712–13; *Representative Government*, 126–7; *Principles of Political Economy*, II, 208ff. (II, i, 3).   [218] "The French Revolution of 1848," 388–91.

[219] See *Principles of Political Economy*, II, xcii (Preface to 2nd ed.), xciii (Preface to 3rd ed.), III, 201–3 (II, i, 2), 758–96 (IV, vii); *Autobiography*, 164; *Earlier Letters*, XIII, 740–1 (Nov., 1848).

ticability of means. Here again the developing, de-centralized forms of socialism have advantages over the imposed, centralized forms. "The *practicability* ... of Socialism, on the scale of Mr. Owen's or M. Fourier's villages, admits of no dispute. The attempt to manage the whole production of a nation by one central organization is a totally different matter. . . ." [220]

Mill's change of attitude towards Fourier is typical of the movement of his thought. Writing to Carlyle in 1833, he jeers at this Fourier, who plans to convert the sea into lemonade.[221] Even in 1849 his misspelling of Fourier's name indicates a casual acquaintance with his thought, but by 1852 his enthusiasm has grown, evidently in proportion to his knowledge, and it remained with him, to be expressed equally strongly in his "Chapters on Socialism." [222] His praise is based on two aspects of Fourierism: it is both more conducive to social utility in the fullest sense, and more in tune with the present state of human cultivation, than other socialist schemes. In his words, "the picture of a Fourierist community is both attractive in itself and requires less from common humanity than any other known system of Socialism. . . ." [223] Several aspects are isolated for praise in the *Principles of Political Economy*: the Fourierists do not intend to abolish private property or inheritance (the latter of which Mill is happy to modify drastically); they plan to reward members of their small and voluntary communities not solely for labour, which however will receive 5/12ths of the economic returns. Capital will receive 4/12ths, and talent 3/12ths. The leaders of the community are to be elected, and will not have complete command over the lives of their fellows, who can spend their incomes as they wish, and live in separate accommodation at their pleasure. The main pecuniary benefit looked for is a saving of distributors' and middle-men's fees. Only members of the community are involved in personal or pecuniary risk, and the plans may be implemented on a moderate scale, not causing havoc in existing social arrangements. Mill concludes:

[220] "Chapters on Socialism," 738. Cf. *Principles of Political Economy*, II, 203 (II, i, 3).

[221] *Earlier Letters*, XII, 193 (25/11/33).

[222] *Principles of Political Economy*, II, 211ff. (II, i, 4); "Chapters on Socialism," 719ff., 748.

[223] "Chapters on Socialism," 748. So Mill objects to the Saint-Simonian type of socialism as authoritative; too much paternalism and too much intrusion into private affairs is included in their scheme (*Principles of Political Economy*, II, 211 [II, i, 4]).

Even from so brief an outline, it must be evident that this system does no violence to any of the general laws by which human action, even in the present imperfect state of moral and intellectual cultivation, is influenced; and that it would be extremely rash to pronounce it incapable of success, or unfitted to realize a great part of the hopes founded on it by its partisans.[224]

Mill's approval depends on a recognition of the need for individual freedom, both in joining a scheme and after joining it. Here again lies the superiority of village communities over state organization. But even within the village, it is apparent that more interference with private life might ensue than would be beneficial.[225] One way of avoiding this danger would be voluntary choice in joining like-minded groups, but Mill is not content with this weak argument.[226]

The question really is, as it should be, an open one, and experience will determine how much support should be given to communal schemes, even when one sees their development as conducive to the greatest happiness. For one question always remains to be asked: are human liberty and spontaneity compatible with socialism? It must be asked, for after "the means of subsistence are assured, the next in strength of the personal wants of human beings is liberty; and . . . it increases instead of diminishing in intensity, as the intelligence and moral faculties are more developed."[227] Again no ideological restrictions should be allowed to confine and control the beneficial organization of society. Socialists always compare, Mill points out, their ideal schemes with the present bad state of free enterprise, but capitalism is in a developing, not a stationary condition, and its future course may render it more conducive than socialism to the greatest good of the greatest number. Until, therefore, mankind has greatly improved in understanding of its problems, and in moral awareness, public-spirited men are well advised to expend effort on bettering the existing system.[228] Mill, who had debated at length with the Owenites in 1825, notes in 1834 that Owen helps out his case "by including in his enumeration not only the evils inseparable from the institution itself, but all those which are actually attendant on it in its present form, however easily remediable."[229] "The principle of private

[224] *Principles of Political Economy*, II, 213 (II, i, 4).
[225] See "Chapters on Socialism," 745-6.   [226] See *ibid.*, 746.
[227] *Principles of Political Economy*, II, 208 (II, i, 3).
[228] See *ibid.*, 207-8 (II, i, 3), 214 (II, i, 4); "Chapters on Socialism," 736; "The French Revolution of 1848," 394-5.   [229] "On Punishment," 734.

property," he says in 1848, fourteen years later, "has never yet had a fair trial in any country; and less so, perhaps, in this country than in some others." [230] He is constantly aware, then, that the classic arguments cannot be settled by theoretical discussions. Will men labour for the social good when their own immediate interest appears to conflict with it?[231] Will socialism provide better moral and intellectual education? Will it result in a more rational approach to the population problem, so crucial for Mill?[232] None of these questions can be answered *a priori* from consideration of human nature. Experience must supply the facts. There is time, he argues, "for the question to work itself out on an experimental scale, by actual trial. I believe we shall find that no other test is possible of the practicability or beneficial operation of Socialist arrange- ments. . . ." [233] The government ought to provide loans to experimental communities, even when the chance of failure is obvious. For only through trial can men be persuaded of the impracticability of their schemes, and the poorer classes will always be restless until given an opportunity to control their economic destiny. A national experiment, "by the high moral qualities that would be elicited in the endeavour to make it succeed, and by the instruction that would radiate from its failure, would be an equivalent for the expenditure of many millions on any of the things which are commonly called popular education." [234] Other measures, such as co-operative medical practice and national insurance, Mill advocates as trial measures on a voluntary basis.[235]

When Mill's attitude towards co-operation is put against his attitude to competition, an apparent and much-commented-on inconsistency arises. Again it is explicable – if not excusable to extreme advocates of either position – by reference to his view of social change and his demand for experimental verification. Competition, it would appear, is essential in an economy concerned to increase production, but eventually, Mill be- lieves, a stationary economic state (possible only with a stationary popu- lation) will be reached in which, presumably, productive techniques will be fully utilized.[236] Whether he held that further increases in production

[230] *Principles of Political Economy*, II, 207 (II, i, 3), and III, 986 (Appendix A).
[231] See *ibid.*, II, 204 (II, i, 3); "Chapters on Socialism," 739ff.; "The French Revolu- tion of 1848," 389.   [232] *Principles of Political Economy*, II, 206 (II, i, 3).
[233] "Chapters on Socialism," 736.   [234] "The French Revolution of 1848," 391.
[235] See "Civilisation," 189–90, where co-operation among literary men is also re- commended; *Letters* (ed. Elliot), II, 109 (22/4/68).
[236] *Principles of Political Economy*, III, 752–3 (IV, vi, 1), 890–1 (V, ix, 2).

would be impossible or unnecessary is not clear, but it is clear that he thought that competition in the stationary state would not be desirable. His classic statement is in his *Principles of Political Economy* :

I confess I am not charmed with the ideal of life held out by those who think that the normal state of human beings is that of struggling to get on; that the trampling, crushing, elbowing, and treading on each other's heels, which form the existing type of social life, are the most desirable lot of human kind, or anything but the disagreeable symptoms of one of the phases of industrial progress.[237]

With just distribution established, and poverty eradicated, mankind's happiness would no longer depend on economic status, and individuals could concentrate on worthier ends. The "diffusion of wealth, and not its concentration, is desirable," Mill avers, and "the more wholesome state of society is not that in which immense fortunes are possessed by a few and coveted by all, but that in which the greatest possible numbers possess and are contented with a moderate competency, which all may hope to acquire. . . ." [238] This view is quite consistent with his attitude towards personal happiness, as is his belief that other economic motives will come to replace the "crude stimuli" necessary in the present imperfect state of human nature. Industrial improvements, for example, will be designed to reduce labour, not to increase wealth.[239] But to try to make a short-cut through history by imposing a pattern of state socialism would be unwise, for successive approximations to the optimum state can only be reached by actual trials of strength between the opposing systems.

Only in his discussion of landed property are Mill's concessions to state socialism at all important. His early training in Ricardian economics and Benthamite politics taught him to regard the land-owning class as one of the chief obstacles to social progress, not only because it desired to maintain the injustice of the economic *status quo*, but also because of its essential inutility. While in general Mill's attitude to land is in accordance with his normal treatment of social topics, he tends to press the argument more strongly against his constant political opponents, the land-owners, than against his frequent allies, the industrial and commercial classes. He draws a distinction between the two forms of property :

[237] *Ibid.,* 754 (IV, vi, 2).   [238] *Ibid.,* 891 (V, ix, 2).   [239] *Ibid.,* 754-7 (IV, vi, 2).

To me it seems almost an axiom that property in land should be interpreted strictly, and that the balance in all cases of doubt should incline against the proprietor. The reverse is the case with property in moveables, and in all things the product of labour: over these, the owner's power both of use and of exclusion should be absolute, except where positive evil to others would result from it: but in the case of land, no exclusive right should be permitted in any individual, which cannot be shown to be productive of positive good.[240]

Land, Mill argues, is a monopoly of nature and like all monopolies may be controlled by the state for the public good.[241] The community has a proprietary right to all land, and this it may assert by appropriating land to beneficial purposes.[242] It may be argued that this is the proper attitude to all property; why should the ownership of land alone have to be justified by considerations of social utility? Mill is not quite so open to attack as this summary would indicate, for he presents arguments showing that, just as private ownership of capital, under certain conditions, is conducive to social utility, so private ownership of land, under existing conditions, is not so conducive. The interest of the landlord is not always bound up with the efficient cultivation of his land,[243] and the accumulation of wealth in a few non-labouring hands has a harmful social effect. This last is one of Mill's main points: what, he asks, have the proprietors of the Grosvenor, Portman, and Portland estates "done, that this increase of wealth, produced by other people's labour and enterprise, should fall into their mouths as they sleep, instead of being applied to the public necessities of those who created it?"[244] Not only the accumulation as such, but its basis in unearned increment is harmful. If the landlord labours for his wealth, then he is benefitting society, at least so far as production is concerned. Mill agrees with Comte "that in the future there will be no class of landlords living at ease on their rents, but every landlord will be a capitalist trained to agriculture, himself superintending

[240] *Ibid.*, II, 231–2 (II, ii, 6). See Mill's early wariness in "Writings of Junius Redivivus," *Tait's Edinburgh Magazine*, 3 (1833), 352, and cf. "The Right of Property in Land," *Dissertations and Discussions*, IV, 289; "Coleridge," 455; "Chapters on Socialism," 736; "Letters of John Stuart Mill to Charles Eliot Norton," *Transactions of the Massachusetts Historical Society*, 1916, 24–5 (26/6/70).

[241] "Leslie on the Land Question," *Works*, V, 672.

[242] "Coleridge," 457; "Corporation and Church Property," 208; "Speech on Land Tenure Reform," 255; "Maine on Village Communities," 141–2; *Principles of Political Economy*, III, 819–21 (V, ii, 5).

[243] See "The Right of Property in Land," 289ff.; "Leslie on the Land Question," 673.

[244] "Advice to Land Reformers," *Dissertations and Discussions*, IV, 275.

and directing the cultivation of his estate. No one but he who guides the work, should have the control of the tools." [245]

Mill is not charmed by the picture, conjured up in its best form by Coleridge, of a property-owning class conscious of its duties to the state, and working to forward the good of the whole through its own particular interest of "Permanence," even at the expense of personal gain.[246] His objection to a master-servant relation is too strong for him to accept the new Tory ideas, whether seen in Carlyle, Coleridge, or Disraeli.[247]

Even if production is beneficially increased through such devotion to the land, distribution, Mill's main concern, would still be unfair. But while the state would be justified by utility in appropriating all land to ensure a just distribution of produce, Mill's distrust of centralization is too strong for him to advocate such a measure. "I agree with you," he writes to Alexander Campbell, "'that the land ought to belong to the nation at large, but I think it will be a generation or two before the progress of public intelligence and morality will permit so great a concern to be entrusted to public authorities without greater abuses than *necessarily* attach to private property in land." [248] But the state may and should exercise control over land ownership.[249] The Land Tenure Association, of which Mill was the active Chairman, in proposing not "the abolition of landed property, but its reform," worked principally for the removal of the law of primogeniture, the limitation or prohibition of further private accumulation of land, the heavy taxation of unearned increment, the encouragement of small cultivators and of co-operative agriculture on state-owned land, and the preservation and control of waste lands by the state.[250] If the present landlords found taxation too onerous, they should have the option of selling their land to the state at a fair market price, and full compensation should be paid for property necessarily appropriated.[251] This programme reflects Mill's belief that the present condition of intelligence and morality cannot ensure good management by the state, just as it cannot ensure co-operation elsewhere, and Mill

[245] *Auguste Comte and Positivism*, 161.
[246] See "Coleridge," 447; and *Principles of Political Economy*, II, 228–32 (II, ii, 6).
[247] See *Principles of Political Economy*, III, 759–62 (IV, vii, 1).
[248] *Letters* (ed. Elliot), II, 243 (28/2/70). Cf. "Speech on Land Tenure Reform," 256.
[249] *Letters* (ed. Elliot), II, 258 (26/6/70).
[250] "Land Tenure Reform," *Works*, V, 689–95.
[251] *Autobiography*, 206–7; "Speech on Land Tenure Reform," 255.

would be happy to postpone indefinitely the day when the state would own all land. The management of waste lands is quite enough at present: "At all events," Mill says, "I think we had better make a beginning with that, and give a thorough trial to collective before we substitute it for individual management." [252] Once again he is insisting on experiential validation of theory – proof is not a deductive process alone, but depends on a conciliation of induction and deduction. He consequently favours moderation, advocating "an honest attempt to find a middle ground of compromise, which, avoiding individual injustice, and sparing past acquisitions, shall maintain the right of the entire community to all that it has not yet parted with, and finally close the door to any further private appropriation of what should belong to the public." [253]

His concern with social laws is also shown in his observation that in England, "for some time past, the idea of absolute property in land has been sensibly weakened, and the tendency of the time is progressively inclining towards the opinion that proprietary rights in the mere raw material of the globe should not be absolute, but limited." [254] One of the principal causes of this tendency is the growing strength of the lower classes, who will not be content with less than the moderate plan of the Land Tenure Reform Association. If the upper classes, whose power is diminishing in any event, try to deny these demands, they will lose all they possess in a social upheaval.[255] Their own interest, as well as the interest of the poor and the general interest, would best be fulfilled therefore by the moderate proposals of the Association.

Much of Mill's writing on land reform concerns small peasant holdings, and Leslie Stephen remarks that his proposals here suggest a movement away from his general attitude towards tenure.[256] In fact, however, Mill is displaying his usual view that, in Burke's phrase, circumstances alter cases. Historical, geographical, and cultural relativity mark his thought here as elsewhere. The peasant holdings advocated by him are intended for the Irish peasants, who are in his view so deprived as to be

---

[252] "Speech on Land Tenure Reform," 256. [253] *Ibid.*, 265.

[254] "Maine on Village Communities," 146.

[255] See, e.g., Mill-Taylor Collection, III, letters to Fawcett (1/1/66 and 24/10/69), f.44, ff.72–4; "Speech on Land Tenure Reform," 265. Mill's attitude here is reminiscent of that of the Philosophic Radicals towards the Reform Bill of 1832; Joseph Hamburger, *James Mill and the Art of Revolution* (Yale, 1963), *passim.*

[256] *The English Utilitarians*, III, 190–1, 232–3.

barely human. Before they can become cultured enough for higher reforms, they need to be stung into life by the crude stimulus afforded by
practised self-interest. Their brutal, lazy, and servile habits must be eradicated by giving them something to work and hope for, most simply by
giving them land on long and secure tenure. Then, when they have learned
to be men they may be ready, like the English, to become good men and
co-operative. In England, on the other hand, the lesson of selfishness has
been well and truly learned, and other considerations, such as the ability
to manage beneficially and efficiently, need attention. The son did not
forget the lessons taught by his father's critics: there are no universal
political, social, or economic panaceas.

Mill early revealed a sympathy with the working classes which remained with him throughout his life, although his acquaintance with
workers was slight until his middle years, and was never intimate. He
believed that justice, one of the main components of utility, was not
realized in a society divided between those who labour and those who
profit, and he saw that the voiceless masses needed champions. If, he
argues at one point, the Whigs stand for the principle of liberty in the
constitution, and the Tories for authority, the Radicals have a unique
responsibility to protect the interests of the poor. The Radicals' "principle
of government" is, therefore, "until Universal Suffrage shall be possible, to
do everything for the good of the working classes, which it would be
necessary to do if there were Universal Suffrage." [257] The dream of a
Radical Party faded, but Mill did not give up this task. He cultivated
correspondence with some working-class leaders, and supported their
case financially, in evidence before the Slaney Committee, in his writings,
and during his brief parliamentary career on the floor of the House. He
earnestly advocated parliamentary representation for them, arguing that
their interests could not be properly represented by men who shared
neither their outlook nor their desires; in this respect, again, he shows an
increased understanding over his early position and that of the Philosophic Radicals, who thought the middle class well qualified to interpret
and represent lower-class interests.

Behind Mill's support for the labourers lies, of course, his belief in
general utility. The interest of the great mass of the people, the workers,
obviously is of vast importance in calculating the general interest. Mill's
remarks in "Thornton on Labour and its Claims" illustrate this point:

[257] "Parties and the Ministry," 18.

The heartiness of Mr. Thornton's devotion to the interest of the labouring classes (or, it should rather be said, to the interest of human nature as embodied in them), is manifested throughout the work. . . . It is not enough that they should no longer be objects of pity. The conditions of a positively happy and dignified existence are what he demands for them, as well as for every other portion of the human race.[258]

The qualifications in the parenthesis and the last phrase are as important as the general approval. The labouring poor are worthy of sympathy, but there should be no delusions about their present state. The best of them exhibit good qualities, but they have not yet been corrupted by power.[259] As a whole, the labouring classes are no better than they can be expected to be, for morality depends largely upon cultivated reason, and their mental development has scarcely commenced.[260] But Mill, like Thornton, has opinions "in every respect as favourable to the claims of the labouring classes as is consistent with the regard due to the permanent interest of the race."[261] The best possible state of society requires that the labourers should receive as much reward, in terms of the best understanding of the principle of utility, as is equitable and just, taking into account the exigencies of existence and conflicting utilities.[262] But realism is necessary: men are at present grossly unequal in capacities, and demands for justice cannot make them equal. Intelligent friends of the working classes should work to amend the social condition in which men are born into situations which make social and economic inequality inevitable.[263] Mill is a friend to labour, but not an uncritical friend; he wishes labour to have its reward, but not more than its reward; he keeps his eye on the practical, not on the abstract and ideal. As Bain remarks, both Mills "were alike distinguished both for their sympathies with the working class, and for refusing to feed them with false hopes."[264] And while the younger Mill saw that the working class needed its own representatives to speak for it, he no less than his father thought that their improvement would make them, in effect, middle class, and the process would give them new insights into social problems, as well as wider and better interests. In this way their complaints against social injustice will

[258] *Works*, V, 650n.   [259] *Letters* (ed. Elliot), II, 45 (25/9/65).
[260] *Principles of Political Economy*, II, 107–10 (I, vii, 5).
[261] "Thornton on Labour and its Claims," 658.   [262] *Ibid.*
[263] "Endowments," 628.   [264] Bain, *James Mill*, 446.

be altered and, if poverty is finally eliminated, will disappear. Even though he is less happy than his father about the mental and moral condition of the middle class, Mill still sees it as the only possible leader of the lower orders until they approximate to a higher condition. The coming democracy will be, as it should be, a middle-class one, like the American.[265]

One of Mill's principal worries is that the power of numbers will be felt in government before the workers have demonstrated their ability to govern themselves – and others. As he remarks in *Thoughts on Parliamentary Reform*, "no lover of improvement can desire that the *predominant* power should be turned over to persons in the mental and moral condition of the English working classes . . .;"[266] but democracy is coming. "High wages and universal reading are the two elements of democracy; where they co-exist, all government, except the government of public opinion, is impossible."[267] The preliminary conditions of enlightenment, that is, will be taken for the thing itself. Prepared or not, he says, the working classes cannot be long prevented from exerting the power which they have always potentially held.[268] Only organization is now necessary. One of the most serious and yet almost certain results of the increasing power of the working classes will be a wide-spread acceptance of anti-property doctrines, and socialist ideas of all shades and colours.[269] Mill's interest in socialism is of course largely conditioned by his belief that the labourers will reach out to embrace socialist doctrines which promise them what they have always been denied. Although he wishes them to adopt the better middle-class habits and beliefs, he cannot, as has been seen, accept his father's belief that the labourers will desire to identify their interest with that of the middle class.[270] While there is little danger that the majority will think it to their advantage to weaken the security of property, they will probably tax the wealthy to a greater extent than

[265] "Tocqueville," 20–1.

[266] *Thoughts on Parliamentary Reform*, 26. Cf. *ibid.*, 44, quoted in note 177 above.

[267] "State of Society in America," *London and Westminster Review*, 2 & 31 (1836), 372.

[268] See "Civilisation," 173–4; "Parliamentary Proceedings of the Session," 516; "Claims of Labour," *Works*, V, 370; "Chapters on Socialism," 706ff.; *Principles of Political Economy*, II, 357 (II, xii, 2).

[269] See *Principles of Political Economy*, II, 202 (II, i, 2); "Chapters on Socialism," 706ff. Cf. Helen Taylor's remarks in her introduction to the latter, 705.

[270] Cf. Anschutz, *Philosophy of J. S. Mill*, 35.

is truly expedient, and institute other measures, such as equal pay in industry, not beneficial to society.[271]

The pressure of circumstances, then, forcing careful consideration of the means to the ideal, appears to have led Mill to his revaluation of socialism; the nature of the ideal itself was not unimportant, but he was trained to resist its appeal while it remained chimerical. By the middle of the century the situation had changed, and with it Mill's attitude:

It is of the utmost importance that all reflecting persons should take into early consideration what these popular political creeds are likely to be, and that every single article of them should be brought under the fullest light of investigation and discussion, so that, if possible, when the time shall be ripe, whatever is right in them may be adopted, and what is wrong rejected by general consent, and that instead of a hostile conflict, physical or only moral, between the old and the new, the best parts of both may be combined in a renovated social fabric.[272]

Mill himself takes "these popular creeds" into consideration, and suggests that "reflecting persons" can do much to help the working classes to fit themselves for the society that, in large measure, will be theirs.

One necessary step, already mentioned, is the representation of their interest in parliament, and in view of the importance of this matter to Mill and to the nation at the time, a few more words are needed. The working classes would of course be no better, and perhaps worse, as representatives of the national interest,[273] especially at first, but they must none the less be allowed to take their place in the nation's forum. Not for the sake of class interests, he says, he wishes some of the elite of the working classes in the House:

Class legislation for the working classes is as much to be deprecated as class legislation for any other class. But the most numerous of all classes ought not to be without, what every other class has – representatives in Parliament who can speak from their own knowledge of the wants, the grievances, & the modes of thought & feeling of their class – of all which, Parliament ought to be fully informed, to enable it to legislate wisely and justly not for class interests but for the general interest; & no other persons however deservedly trusted by the working classes can speak on these subjects with either the same knowledge or the same authority as those who, being in other respects qualified, are themselves working men.[274]

[271] *Representative Government*, 120–1.   [272] "Chapters on Socialism," 707–8.
[273] Mill-Taylor Collection, III (2/12/64), f.36.
[274] *Ibid.*, I, #120 (10/11/68), ff.289v, 290r (draft).

In the future there will be a great danger of biassed majority rule, and precautions must be introduced to forestall this danger, but in the meantime the pressing grievance involved in the non-recognition of social obligations towards the working class is more important.[275] Furthermore, the habit of political activity will play an important part in the workers' education, and their presence in parliament would also forward other legislation important for social improvement. "Very few years of a real working-class representation would have passed over our heads before there would be in every parish a school rate, and the school doors freely open to all the world; and in one generation from that time England would be an educated nation." [276]

Education is indeed the one thing necessary for the workers.[277] Mill believes that, apart from considerations of utility, socialism is slightly more probable as the future state of social organization because of the workers' interest in economic equality, and he sees no danger to utility in this tendency, so long as the people are ready for the obligations imposed on them by a communal system. But they are not now ready. Here is found the most important limitation on his socialism, as he indicates most clearly in the Preface to the 3rd edition (1852) of his *Principles of Political Economy*:

The only objection [to Socialism] to which any great importance will be found to be attached in the present edition, is the unprepared state of mankind in general, and of the labouring classes in particular; their extreme unfitness at present for any order of things, which would make any considerable demand on either their intellect or their virtue. It appears to me that the great end of social improvement should be to fit mankind by cultivation, for a state of society combining the greatest personal freedom with that just distribution of the fruits of labour, which the present laws of property do not profess to aim at. Whether, when this state of mental and moral cultivation shall be attained, individual property in some form (though a form very remote from the present) or community of ownership in the instruments of production and a regulated division of the produce, will afford the circumstances most favourable to happiness, and best calculated to bring human nature to its greatest perfection, is a question which must be left, as it safely may, to the people of that time to decide. Those of the present are not competent to decide it.[278]

[275] See "Notes on the Newspapers," 436. [276] Mill-Taylor Collection, XLV, #8, f.36.
[277] See *Principles of Political Economy*, II, 183–4 (I, xii, 3).
[278] *Ibid.*, xciii. Cf. the letters written in the same year to Soetbeer and Rau, *Letters* (ed. Elliot), I, 167, 171.

Experience must first show that men are capable of working for others, for the community or the nation, before society can be organized in accordance with such an assumption. Mill believes that the demonstration probably will be forthcoming,[279] but the experience is necessary, for the change in moral temper required is enormous. It cannot be achieved by "an Act of Parliament, but must be, on the most favourable supposition, a work of considerable time." [280] He expresses, in one place, views remarkably like those of Ruskin as well as Carlyle, in discussing the practicability of socialism; no matter how the question is answered in the future, he says, the true moral implications of labour remain utilitarian – each should work for all. "Until labourers and employers perform the work of industry in the spirit in which soldiers perform that of an army, industry will never be moralized, and military life will remain, what, in spite of the anti-social character of its direct object, it has hitherto been – the chief school of moral co-operation." [281] But for Mill the army must be a voluntary one. Industry can be socially organized and controlled only by people "who will make great temporary sacrifices such as can only be inspired by a generous feeling for the public good or a disinterested devotion to an idea, not by the mere desire of more pay and less work." [282] A gradual development of the moral nature of man, requiring for its fulfilment many a long year of trial and instruction, is a basic essential of the perfect socialist society, as of the perfect utilitarian society. The same sort of man is required for both, whether or not experience proves them to be identical.

Those interested in social advance, then, should work for the intellectual and moral improvement of the deprived. One of the most important lessons to be impressed on the poor is that of the control of population; in fact, if the poor could be persuaded voluntarily to limit their numbers, so much suffering would vanish that socialistic schemes might not be needed. The Malthusians, Mill is concerned to point out, are not hard-hearted enemies of the poor, but their realistic friends.[283] Before Malthus poverty was, Mill holds, largely inexplicable, and strive as charitable philanthropists might, they could not solve a problem which they could not understand. Now that the explanation is to hand, a solu-

---

[279] *Representative Government*, 55.   [280] "Chapters on Socialism," 750.
[281] *Auguste Comte and Positivism*, 149.
[282] *Letters* (ed. Eliot), I, 172 (7/7/52). Cf. "Claims of Labour," 375.
[283] "Claims of Labour," 366, 368.

tion can be seen which will result in a major reduction of suffering, if man can but learn to control his "brute instincts" and "natural inclinations." [284]

Uninformed general philanthropy, in Mill's view, whether individual or governmental, is dangerous, for knowledge and circumspection as well as zeal are necessary. The poor, he says, "ought on proper conditions to be shielded, we hope they already are so, by public or private charity, from actual want of mere necessaries, and from any other extreme of bodily suffering," [285] but such charity only alleviates; it does not cure or prevent the disease. Mill gives his considered opinion in "The Claims of Labour," and although it sounds somewhat harsh in comparison with some of his comments on the poor its doctrine is seen on examination to be in complete accord with those he expresses elsewhere. He gives recognition to the growing interest in the condition of the labouring classes, but suggests that the upper classes are attracted just as much by the latest fad as by conscience or self-interest, in advocating aid. As usual, Mill attributes much of the stir to social change, particularly in this case to the stimulus given to social reformers by the passing of the Reform Bill. Ideas, such as those presented by Carlyle in *Past and Present* and *Chartism*, plus the facts, presented really for the first time in the Poor Law Commissioners' reports, plus circumstances, including depression and the Corn Law struggles, have altered the attitude of the ruling classes. But this new attitude is too paternal, too protective, to be of much utility: "the liberty of action of independent citizens" cannot be combined "with the immunities of slaves." [286]

The provisions of the much reviled Poor Law of 1834 are in the long run not only more practical but also kinder than paternalistic schemes, for they tend to produce self-reliant workers who can help themselves to rise in the world. He never departed from the opinion expressed in one of his "Notes on the Newspapers" in the year of the Poor Law:

The condition of a pauper must cease to be, as it has been made, an object of desire and envy to the independent labourer. Relief must be given; no one must be allowed to starve; the necessaries of life and health must be tendered to all who apply for them; but to all who are capable of work they must be tendered on such terms, as shall make the necessity of accepting them be regarded as a

[284] *Principles of Political Economy*, II, 367 (II, xiii, 1).
[285] "Claims of Labour," 375; "on proper conditions" was added in 1859.
[286] *Ibid.*, 374.

misfortune; and shall induce the labourer to apply for them only when he cannot help it, and to take the first opportunity of again shifting for himself. To this end, relief must be given only in exchange for labour, and labour at least as irksome and severe as that of the least fortunate among the independent labourers: relief, moreover, must be confined to necessaries. Indulgences, even those which happily the very poorest class of labourers, when in full employment, are able occasionally to allow themselves, must be rigidly withheld.[287]

The poor are to inherit the earth, but they must first be made fit for their inheritance. The more fortunate and educated classes must see the importance of one condition of aid above all others: it must be designed to make further help less necessary, to make the recipient better able to look after his own interests. No scheme which does not aim morally to influence the minds and habits of the people can be of use. Looked at in this way, the best that can be done is to have just laws, and universal education.[288] Justice, that is, is more essential than mercy.[289] Benevolence is of course not immoral in itself, indeed it is an attribute of the moral man, but it creates, when practised in the wrong way, dependence, servility, and laziness. Mill points out that "it is one thing to tell the rich that they ought to take care of the poor, and another thing to tell the poor that the rich ought to take care of them. . . ." [290] As to the education of the poor, it must not be seen as a matter of mere book-learning, for the whole of a man's life, his occupation, social environment, relations with others, contributes to his character.[291] None the less, formal education must be greatly improved. Secularism and the lower-class fear of "over-education" should be counteracted, and cheap libraries provided. Industrial schools should also be established, not only to train workmen, but also to develop human beings.

One of the most essential elements in the character of a worthy citizen, overlooked by the present society, is the ability to co-operate for mutual benefit; here just laws can aid the working classes and the whole society by making it possible for men to learn to co-operate while materially benefitting themselves, and without any social upheaval. In advocating co-operative ventures Mill brings together his main themes: utility is gradually forwarded, through moral and intellectual improvement, by means of a variety of voluntary enterprises that demonstrate their practicability by working in accordance with the known laws of social de-

[287] "Notes on the Newspapers," 361.   [288] "Claims of Labour," 387.
[289] Ibid.   [290] Ibid., 376.   [291] Ibid.

velopment and human nature, all the while preserving the framework of society and altering but not destroying institutions. Furthermore, a minimum of effort is required from the state, for what must be done lessens the need for further state activity, and yet is simple: the passing of laws permitting the easy formation of working-men's associations. One of the great advantages of co-operative ventures is that they can be founded in a society as it now is, and can therefore prove their case through competition with capitalist ventures.[292] Writing to Fawcett in 1863 about a discussion the latter had on co-operatives, Mill says:

I suppose what your opponents questioned was merely the probability of its success in the more difficult kinds of industrial enterprise. Of such a doubt one can only say, Solvitur (or *Solvetur*) *ambulando*. The thing is practicable or not, according to the intellectual and moral qualities of those who attempt it. Doubtless many will attempt it and fail, but some, and in the end, many, will succeed. It is not necessary that all should. The success of co-operation on any large scale, will establish a practical minimum of wages, and will strike at the root of the opposition of apparent interest between employers and labourers, since whatever profit the capitalist can obtain in the face of co-operation, must be a mere equivalent for the advantage the enterprise derives from his capital, skill, and unity of management.[293]

It should be noted that Mill is sceptical of the ability of co-operatives to succeed without outside capital, whether obtained from government or by private loan.[294] Interest is an equitable recognition of the capitalist's abstinence; the best situation is one in which the workmen themselves gather enough capital to permit profitable operation, for then the full rewards can be distributed among themselves – but there should be a reward for investment. In addition, the skill of management deserves reward; skill will not be forthcoming without reward, and failure will ensue. If the personal interest of the manager is not bound up with the success of the organization, then once more there is likelihood of inefficient supervision and inadequate initiative, as in many joint-stock companies.

Like socialist schemes in general, co-operatives are likely to founder

[292] "Chapters on Socialism," 732–3.
[293] Mill-Taylor Collection, III, ff.29–30 (17/5/63). Cf. his similar remarks on Industrial Partnerships, *Principles of Political Economy*, III, 903–4 (V, ix, 7) and communist communities, "Chapters on Socialism," 747–8.
[294] "Thornton on Labour and its Claims," 656.

because of the unprepared state of human feelings, affections, will, and intellect.

To be independent of master manufacturers, to work for themselves and divide the whole produce of their labour is a worthy object of ambition, but it is only fit for, and can only succeed with people who can labour for the community of which they are a part with the same energy and zeal as if labouring for their own private and separate interest (the opposite is now the case), and who, instead of expecting immediately more pay and less work, are willing to submit to any privation until they have effected their emancipation.[295]

Initial successes resulting from the enthusiasm and devotion of the founders are likely,[296] and furthermore, as only the best and least selfish of individuals are likely to join in the first instance, the earliest examples probably will have more success than many of the later.[297]

All these criticisms, it should be remembered, are offered by a friendly critic, who really believes in the efficacy of co-operatives. Mill expects two great economic benefits from such schemes, benefits large enough to offset the difficulties: the first, relating particularly to the interest of the workmen, is the improved distribution of wealth through a more equitable distribution of profits;[298] the second, pertaining to the whole community, is the increased production resulting from the workers' interest being associated with profit.[299] The second depends, of course, on the first.

Modifications of remuneration, such as profit-sharing and piecework, not involving the ownership of the capital by the workers, had an immediate appeal for Mill, because they not only could work within the existing economic framework, but could also meet the principal objection which producers' co-operatives are designed to meet.[300] Piecework is a compromise between justice and practicability; it recognizes the benefit to be gained for society through the utilization of selfishness. It is, there-

[295] *Letters* (ed. Elliot), I, 166–7 (7/1/52).

[296] "The French Revolution of 1848," 394.

[297] Cf. Mill's remarks on such model factories as that of Samuel Greg who, Mill notes, had to get rid of his "aborigines": "It is in the nature of things that employers so much beyond the average should gather round them better labourers than the average, and retain them, while so eligible a lot is not to be had elsewhere. But ordinary human nature is so poor a thing, that the same attachment and influence would not, with the same certainty, attend similar conduct, if it no longer formed a contrast with the indifference of other employers." ("Claims of Labour," 382.)

[298] *Ibid.*, 382, 385–6.

[299] "Chapters on Socialism," 742–3; "Thornton on Labour and its Claims," 666–7.

[300] See "Chapters on Socialism," 743.

fore, in Mill's opinion, "highly expedient; and until education shall have
been entirely regenerated, is far more likely to prove immediately successful, than an attempt at a higher ideal." [301] Industrial Partnership or
profit-sharing, he points out, is an effective means of identifying the
workers' interest with the success of the enterprise, and so of raising
them from a dependent to a self-dependent position. He is convinced that
the industrial economy which divides society absolutely into two portions, the
payers of wages and the receivers of them, the first counted by thousands and
the last by millions, is neither fit for, nor capable of, indefinite duration : and
the possibility of changing this system for one of combination without dependence, and unity of interest instead of organized hostility, depends altogether
upon the future developments of the Partnership principle.[302]

In "The Claims of Labour" and "Thornton on Labour and its Claims,"
as well as in his *Principles of Political Economy*, Mill stresses the role
of Industrial Partnerships,[303] but in his review of Thornton, the latest of
the three, he indicates more clearly his belief that such partnerships are
transitional, and will ultimately give way to, or be transformed into,
completely co-operative ventures. In a letter written in 1869 he makes
the same point :

We should hope, indeed, ultimately to arrive at a state of industry in which
the workpeople as a body will either themselves own the capital, or hire it
from its owners. Industrial partnerships, however, are not only a valuable
preparation for that state, and transition to it, but might probably for a long
time exist by the side of it with great advantage; if only because their competition would prevent co-operative associations of workmen from degenerating, as
I grieve to say they often do, into close joint-stock companies, in which the
workmen who founded them keep all the profits to themselves.[304]

He grieves because co-operation is for him far more than an economic
measure to prevent fraud,[305] to distribute profits more justly, to increase
profits, and to reduce the waste of distributors' costs : it is a great means
of moral education. Active sympathy for others, resulting in action for
their benefit, magnified until it includes the good of the whole, is the
ultimate aim, and in the utilitarian society people will work together
of their own accord for social ends. Such results are only to be achieved
through cultivation; as Mill says, "Co-operation, like other difficult things,

[301] *Principles of Political Economy*, II, 210 (II, i, 4).   [302] *Ibid.*, III, 896 (V, ix, 5).
[303] See "Claims of Labour," 382; "Thornton on Labour and its Claims," 666–7;
Principles of Political Economy, II, i, and IV, vii, *passim*.
[304] *Letters* (ed. Elliot), II, 230–1 (11/12/69).   [305] "Chapters on Socialism," 732.

can be learnt only by practice: and to be capable of it in great things, a people must be gradually trained to it in small. Now, the whole course of advancing civilization is a series of such training."[306] Producers' and consumers' co-operatives are only particular forms of the larger co-operative growth of society, the chief characteristic of "advancing civilization," manifested in divers societies for divers purposes, in municipal government, in the division of labour, even in the often objectionable joint-stock companies;[307] but they are important forms, for they reach the segment of society least affected by other forms of co-operation, and yet the one destined to control the political, social, and economic future of the country. If the workers learn the lesson, all may be gained. They should, therefore, be encouraged to form co-operatives for their own and the country's moral as well as economic benefit.

One more reason for co-operative experiments is advanced by Mill: failure, like success, will bring improved conditions, for mistakes in theory will be made apparent to the workers, who will then be more content to accept the perhaps hard facts of existence.[308] The value of capital, for example, and the necessity of unified management might be impressed on previously sceptical workers.[309] In the light of widened experience, again, the workers might well learn the important lesson of Malthus, and by limiting their numbers begin on the only permanent solution of the problem of poverty. The elevation of character necessary for the final society, as well as the recognition of the limitations imposed by the physical laws of the universe are both forwarded by co-operative ventures – such a double recommendation surely justifies their encouragement.[310] Mill's

[306] "Civilization," 167.

[307] See *Principles of Political Economy*, III, 708 (IV, i, 2); "Civilization," 170.

[308] See "Notes on the Newspapers," 248.

[309] See "Claims of Labour," 385. James Mill's attitude, according to his son, was similar; when Holyoake asked for information about the relations between Owen and James Mill, John Mill replied that his father "knew Robert Owen well & had frequent oral discussions with him: of written ones I know nothing." James Mill, he continues, thought that Owen's Communistic Associations could not succeed, "but he always said they were entitled to a fair & complete trial." (Mill-Taylor Collection, II, #255, f.589v.)

[310] Mill practised what he preached when he came to the support of the Wolverhampton Plate Lock Co-operators in the press and with a cash donation. Characteristically, he saw that his donation would not do good by itself, and he tried to get more wide-spread support, all the time making reservations based on his view of the enterprise's practicability. "It is but little that I could in any case do to aid them," he writes to Fawcett, "but even a little is sometimes useful; it is however

large enthusiasm is expressed in a letter of 1869: "The emancipation of women and co-operative production are, I fully believe, the two great changes that will regenerate society." [311]

After this discussion and analysis, it may be profitable to return again to the question posed at the beginning of this section: to what extent was Mill a socialist? The answer, it is hoped, will now be clearer. Mill believed that a mad rush for wealth is harmful to the best elements in human nature, and he believed that capitalism as it existed in his time nourished the desire for crass worldly advantage: socialism repudiates such a desire. Capitalism had hitherto thrived on economic inequality, with a large gulf between the two nations of rich and poor: socialism aims at the abolition of great economic differences. Capitalism, as then established, led men to pursue their own interest at the expense of the community's: socialism puts the general interest first. So far, it is obvious, Mill's sympathy would be with socialism. But only so far, for the contrast here developed is between ideal socialism and contemporary capitalism. One great advantage that capitalism has is that it is forced, by its own theory, to be pragmatic. Success in the business world (apart from force and fraud, which should be legally prevented) depends on practical wisdom, and attention to the realities of life. Furthermore, capitalism is changing and, in accordance with the laws of society and political economy, tends of itself in a non-monopolistic system to equalize fortunes.[312] In Mill's view:

That all should indeed start on perfectly equal terms, is inconsistent with any law of private property: but if as much pains as has been taken to aggravate the inequality of chances arising from the natural working of the principle, had been taken to temper that inequality by every means not subversive of the principle itself; if the tendency of legislation had been to favour the diffusion, instead of the concentration of wealth – to encourage the subdivision of the large masses, instead of striving to keep them together; the principle of individual property would have been found to have no necessary connexion with the

---

an unthrifty mode of using one's means of doing good, to bolster up particular experiments of social improvement, if they have not in themselves the conditions of success." (Mill-Taylor Collection, LVII, #33 [8/11/68].) He really continued his active support only because he thought that the body was being subjected to unfair competition. See *ibid.*, III, f.39 (22/3/65); XLVIII, #49 (7/4/65); LVII A (22/3/65 and 12/4/65); and *Co-operator*, 5 (1865), 161.

[311] *Letters* (ed. Elliot), II, 172 (1/1/69).   [312] "Chapters on Socialism," 729-30.

physical and social evils which almost all Socialist writers assume to be inseparable from it.[313]

If poverty could be reduced to a negligible amount (the population problem being solved),[314] and the people educated, the discussion would be thrown back on a different set of considerations, for the utility of socialism lies in its promise to do away with poverty.[315] But will it in fact do so? Or can capitalism do so more quickly and with less disruption? If capitalism is not at a disadvantage here, it may be found to have important advantages elsewhere, the greatest of which may well prove to be the encouragement of spontaneity and the preservation of an atmosphere of freedom. Whatever the promise of socialism, its implementation might well, like Comte's version of the Religion of Humanity, impede utility by leaving all to public opinion and nothing to individuals. Referring to socialist systems, Mill says:

The question is, whether there would be any asylum left for individuality of character; whether public opinion would not be a tyrannical yoke; whether the absolute dependence of each on all, the surveillance of each by all, would not grind all down into a tame uniformity of thoughts, feelings, and actions. This is already one of the glaring evils of the existing state of society, notwithstanding a much greater diversity of education and pursuits, and a much less absolute dependence of the individual on the mass, than would exist in the Communistic régime. No society in which eccentricity is a matter of reproach, can be in a wholesome state. It is yet to be ascertained whether the Communistic scheme would be consistent with that multiform development of human nature, those manifold unlikenesses, that diversity of tastes and talents, and variety of intellectual points of view, which not only form a great part of the interest of human life, but by bringing intellects into stimulating collision, and by presenting to each innumerable notions that he would not have conceived of himself, are the mainsprings of mental and moral progression.[316]

Socialism, while promoting the salutary stationary state in respect of wealth, may thus bring also the sterile stationary state in respect of intellect and morals. The moralization of man is quite possibly proceeding independently of the economic organization of society, and a better

[313] *Principles of Political Economy*, II, 207–8 (II, i, 3); cf. *ibid.*, III, 986 (Appendix A).
[314] In "The French Revolution of 1848," 386–7, Mill implies that there is little to choose between free enterprise and socialism with regard to the population problem; in "Chapters on Socialism," 728–9, he shifts slightly, but only slightly, remarking that socialism may have some advantages.
[315] See *Principles of Political Economy*, II, 206 (II, i, 3).   [316] *Ibid.*, 209 (II, i, 3).

condition of moral feeling may therefore arrive along with, although not as a consequence of, a better capitalist system.

Finally, capitalism has shown something of what it can do for good as well as for evil, and socialism remains an untried theory. One of its worst defects is its unrealistic view of the benefits to be expected automatically from the equalization of fortunes. The labourers' share, Mill saw, would be little increased by mere appropriation of the capitalists'. The suppression of unnecessary distributors and other "parasites of industry" would, however, have a noticeable effect, as would land reform.[317] Economics, in truth, has less effect on society than socialists believe; since the whole complex state of civilization results from the similarly complex state which preceded it, the freedom of the market cannot be responsible for all existing injustices.

There are arguments from reason and desire on both sides, and the superiority of one system or the other waits in reality for the verdict of history. As in other cases, Mill does not hesitate to work for what he considers the good in any form, but leaves the decision to the future: "We are too ignorant either of what individual agency in its best form, or Socialism in its best form, can accomplish, to be qualified to decide which of the two will be the ultimate form of human society." [318] If one persists in asking whether Mill is an advocate of socialism or of free enterprise the answer, in terms of his dependence on experience, is that he is both – and neither.[319] He cannot decide on the available evidence which is more conducive to the greatest good of the greatest number, and so he is neither socialist nor capitalist; he wishes to leave avenues of development open for each, and actively supports what he holds to be the best tendencies in each, and so he is both.

One's view of Mill as a socialist ultimately waits on the answer to that annoyingly necessary question: Compared to what? Compared to his father and Bentham, to the classical economists, to the public and almost all the informed opinion of his time, and to modern defenders of capitalism, he is socialist. Compared to present-day socialists, to their practical and theoretical forerunners (Mill's contemporaries), he is capitalist. But he too is a forerunner: Fabianism draws from many sources, but almost all its tenets are to be found somewhere in Mill's writings. It is a rela-

[317] "Chapters on Socialism," 735–6.
[318] *Principles of Political Economy*, II, 208 (II, i, 3); cf. *ibid.*, xciii (Preface to 3rd ed.).
[319] See also Appendix, 275–6 below.

tivist doctrine, looking to a gradual implementation of practical measures, precisely defined in detail, and designed for present problems; it rejects class war, and seeks to propagate itself through persuasion and not through violence; it leaves room for the individual, and for moral development; its aims are those moderate ones of which Mill approved, the gradual orientation to public service of land and industrial revenue; it is also socialist. The evidence would seem to indicate that Mill was what he said he was, a qualified socialist. And the conclusion is not surprising, for when all the evidence is examined, he is seen also to be a qualified democrat, and even a qualified libertarian. Only in the ultimate area where experience can afford no proof, that is, in the acceptance of a *summum bonum*, do the qualifications disappear: in his own terms, he is an unqualified utilitarian. Though his conviction and understanding of utility were deeper, and his sympathies broader, his end was in his beginning.

Appendix

Darwin and Marx

AMONG MILL'S famous contemporaries, there are two in particular on whom one would expect him to have expressed views – Darwin and Marx. Although he had very little to say about Darwin, he was aware of the developmental and evolutionary theories of his age, and Helen Taylor comments in her "Introductory Notice" to *Three Essays on Religion* (viii) that Mill would certainly have referred to the Darwinian theory had his essays on "Nature" and the "Utility of Religion" been written later or revised. Mill's attitude towards developmental theories is best seen in relation to his views on hypothesis. In the rush to adopt evolutionary explanations of all and sundry phenomena, including some areas such as literature which are far removed from any real involvement in problems of "natural selection," many nineteenth-century and early twentieth-century critics of Mill condemned his apparent ignorance of the importance of evolution. So they attempted to explain the inadequacies of his theories, particularly in the sociological area. Though Darwinism has come under criticism, and failure to adopt his hypothesis in its simple form now seems less damning, the criticisms of Mill are still outstanding, and it is of some interest to see just what, if anything, he thought of Darwin's theory.

It soon becomes apparent that he knew of it, and was aware of some of the difficulties in accepting it. In his *Logic*, after discussing the worth of hypotheses such as Gall's, he continues: "Mr. Darwin's remarkable speculation on the Origin of Species is another unimpeachable example of a legitimate hypothesis. What he terms 'natural selection' is not only a *vera causa*, but one proved to be capable of producing effects of the same kind with those which the hypothesis ascribes to it : the question of possibility is entirely one of degree. It is unreasonable to accuse Mr. Darwin (as has been done) of violating the rules of Induction. The rules of Induction are concerned with the conditions of Proof. Mr. Darwin has never pretended that his doctrine was proved. He was not bound by the rules of Induction, but by those of Hypothesis. And these last have seldom been more completely fulfilled. He has opened a path of inquiry full of promise, the results of which none can foresee. And is it not a wonderful feat of scientific knowledge and ingenuity to have rendered so bold a suggestion, which the first impulse of every one was to reject at once, admissible and discussable, even as a conjecture?" (II, 19n.; III, xiv, 5. Added in the 5th ed., 1862.) As early as 11 April, 1860, he mentioned Darwin's theory in a letter to Bain, remarking *inter alia* that although Darwin "cannot be said to have proved the truth of his doctrine, he does seem to have proved that it *may* be true ..." (*Letters* [ed. Elliot], I, 236).

The particular application of evolution which most interested Mill was the explanation of the presence in animal species of organs bearing more than an apparently accidental relation to each other. Writing to J. E. Cairnes in 1871, he says: "With regard to those parts of coexistence which as you say 'have a manifest adaptation to each other as the teeth, stomach and claws of an animal,' these are the ones which seem to me to be *par excellence* referable to causation; they are probably explicable by natural selection, or some other form of the evolution theory. Undoubtedly they may be used as a basis for deductions, but so may all empirical laws, within definite limits of time, place, and circumstance" (Mill-Taylor Collection, LV, f.179r&v). He never admitted the hypothesis to have been proved, for in his "Theism" he holds, as he held throughout the latter part of his life, that the best explanation of such phenomena as the connection of the "wonderful mechanism of the eye" with the "fact of sight," is creative foresight.

The argument from design is the only proof for the existence of a deity which he will admit, but, after stressing the strength of this argument, he still finds room for a lengthy, and realistic, account of Darwin's hypothesis. As well as creative foresight, he says, there is another possible explanation of the connection between the eye and sight, an explanation "on which attention has been greatly fixed by recent speculations, and the reality of which cannot be called in question, though its adequacy to account for such truly admirable combinations as some of those in Nature, is still and will probably long remain problematical. This is the principle of 'the survival of the fittest.' " Mill goes on to say : "This principle does not pretend to account for the commencement of sensation or of animal or vegetable life. But assuming the existence of some one or more very low forms of organic life, in which there are no complex adaptations nor any marked appearances of contrivance, and supposing, as experience warrants us in doing, that many small variations from those simple types would be thrown out in all directions, which would be transmissible by inheritance, and of which some would be advantageous to the creature in its struggle for existence and others disadvantageous, the forms which are advantageous would always tend to survive and those which are disadvantageous to perish. And thus there would be a constant though slow general improvement of the type as it branched out into many different varieties, adapting it to different media and modes of existence, until it might possibly, in countless ages, attain to the most advanced examples which now exist. . . . Of this theory when pushed to [an] extreme point, all that can now be said is that it is not so absurd as it looks, and that the analogies which have been discovered in experience, favourable to its possibility, far exceed what any one could have supposed beforehand. Whether it will ever be possible to say more than this, is at present uncertain. The theory if admitted would be in no way whatever inconsistent with Creation. But it must be acknowledged that it would greatly attenuate the evidence for it." (*Three Essays on Religion*, 172–4.) In fact, Mill displays an admirable caution, and he has no need for a *volte face* such as Huxley's in his Romanes Lecture, for he never places any confidence in the beneficial operation of natural processes. His "Nature" reveals quite clearly that he was in no danger of ascribing ethical qualities to an objective and non-human process. He makes reference to the Spencerian type of evolutionary belief in letters to Spencer, and in his *Inaugural Address*: "The growth of a plant or animal from the first germ is the typical specimen of a phenomenon which rules through the whole course of the history of man and society – increase of function, through expansion and differentiation of structure by internal forces" (62).

About Marx Mill undoubtedly knew little, but in fact Marx was little known in England up to the time of Mill's death. As noted in the text,

Mill, like his contemporaries, does not distinguish as we would between Socialism and Communism, using the terms interchangeably for the most part to refer to kinds of "Association." When he does discriminate, as in his *Principles of Political Economy* (II, 210; II, i, 4), he uses Communist to mean that social organization which implies an absolute equalization of labour and wealth, the "extreme limit of Socialism." It has frequently been observed that Mill apparently had no knowledge of the writings of Marx and Engels (see, e.g., Cole, *Socialist Thought: The Forerunners, 1789–1859*, 313; Stephen, *The English Utilitarians*, III, 224; Schapiro, "John Stuart Mill, Pioneer of Democratic Liberalism in England," 127–60), but L. S. Feuer has traced the references in Mill's published letters to attitudes, persons, organizations, and publications which are associated with Marx and Engels ("John Stuart Mill and Marxian Socialism," 297–303; the relevant letters are in Elliot's edition, II, 78, 147, 152, 268, 334, 347). The list is not impressive, and it is clear that Mill, knowing little, attached little importance to the doctrines of Marxism. However, it seems likely that, had he lived to complete his "Chapters on Socialism," he would have paid more attention to Communist theory.

That there are major differences of opinion between him and the Marxists is obvious, and speculation is largely futile, but some points may be mentioned. First, Mill objects strenuously to the idea of violent revolution ("State of Politics in 1836," 271; "The Close of the Session," 607; "Currency Juggle," 191–2; "Notes on the Newspapers," 311–2; *Letters* [ed. Elliot], II, 347–8 (4/10/72]). A revolution he desired, but primarily a moral and intellectual revolution. Secondly, he sees no need for, or true evidence of, a class war, and the dictatorship of the proletariat, in the workers' present condition, would be to him puerile nonsense (*Letters* [ed. Elliot], II, 122–3, 334). Thirdly, specific criticisms of too much dependence on central control and too little attempt to delineate the institutions of the communist state are hinted at by Mill in his direct references to Marxist doctrines (*ibid.*, 334–5). More important differences lie behind, and may be inferred: Mill's dialectic of history, depending for advance on intellect, idea, and individual, although acknowledging the importance of social and economic factors, is not compatible with economic determinism. And, not to labour the issue, from Mill's point of view Marx, like Comte, would be guilty of ignoring the conditions of proof, generalizing from insufficient data, and designing an authoritative system without sufficient regard for basic human needs and variety.

Bibliography

THE FOLLOWING LIST includes only those works drawn on in the text. For Mill's writings, see *Bibliography of the Published Writings of John Stuart Mill*, ed. Ney MacMinn, J. R. Hainds, and J. M. McCrimmon (Evanston: Northwestern University Press, 1945); for writings on Mill, see *The Mill News Letter* (Toronto: University of Toronto Press in association with Victoria College, 1965–ff.), no. 1 ff., and Keitaro Amano, "John Stuart Mill," *Bibliography of the Classical Economists*, Vol. III, Part 4 (Tokyo: Science Council of Japan, 1964).

I. Writings of J. S. Mill

"Advice to Land Reformers," *Dissertations and Discussions*, IV, 266–77.
"Alfred de Vigny," *ibid.*, I, 287–329.
"Aphorisms," *ibid.*, 206–10.
"Appendix," *ibid.*, 467–74. (Reprinted from "Rationale of Representation,"
    347–9, and "Tocqueville on Democracy in America" [1835],110–112n.)
"Armand Carrel," *ibid.*, 211–83.
Auguste Comte and Positivism. 2nd ed. London: Trübner, 1866.
Autobiography. New York: Columbia University Press, 1924.
"Bailey on Berkeley's Theory of Vision," *Dissertations and Discussions*, II,
    94–119.
"Bain's Psychology," *ibid.*, III, 97–152.
"Bentham," *ibid.*, I, 330–92.
"Blakey's History of Moral Science," *Monthly Repository*, 7 (1833), 661–9.
"Carlyle's French Revolution," *London and Westminster Review*, 5 & 27 (1837),
    17–53.
"Centralisation," *Edinburgh Review*, 115 (1862), 323–58.
"Chapters on Socialism," in *Collected Works*, V (Toronto: University of
    Toronto Press, 1967), 705–53.
"Civilization," *Dissertations and Discussions*, I, 160–205.
"The Claims of Labour," in *Collected Works*, V, 363–89.

"Close of the Session," *Monthly Repository*, 8 (1834), 605–9.

"Coleridge," *Dissertations and Discussions*, I, 393–466.

Considerations on Representative Government. 3rd ed. London: Longman, Green, Longman, Roberts, and Green, 1865.

"The Contest in America," *Dissertations and Discussions*, III, 179–205.

"Corporation and Church Property," in *Collected Works*, IV (Toronto: University of Toronto Press, 1967), 193–222.

Correspondance inédite avec Gustave d'Eichthal. Ed. E. d'Eichthal. Paris: Germer-Baillière, 1898.

"The Currency Juggle," in *Collected Works*, IV, 181–92.

"Death of Jeremy Bentham," *Examiner*, 10 June, 1832, 371–2.

"The Definition of Political Economy," in *Collected Works*, IV, 309–39.

"Diary," in *Letters*, ed. Elliot, II, 357–86.

Dissertations and Discussions. 4 vols. London: Longmans, Green, Reader and Dyer, 1875.

"Duveyrier's Political Views of French Affairs," *Edinburgh Review*, 83 (1846), 453–74.

Earlier Letters. Ed. Francis E. Mineka. *Collected Works*, Vols. XII and XIII. Toronto: University of Toronto Press, 1963.

The Early Draft of J. S. Mill's Autobiography. Ed. Jack Stillinger. Urbana: University of Illinois Press, 1961.

"Endowments," in *Collected Works*, V, 613–29.

"England and Ireland," *Examiner*, 13 May, 1848, 307–8.

An Examination of Sir William Hamilton's Philosophy. 4th ed. London: Longmans, Green, Reader, and Dyer, 1872.

"A Few Observations on the French Revolution," *Dissertations and Discussions*, I, 56–62.

"A Few Words on Non-Intervention," *ibid.*, III, 153–78.

"The French Revolution of 1848," *ibid.*, II, 335–410.

"French Theatre," *Examiner*, 22 May, 1831, 325–6.

"Further Reply to the Debate on Population," *Archiv für Sozialwissenschaft und Sozialpolitik*, 62 (1929), 225–39, 466–7. (This title is incorrect; Mill's is "Closing Speech on the Co-operative System.")

"The Game Laws," *Westminster Review*, 5 (1826), 1–22.

"Grote's Aristotle," *Dissertations and Discussions*, IV, 188–230.

"Grote's History of Greece," *ibid.*, II, 510–54.

"Grote's Plato," *ibid.*, III, 275–379.

"Guizot's Essays and Lectures on History," *ibid.*, II, 218–82.

Inaugural Address at St. Andrews. London: Longmans, Green, Reader, and Dyer, 1867.

"The Income and Property Tax," in *Collected Works*, V, 549–98.

"Mr. John Stuart Mill," in "Papers relating to the Re-organization of the Civil Service," *Parliamentary Papers*, 1854–55, XX, 92–8.

"Land Tenure Reform," in *Collected Works*, V, 687–95.

"Law of Libel and Liberty of the Press," *Westminster Review*, 3 (1825), 285–321.

"Leslie on the Land Question," in *Collected Works*, V, 669–85.

"Letter to the Editor," *Edinburgh Review*, 79 (1844), 267–71.

Letters. Ed. Hugh S. R. Elliot. 2 vols. London : Longmans, Green, 1910.

"Letters of John Stuart Mill to Charles Eliot Norton," *Transactions of the Massachusetts Historical Society*, 1916, 11–25.

"Lord Durham's Return," *London and Westminster Review*, 32 (1838), 241–60.

"Maine on Village Communities," *Dissertations and Discussions*, IV, 130–53.

"Michelet's History of France," *ibid.*, II, 120–80.

"Miss Martineau's Summary of Political Economy," in *Collected Works*, IV, 223–8.

"The Negro Question," *Fraser's Magazine*, 41 (1850), 25–31.

"Newman's Political Economy," in *Collected Works*, V, 439–57.

"Notes on the Newspapers," *Monthly Repository*, 8 (1834), 161–76, 233–48, 309–12, 354–75, 435–56, 521–8, 589–600, 656–65.

"Notes on Some of the More Popular Dialogues of Plato," *ibid.*, 8 (1834), 89–99, 203–11, 404–20, 633–46, 691–710, 802–15, 829–42; 9 (1835), 112–21, 169–78.

"On Genius," *ibid.*, 6 (1832), 649–59.

On Liberty. London : Parker, 1859.

"On Punishment," *Monthly Repository*, 8 (1834), 734–6.

"Parliamentary Proceedings of the Session," *London and Westminster Review*, 1 & 30 (1835), 512–24.

"Parties and the Ministry," *ibid.*, 6 & 28 (1837), 1–26.

"Pemberton" (unheaded notice), *Examiner*, 3 June, 1832, 358.

"Periodical Literature : Edinburgh Review," *Westminster Review*, 1 (1824), 505–41.

"Postscript," *London and Westminster Review*, 1 & 30 (1835), 254–6.

"Postscript : The Close of the Session," *ibid.*, 2 & 31 (1835), 270–7.

"Preface," *Dissertations and Discussions*, I, iii–vi.

Principles of Political Economy. Collected Works, Vols. II and III. Toronto : University of Toronto Press, 1965.

"Public Responsibility and the Ballot," *The Reader*, 5 (29 Apr., 1865), 474–5.

"Question of Population," *Black Dwarf*, 11 (27 Nov. and 10 Dec., 1823), 748–56, 791–8.

"Radical Party in Canada," *London and Westminster Review*, 6 & 28 (1838), 502–33.

"Rationale of Representation," *ibid.*,1 & 30 (1835), 341–71.

"Recent Writers on Reform," *Dissertations and Discussions*, III, 47–96.

"Regulation of the London Water Supply," in *Collected Works*, V, 431–7.

"Remarks on Bentham's Philosophy," in Edward Lytton Bulwer, *England and the English*. 2 vols. London : Bentley, 1833, II, 321–44.

"The Right of Property in Land," *Dissertations and Discussions*, IV, 288–302.

"Sedgwick's Discourse," *ibid.*, I, 95–159.

"The Silk Trade," in *Collected Works*, IV, 125–39.

"Speech on the British Constitution," in *Autobiography*, ed. H. J. Laski. London: Oxford University Press, 1924, 275–87.

"Speech on the Church," *ibid.*, 310–30.

"Speech on the Influence of the Aristocracy," *Archiv für Sozialwissenschaft und Sozialpolitik*, 62 (1929), 239–50.

"Speech on Land Tenure Reform," *Dissertations and Discussions*, IV, 251–65.

Speech on Personal Representation. London: Henderson, Rait, and Fenton, 1867.

"Speech on the Present State of Literature" (1827), *Adelphi*, 1 (1924), 681–93.

"Speech on the Utility of Knowledge," in *Autobiography*, ed. Laski, 266–74.

The Spirit of the Age. Ed. F. A. Hayek. Chicago: University of Chicago Press, 1942.

"State of Politics in 1836," *London and Westminster Review*, 3 & 25 (1836), 271–8.

"State of Society in America," *ibid.*, 2 & 31 (1836), 365–89.

The Subjection of Women. London: Longmans, Green, Reader, and Dyer, 1869.

A System of Logic, Ratiocinative and Inductive. 8th ed. London: Longmans, Green, Reader, and Dyer, 1872.

"Tennyson's Poems," *London and Westminster Review*, 1 & 30 (1835), 402–24.

"Thornton on Labour and its Claims," in *Collected Works*, V, 631–68.

Thoughts on Parliamentary Reform, in *Dissertations and Discussions*, III, 1–46.

Three Essays on Religion. London: Longmans, Green, Reader, and Dyer, 1874.

"Tocqueville on Democracy in America," *Dissertations and Discussions*, II, 1–83.

"Tocqueville on Democracy in America," *London and Westminster Review*, 1 & 30 (1835), 85–129.

"The Two Kinds of Poetry," *Monthly Repository*, 7 (1833), 714–24.

"Two Letters concerning the Co-operative Platelock Makers of Wolverhampton," *Co-operator*, 5 (1865), 161.

"Use and Abuse of Political Terms," *Tait's Edinburgh Magazine*, 1 (1832), 164–72.

Utilitarianism. 3rd ed. London: Longmans, Green, Reader, and Dyer, 1867.

"Walsh's Contemporary History," *London and Westminster Review*, 3 & 25 (1836), 281–300.

"War Expenditure," in *Collected Works*, IV, 1–23.

"What is Poetry?" *Monthly Repository*, 7 (1833), 60–70.

"Whewell on Moral Philosophy," *Dissertations and Discussions*, II, 450–509.

"Writings of Junius Redivivus," *Monthly Repository*, 7 (1833), 262–70.

"Writings of Junius Redivivus," *Tait's Edinburgh Magazine*, 3 (1833), 347–54.

II. Secondary Sources

Abrams, Meyer H. *The Mirror and the Lamp.* New York: Oxford University Press, 1953.

Alexander, Edward. *Arnold and Mill.* New York: Columbia University Press, 1965.

Anschutz, R. P. *The Philosophy of J. S. Mill.* Oxford : Clarendon Press, 1953.

Atkinson, Charles M. *Jeremy Bentham.* London : Methuen, 1905.

Bain, Alexander. *James Mill.* London : Longmans, Green, 1882.

———— *John Stuart Mill.* London : Longmans, Green, 1882.

Bentham, Jeremy. *Rationale of Judicial Evidence.* Ed. J. S. Mill. 5 vols. London : Hunt and Clarke, 1827.

———— *Works.* Ed. John Bowring. 11 vols. Edinburgh : Tait, 1843.

Borchard, Ruth. *John Stuart Mill the Man.* London : Watts, 1957.

Bowring, John. *Deontology.* (Ed. from Bentham's MSS.) 2 vols. London : Longman, Rees, Orme, Brown, Green, and Longman, 1834.

Britton, Karl. *John Stuart Mill.* London : Penguin, 1953.

———— and John M. Robson. "Mill's Debating Speeches," *Mill News Letter,* 1 (1965), 2–6.

Carlyle, Thomas. *Chartism.* London : Fraser, 1840.

———— *The French Revolution.* 3 vols. London : Fraser, 1837.

———— *Miscellaneous and Critical Essays.* 7 vols. London : Chapman and Hall, 1872.

———— *On Heroes, Hero-Worship, and the Heroic in History.* London : Fraser, 1841.

———— *Past and Present.* London : Chapman and Hall, 1843.

———— "Repeal of the Union," *Examiner,* 29 Apr., 1848, 275–6.

———— *Sartor Resartus.* London : Saunders and Otley, 1838.

Catlin, George. *History of the Political Philosophers.* London : Allen and Unwin, 1950.

Cole, G. D. H. *Socialist Thought: The Forerunners, 1789–1859.* London : Macmillan, 1953.

Coleridge, Samuel Taylor. *On the Constitution of Church and State, according to the Idea of Each.* London : Hurst and Chance, 1830.

———— *Second Lay Sermon,* in *Works.* London : Bell, 1894.

Comte, Auguste. *Catechism of Positivism.* Trans. Richard Congreve. London : Chapman, 1858.

———— *Cours de philosophie positive.* 2nd ed. 6 vols. Paris : Baillière, 1864.

———— *A General View of Positivism.* Trans. J. H. Bridges. London : Routledge, 1908.

———— *Positive Philosophy.* Trans. Harriet Martineau. 2 vols. London : Trübner, 1875.

———— *Système de politique positive.* Paris : Saint-Simon, 1824.

Courtney, W. L. *The Life of John Stuart Mill.* London : Scott, 1889.

Dicey, A. V. *Lectures on the Relation between Law and Public Opinion in England during the Nineteenth Century.* London : Macmillan, 1905.

Everett, C. W. *The Education of Jeremy Bentham.* New York : Columbia University Press, 1931.

Feuer, L. S. "John Stuart Mill and Marxian Socialism," *Journal of the History of Ideas,* 10 (1949), 297–303.

———— *Psychoanalysis and Ethics.* Springfield : Thomas, 1955.

Fox, Caroline. *Memories of Old Friends.* 2nd ed. 2 vols. London : Smith, Elder, 1882.

Garnett, Richard. *Life of Carlyle.* London : Scott, 1887.

Grote, George ("Philip Beauchamp"). *Analysis of the Influence of Natural Religion on the Temporal Happiness of Mankind.* (From the MSS of Jeremy Bentham.) London : Carlile, 1822.

Halévy, Elie. *The Growth of Philosophic Radicalism.* London : Faber and Faber, 1952.

Hamburger, Joseph. *James Mill and the Art of Revolution.* New Haven : Yale University Press, 1963.

Hare, Thomas. *The Election of Representatives, Parliamentary and Municipal.* London : Longmans, Green, Reader, and Dyer, 1873.

────── *The Machinery of Representation.* London : Maxwell, 1857.

Hayek, F. A. *John Stuart Mill and Harriet Taylor.* London : Routledge and Kegan Paul, 1951.

Himmelfarb, Gertrude, ed. *Essays on Politics and Culture by John Stuart Mill.* New York : Doubleday, 1962.

──────"The Two Mills," *The New Leader,* 10 May, 1965, 26–9.

Kubitz, Oskar A. *The Development of John Stuart Mill's System of Logic, Illinois Studies in the Social Sciences,* 18 (1932), 1–310.

Leader, R. E., ed. *Life and Letters of J. A. Roebuck.* London : Arnold, 1897.

Levi, A. W. "The 'Mental Crisis' of John Stuart Mill," *Psychoanalytic Review,* 32 (1945), 86–101.

────── "A Study in the Social Philosophy of John Stuart Mill." Ph.D. thesis, University of Chicago, 1940.

Lévy-Bruhl, L., ed. *Lettres inédites de John Stuart Mill à Auguste Comte.* Paris : Germer-Baillière, 1899.

Lindley, Dwight. "The Saint-Simonians, Carlyle, and Mill; a Study in the History of Ideas." Ph.D. thesis, Columbia University, 1958.

Macaulay, T. B. "Bentham's Defence of Mill," *Edinburgh Review,* 49 (1829), 273–99.

──────"Mr Mill's Essay on Government," *ibid.,* 159–89.

────── "Utilitarian Theory of Government, and the 'Greatest Happiness Principle,'" *ibid.,* 50 (1829), 99–125.

Mack, Mary. *Jeremy Bentham.* London : Heinemann, 1962.

Mill, Anna J. *John Mill's Boyhood Visit to France.* Toronto : University of Toronto Press, 1960.

────── "J. S. Mill's Visit to Wordsworth, 1831," *Modern Language Review,* 44 (1949), 341–50.

Mill, Harriet Hardy (Taylor). "The Enfranchisement of Women," in J. S. Mill, *Dissertations and Discussions,* II, 411–49.

Mill, James. *Analysis of the Phenomena of the Human Mind.* Ed. J. S. Mill. 2 vols. London : Longmans, Green, Reader, and Dyer, 1869.

────── "The Ballot," *Westminster Review,* 13 (1830), 1–39.

———— "Education," in *Essays*. London : n.p., n.d.

———— *An Essay on Government*, in *ibid*.

———— *A Fragment on Mackintosh*. London : Baldwin and Cradock, 1835.

———— *History of British India*. 3 vols. London : Baldwin, Cradock, and Joy, 1817.

————"Periodical Literature," *Westminster Review*, 1 (1824), 206–49.

Milne, A. Taylor. *Catalogue of the Manuscripts of Jeremy Bentham in the Library of University College, London*. 2nd ed. London, 1962.

Mineka, Francis E. "The *Autobiography* and the Lady," *University of Toronto Quarterly*, 32 (1963), 301–6.

Morley, John. *Life of Gladstone*. 3 vols. London : Macmillan, 1903.

Muirhead, J. H. *Coleridge as Philosopher*. London : Allen and Unwin, 1930.

Neff, Emery. *Carlyle and Mill*. New York : Columbia University Press, 1926.

Nesbitt, G. L. *Benthamite Reviewing*. New York : Columbia University Press, 1934.

Packe, Michael St. J. *The Life of John Stuart Mill*. London : Secker and Warburg, 1954.

Palgrave, Francis T. "Mill's *Autobiography*," *Quarterly Review*, 136 (1874), 150–79.

Pappé, H. O. *John Stuart Mill and the Harriet Taylor Myth*. London : Cambridge University Press, 1960.

Pringle-Pattison, A. Seth. *The Philosophical Radicals*. Edinburgh : Blackwood, 1907.

Ricardo, David. *Works*, Vol. VI. Ed. P. Sraffa. Cambridge : Cambridge University Press, 1952.

Robson, John M. "John Stuart Mill and Jeremy Bentham, with Some Observations on James Mill," in M. MacLure and F. W. Watt, eds. *Essays in English Literature from the Renaissance to the Victorian Age*. Toronto : University of Toronto Press, 1964, 245–68.

———— "John Stuart Mill and Matthew Arnold," *Humanities Association Bulletin*, 34 (1961), 20–32.

———— "John Stuart Mill's Theory of Poetry," *University of Toronto Quarterly*, 29 (1960), 420–38.

Romilly, Samuel Henry, ed. *The Romilly-Edgeworth Letters, 1813–1818*. London : Murray, 1936.

Russell, Bertrand and Patricia, eds. *The Amberley Papers*. 2 vols. London : Hogarth, 1937.

Schapiro, J. S. "John Stuart Mill, Pioneer of Democratic Liberalism in England," *Journal of the History of Ideas*, 4 (1943), 127–60.

Semmel, Bernard. *The Governor Eyre Controversy*. London : MacGibbon and Kee, 1962.

Sidgwick, Henry. "Bentham and Benthamism in Politics and Ethics," *Fortnightly Review*, n.s. 21 (1877), 627–52.

Smith, Leveson. *Remarks upon an Essay on Government*. London : Ridgway, 1827.

Stephen, Leslie. *The English Utilitarians.* 3 vols. London; Duckworth, 1900.

Strachey, Lytton, and Roger Fulford, eds. *Greville Memoirs, 1814–60.* 8 vols. London : Macmillan, 1938.

Taylor, Henry. *Autobiography.* 2 vols. London : Longmans, Green, 1885.

Tocqueville, Alexis de. *Democracy in America.* Trans. Henry Reeve. 2 vols. London : Longman, Green, Longman, and Roberts, 1862.

—— *Œuvres complètes,* Vol. VI. Ed. J.-P. Mayer. Paris : Gallimard, 1954.

Wallas, Graham. "Bentham as Political Inventor," *Contemporary Review,* 129 (1926), 308–19.

—— *Francis Place.* London : Allen and Unwin, 1918.

—— "Jeremy Bentham," *Political Science Quarterly,* 38 (1923), 45–56.

Weinberg, Adelaide. *Theodor Gomperz and John Stuart Mill.* Geneva : Droz, 1963.

Whittaker, Thomas. *Report on the Bentham MSS. at University College, London, with Catalogue.* London, 1892.

Index

Mill, John Stuart (cont.)
132, 135, 137, 142, 152–3, 156n, 172,
187, 193, 224, 233–6, 239–40, 244;
reassessment by JSM of his intellectual
inheritance 14, 24–7, 32–49, 70–1, 75–7,
84, 87, 89–91, 94, 100, 107–8, 126–7,
131, 135–6, 140, 143–4, 167, 170
  Carlyle (and reassessment of
influence) 70, 76, 80–95, 114, 119, 190;
correspondence of JSM with TC 27n,
28–9, 32, 34n, 64, 79, 81–8, 128, 153, 249
  Coleridge 70–7, 82n, 85, 94, 103,
105, 107–8, 114, 140–1, 145–6, 187, 198,
209, 225–6, 229, 241
  Comte (and reassessment of
influence) 70, 75, 95–105, 108, 114, 138,
154, 164, 166, 168, 171, 177–8, 190, 208,
210, 221–4, 239–40, 253, 269, 276
  Harriet Taylor Mill 30, 50–68, 83,
114, 127, 137, 226n, 228, 234, 248;
JSM's eulogies of HTM 51–4, 56, 64, 96;
"joint productions" of JSM and HTM
55n, 56–9, 61–6, 67–8, 226n
  Saint-Simonians (and reassessment
of influence) 65n, 70–1, 74–80, 94, 101,
103, 105, 107–8, 114, 166, 176–7, 187,
195, 198, 221–2, 238–40
  Tocqueville 70, 105–14, 178–9, 244;
correspondence of JSM with T 106,
108–11
  major areas of thought:
  economic 84, 103n, 269–70;
capitalism vs. socialism 250–2, 256,
260–1, 264, 268–70; charity 216, 261–3;
communism 264n, 267n, 269, 275–6, see
also socialism; co-operatives 214–15,
261, 263–8; population 251, 261–2, 267,
269; profit-sharing and piece-work
264n, 265–6; socialism 59–60, 78–80,
110, 113, 136–7, 178–80, 201, 204–6,
245–71, 276; approval of voluntary
association 245–6, 249–51, 261, 263–5,
landed property 252–6, 270–1,
repudiation of state socialism 245–6,
249, 252, 254–5, 276; trade unions
214–16, 230; see also working class
  moral ix, 22–7, 35, 63–7, 87, 91–2,
96, 104, 107, 109–10, 117–59, 174,
179–80, 184–5, 200–4, 206, 208, 221,
228–9, 235, 246–7, 252–3, 256–7, 260–1,
263, 266–71, 276; conscience 149;
"desirable" 155, 157–8; free will 175;
habit 147–8; intellect 151–5, 167–8, 177,
276; justice 132–3, 149, 156, 158, 186,

247–8, 256–8; proof 155–8; qualitative
vs. quantitative 155–7; sympathy
133–9, 152
  political 71–8, 82–4, 96–8, 100–14,
117, 126, 162–3, 178–9, 182–271; amount
of government 202–22, arguments for
laissez-faire 205–8, 213–14,
qualifications of laissez-faire 208–19;
competitive civil service 190, 241–2;
defence of JM 43, 47; democracy
224–33, 236, 238–9, 243–4, 258–60, 271;
elections, ballot 233–5, franchise
225–33, frequency 236, Personal
Representation 190, 199, 228, 231–3,
plural voting 190; end of government
202–4; laissez-faire, see amount of
government; leadership, see
representatives, quality of, liberty,
influence of Carlyle, of Comte, of
Saint-Simonians; local vs. central
government 219–22; method 40–4, see
also views on method; natural rights
41; relativism 204–5, 209, 223, 246, 255,
270–1; representatives, functions
239–44, Legislative Committee 190,
200, 240, 243, methods of selecting
222–35, qualities 222–3, 235–9, 240–4,
259, responsibility to electors 235–6,
239, second chambers 199–200, 240–1
  social 96–100, 103–14, 117, 135–6,
143, 152, 160, 163–80, 182–271, 273;
relativism s.v. political thought
  views on:
  antagonism, see dialectic, method
  aphorisms 192
  "Artist" and "Scientist" x, 27–30,
41, 64–8, 86, 107, 117–18, 134, 145,
159–82, 202, 223, 240, 247
  Church of England 72–3, 75–6, 82,
211–12
  communism s.v. economic
thought
  democracy s.v. political thought,
see also equality
  education 72–3, 195–7, 209–12,
226–8, 244, 251, 260, 263, 266–7, 269
  equality 129, 178–9, 182–4, 201–2,
242, 246–8, 252, 257–60, 268–70, racial
91–3, sexual 55, 87, 268
  "ethology" 141
  evolution 150–1, 273–5
  gradualism 263–4, 268, 271, 276
  history 71, 75–8, 88–90, 96–100,

Utilitarianism 49n, 57, 68, 96n, 118,
123n, 132, 135, 137–8, 142, 144, 146n,
147–9, 150n, 155, 157–8, 246n; walking-
tour journals 24; "Walsh's
Contemporary History" 229n; "War
Expenditure" 169–70; "What is
Poetry?" 27n, 28n, 30; "Whewell"
34–5, 49n, 125, 127n, 133n, 134n, 229;
"Writings of Junius Redivivus"
(*Monthly Repository*) 27n, 121, 126;
"Writings of Junius Redivivus" (*Tait's*)
27n, 253n
Millet, René 222
Milne, A. T., *Catalogue of the MSS of
Bentham* 10n
Milton, John 4, 120
Mineka, Francis E., ed., *J. S. Mill,
Earlier Letters* s.v. JSM; "The
Autobiography and the Lady" 53–4,
57n
Morley, John, *Life of Gladstone* 200n,
237, 242n
Mueller, Iris xi
Muirhead, J. H., *Coleridge as
Philosopher* 72n
Mutual Improvement Society 5, 69n, 195

NAPOLEON BONAPARTE 84
Neff, Emery, *Carlyle and Mill* 10n, 14n,
18n
Nesbitt, G. L., *Benthamite Reviewing*
19n
Newman, J. H. 30
Newton, Sir Isaac 146, 192
Nichol, J. P. 76

OWEN, ROBERT 13, 249–50, 267n

PACKE, MICHAEL, *Life of Mill* 22, 51, 53,
59, 61n
Paley, William 133n, 145
Palgrave, F. 56n
Pappé, H. O. xi; *J. S. Mill and the
Harriet Taylor Myth* 53–4, 56n, 68
Parliamentary Review 22
Pemberton, C. R. 30–1
Peter the Great 43
"Philip Beauchamp" *see* Grote, George
Philosophic Radicals 5–8, 14, 16, 17n, 18,
22, 33, 36, 41, 44, 75, 83, 85–6, 152–3,
224, 229, 231n, 233–4, 237–9, 255n, 256
Philpotts, Henry 82
Place, Francis 11n, 62n
Plato 48, 121, 194, 196–7, 239, 240n

Poor Law 216, 219, 262
Priestley, Joseph 9n
Pringle-Pattison, A. S., *Philosophical
Radicals* 14

RAU, C. D. H. 260
Reform Bill (1832) 22, 77, 82–3, 223–4,
255n, 262
Ricardo, David 5, 7n, 49n, 59, 252
Robson, J.M., "Mill and Arnold" 85n,
247n; "Mill and Bentham" 4n, 6n, 23n,
33n; "Mill's Debating Speeches" 7n;
"Mill's Theory of Poetry" 28n
Roebuck, John 23n, 26n, 69; *Life and
Letters* (ed. Leader) 7
Roland, Mme 87
Romilly, Lady Anne 62n
Romilly-Edgeworth Letters 62n
Rousseau, J.-J. 194
Royal Commission on Trade Unions 216
Ruskin, John 261; *Modern Painters* 120

SAINT-SIMONIANS xi, 48, 50, 69, 95–6, 98,
124, 126, 166, 195, 204–5, 249; influence
on JSM s.v. JSM
Schapiro, J., "John Stuart Mill" 276
Scott, Sir Walter 222
Semmel, B., *The Governor Eyre
Controversy* 93n
Senior, N. W. 49n
Shelley, Percy Bysshe 53, 63; "Ode to
Liberty" 123
Sidgwick H., "Bentham and
Benthamism" 9n
Slaney Committee 256
Smith, Adam 49n
Smith, Leveson, *Remarks upon An Essay
on Government* 24n
Smith, Sydney, "Noodle's Oration" 35
Society for the Diffusion of Useful
Knowledge 81
Socrates 122, 139, 189
Soetbeer, Adolph 260
Southey, Robert 69
Spencer, Herbert 186, 275
Stephen, J. F. 184
Stephen, Leslie, *The English Utilitarians*
10n, 11, 14n, 106, 184, 215n, 255n, 276
Sterling, John 50, 69–70, 94, 127, 145n
Stillinger, Jack, ed. *Early Draft of J. S.
Mill's Autobiography* s.v. JSM

TAYLOR, HELEN 51, 96, 258n, 273; JSM's
high opinion of 96